D 03

EARLY MODERN ENGLISH LIVES

Dedicated to the memory of our colleague and dear friend
Lloyd Davis, 1959-2005

Early Modern English Lives
Autobiography and Self-Representation 1500–1660

Ronald Bedford
University of New England, Australia

Philippa Kelly
University of New South Wales, Australia

ASHGATE

Published by
Ashgate Publishing Limited
Gower House
Croft Road
Aldershot
Hants GU11 3HR
England

Ashgate Publishing Company
Suite 420
101 Cherry Street
Burlington, VT 05401-4405
USA

Ashgate website: http://www.ashgate.com

British Library Cataloguing in Publication Data
Bedford, Ronald, 1959-
Early modern English lives : autobiography and self-representation 1500-1660
    1. Autobiography 2. English prose literature – 16th century – History and criticism
    3. Self in literature 4. England – Biography – History and criticism
    I. Title II. Davis, Lloyd, 1959-2005 III. Kelly, Philippa
    828.3'0809492

Library of Congress Cataloging-in-Publication Data
Bedford, Ronald, 1959-
    Early modern English lives : autobiography and self-representation, 1500-1660 / by Ronald Bedford, Lloyd Davis, and Philippa Kelly.
        p. cm.
    Includes bibliographical references and index.
    ISBN-13: 978-0-7546-5295-3 (alk. paper)
    1. Autobiography. 2. England—Biography—History and criticism. I. Davis, Lloyd, 1959-2005. II. Kelly, Philippa. III. Title.

CT25.B32 2007
920—dc22

2006036043

ISBN: 9-780-7546-5295-3

Printed and bound in Great Britain by Antony Rowe Ltd, Chippenham, Wiltshire.

Contents

List of Figures

Acknowledgments

The authors are indebted to the Australian Research Council for the joint award of a three-year Large Grant which made the research and writing of this project possible. We also gratefully record the assistance of our institutions and the staff of their libraries – the University of New England, the University of Queensland and the University of New South Wales – in supporting and providing facilities for our work. The Australian Universities' Languages and Literature Association congresses have for several years listened to our papers and panels, and we are grateful for those opportunities and for the genially constructive criticism offered by its members. We acknowledge too the generous help of staff at the Henry E. Huntington Library, the Cambridge University Library, the Folger Library, the Bodleian Library, and the University of California at Berkeley Library.

Particular thanks are due to Derek Cohen and Bob White for their initial and continued encouragement, to Anna Bemrose, Belinda Tiffen and Dosia Reichardt for invaluable research assistance, and to all those who attended and contributed to the 'Theory and Practice of Early Modern Autobiography' colloquium held at the Humanities Research Centre, Canberra, in December 2002.

We acknowledge with thanks permission to reproduce material from the National Portrait Gallery, London, Appleby Castle, Cumbria, and the Kunsthistorisches Museum, Vienna. Thanks too to Wesley Hicks and Donna Lee Brien for their expert preparation of final copy, and to the School of English, Communication and Theatre at the University of New England for generously supporting this work. We are especially grateful for the quiet efficiency of Erika Gaffney at Ashgate in what turned out to be a difficult gestation for this book. In August 2005, Lloyd Davis died of a brain tumour, and we – his co-scholars and friends – dedicate the book to his memory, with love and admiration.

Ron Bedford
Philippa Kelly

Introduction

> Going ... to Cranham I was taken ill with a cold which sadly afflicted me for about 3 weekes, but god delivered mee, and gave mee more health, and cheerefulnes and content in himselfe, wife, children, his wayes, my people then formerly; so that my earnest desire is still towards them.
>
> Ralph Josselin, *Diary* [1]

This most unremarkable of diary entries – a brief account by Ralph Josselin of catching a cold on his way to Cranham – provides a way into some features that fuel our study of early modern English autobiography. Firstly, the words, 'cheerfulnes' and 'content', very commonly used terms in the sixteenth and seventeenth centuries and familiar too in our own lexicon, are related to, but distinct from, the post-Rousseau vocabulary of interiority. The *Oxford English Dictionary* finds the earliest usage of the word 'feelings', construed as the 'tender or sensitive side of one's nature', in 1771, while for 'emotional' ('liable to any emotion') the compilers find no record before 1857. 'Egotist' and 'egotism' it cites from 1714, 'self-control' from 1711, 'self-criticism' from 1857, 'self-effacing' from 1902, and 'self-image' from 1939. 'Devastate', a back-formation, is claimed as a first for 1638, though it was not in common parlance until the nineteenth century. It is clear, then, from Josselin's 'cheerfulnes', 'content', 'desire' and 'affliction' – all common enough in sixteenth- and seventeenth-century English – that people in the early modern period did not have a detailed language for experiencing, and describing, individuality as we know it, although the *OED* does cite several words – such as 'touchy' (1605), 'lonely' (1607), 'lonesome' (1647), and 'emotion' in the sense of strong feeling (1660)[2] – as entering English parlance during the seventeenth century. The term 'autobiography', as James Treadwell notes, did not enter the English lexicon until 1797.[3]

In recent decades much debate has circulated concerning the nature, or extent, of agency and autonomy granted to people who lived four centuries ago. Lori Humphrey Newcomb observes the 'particular and contingent histories' that compel literary evaluations to be reliant on 'ingeniously interpre[ted] evidence'[4], while Stephen Greenblatt has turned to psychonalysis to provide a negatively-aligned frame for what we *can* know. In seventeenth-century culture, he argues, 'proprietary rights to the self' were as yet not established, and people were identified by their social roles and their relationship to the community. Identity was conferred by rights to property rather than agency as we understand the word in post-Enlightenment terms.[5] In counterpoint (as distinct from opposition) to this,

Karen Worley Pirnie agrees with Mary Beth Rose that individuality and privacy were indeed gaining public validity[6], a suggestion that Peter Goodall endorses in his analysis of the library or study as a place for contemplation that encouraged private self-reflection.[7] And the broader impact of expanding geographical horizons also shifted the boundaries of individual sensibilities, as Helen Wilcox reminds us:

> In an energetically colonial period, the concept of ownership and self-possession is not unrelated to the discovery and claiming of new worlds; the contemplation and enunciation of individual human personalities constituted voyages of exploration and conquest, too. As Sir Thomas Browne tellingly wrote in his *Religio Medici* (1643), "The World that I regard is my selfe".[8]

All of these opinions – including Greenblatt's, which contests assumptions of individuated agency – allow for the suggestion that self-representation in early modern England seeks to creatively construct the meaning of a life; and that this has less to do with a drive for evacuation (of thought onto paper) than with evaluation (of the sum of one's actions or of a particular life).

In examining the connotation, context and expression of the term 'early modern autobiography', our argument is not that people four centuries ago had a *different* language to express the same emotions that we might entertain today; nor that people were without loneliness and despair, or emotional equivalences, for example, to 'self-critical', 'self-hatred', and so on. Our claim is rather that the absence of a language to describe the intricacies of emotion means also that such intricacies are largely implicit, unanalyzed and therefore not recorded as a part of individual self-identity. Indeed, the very word 'individual' traces a huge arc of interpretation in early modern parlance, from 'indivisible' (unable to be divided) to the very unique features that divide and distinguish one particular person from another. It is not until the nineteenth century that 'individual' settles into an unequivocal mark of singleness and autonomy: *An individual is that which cannot be divided without ceasing to be what it is.*[9]

Given such differences in the language of interiority, what, for Josselin and those living in his period, constitutes 'autobiographical' discourse? What criteria does such discourse bring to an act of self-disclosure, and is it possible to assign to these acts archetypal features of 'selfhood'? An important quality to notice about Josselin's diary entry is the assignment of agency to God. Note the passive 'I' construction that gives the active verb to God: 'I was taken ill with a cold which sadly afflicted me for about 3 weekes, but god delivered mee'. And the very verb 'deliver' conveys a strong sense of providential overhang: relief from a cold involves a contract with God who enfolds devout mortals within his mercy. Agency is at once given over to God and dispensed, as a strictly secondary function, to oneself, the subject who must act rightly in order to *deserve* merciful deliverance. And recovery from a cold involves also an act of faith – Josselin records how his contentedness with God, his wife, and his children is enhanced by deliverance from the ordeal he has been through, so that, in effect, his conception of the catching of a cold offers a rendering, in miniature, of his beliefs about mortality and eternity.

Repeatedly Josselin refers to God as 'preserving' and 'delivering' him: 'God good to mee in my peavce, health plenty in my family wife and children, the Lord preserved us from many grosse sins: the Lord good in mildning of my spirit' (Feb. 23, 1644, p. 34). A running diary, for him, affords a way of recording his faith, of monitoring God's favour, and of chastening himself to the expectation of greater munificence from God. And this is the feature that emerges again and again in the diaries of the period: the expression of an 'I' as bequeathed by God, and thus experienced, as it were, in the third person. The commitment of 'self' to the pages of a journal is always and everywhere a conversation with God, so that one speaks of 'oneself' in the passive voice. Consider Mary Rich, who writes of the increase in devoutness noticed by her friends and family: 'it was no wonder to me that I appeared so altered to them, for I was so much changed to myself that I hardly knew myself, and could say with that converted person, "I am not I"'.[10] It is against the backdrop of spiritual offices and ideals that she distinguishes herself and defines her changes, as if her character were a painting, a continuous work in progress completed by her hand *through* the workings of God. In a different context Richard Rogers, a puritan preacher, lays out his character in consonance with his spiritual offices and obligations:

> I, being this week in Huntingdonshire, went out with our neighbours, 4 or 5 well-disposed men, in good sort, prepared both for prechine and confer[ence] … We bestowed the time by the way comfortably. And at mr. Castles we abode 2 nightes with exceedinge ioy and consolacion together, and so at other places the time was well bestowed. I found no trouble nor distraction of minde by daungerous lustes, ether after the world or etc, which I tooke as a frute of a minde throughly and holily occupied.[11]

Rogers's diary implies a division between thoughts that are compatible with his spiritual offices, and the lustful thoughts that threaten to undermine them. He nominates those generic 'daungerous lustes' in a formulaic phrase – 'ether after the world or etc.' – which wraps up the lusts of 'the flesh and the devil' in an 'or etc', refusing either authorial or readerly entry into that private and interior world. The absence of such anarchic thoughts he takes as a merciful sparing by God, who rewards him with an easeful spirit for 'a minde throughly and holily occupied'. Elsewhere he harshly reprimands himself with reminders to 'governe my selfe' (p. 91), and with assessments of a mind, shirking duty, that leaves itself prey to dangerous lusts:

> I, perceiving my mind not so cheerful nor of so good courage as to be readily disposed to duty … I did this morn[ing], after the reading of some part of my wri[tings], fall to further consideration with my selfe how to frame my mind wil[lingly] to goe under it. I was the easilier drawne to it by calling to mind how graciously the lord hath kept me since my first beginning to preche. (p. 92)

Again 'self-expression' emerges as a combination of divine grace and a mind spared from evil, so that the subject himself is depicted as if in the third person. There are repeated references to the self as both subject and object: 'I shoulde not recover myselfe' (p. 80); 'to solace my selfe with trashe' (p. 81); 'It is wonderful that evr such mistes should be cast before ones eyes, as to be excessively caryed after earthly th[ings], and yet not to see it as a fault, nor ones selfe unsettled' (p. 79); 'I feele my selfe to goe about to rouze upp my selfe' (p. 89). An active-voice ejaculation from mind to paper seems not to merit recording, while the self that Rogers does record – because it is defined along the lines of spiritual obligation – is a carefully sifted composite, acting *upon*, or as a result of, the forces of goodness, weakness or evil.

If this is indeed the case – and especially if it is a general feature of journals in the period – the expression of subjectivity would seem partial and unsatisfying as an analysis of autobiographical self-representation. Consider also John Worthington, who writes: 'I have yet many other things relating to all manner of public affairs and concernments, but my torments, which are too selfish, seaze upon me, and will not suffer me to enlarge'.[12] Enlarging on the private parts – those parts of a self that do not conform to the strict lines of spiritual self-governance – is not something Worthington wishes to do. Is the *only* element of 'autobiography' left us by these authors, therefore, simply a formulaic one, with the author's unique individuality residing in the places he or she deems unsuitable to describe? To make this conclusion would, in our view, be both a generalization and an interpretive imposition, considering that all of the excerpts above concern spiritual life, which discourages authors from a focus on temporal affairs alone. But even if we look to the diary of Elias Ashmole, antiquary, we see, if not a similar overhang of spiritual obligations, indeed a similar sense of detachment from immediate agency. Ashmole writes: 'The cause between me and my wife was heard, where Mr. Serjeant Maynard observed to the Court that there were 800 sheets of dispositions on my wife's part, and not one word proved against me of using her ill, nor ever giving her a bad or provoking word'.[13] Again, this could have been written in the third person, with the passive position detaching the author from the very disquiets and disputes that he records. To suggest that such authors did not *feel* with immediacy would be ridiculous; but certainly, there are conventions of self-expression which make it always, and everywhere, appropriate to record oneself in terms of the structures (and the strictures) of duty and obligation.

In our study of autobiographical self-representation, we argue that in early modern English writings there did not exist the sharp division that is commonly made today between a private 'I' and the social role permitted to the 'I' – as in the paradigmatic figure of 'an autonomous individual testing rules imposed from without against a sensibility nourished from within'.[14] Moreover, we argue that places of private distress or anxiety are not the only 'true' markers of individuality, but rather, places that an early modern author often thinks unfit for the act of description. This speaks a great deal about the purpose and means of autobiographical self-representation: how people wanted their lives to be recorded, what they thought worthy of recording, and how they conceived of individuality as a social concept rather than a model of unique genius.

A return to the social and political history that the record of language can reveal confirms this sense of what is fit and unfit for expression, and of how one is expected to comport oneself. One of the *Oxford English Dictionary*'s most careful, fragile, complex, and lengthy entries is on the word 'self', including its emphatic personal pronouns and very many compounds. One sense of the word (described by the *OED* as '*Chiefly Philos.*[ophical]') is defined as 'that which in a person is really and intrinsically *he* [or *she*] (in contradistinction to what is adventitious); the ego (often identified with the soul or mind as opposed to the body); a permanent subject of successive and varying states of consciousness'. A seventeenth-century use of this 'self' is cited from Thomas Traherne: 'A secret self I had enclos'd within, / That was not bounded with my clothes or skin' – a couplet echoing the interiority claimed by Hamlet's 'For I have that within that passeth show'. Compounds in which *self-* is in the adjective relation – as for example with the sense 'inherent in, depending upon, or proceeding from oneself, one's own nature etc.; belonging to oneself as an independent creature' – attract one of the *OED*'s occasional excursions into cultural history: 'in the 17thC often *spec.* [specifically] dependent or relying upon one's own efforts or merits apart from the grace of God'. Florio's *Montaigne* (1603) mocks those who 'self-conceitedly ... over-esteeme what they possess above others'; from the London playhouses Marlowe's Faustus is shown 'swolne with cunning of a selfe-conceit' (*Dr Faustus*, 1588–89, 1.i. 20), the Prologue in Shakespeare's *Henry V* praises those 'Free from vain-nesse, and selfe-glorious pride' (1599), Beaumont and Fletcher's *A King and No King* (1611) rebukes a 'too self-glorious temper' (4. ii); and preachers like Isaac Bargrave offer 'A Sermon against Selfe Policy, preached at White-Hall in Lent, 1621'. The compound 'self-conceited', 'now somewhat *rare*', was, says the *OED*, 'freq[uent] in 17thC', and of course in a distinctively pejorative sense. Both religiously, in the Protestant and predominantly Calvinist atmosphere of the late sixteenth and seventeenth centuries in England, and socially, in the carefully and visibly stratified society of the period, even to speak of the 'self' could, it would seem, risk spiritual, social, and semantic malfeasance. 'Great liberty I have geven my selfe,' writes Richard Rogers, 'and with my godlines I well remember much slightnes hath been adioned, so that much froth is in our best actions when we lead our lives after so common a manner' (p. 59).

For modern readers, one of the more startling reminders of both this distinctively early modern self-regard and the detached model of agency that accompanies it may be found in Lady Anne Clifford's pleasurable description of her appearance.

> I was verie happie in my first Constitution, both in my mynd and Bodye. Both for internall and externall Endowments, for never was there Childe more equallie resembleing both Father and Mother than myself. The Collour of myne eyes was Black

lyke my father's, and the form and aspect of them was quick and lively like my
Mother's. The haire of myne head was Browne and thick, and so long that it reached to
the Calfe of my Legges when I stood upright, with a peake of haire on my forehead and
a Dimple in my Chynne lyke my Father, full Cheekes and round face lyke my Mother,
and an exquisite shape of Bodie resembling my Father.[15]

The perfect harmony of features and frame constitutes, firstly, an act of homage to
her parents, who have married their finest traits in the person of their daughter.
Secondly, through this physical harmony Clifford assigns to *herself* the composite
balance that is the ideal for a lady of Jacobean times. Every feature, pleasing in
itself (following the Petrarchan style of separating out body parts the more to
admire them), slots into place within an admirable whole, the model for ideal
female comportment.[16] What might be deemed vanity, then, is given an entirely
more significant meaning when placed in context with Clifford's cognizance of the
family line of which she is a part, and within which she spends half her life battling
to secure her rightful place. The child of an estranged couple – so much so that her
father defies existing property laws to bequeath his estate to his uncle rather than to
his wife or child – she retrieves from her parents a harmony of physical features
that makes of them fitting antecedents for herself; she is also careful to
memorialize for her descendants her own person as a model of female
comportment. (Indeed, so fervently is she committed to this that in her fifty-sixth
year she commissions a Great Painting that portrays her in triptych against a noble
lineage.) Her description of her physical perfection is thus less about self-love, or
self-enthrallment, than about an ever-vigilant awareness of herself as a part of an
elaborate family portrait, and herself, *in herself*, as a composite model.

*   *   *   *

Studies of autobiography frequently assume an essential value or trajectory as
intrinsic to autobiographical discourse – whether they adopt a formalist-stylistic
approach (Sturrock[17], Olney[18] and Spengemann[19]), a historical one (Ebner[20],
Spacks[21], Mascuch[22]), feminist perspectives (Miller[23]) or postmodern viewpoints
(Elbaz[24]). 'In the interests of defining a cohesive genre,' observes Felicity
Nussbaum, the 'fragmentary nature of the texts is often ignored'[25] and, moreover,
studies tend to mirror the humanist tendency to model discourse as cogent,
univocal, gathered and controlled, while submerging the strains that might run
through and beneath it.[26] The subject of identity and self-representation has in
recent decades been the focus of much debate and revisionary work (for example,
Nussbaum[27], Gagnier[28], Folkenflik[29] and several collections of essays[30]), which
posits the self – in some ways an anachronistic concept for much of the early
modern period – as but one effect of numerous discourses and institutions that
construct subjectivity as a nexus: as, in other words, a volatile intersection of
identities, roles, actions and beliefs.
    Many recent accounts of the interplay between subjectivity and textuality –

including specific conceptions of sexuality, gender, class, race, nationalism, capitalism and religion – have reshaped understandings of literary and nonliterary characterization, allowing for understandings of premises of essentializing perspectives as well as of the social and rhetorical frameworks in which selfhood is represented. Shari Benstock, for example, critically unravels the premises of the autobiographical conception 'that there is such a thing as the "self" and that it is "knowable". This coming-to-knowledge of the self constitutes both the desire that initiates the autobiographical act and the goal toward which autobiography directs itself'.[31] In order to move the debate away from restrictively oppositional terms, Paul John Eakin discusses the tensions between 'relational and autonomous modes of identity'.[32] Jerome Bruner's theory of autobiographical process as publicly negotiable, a 'conversation of lives' carried on between authors and readers, whose utterances and responses inform each other, provides a useful sense of the social and ethical dialogue through which early modern identity is experienced and represented among its first writers and readers.[33] Such criticism encourages the conception that autobiographical works constantly engage with the shifting and developing roles and identities played by their authors and by their readers. Scholars now suggest profoundly intricate ways in which identity is informed by multiple, competing, and often conflicting personal and group practices. Individual 'selfhood' is but one effect – contested, uncertain, and often transient – of such practices.

Much productive speculation has circulated too around the notions of 'interiority' and 'inwardness' (and their complementary opposites), exploring the nature of the early modern experience of interiority and its discursive expression. Katherine Eisaman Maus, for example, begins her study, *Inwardness and Theater in the English Renaissance,* with a brief discussion of recent views about early modern selfhood and how it might be constituted.[34] Some critics, like Eisaman Maus herself, or Debora Shuger, argue that people of that period were very much preoccupied with individuality, that is, with the connection between public selves and private, interior motivations, however complex and negotiable those connections might be.[35] Above all the theatre – that sudden explosion of public personation and (especially in Shakespearean theatre) publicly performed introspection – is seen as precipitating a changing self-awareness: Joel Fineman sees in Shakespeare's *Sonnets* the creation of the modern subject, while Harold Bloom credits Shakespeare with 'the invention of the human'.[36] Others contend, however, that interiority constitutes a retrospective contemporary imposition on the historical subjects of the early modern period; that Shakespeare, in his recognition of interiority, was an anachronistic prophet who looked forward to our own later, evolutionary sophistication, and that writers and artists of the time were commonly concerned not with individuation, but with reflections of social themes.[37]

While our study here does not claim an overarching method that embraces multiplicity while avoiding the constraints of specific perspectival channels, it does seek to explore the concept and practice of self-representation in terms of specific themes (the iconography of clocks and mirrors), activities (travel, war, the making of wills[38], and attributes (gender). In doing so it seeks to make room for, or to understand, the 'variety of categories of ... person[hood] or conceptions of the self' available in the early modern period[39], as well as the kinds of perceptual constraints that may be imposed by perspectival groupings. To this end, we have several figures (Thomas Whythorne, for example, or Anne Clifford, Sir Thomas Elyot, or Ralph Josselin) who reappear in different chapters, interacting with the diverse figures who, for reasons of space as well as discussional development, might appear in our study in only one context. We will also link the structures of our conceptual frameworks themselves, showing ways in which they interlink with, and expand upon, each other.

We begin with a two-part analysis of the ways in which time was conceived of and expressed in the early modern period, particularly in life-writing and discourses of the 'self'. We will explore the crucially important concept of double-time that informed all activities at all levels of a society that was still – despite the changes in understandings of the world, the universe, and the secular autonomy of individuals – heavily steeped in providential design. The book's next section, 'Reflections: Selves and Others', begins with a chapter (Chapter Three) discussing early modern English travellers: their reasons for travelling to Europe, Asia and parts of the New World, the expectations they took with them, the perspectives they recorded, and the insights with which they returned. Always and everywhere, English travellers (despite occasionally expressed frustrations about the English economy and manners, etc.) remained confident of their national superiority, and the aim, on return, was to incorporate in one's demeanor subtle foreign excellencies without disrupting, in any manner, one's ideal 'English' comportment. In Chapter Four we move from selves looking outward to selves looking inward, turning to the mirror, the source of emblematic self-images for a host of textual representations. Chapter Four juxtaposes the kinds of clarities and obscurities that make mirror-based identity structures valuable to a study of self-representation.

Comprising Part Three of the book, Chapters Five and Six address the social formations that underlie, and are challenged by, the experiences of selves at war. These chapters seek to analyze through particular texts the ways in which writers in circumstances of warfare grapple with self-identity; and to understand this struggle in both individual and civic terms. Part Four of the study ('Women and Life-Writing') looks at the recording of women's lives and their legacies left at death. Chapter Seven examines representations of selfhood in the writings of three women of social rank, one writing in Elizabethan and two in Jacobean times. The chapter pursues an understanding of the influence of religion, codes of comportment and economic concerns on the constraints and liberties that inform such women's self-conceptions. Chapter Eight is devoted to the subject of women's wills, discussing the way in which death – and one's preparation for it – can be read into a narrative that helps us to better understand early modern women's lives.

Through our study of self-representation in the early modern period we hope to contribute to understandings of 'the self' in sixteenth- and seventeenth-century

England. Our interest is in unearthing and illustrating the many presuppositions and contradictions that informed meanings of 'individuality', meanings that were not firm and incontrovertible, but, instead, volatile and socially dynamic. We seek to illustrate the ways in which such meanings played out in people's lives, affecting their social mobility, their idea of gendered expectations, their conceptions of foreign lands and behaviours, their understandings of nationhood and community and their beliefs about the meaning of a temporal life in relationship to the life out of time to which they were inevitably headed. And our access to such meanings can be granted only through their acts of inscription. The seventeenth-century antiquary, annalist and multiple biographer Thomas Fuller, explaining 'The Design' of his compendious *The Worthies of England* (1662), suggests why that act of inscription, by an individual self or another on their behalf, should be of such vital concern:

> It hath been the lawful desire of men in all ages to perpetuate their memories, thereby in some sort revenging themselves of mortality, though few have found out effectual means to perform it. For monuments made of wood are subject to be burnt; of glass, to be broken; of soft stone, to moulder; of marble and metal (if escaping the teeth of time) to be demolished by the hand of covetousness; so that, in my apprehension, the safest way to secure a memory from oblivion is (next to his own virtues) by committing the same in writing to posterity.[40]

Notes

1   *The Diary of Ralph Josselin, 1616–1683*, ed. Alan Macfarlane (London: Oxford University Press, for the British Academy, 1976), 29 March 1644, p. 15.
2   'Emotion', as 'physical stirring', was first recorded in 1579, and it was used to describe 'any feeling generally' in 1808. *Oxford English Dictionary* (Oxford, 1933).
3   James Treadwell, *Autobiographical Writing and British Literature, 1783–1834* (Oxford: Oxford University Press, 2005), p. 3.
4   Lori Humphrey Newcomb, 'The Triumph of Time: The Fortunate Readers of Robert Greene's *Pandosto*', in *Texts and Cultural Change in Early Modern England*, ed. Cedric C. Brown and Arthur Marotti (Basingstoke: Macmillan, 1997), p. 95.
5   Stephen Greenblatt, 'Psychoanalysis and Renaissance Culture', in *Literary Theory/Renaissance Texts*, ed. Patricia Parker and David Quint (Baltimore: Johns Hopkins University Press, 1986), pp. 210–24.
6   Karen Worley Pirnie, 'Moulsworth, Freud and Lacan', in *'The Birthday of My Self': Martha Moulsworth, Renaissance Poet*, ed. Ann Depas-Orange and Robert C. Evans (Princeton: Critical Matrix, 1996), p. 84.

7   Peter Goodall, 'The Author in the Study: Self-Representation as Reader and Writer in the Medieval and Early Modern Period', in *Early Modern Autobiography: Theories, Genres, Practices*, ed. Ronald Bedford, Lloyd Davis and Philippa Kelly (Ann Arbor: University of Michigan Press, 2006). For an argument closer to Greenblatt's suggestion of the absence of 'individual' agency, see Conal Condren's essay in the same volume: 'Specifying the Subject in Early Modern Autobiography'.

8   Helen Wilcox, '"The birth day of my selfe": John Donne, Martha Moulsworth and the emergence of individual identity', in *Sixteenth-Century Identities*, ed. A.J. Piesse (Manchester: Manchester University Press, 2000), p. 157.

9   William Thomson, *Outline of the Laws of Thought*, 1860, §56.86. Entry under 'individual', *OED*, vol. 5, p. 223.

10 Mary E. Palgrave, *Saintly Lives: Mary Rich, Countess of Warwick* (London: Dent, 1901), p. 133.

11 *Two Elizabethan Puritan Diaries by Richard Rogers and Samuel Ward*, ed. M.M. Knappen (Gloucester, Mass.: Peter Smith, 1966), p. 90.

12 *The Diary and Correspondence of Dr. John Worthington*, ed. James Crossley (Manchester: Chetham Society, 1847), p. 189.

13 *The Diary and Will of Elias Ashmole*, ed. and extended from the original manuscripts by R.T. Gunther (Oxford: Oxford University Press, 1927), p. 60.

14 *Representations of the Self from the Renaissance to Romanticism*, ed. Patrick Coleman, Jayne Lewis and Jill Kowalik (Cambridge: Cambridge University Press, 2000), p. 3.

15 In the prologue to *The Diaries of Lady Anne Clifford* (Wolfeboro Falls: Alan Sutton, 1991, pp. 1–2), the editor, David Clifford, cites this passage from Lady Anne's Great Books. For more on this passage, see Chapter 7 of our study.

16 One of the most vividly concise accounts of the composite female figure – extolled in the verses of Petrarch, and featuring a 'beautiful monste[r] composed of every individual perfection' – remains that described by Nancy J. Vickers in 'Diana Described: Scattered Women and Scattered Rhymes', *Critical Inquiry* 8 (2), Winter 1981, p. 277. Vickers describes the Petrarchan depiction of women as 'a composite of details ... Laura's whole body was at times less than some of its parts' (p. 267), which formed the model for European gentlewomen.

17 John Sturrock, in *The Language of Autobiography: Studies in the First Person Singular* (Cambridge: Cambridge University Press, 1993), argues that certain autobiographical works are important simply because of their 'quality', not because of the schematics imposed by canon-makers (p. 19). And yet he also attempts to steer analysis away from the search for the 'autobiographical hero' of individuation and singularization (pp. 289–91).

18 James Olney, *Metaphors of Self: The Meaning of Autobiography* (Princeton: Princeton University Press, 1972). Olney endorses the didactic value of autobiography (p. vii.) Many critics insist on the edifying value of autobiographical self-disclosure, whether it does so by 'celebrat[ing] the autonomous individual and the universalizing life story' or 'serv[ing] a larger purpose of valorizing the lives of ordinary, often marginalized subjects'. *Getting a Life: Everyday Uses of Autobiography*, ed. Sidonie Smith and Julia Watson (Minneapolis: University of Minnesota Press, 1996), pp. 3, 161.

19 William C. Spengemann, *The Forms of Autobiography: Episodes in the History of a Literary Genre* (New Haven: Yale University Press, 1980).

20 Dean Ebner, *Autobiography in Seventeenth-Century England: Theology and the Self* (The Hague: Mouton, 1971).

21 Patricia Ann Meyer Spacks, *Imagining a Self: Autobiography and Novel in Eighteenth-Century England* (Cambridge, Mass.: Harvard University Press, 1976).

22 Michael Mascuch traces 'the stirrings of a personal voice and an individual self-identity' from its beginnings in the mid-seventeenth century, when the 'concept of personality is still latent, and altogether pious … [b]ut a tendency to place the person before the piety had begun to emerge'. *Origins of the Individualist Self: Autobiography and Self-Identity in England, 1591–1791* (Cambridge: Polity Press, 1997), p. 96.

23 Nancy K. Miller, *Getting Personal: Feminist Occasions and other Autobiographical Acts* (New York: Routledge, 1991).

24 Robert Elbaz, *The Changing Nature of the Self: A Critical Study of the Autobiographical Discourse* (London; Sydney: Croom Helm, 1988).

25 Felicity Nussbaum, *The Autobiographical Subject: Gender and Ideology in Eighteenth-Century England* (Baltimore: Johns Hopkins University Press, 1989), p. 22.

26 For more on the subject of humanism, see Elizabeth Heale, *Autobiography and Authorship in Renaissance Verse: Chronicles of the Self* (Basingstoke: Palgrave Macmillan, 2003), p. 3.

27 Felicity Nussbaum feels that autobiography can be conceived as a textual practice in which 'women and men, privately and publicly, experiment with interdiscourses and the corresponding subject positions to broach the uncertainties of identity. … Such texts may work simultaneously for and against the ideologies of identity which prevail'. *The Autobiographical Subject*, p. 37.

28 Regenia Gagnier. *Subjectivities: A History of Self-Representation in Britain, 1832–1920* (New York: Oxford University Press, 1991).

29 See Robert Folkenflick's important analysis of intersubjectivity: 'Introduction: The Institution of Autobiography', in *The Culture of Autobiography: Constructions of Self-Representation*, ed. Robert Folkenflik (Stanford: Stanford University Press, 1993), p. 234.

30 See *Representations*, ed. Coleman, Lewis and Kowalik, 'Introduction', pp. 3–15.

31 Shari Benstock, 'Authorizing the Autobiographical', in *The Private Self: Theory and Practice of Women's Autobiographical Writings*, ed. Shari Benstock (London: Routledge, 1998), p. 11.

32 Paul John Eakin, *How Our Lives Become Stories: Making Selves* (Ithaca: Cornell University Press, 1999), p. 181.

33 Jerome Bruner, 'The Autobiographical Process', in *The Culture of Autobiography*, ed. Robert Folkenflik, pp. 38–56.

34 Katherine Eisaman Maus, *Inwardness and Theatre in the English Renaissance* (Chicago: University of Chicago Press, 1999). See in particular pp. 1–34.

35 Debora Shuger 'Life-writing in Seventeenth-century England', in *Representations*, ed. Coleman, Lewis and Kowalik, pp. 73–4.

36 Joel Fineman, *Shakespeare's Perjured Eye: The Invention of Poetic Subjectivity in the Sonnets* (Berkeley: University of California Press, 1986); Harold Bloom, *Shakespeare: the Invention of the Human* (New York: Riverhead Books, 1998).

37 See, for example, Francis Barker, *The Tremulous Private Body: Essays in Subjection* (London: Methuen, 1984).

38 Elizabeth Heale displays, for example, the complex strains of motivation that underpin the making of a 'will' or final testament: it is 'a recognition of the final dissolution of the self in death, and a written trace of self-assertion'. *Autobiography and Authorship*, p. 171.

39 Peter Burke, 'Representations of the Self from Petrarch to Descartes', in *Rewriting the Self: Histories from the Renaissance to the Present*, ed. Roy Porter (London: Routledge, 1997), p. 28.
40 Thomas Fuller, *The Worthies of England* (London, 1662); ed. John Freeman (London: George Allen & Unwin, 1952), p. 1.

PART 1
Early Modern Autobiography and Time

Chapter 1

A Life in Time

Marking Time: A Musician's Life

In what has been commonly regarded as one of the earliest examples of 'modern' autobiographical writing in English – in the sense of a sustained life-narrative consciously designed with a beginning, middle, and end[1] – Thomas Whythorne's manuscript, written about 1576 and discovered in 1955, 'lay[s] open unto you the most part of all my private affairs and secrets', and is structured along the 'ages of man' divisions. The full title of Whythorne's combined life story and collection of musical compositions is: 'A book of songs and sonetts, with longe discourses sett with them, of the chylds lyfe, togyther with A yoong mans lyfe, and entring into the old mans lyfe. devysed and written with A new Orthografye by Thomas Whythorne, gent'. Whythorne not only modifies normal orthography – a quixotic attempt to produce a phonetic spelling, not a Pepysian encryption – but, more interestingly, he abandons the day-of-the-week, date and year chronology of the customary diary or journal. At a stroke he generates instead what appears as a more 'novelistic' narrative mode structured upon 'events', circumstantial and psychological, extended over large temporal units, and providing opportunities for cross-reference, reflection and didacticism. These temporal units are both familiar and ancient, deriving from the division of a life into ages: seven is the most common – by analogy, as St Augustine has it[2], with the seven ages of world history, itself deriving from the seven days of creation – though the number can vary between four and ten: in his autobiography Whythorne, his life still of course in progress, has only three.

The most familiar and resonant example of this schema is probably Jacques's catalogue in *As You Like It*, sources for which, as for Whythorne's device too, may be found in Sir Thomas Elyot's *Castel of Helth* (1534) or Marcellus Palengenius's *Zodiacus Vitae*, translated by Barnaby Googe in 1565 and a well-known school text.[3] The addition in Jacques's speech of the *theatrum mundi* metaphor – 'All the world's a stage' – reinforces Jacques's own pessimism with an overarching determinism – men and women are 'merely players' and the successive parts they play are already assigned and written for them – which is consonant both with the dominant theological ethos of Calvinism of the time and Jacques's particular brand of cynicism. Whythorne's ages of a life can give rise to lengthy moral excursions, doggerel verses and accumulated biblical quotations on, for example, the subject of bringing up children. Yet the purpose of his approach is not so much to provide opportunity for instruction but the solution to a technical problem, a means of constructing an autobiography that will liberate both author and reader from the metrics of the mere calendar entry. It is also made clear in Whythorne's address to the reader on the first page of his manuscript that his subject, in this account of his 'whole life to this day', is *time* and its effects on the human personality: 'When ye have considered of this hereafter written, ye shall perceive that as I have changed from time to time, by Time, so altered mine affections and delights'. Thus 'time' for Whythorne is the agency of growth, change and alteration, but its relation to inscription, the act of writing, is one that paradoxically allows for the *capture* of that change, making it available for recording and for retrospective consideration and perception.

Whythorne's other ingenious structural device or *aide-memoir* is to refer to the manuscript of his chronologically sequenced Songs and Sonnets in the ordering of his life story. The appearances of most of these many verses in his text are prefaced by phrases such as 'wherefore to ease my heart I wrote as followeth', or 'whereupon I made this sonnet following'. His larger narrative moves successively through the age of childhood "from the infancy until fifteen", the age of 'adolescency' ('the first part of the young man's age' from 16 to 25), and the age of *juventute* from 25 to 39. According to some models, 'old age' began at 40, to others *senectute* began with the sixtieth year: Whythorne himself was about forty eight when he wrote the autobiography.[4] His modern editor suggests that the use made of this framework is unique in early autobiographical practice, and is a significant example of Whythorne's originality in the endeavour to construct a life.[5]

The life thus constructed is of course precisely that: a discursive artifact. Recent commentary on Whythorne has highlighted particularly the tension between his projected role as would-be courtier, writing and performing amorous ditties for female patrons, and his desire to appear as the moral gentleman – roles which reveal, it is argued, the uncertainty of his social situation as both employed tutor and gentleman musician.[6] The emphasis here, however, is less on Whythorne's sense of economic and social marginality and more on his characteristic tendency, as Anne Ferry describes it, 'to see himself not as a unique individual but as a particular instance of the general condition of man'.[7] To a sensibility like Whythorne's – and in this he seems entirely representative of his age – the agency which constructs the life may appear to be the individual author but is in fact a combination of a series of social and moral generalities assembled from the Bible, ancient authors, and everyday proverbs, to whose collective injunctions and wisdom he, like everyone else he supposes, seeks to conform. And in shaping his life, the temporal process itself is always predominant, however ingeniously its musician author may appear to be beating time.

A characteristic passage from Whythorne makes this point with great clarity. He is contemplating having a second portrait painted of himself now that he is twelve years older than his 'last counterfeit', and he notes how he 'was much changed from that I was at that time, as by the long and fullness of my beard, the wrinkles on my face, and the hollowness of mine eye' – thoughts which provoke the following verse and commentary:

> *Who that will weigh, of ages all,*
> *Their change of shapes from time to time,*
> *What childish thoughts to younglings fall,*
> *As years wax ripe how they do climb,*
> *May well in mind this sentence call:*
> *As time doth alter every wight,*
> *So every age hath his delight.*

This foresaid cause of writing of the ages of mankind brought now to my remembrance that which I wrote before touching the childish years, the adolescency and the juventute or young man's age. And therefore I considering with myself that I was now above thirty years of age and growing toward the age of forty, at the which years begins the first part of the old man's age, I took occasion to write thereof this sonnet following:

> *The force of youth is well nigh past,*
> *Where heat and strength of late took place,*
> *And now is coming in all haste*
> *The cold, weak age for to deface*
> *The show of youth. Wherefore I must*
> *Yield to my chance and thrall my lust.*
> *Now farewell youth and all thy toys:*
> *I will go seek more certain joys.*[8]

What is to be emphasized here is the very *unremarkableness* of Whythorne's sentiments: they are of course among the most repeated commonplaces of Elizabethan and Jacobean writing and culture. To be sure, Whythorne as active subject adds that he looked after his diet and exercise, and 'did not continually use anything that should deface my show of youth or bring untimely age upon me, wherefore I was judged of many which did not know my years to be always younger than I was indeed'.[9] This may have a modern ring to it and remind us of the utter seriousness of our own culture's vast investments in such a project, but Whythorne is not fooled by his momentary vanity. It is clear that he has thoroughly internalized those commonplaces of life's brevity and of the stations marking the Gradual or progress towards eternity: the awareness of Time's bending sickle is everywhere evident in his verbosely pedantic prose, both explicitly, for instance, when in London during the plague, 'whereby I looked every minute of an hour when I should be visited as the rest were'[10], and in more subterranean indications. Within a handful of paragraphs we have, for example, the nervously, even obsessively, iterated locutions, 'after I had been a certain time', 'from time to time to see how time doth alter them', 'for the time present', 'as it was in time past', 'to see how time doth alter them from time to time', 'I being at this time', 'that I was at that time', 'thus having passed my time', 'the loss of my time', 'within a short time', 'by that time that I had passed my time', and so on.[11] Whythorne's sensitivity to chronology can move from the macro-time of the seven ages of man to the micro-time of the ticking of minute after minute.

Whether the structuring of early modern life-writing takes the form of the unreflective diary entry against day and month and year or an alternative organization of a life like Whythorne's, the sense of subservience to a larger 'plot' is always strong. Almost inevitably, Whythorne's depression after rebuffs to his self-esteem takes the form of reflection 'on the old saying, "This world is but a scaffold for us to play our comedies and tragedies upon"'. Whythorne confirms and acquiesces in a sense of the ordinariness, the *un-uniqueness*, of every individual: everyone marks time to the clock and calendar; everyone processes, with varying degrees of success or dignity, through the allotted ages of a life. Belief in the power of certain numbers, notably seven and three, meant that some ages in this process were fraught with special danger. A couple of generations on from Whythorne, the nonconformist minister Philip Henry's diary furnishes a characteristic instance of the sense of a life lived against a temporal backdrop with whose segments and divisions the individual is most likely to conform but which he or she may, providentially, manage to evade or survive. Echoing the emperor Augustus, who is supposed to have expressed considerable relief 'at having survived my climacteric, the sixty-third year'[12], Philip Henry's progress towards his last days are described by his son Matthew:

> When he was in the Sixty third Year of his Age, which is commonly called the Grand Climacterick, and hath been to many the Dying Year and was so to his Father, he numbred the days of it, from August 24 1693 to August 24 1694, when he finished it. And when he concluded it, he thus wrote in his Diary This Day finisheth my commonly Dying-Year, which I have numbred the Days of, and should now apply my Heart, more than ever to Heavenly Wisdom.[13]

Further, what is proper to us as individuals – as in Whythorne's promise to reveal 'my private affairs and secrets' – is articulated through a universally shared temporal continuum, not merely discursive or rhetorical but actively suggesting pre-emption and inevitability rather than agency and choice. Whythorne escapes the mere calendar only to substitute, inevitably, an alternative temporal determinant.

In life-writing such as Whythorne's or Henry's the sense that a convincingly autonomous subject is being depicted is further diluted by the social determinism evident in two of Whythorne's more characteristic discursive strategies. Firstly, interpolated poems and songs – so distinctive a feature of his autobiography – are singled out by Whythorne in his address to the unnamed friend for whom ostensibly the life story is written: 'I did think it needful not only to show you the cause why I wrote them [the poems] but also to open my secret meaning in divers of them'.[14] And yet, despite the citing of often distraught and poignant narrative moments and motives for the writing of the poems, they themselves invariably emerge not as vehicles of personal revelation but as conventionally anonymous verse for general public consumption. Secondly, and with a similar effect, his individual life story is paradoxically vocalized, by proxy as it were, through an accumulation of biblical phrases, folk-wisdom from compendia, familiar saws from Erasmus's *Adagia*, worn-out sayings of all sorts, and a huge linguistic investment in proverbial or pseudo-proverbial phrases. For paragraphs at a time he appears to be depicting himself in a ventriloquized omnivocal vulgate in which the individual voice struggles for breath – or, of course, into whose very anonymity it may retreat and hide. And yet rather than reenacting the familiar New Historicist motif of the individual subordinated by the moral and social, Whythorne's self-depiction seems to suggest that the individual 'knows' himself *only* through these social moments. A sense of self emerges from a conglomerate of impressions and apprehensions about the swiftness of time passing and the externally documented milestones of a life. Thus, the self is not something privately held and inwardly focused, separable from these social moments and *topoi*, but is understood as a rhythmic part of, and participation in them.

A sense of communal identity and solidarity which Whythorne's autobiography insists upon – even its novel orthography is at least *designed* as a contribution to easier communication – may be seen as indicative of a period when generally speaking – and unlike our own time – most people did not have to find a place in the world but inherited it and knew what it was; when there was a deep sense that everything did in fact hang together; when the natural human desire for accountability, predictability and inevitability – including the comforting bad faith of 'if we can't help it, we can't help it' – could be satisfied at every turn. The world of early modern England, as also of generations of medieval and Renaissance Europe, was one in which every item of experience, from the weather to the fall of princes, was seen as providentially disposed, and which no one but the occasional paranoid or heretic would ever suggest was merely chaotic, unpatterned, random. For a culture steeped in the great determinisms of providentialism and Calvinist theology the exact nature of human agency would always be problematic[15]: a sense of individual autonomy could be simultaneously enhanced and erased by the paradoxical conviction that one was both part of the plan, or the plot, or the 'meaning', and that one was also – like everything else in the creation – bounded and placed, subject to the rules of the game, and hence nothing unique, nothing special. Whythorne's simultaneous self-advertisement and self-negation points to the paradox of a socially and theologically determined early modern world whose temporal paradigms are indelibly blue-printed upon every individual, but whose subjects nevertheless seek, through self-representation in diary, journal, life-writing, or portraiture, to discover and measure the extent both of their authenticity and autonomy and of their relation at any given moment to the inevitable succession of birth, maturity and death. This characteristic early modern, or rather premodern, dualism, which is so evident in Whythorne's representations of himself, may be located in some of the tensions which much life-writing exhibits yet tends to keep separate: in the division, for instance, between classical and Christian moral frames, in the exercise of self-determination towards worldly success and achievement restrained by a sense of its temporizing nature, or (to quote Debora Shuger's colourful phrasing) between 'the forum in which men strut, shove, and butt horns, and the closet in which they kneel to beg forgiveness for their sins'.[16]

As Whythorne's autobiography proceeds, the 'blood of youth', the encounters with importunate or deceiving widows, the disappointed hopes, and the negotiations of salary and personal status, increasingly give way to zealous discussions of sin and salvation parroting dozens of Tudor sermons and interspersed with heavily didactic verses. Whythorne's thoughts also turn to what he may leave after him. Following the period covered by the account of his life, a marriage is recorded on 5 May 1577, between Thomas Whythorne and 'Elizabeth Stoughton, spinster'. When Whythorne died aged sixty-seven in 1596, his nuncupative will proved that he had no surviving children. In his autobiography he recalls his labours to produce a copy for the printer of the five part-books of his songs, which he calls his children, 'which my head brought forth' – a phrase echoed by Shakespeare's Sonnet 77 in those metaphorical 'children nurs'd, deliver'd from thy brain' and recorded, to the defeat of time, in 'thy book'. Whythorne decided to push the analogy between his songs and children further: 'because they should bear my name', he wrote, 'I could do no less than set in every one of them their father's picture or counterfeit, to represent to those who should use the children the form and favour of their parent'. Since Whythorne had just had a new portrait of himself painted in 1569, he arranged to have a woodcut made from it and adorned with the coat of arms

> left to me by my poor ancestors, with which, though they have left me no great revenues to support and maintain them with, yet they have left me a remem-brance that I am as free a man born both on my father's and my mother's side as he who may spend thousands of pounds of yearly inheritance.[17]

Thus, as his songs are sung and his life story is read, their father's authorship and identity are stamped alongside a coat of arms which, despite penury, establishes social position, and in an image which embodies both Whythorne himself and his own father and mother.

Consideration of Thomas Whythorne's autobiography raises a number of issues that constitute the primary concerns of this and the following chapter on time and selfhood. Firstly, Whythorne's sensitivity to dates and calendars and time passing foregrounds the *measurement* of time, and we shall explore the role and functioning of timepieces as they were perceived and glossed in the period in the next section entitled 'Clocks and Selfhood'. Secondly, Whythorne expresses both conceptually and stylistically many of the tensions in early modern life-writing between the individual self and society and between autonomy and determinism, or the opposing and intersecting regimens of the temporal world and the eternal. These tensions, we argue, are characteristic of much early modern self-representation. They will be discussed particularly in the section 'God-time and the

Self', and illustrated through consideration of a number of autobiographical texts, particularly the diary of Ralph Josselin. In the next chapter, in which issues of autobiography and temporality are further considered, it is argued that the locators of time and space seem to be regarded in the period as in some sense always double (both 'here' and 'elsewhere'), and thus the individual as equally in some sense double too, so that a conception of time and the depiction of a self are constantly informing and mediating each other. Thomas Whythorne, as we have seen already, has some interesting things to say about another nontextual kind of self-representation, and that is the portrait. We conclude Part One with a section exploring 'the Self and the Portrait' which follows Whythorne's account of his own portraits and considers other examples of early modern memorial portraiture in their negotiations with issues of time, death, and self-representation.

Clocks and Selfhood

'Lighten our darkness we beseech thee, O Lord; and by thy great mercy defend us from all perils and dangers of this night.' These familiar words of the *Book of Common Prayer*'s Third Collect for Evening Prayer signal both an Elizabethan sense of the profound difference between day and night and the relativity of our present temporal arrangement of dividing day and night together into twenty-four hours of equal length which, though familiar to early astronomers, was far from being a universal datum. It was not employed in civil life in Europe until the fourteenth century, coinciding with the appearance of public mechanical clocks. Yet while uniform practices in the chronology of years and in dating had been widely established by the early modern period, the time 'told' by such clocks was not of course 'World Time', but local or regional time, the times of unconnected 'urban monads' or the various 'burgher times', after their origin with the local city burghers.[18] Moreover, those clocks were not quite ours: until the middle of the seventeenth century clocks most often had only one hand and the dial was divided into hours and quarters. In post-industrial life timekeeping is also bookkeeping, the crucial dimension without which economic productivity and profitability are effectively unmeasurable, and without which uniform rates of pay are unnegotiable. And it is also a primary means by which modern and postmodern subjects both orientate and define themselves.[19] With what kind of sensibility, it may then be asked, did early modern individuals regard time, and – to use Norbert Elias's term – with what 'self-regulating' effects?[20] And how did these effects contribute to the construction and representation of self-identity?

Many of the complex and ubiquitous technologies of time so familiar to modern subjects and scholars were of course quite absent from the daily lives and experience of those whose writings we are considering. It is thus difficult to imagine the social world of those who lack the ever-alert compulsion to know the time, or who seek to 'know' it in ways different from the needs that compel our own conformity. Here we seek to explore some of the conditions and assumptions through which early modern subjects tended to depict themselves in relation to time, not only metaphysically or religiously, but also in relation to the discursive apparatus itself (that is, ink, paper, books, and the calendar) and to the genres and conventions through which that representation is structured. In the various rubrics and forms that early modern life-writing takes – in memoirs, diaries, epistolary collections, or 'autobiographical' sketches – the recording of events, from the most functional and laconic of journals or account books to the extended narrative of a life, depends upon a habitus of social time which renders the articulation of diary, journal or diurnal possible. Yet the common articulation itself does not reveal what that notion of time meant to sixteenth- and seventeenth-century subjects, nor how they assumed different kinds of self-meaning in relation to it. Much recent work has been done on early modern subject-formation in relation to such discourses as those of politics, both national and domestic, of class and the hierarchies of power, of classical and Christian ethics, of gender and women's writing, of devotional self-representation and self-appraisal, and of rhetorical self-performance. In almost every field of enquiry difficulties have emerged for the modern or postmodern scholar in the search for distinctions familiarly recognizable to us: between, for example, the private and the public spheres, or the 'inwardness' and the 'outwardness' of gestures of self-revelation, or indeed for a coherent notion of psychological self-portraiture itself.[21] Similar caveats will emerge in the expressions of temporality in the period and their relation to both the perception and the construction of a 'self' and its 'life'.

   That is to say, the question of time and its paradoxes can raise different issues at different cultural moments, and we are concerned here with some of the ways in which early modern subjects were able to write about themselves in their cultural moment through references to time, or were able to use notions of time to shape their sense of themselves both conceptually and textually. Any acts of memory or commemoration or archival recording – the oral recital, the gravestone which, according to Sir Thomas Browne, 'tells truth scarce forty years' (*Urne Buriall*, 1658), the permanent or semipermanent inked inscriptions in diary, diurnal, journal or memoir – imply assumptions, both in their moment of origin and in their subsequent 'readings' over time, about the nature of selfhood in relation to temporal processes. These assumptions derive from various notions of time as much as of selfhood: as objective phenomena of natural creation, like space or gravity; or as innate forms of experience peculiar to human consciousnesses; or as symbolic systems akin to other socially constructed and learned exchanges, such as language or money. In what ways does the expiration of seconds, minutes and hours affect subjectivity and selfhood? And what sort of time should be referred to – astronomical, biological, cosmic, theological, or the time pertaining to sub-particle physics? If it is simply clock time that should concern us we might ask: what is a clock for, and what exactly *does* the clock tell when it tells the time, and to whom?

   In a self-dramatizing and striking series of metaphors, the deposed Richard II compares himself to the broken musical time of a 'disordered string', and then himself, mind and body, to a clock:

> I wasted time, and now doth time waste me,
> For now hath time made me his numb'ring clock.
> My thoughts are minutes, and with sighs they jar
> Their watches on unto mine eyes, the outward watch
> Whereto my finger, like a dial's point,
> Is pointing still in cleansing them from tears.
> Now, sir, the sounds that tell what hour it is
> Are clamorous groans that strike upon my heart,
> Which is the bell.   (*Richard II*, V. v. 49–57.)[22]

The extended metaphor theatrically captures a sense of the intimate and thoroughly internalized reciprocity between the self and time, and derives its power here not so much from its ingenuity as a conceit but rather from its familiarity. Early modern subjects frequently record a sense of the body as a timepiece in contexts that are nondramatic and in voices that are 'autobiographical'. While the simple candle-clock, sundial or hourglass can provoke conventional lessons of mortality, more complex analogies (like Richard II's) can be sustained between the self and the mechanical operations of the clock. It is useful, then, in suggesting what time-indication may have meant socially and personally in early modern culture, to look in more detail at some timepieces, including early 'numb'ring' clocks.

The Wells Cathedral clock, Somerset, and the astronomical clock in Wimborne Minster, Dorset, are both among the most ancient working clocks in Europe. In the Wells clock the inside dials and figures are of the same period and make its clock face probably the oldest surviving original one anywhere. What does it say? At the dial's centre a small ball indicates the Earth, around which the Moon and the Sun revolve and from which expanding concentric circles indicate the days of the month, the minutes, and the hours. An inscription on the face reads, *Sphericus archetypum globus hic monstrat microcosmum*, or 'this rounded ball displays a model of the universe in miniature'. The single mechanism runs this clock face inside the church building, plus a turret above it in which four jousting wooden knights revolve in combat every quarter-hour, and a large military figure in a sentry box in the triforium which strikes bells at the hours and quarters. The mechanism also runs an outside clock face on the north transept, where two four-foot high knights in armour act as quarter-jacks. Leaving aside the ingenious and even frivolous entertainment provided by the clock's many accessories (which can be accounted for, it seems, like many medieval misericords or gargoyles, only by appeal to a sense of fun), the sole purpose of the commissioning and construction of this cutting-edge technology was to ensure that canons, vicars choral and choristers started services punctually – by the late thirteenth century services had become numerous and very elaborate both in the Quire and in the multitude of subsidiary chapels. The outside clock could be seen by the steward of the vicars choral in their hall opposite, and could be heard by the servants of canons in their houses nearby, while the rest of the city could hear the hour bell at the top of the central tower of the cathedral. The Wimborne astronomical dial or *orelegium*, orloge, oriel, or horal, about five feet square, is also constructed on the Ptolemaic system. The Earth is a green ball at the centre, the Moon revolves against a black sky dotted with silver stars, and along the outer ring of blue sky the Sun marks the hour against black and gold numerals at the dial's edge.[23]

In late medieval and early modern England the visible and multiple movements of such clocks reveal to people the position they and others at present occupy in the great flow of cosmic and worldly events beyond the liturgical precincts of the clock itself. The symbols on the clock face transmit the time not only for the observers but also for the society and world to which they belong. The clocks will tell people how long they have taken to get to that place from another, or how long to the start of the next church office. The changing constellations inform viewers of the present position of the endlessly moving natural phenomena, the Sun, the Moon, and the Earth. The question of how the displays of these public timekeepers affected the observers' sense of *themselves* can partly be answered by noting their highly engineered intentionality. Gerhard Dohrn-Van Rossum's description of 'monumental astronomical clocks' in late medieval Strasburg, or Chartres, or in St Paul's Cathedral in London, is most helpful in revealing their implications: as their 'astronomical and calendrical dials were rotated, kings moved past the Virgin Mary and bowed down, cocks flapped their wings and crowed, moveable skeletons appeared as reminders of death'. He comments that these replicas of the starry heavens 'surely did not fail to have an effect on the viewer's conception of time', and presumably contributed significantly to a viewer's sense of his or her own participation in these tableaux. However, Dohrn-Van Rossum also contends that this 'mechanization of the liturgy' was of no importance in terms of modern timekeeping or time-indication, and 'when people looked at these mechanisms they were not looking at the clock'.[24] Why weren't they, we might ask? They were not perhaps, like post-industrial subjects, looking at the clock merely to know the time, but were responding to a range of simultaneous temporal complexities that were indicated by the revolution of the single arm. Such clocks do not mark – as modern clocks arguably do – an alienation between the natural and the social, or between desire and duty, or, paradoxically, between the individual and the community. Rather, they affirm an awareness of time and its symbols as embracing a wide network of relationships in which the individual, the social and the nonhuman natural planes are all interconnected.[25]

The 'message' of such timekeepers – in addition to their summons to worship – is thus not primarily the regulation of work-time but seems designed to effect the moral and religious instruction of those who contemplate them. Countless exhortations in tracts and sermons of the period see timepieces as commentary on both the brevity of life and on time as the gateway to eternity, with consequent warnings against individual vanity and self-regard. Aphorisms and verses, such as Henry King's *Sic Vita* (1640) (which provided a popular model for imitation and parody), or John Hall's self-instructive contemplation 'On an Houre-glasse'

(1646), can of course be matched by innumerable mottoes, in English and Latin, on public and domestic sundials and clocks themselves: 'Prepare to die', 'Consider your latter end', 'I shall return, but never thou', or *Hora est Orandi* ('It is the hour for prayer'), and so on. Such 'sentences' arguably not only instruct (in the sense of prodding at what is already known) but also construct in individuals what is considered to be an *appropriate* response, encouraging self-identification with the spectacle of temporal procession. For every motto urging worldly 'busyness' others warn of the world to come and thus of the individual's exposure, and many combine the two. They also frequently bring together the clock and the mirror – that other Tudor and Stuart motif of self-examination and self-regulation. And the combined notions of 'time' and of 'reflection', as expressed in the material artifacts of clock and mirror and their reciprocal tropes of self-understanding, suggest some ways in which early modern English people expressed ideas of time and selfhood.

For example, a typical seventeenth-century English sundial exhorts:

From ye dial learn ye hours,
From ye mirror learn ye years;
But length of life learn from ye flowers,
How short our time appears.[26]

This sort of device is equally familiar in quasi-autobiographical sonnet writing, notably in Shakespeare's *Sonnets* (Sonnet 77, for example, presents a triad of glass, dial, and blank paper, on which what is learned may be inscribed), but it occurs in many others too. Fulke Greville, for instance, merges the images of mirror and clock (or time) into a single focus by arguing, via St Paul, that at death the human soul, or personality, flees the body in order 'To see it selfe in that eternal Glasse,/ Where time doth end' – that is, its true self beyond momentary reflections and beyond time, where 'all to come, is one with all that was' (*Sonnets from Caelica*, 87, pub. 1633). Motifs of resistance to life's brevity and time's scythe may include the production of poems and songs, or books, or portraits, or children, but the overwhelming consciousness is, firstly, of an ever-advancing, never-returning 'progress' through successive individual entropy and loss; and secondly, of an awareness, or belief, that time is only temporary. Thus there is a sense in which all inscription, including both life-writing and artistic self-depiction or portraiture, is an attempted solution to a technical problem, that is, the problem of the apparent and constant motion of time. As far as the self is concerned in this motion, the consciousness of a final destination in which time will no longer exist is usually followed by the question of what then will happen to the 'self'.

Of many possible instances in Tudor and Stuart literary culture, two particularly resonant and well-known examples of responses to time and selfhood can be seen in short seventeenth-century poems by Edward Herbert and by John Milton. One arises from a familiarly domestic moment of insomnia, the other from devising a motto for a clock, and both expand into philosophical 'argument' about the nature of time and individuality. They both, too, read the clock into the self, and the self into the clock. Edward, Lord Herbert, in his poem, 'To his Watch, when he could not sleep', listens to the 'uncessant minutes' that 'tell / The time that tells our life' and act as 'Death's Auditors', adding up cumulatively to the *whole* of a life – though Herbert's actual written autobiographical audit of his own life itself in fact broke off prematurely.[27] In his night time meditation those fleeting minutes, that 'both divide / And summ' a life, finally make

> what's new,
> Ill and good, old, for as we die in you,
> You die in Time, Time in Eternity. (*Poems*, pub. 1665)

As in the frequent analogy between the body's pulse and the clock, or liturgical time ('The beating of thy pulse (when thou art well) / Is just the tolling of thy Passing Bell', Henry King, 'My Midnight Meditation', *Poems*, 1657), so the ticking of the watch in Herbert's genre poem mimics the ticking of a life and points to a 'time' when both will stop. The audit to come is not explicitly figured in the poem's ending (which in fact expands into a denial of an ending), but the future of the individual self in that eternity is implicit with anxiety and warning.

In his autobiography Herbert reflects on his own original 'newness' as an infant and wonders how *he*, the particularized and individual baby Edward, came to be himself:

> When I came to talke One of the first Inquiries I made was, How I came into this world; I tould my Nurse keeper and others I found my selfe here indeede but for what Cause or beginning or by what meanes I could not ymagine; But for this as I was laught at by my Nurse and some other women that were present soe I was wondered at by others who said they never heard Childe but my selfe aske that Question.

He inserts at this point a poem, in his customary tortuous Latin, made 'since that tyme', exploring the development of the individual person through time and the role of the 'Vis Plastica or Formatrix', as he calls it, that infused vigorous energy into the foetus, shaped the body with 'slender, projecting limbs', 'wrought the marvellous structure of the senses', and furnished a 'shelter for the mind, which, gliding down from Heaven, assumed its own functions and, as a sort of indication of future destiny, brought the whole slothful mass into order and made it useful'. The drift of the poem, and of Herbert's explanatory comments, is to assert a conformity between the innate faculties of human minds and the transcendent and imperishable character (neither 'new' nor 'old') of 'the Perfect, Eternal and Infinite'. This conformity between our faculties and the eternal moral verities (he cites 'Hope, Faith, Love, and Joy') proves that our individual destiny is in 'a more happy estate' than this temporal world, where knowledge of such verities is continually disappointed or frustrated. Contemplating the mysteries of birth, death, the body, and selfhood, Herbert writes:

[W]hen I came to riper yeares I made this Observation which afterwards a little Comforted mee, that as I found my selfe in possession of this life without knowing any thing of the Pangs and throwes my Mother suffered when yet doubtlesse they did noe less presse and afflict mee then her, soe I hope my Soule shall passe to a better life then this without being sensible of the Anguish and paines my body shall feele in death, For as I believe then I shalbee transmitted to a more happy estate by Gods Greate Grace I am confident I shall noe more knowe how I came out of this worlde then how I came into it.[28]

Just as the foetus growing in the womb had no need of 'Eyes, Eares and other senses' until after birth, so our possession of moral and intellectual faculties – 'which are', Herbert disenchantedly claims, 'almost as uselesse for this life as the abovenamed senses were for the Mothers wombe' – is the sure indication to Herbert that the temporal experience of mortal years is for the individual only a step to another kind of birth.

Milton, too, finds meaning for the self, mediated by the mechanical operations of the clock, in the mysteries of immortality. The manuscript of Milton's poem 'On Time' (written probably about 1633) shows that the original heading, later deleted, was 'set on a clock case', and its 'lazy leaden-stepping hours' and 'the heavy plummet's pace' refer to the movement of the lead weight in regular jerks or steps as the clock's escapement functions. (A reading of both Herbert's 'To his Watch' and Milton's poem benefit from the addition of sound effects.) But when time is no longer and we are in a place where 'we shall for ever sit' ('Triumphing over Death, and Chance, and thee O Time'), we 'shall greet our bliss / With an individual kiss'. The last phrase is perhaps slightly odd and has caused some discussion among critics: by it Milton arguably means here *not* the common seventeenth-century meaning of individual as 'inseparable' (that is, a kiss that cannot be divided), but rather that each shall kiss the other *as* an individual, self-knowing person. The suggestion is that Milton (like Herbert) is contributing to a controversy, still active in the seventeenth century, over the Averroist's denial of personal immortality, and is arguing that each person, conscious of its selfhood, will rise from the dead with the same identity as in life.[29]

Herbert's ticking watch and Milton's thumping clock-case are useful in the ways they illustrate what clocks *do*, and how they function at both a social and an individual level. The emblematic clock marks the two 'temporalities' of the physical, circumstantial world and of the numinous, spiritual realm, and its symbolic notation almost forces viewers to engage with its claims upon themselves. When he writes of himself, Herbert is moved to a vanity in his own precociousness and to optimism about the human personality's eternal constitution, while in Milton's poem the issue of individual identity and its persistence is specifically contested in a horological context. Clocks thus appear to mark a paradox, affirming both the 'thisness' of one's physical being and, like mirrors, gesturing toward the unfathomable. In relation to early modern selfhood and self-representation, they help to make people 'known' to themselves, marking a physical and temporal presence – 'I am here, and now' – while simultaneously suggesting a sense in which this physical presence once did not and will no longer exist. They generate claims and counter-claims regarding the nature of the self's origin and survival. In this way early modern clocks, like mirrors, are emblems of both of self-recognition and of metaphysical anxiety (see Chapter 4).

God's Time and the Self

Almost inevitably for modern readers the most familiar touchstones or *exempla* of early modern sensibilities regarding a whole range of topics seem to reside in Shakespeare's works. While it is our aim here to counter this inevitability by emphasizing responses to time and selfhood in nondramatic and autobiographical contexts, it is hard to put aside those famous set speeches on self-identity and time, such as Richard II's body-clock or Macbeth's sense of the not quite endless procession of tomorrows. It could, however, be argued that such speeches and other well-known dramatic moments, such as Faustus being pursued by the chiming clock, themselves derive from a complex awareness of time and the self which is also accessible in more ordinary self-representational texts. While all such works share common sources in religious discourse, autobiographical texts reveal time-and-self issues in ways that are especially interesting and significant. One particular kind of 'Shakespearian' *sententia* on time needs attention, however, both because of its familiarity and particularly because of its conceptual hostility to views of time and the self that are vital to the autobiographical enterprise. And it may not, perhaps, be an accident that it is a trickster, disguiser, and self-denier who voices this anti-autobiographical argument.

In *Troilus and Cressida* Ulysses, purveyor of elaborately packaged and self-serving commonplaces such as the undesirability of anarchy (I, iii) or the fragility of reputation (III, iii), discourses to Achilles on the nature of time. Ulysses' speech here – like his celebrated account of order – is filled with quotable quotes, or 'sentences':

> Time hath, my lord,
> A wallet at his back, wherein he puts
> Alms for oblivion ...
> For Time is like a fashionable host
> That slightly shakes his parting guest by th' hand,
> And, with his arms outstretched, as he would fly,
> Grasps in the comer ...
> For beauty, wit,
> High birth, vigour of bone, desert in service,
> Love, friendship, charity, are subjects all
> To envious and calumniating time.   (III, iii, 139–68)

In his needling of Achilles, Ulysses comments upon the human propensity for novelty and its chronic shortness of memory. 'The present eye praises the present object', so do not sit back on your past laurels. Ulysses' point of view has a compelling logic, and its message that time, in the sense of Opportunity or *Occasio*, must be seized, from Brutus's 'There is a tide in the affairs of men' to the familiar *carpe diem* motif, is a recurrent theme of Renaissance pragmatism, both in its transactions with the classical tradition and in the injunctions of preachers to seize upon the opportunities of 'God's time'.[30] Yet, like the tendentious justification of the status quo in Ulysses' public address on order, or the smoke-and-mirrors account of the optics of reflection preceding the speech on time, this description of the nature of time can be deconstructed to expose its opposite. Though for some Ulysses' words in the play may be adduced as evidence of some deep-seated Elizabethan 'world picture', far from elaborating the received wisdom about time and memory, they serve only to define their complexity. Ulysses' aggressively lock-down rhetoric renders all revolution destructive (ironical enough in a post-Reformation context), makes the only recognition of one's value which counts that of one's peers (a doctrine singularly at odds with both Protestantism and Catholicism), and conceives of the present as always o'ertopping the past, and of the past itself as consigned to some cosmic dustbin.

Ulysses' unreliability, or partiality, as an expositor of early modern views of time and the self is exposed by that very 'autobiographical impulse' which is the subject of this study. Indeed, it is Achilles who, after Ulysses' harangue, ignores the merely pragmatic self-and-opportunity homily and comes up with a more searching model of self-analysis: 'My mind is troubled like a fountain stirred', he says, 'And I myself see not the bottom of it' (III, iii, 295–6). In separating 'I myself' and 'my mind' in this way, Achilles imagines himself, like a Freudian subject (or of course like a Shakespearian character) looking into his own mind and seeking to understand 'it' (himself) in a paradigm which, however illogical, implies constant dialogue and negotiation with one's self about one's self. As Achilles personifies himself on the stage of his own imagination, looking into the fountain of his own mind, he is somehow liberated from that solely predatory 'time' insisted on by Ulysses that destroys reputations and disintegrates personalities. And it is this examination, or representation, of the self by the self – whether reflective, ironical, self-excusing or, like Achilles, merely confused – that makes autobiographical practice possible. Further, as the examples we adduce of textual self-exploration and portraiture clearly indicate, there is no such thing as time's dustbin – indeed, in the shared construction of ideas of eternity and the self which we follow, the notion is an incoherent one, or coherent only *ad hominem*. Ulysses' speech offers a key counter-view of time's processes that helps us to recognize the importance of ideas of time and the self to both the *desire* to write a life, or part of a life, and to the *manner* in which that life might be constructed. In the activity of life-writing, those 'scraps' of 'deeds past' are not 'devour'd / As fast as they are made, / Forgot as soon as done', as Ulysses maintains. On the contrary, they are preserved by inscription, organization and reflection; virtue does indeed 'seek / Remuneration for the thing it was', and the recognition that all particular present moments 'are made and moulded of things past' is critical to the search for what it is that is at the bottom of one's mind, to representations of the self.

Early modern life-writing and its material product can emerge in a number of forms: a diary or journal such as Ralph Josselin's, neatly entered into a book of blank paper like that presented in Shakespeare's Sonnet 77 and bound in calf; Philip Henry's 22 years of diaries written in interleaved Goldsmith's Almanacks with a crow-quill; Major John Saunderson's Civil War diary written almost literally on the hoof in the interleaves of a copy of William Lilly's astrological observations and conjectures, *Merlini Anglici Ephemeris* (1648); or the Essex lawyer Sir John Archer's diary, squeezed in cramped contractions into the spaces between the weather predictions and interest tables of a series of lawyer's Almanacs. Motives for the writing of such journals may sometimes be explicit, such as the memorial for one's descendants, or the instruction of Christian readers; they may be reconstructed by others on behalf of their authors; or in other contexts the motives may be quite elusive, especially where manuscripts are secreted and apparently unread by anyone but their writer.[31] Yet their material forms are all by analogy a kind of synopticon, viewings of a life, or a part of a life, simultaneously, their only imitation of time-as-sequence lying in the serial mode of composition and the turning of pages. Thus the completed 'narrative' contained in the material artifact of the journal or autobiography may be seen both as an exercise in continuous self-appraisal over time and also as a response to the injunction *Ne quid pereat* (let nothing be lost). Its form is both a 'for-God's-eyes-primarily' story, and also responsive to and mimetic of a 'God's-eye-only' view of an eternally present and timeless universe, an eternal Now 'Wherein past, present, future He beholds' (Milton, *Paradise Lost*, 3.78). In most journals the sense of dual time frames is implicit or subdued – and may even, in pragmatic work or account books, seem to be totally absent. But the routinely 'pious' gesture of an entry such as, 'I received some mony from my tenant Brewer, this is gods goodnes when anything yields increase' (from *The Diary of Ralph Josselin*, to be discussed below) betrays an instinctive acknowledgement of what Basil Willey once called 'the metaphysical flicker from world to world', and implies a dimension lying beyond the mundane sequence of investment and profit (or loss).

Sir Thomas Browne's autobiographical *Religio Medici* (1643) describes this dimension mathematically, arguing the excessive modesty of the biblical claim that in the sight of God a thousand years are only a day (2 Peter 3):

> For to speak like a Philosopher, those continued instances of time which flow into a thousand yeares, make not to him one moment; what to us is to come, to his Eternitie is present, his whole duration being but one permanent point without succession, parts, flux, or division.

'Time', claims Browne, 'we may comprehend, 'tis but five dayes elder then our selves', but 'in eternity there is no distinction of Tenses'. The believing writer,

Browne's perspective suggests, may through faith and the creative, mimetic act of inscription annihilate the human sense of the procession of time. Such an act appears to have achieved that for Browne, whose 'memory' of the future allows him to conclude that

> that terrible terme *Predestination*, which hath troubled so many weake heads to conceive, and the wisest to explaine, is in respect of God no prescious determination of our estates to come, but a definitive blast of his will already fulfilled, and at the instant that he first decreed it; for to his eternitie which is indivisible, and altogether, the last Trumpe is already sounded, the reprobates in the flame, and the blessed in *Abrahams* bosome. [32]

For Browne this paradox of the timelessness of time allows for the imaginative location of himself, somehow, *in* that timeless dimension, offering relief from what he sees as the horrors of Calvinist dogma. The effort to find a self-location in terms of time, space and providential determination is, as we shall argue, a primary feature in the orientation of thought of many less eloquent, or less philosophical, chroniclers of the early modern experience of 'a life' and its ethical, behavioural and representational dilemmas.

'This weeke god was good to mee': Ralph Josselin's Diary

Ralph Josselin was vicar of Earls Colne, Essex, from 1641 until his death in 1683, and his diary, 182 pages of close, often abbreviated, handwriting on both sides of the paper and bound in leather, begins with an account of his childhood and youth from his birth in 1616.[33] Unlike Whythorne's retrospectively structured narrative, Josselin's is a regular diary, building a life entry by entry through accumulation of daily, monthly and yearly detail. The exception of course is in the material of Josselin's early life, composed prior to the start of the diary proper beginning after his marriage in 1640, and which is headed: 'A thankfull observacion of divine providence and goodness towards mee and a summary view of my life: by mee Ralph Josselin'. In such a formulation the tension between providence and human agency is immediately foregrounded: though it may be 'my life', the life itself is the work of divine providence, while only the *account* of it is entirely the work and responsibility of its subject. And that account is written under the scrutiny and judgment of God. Josselin was a man of puritan and parliamentarian sympathies who nevertheless, like so many of his 'puritan' compatriots, welcomed the return of Charles Stuart as king. In the Civil Wars he served with the parliamentary army as a chaplain on two occasions, though disapproving of the king's death and later praying, 'god forgive my ignorant acting in the troubles against the King, and his family' (28 March 1656, p. 365). He showed commitment for a while to millenarian beliefs, had Quaker sympathies, and lived through the Restoration on the borderline of nonconformity. Characteristic of English Protestant sensibility, and especially of those with Josselin's uncertain allegiances, is the constant tipping of the hat, as it were, to the providence which is both the disposer of all things and, from the point of view of the diarist, the ultimate reader of the journal's accumulating manuscript pages. Josselin's invariable and almost hypnotic locution commencing each diary entry is, 'All this weeke god was good to mee and mine', 'This weeke the Lord was gratious to mee and mine', 'This day god good to mee', and so on. In his account of his childhood he records how

> In my infancy I had a gratious eye of providency watching over mee, preserving me from dangers by fire, a remembrance I shall carry to my grave on my right thigh, by knives being stabd in the forehead by my second sister, a wild child but now I hope god hath tamed and sanctifyed her spi[rit,] falls from horse, water and many casualtyes. (p. 1.)

The nimbleness of mind and animal energy of adolescence is recalled with a guilty admiration, but the emergent self and its fantasy life, territorial or sexual, is subjected to the inevitable censure:

> I was much delighted with Cosmography taking it from my Father. I would project wayes of receiving vaste est[ates] and then lay it out in stately buildings, castles. libraryes: colledges and such like: and withal which [was] worse oh the strange prodigious uncleane lusts when I was yet a child. How often have [I] walkt with delight to meditate upon such courses being well acquainted with those sens[ations] by bookes which I had. yett I blesse god who kept mee from all outward uncleanesse. praise bee [to] him, and for this I desire to loath and abhorre my selfe. (p. 2.)

The sense of the pervasiveness of divine interest, from Josselin's son falling off a chair and yet providentially failing to break his skull (30 December 1645, p. 53) to the 'mercifull providence' of the provision by Robert Potter, having 'tryed all my friends', of a horse (6 March 1646, p. 88), can give occasion for homiletic reflections, such as the entry for 5 September 1644: 'Stung I was with a bee on my nose, I presently pluckt out the sting, and layd on honey, so that my face swelled not, thus divine providence reaches to the lowest things. lett not sin oh Lord that dreadfull sting bee able to poison mee' (p. 19).

There appears to be little space in such a prescribed and, literally, supervised world for individual agency that does not risk spilling over into various degrees of wickedness and sin – a pathology vividly evident, for example, in the 'canonical' autobiographical writings of John Bunyan. We can add to this abiding sense of a providential universe, in which the bitter military engagements of the Civil Wars are invariably noted by Josselin – as indeed by every national newspaper and broadsheet – as a series of divine punches and counter-punches, the particular circumstances of Josselin's life. He had a large and extended complex of relatives and a deep involvement in the ties of family life – his wife had ten live births during 1642–1663, and survived her husband. He was a member of a church under constant siege and turmoil whose quotidian duties required of him the conduct of baptisms, marriages, burials – including a number of his own children – and the visitation of the sick and dying. He had further social roles as landowner and farmer, always vulnerable to the weather and the harvest and the price of commodities. All these, together with his minutely, even obsessively, recorded details of his own and others' – often fatal – ailments and diseases[34] make it easy to understand why the self represented in this diary is characterized more as victim than agent, as observer and sufferer rather than chooser and determinant, a person to whom 'things' happen and who is ever willing to forfeit any act that may have the appearance of autonomy.

That Josselin is representative here of a typical early modern English *mentalité* perceptible both in the individual and at the level of state politics is underwritten by entries such as that for 29 March 1644: 'keeping a day of Humiliacon at my Lady Honywoods while we were praying god was making Waller victorious over Hopton' (p. 15). Throughout the early 1640s entries indicating 'a day of humiliacon' or a 'Day of Publique himiliacion' occur with great frequency, and indicate not only private devotions but also adherence to a public day of fasting and prayer, prescribed by the state. In Essex, Josselin hears of the execution of King Charles: 'Heard K.C. was executed ... this day was a fast, a very cold day' (31 January 1648/9), and he broods on the event for several days before his next entry:

> I was much troubled with the blacke providence of putting the King to death; my teares were not restrained at the passages about his death; the Lord in his mercy lay it not as a sinne to the charge of the kingdome, but in mercy do us good by the same; the small poxe on some familyes of the towne but spreadeth not, to God be the glory therof: this weeke I could do nothing neither in my Hebrew, nor in my reconciler. (4 February 1648/9)

Josselin's disturbance is evident not merely in his inability to concentrate but in the way he seems forced to confront in the king's death a frighteningly Manichaean notion of a 'blacke providence' whose issue is 'a sinne'. He casts around for more acceptable supernatural interventions such as the containment of smallpox, but his deep anxiety will not abate. He dismisses 'passionate' talk about the execution, and concludes the entry with a prophetic flourish:

> The death of the king talked much of, very many men of weaker sort of christians in divers places passionate concerning it, but so ungroundedly, that it would make any bleed to observe it, the lord hath some great thing to doe, feare and tremble att it oh England. (4 February 1648/9)

The same self-humiliation and trembling may well be required of the individual. Following the death of his ten-day old baby son Ralph, Josselin chastises himself: 'Whereas I have walked with much vanitie in my thoughts and resolved against it and served divers lusts too much in thought, and in actions, wheras both body and soule should bee the lords who hath called mee to holynes, god hath taken away a sonne' (p. 114). But the day before, 22 February 1647, Josselin had experienced a moment of reassurance dependent upon a change of temporal perspective. Through the words of the Burial of the Dead, which he must have intoned countless times, he records a glimpse through the eye of faith of a different kind of time:

> Thes 2 dayes were such as I never knewe before; the former for the death, and this for the burial of my deare sonne whom I layed in the chancell on the North side of the great Tombe; there thy bones rest out of my sight, but thy soule liveth in thy and my gods sight, and soule and body shall assuredly arise to injoy god, and thes eyes of mine shall see it: yea and my god shall make mee see this dealing of his to bee for the best. (p. 114)

The crushing rebuke in this world for vanity and lust committed in this world will be 'explained' on the other side, where his son's soul and resurrected body will be seen (the act of *seeing* is insisted on), and so too will God's plan.

During the years 1647–1657 Josselin seems to have been a convinced millenarian. Certainly the number of diary entries speculating on the Second Coming of Christ are among his most sustained pieces of writing. Like all millenarian speculations, they involve complex varieties of temporal arithmetic and compilations of numbers from both apocalyptic biblical texts and from scrutiny of secular history. The diary vividly presents the contrast between an awareness of an overarching cosmically ordered time-keeping whose chronology is marked by vast temporal units burning towards a chosen point of time – 'Three famous ruines are of the Romane Empire, the 1st 365: the 2^d 45 yeares after that: 410: the 3^d. 45. yeares after that viz: 455: in the two last the City was taken and in part burnt. if wee adde Daniels 1290. yeares to 365: yeares: it is', Josselin triumphantly asserts, '1656' (2 January 1650, p. 230) – and the unstudied daily ordinariness of adjacent entries such as: 'bargained with old Taylor to sett up leantoo's to my barne for cowes and strawe and horse', or 'at night my tooth began to ake on the left side'. In similar fashion his recordings of critical moments in the nation's life are assimilated into an ongoing concern with his suppurating navel, windows broken by the wind, mildew on the wheat, or miserly neighbours. His entry for 27 February 1656 records 'confident reports that Cromwell was proclaimed King, said also wee shall have an house of lords'; and he adds, with a gesture skywards as it were, 'some great alteration is in hand, but what it will bee time will discover, only he hath outwitted his coactors in former designes, and no doubt his purpose is the like, but none can outwit the almighty'. In another key, or from a purely mundane temporal dimension, a marginal annotation against that entry on wily Cromwell delightedly records that 'wee and others had damaske rose buds in February' (p. 392). In Josselin's text, as in so many early modern texts of both self-representation in journals and autobiographies and of the presentation of other selves in drama and imaginative literature, there always seem to be two time scales to attend to, each constantly interacting with the other: one the *chronos* of watches and clocks and lunar and solstitial calendars, the other the *kairos* of God's time-keeping into which all terrestrial chronologies will be subsumed.

It is clear that conformity or otherwise to the plan, whether by apparent choice or mere default, is not an option, and though a man of Josselin's temperament may find such determinism a source of comfort, it cannot prevent bad dreams. Particularly through the 1650s Josselin had many bad nights, and his frank recording of some fifteen or sixteen dreams marks a significant point of interest of his diary. Although he does not attempt to 'theorise' his dreaming, several of the dreams, coming from the temporally fractured world of the dormant brain, speak eloquently of suppressed fears of inadequacy or delinquency. In one he dreams he is in church, taking communion, but he does not go home to dinner, nor does his wife care whether he does or not; he is still there for afternoon service, but without his proper vestments on and filled with shame:

> I stoopt down and put a handkerchiefe about my necke (to conceale my wives neglect) I begun to sing, but could not read the psalms, nor sing, nor none sing with mee, the book was a strangers, I laboured for my own bible but could not come by it. (23 March 1655, p. 364)

The sense of personal abandonment here, of being utterly alone – and, indeed, of being erased and supplanted by another, a stranger – is transformed into a softly glowing and yet ambiguous anticipation of martyrdom in the blessed company of the saints as Josselin transcribes his dream of the night of 15 February 1657:

> I dreamed at night I was condemned to die for religion, another minister with mee and some women also, I was somewhat afraid at first in my spirit afterwards very comfortable, I was in wonderfull large roome matted, but I awaked before execution. (p. 419)

The detail of the large room with its matting floor is startling with the clarity and irrelevance of dreams, but Jossselin is left in the morning, like K in Kafka's *The Trial*, unable to discover the nature of the charges or the reasons for his condemnation; for, he adds, 'I remember not the points on which done'.

In the last decade or so of the journal Josselin's entries grow briefer, the handwriting more shapeless. Among 'Josselins Sayings' bound into the end papers of the volume are some reflections on time and mortality, among them Josselin's calculation of his own apotheosis, a calculation derived from superimposing the span of a man's life on the seven days of the week to predict a final arrival at an eternal Sabbath: 'if mans age bee 70: then I now being in my 58. am almost at my friday midnight, lord fitt mee for a blessed sabbath at hand' (p. 657). In the diary itself, like the emperor Augustus and like Philip Henry, Josselin gratefully survives his 'critical and dangerous' sixty-third year (26 January 1679, p. 626), dying in 1683 at the almost perhaps very early Sunday morning age of 67.

Notes

1   The phrase is James M. Osborn's, editor of *The Autobiography of Thomas Whythorne* (Oxford: Clarendon Press, 1961), Preface, p. v.

2   *Patrologia Latina*, vol. 34, cols. 190–94.

3   See J.E. Hankins, *Shakespeare's Derived Imagery* (Lawrence: University of Kansas Press, 1953), pp. 15–28, and Alan Brissenden (ed.), *As You Like It*, World's Classics (Oxford: Oxford University Press, 1994), p. 150n. For general surveys of 'the ages of man' motif, see J.A. Burrow, *The Ages of Man: A Study of Medieval Writing and Thought* (Oxford: Clarendon Press, 1986), and Mary Dove, *The Perfect Age of Man's Life* (Cambridge: Cambridge University Press, 1986), in which Whythorne is referred to, p. 27.

4   Whythorne, *Autobiography*, modern spelling and abbreviated edition, ed. James M. Osborn (London: Oxford University Press, 1962), pp. 11, 66, 117–18. Elizabeth Heale, in *Autobiography and Authorship in Renaissance Verse* (London: Palgrave, 2003), argues for Whythorne's original orthography as 'an integral part of the self-presentation of the writer' (p. 179, n. 2), but while acknowledging this argument we have preferred to quote from Osborn's much more accessible 1962 edition.

5   Osborn, 1961, lix.

6   Elizabeth Heale, 'Songs, Sonnets and Autobiography: Self-Representation in Sixteenth-Century Verse Miscellanies', in *Betraying Our Selves: Forms of Self-Representation in Early Modern English Texts*, ed. Henk Dragstra, Sheila Ottway and Helen Wilcox (London: Macmillan, 2000), pp. 59–75. See also Andrew Mousely, 'Renaissance Selves and Life Writing: The *Autobiography* of Thomas Whythorne', *Forum* 26 (1990): 222–30.

7   Anne Davidson Ferry, *The 'Inward' Language: Sonnets of Wyatt, Sidney, Shakespeare, Donne* (Chicago: University of Chicago Press, 1983), p. 37.

8   Osborn, 1962, p. 117.

9   Osborn, 1962, pp. 117–18.

10 Osborn, 1962, pp. 127–8.

11 Osborn, 1962, pp. 120–28.

12 Aulus Gellius, *Noctes Atticae*, 15.7.3; for which see *The Oxford Classical Dictionary*, ed. S. Hornblower and A. Spawforth, 3rd edition (Oxford University Press, 1996), pp. 627–8.

13 *Diaries and Letters of Philip Henry, MA, of Broad Oak, Flintshire, A.D. 1631–1696*, ed. Matthew Henry Lee, M.A., Vicar of Hanmer (London: Kegan Paul, Trench and Co., 1882), p. 376.

14 Osborn, 1962, p. 1.

15 Alistair Fox argues that 'by the late 1560s the discourse generated by this fervent Calvinist Protestantism ... had become unquestionably the most powerful and dominant normative discourse in Elizabethan England'. *The English Renaissance: Identity and Representation in Elizabethan England* (Oxford: Blackwell, 1997), p. 63.

16 See Debora Shuger's brief but penetrating essay, 'Life-writing in Seventeenth-Century England', in *Representations of the Self from the Renaissance to Romanticism*, ed. Patrick Coleman, Jayne Lewis, and Jill Kowalik (Cambridge: Cambridge University Press, 2000), pp. 73–4.

17 Osborn, 1962, pp. 211–12.

18 See Gerhard Dohrn-Van Rossum, *History of the Hour: Clocks and Modern Temporal*

Orders, trans. Thomas Dunlap (Chicago and London: University of Chicago Press, 1996), p. 323; G.J. Whitrow, 'Time and Measurement', in *Dictionary of the History of Ideas* (Scribner: New York, 1973).

19 On the sociology of timekeeping, Norbert Elias argues that in modern working life, the external social compulsion of time represents a 'complex system of self-regulation … within individual people as regards time, with a correspondingly acute individual sensibility towards time'. Norbert Elias, *Time: An Essay*, trans. Edmund Jephcott (Oxford: Blackwell, 1992), p. 22.

20 Such questions have, of course, been put many times: for example, in Frederick M. Turner's *Shakespeare and the Nature of Time* (Oxford: Oxford University Press, 1971), or by Ricardo J. Quinones, whose *The Renaissance Discovery of Time* (Cambridge Mass.: Harvard University Press, 1972) was severely critiqued in G.F. Waller's very useful *The Strong Necessity of Time: The Philosophy of Time in Shakespeare and Elizabethan Literature* (The Hague: Mouton, 1976); or Linda Woodbridge, 'Shakespeare and the Carnival of Time' in her *The Scythe of Saturn: Shakespeare and Magical Thinking* (Urbana and Chicago: University of Illinois Press, 1994), pp. 265–325. Specialist studies recording and exploring the Renaissance sense of time, contingency and mutability tend to be of three kinds (leaving aside esoteric contributions such as Alastair Fowler's *Spenser and the Numbers of Time* [London: Routledge and Kegan Paul, 1964]): those like Quinones that rely on an impressionistic, quasi-Burkhardtian historiography; those primarily concerned with plotting the emergence of 'modern time'; and literary studies generally directed towards the explication of canonical texts and, overwhelmingly, Shakespeare's sonnets and plays.

21 See Shuger, 'Life Writing', pp. 63–78.

22 All quotations from Shakespeare's plays here are from *The Norton Shakespeare*, ed. Stephen Greenblatt et al. (New York and London: Norton, 1997).

23 See F. Neale and A. Lovell, *Wells Cathedral Clock* (Wells: Wells Cathedral Publications, 1998); Edward Stanham, *The Astronomical Clock in Wimborne Minster Dorset* (Woodmansterne Publications Ltd., 1988). Also F.C. Haber, 'The Cathedral Clock and the Cosmological Clock Metaphor', *KronoScope Journal for the Study of Time*, Leyden: Brill, n.d. II. p. 399.

24 Dohrn-Van Rossum, *History of the Hour*, pp. 107–8. He refers for this argument and its phrasing to Klaus Maurice, *Die deutsche Räderurh. Zur Kunst und Technik des mechanischen Zeitmessers im deutschen Sprachrauum*, 2 vols (Munich, 1976), 1, p. 38ff.

25 Norbert Elias, *Time: An Essay*, pp. 14–15.

26 Recorded, along with many other examples, in T. Geoffrey W. Henslow's illustrated *Ye Sundial Booke* (London: W. & G. Foyle, 1935).

27 Herbert's extrovert autobiography, written c. 1645 when he was about sixty, stops in mid-life at the point where frustrated ambition, debt, and courtly neglect set in. *The Life of Edward, First Lord Herbert of Cherbury, written by himself*, ed. J.M. Shuttleworth (London: Oxford University Press, 1976).

28 *The Life*, pp. 11–13. The Latin poem, here entitled 'VITA', is alternatively titled 'De Vita Humana Philosophica Disquisitio' and derives from the 1645 and 1656 editions of Herbert's *De Causis Errorum*. An English translation is given in Shuttleworth, pp. 136–7.

29 See *Milton's Complete Shorter Poems*, ed. John Carey (London: Longman, 1971), pp. 165–6.

30 See, e.g., Sharon A. Beehler, '"Confederate Season": Shakespeare and the Elizabethan Understanding of *Kairos*', in *Shakespeare Matters: History, Teaching, Performance*, ed. Lloyd Davis (Newark: University of Delaware Press, 2003), pp. 74–88.

31 The precarious survival of some journals may be illustrated by Nehemiah Wallington, whose handwritten quarto of 518 pages, 'A Record of the Mercies of God, or a Thankful Remembrance' is prefaced by this introduction explaining his reasons for recording his life: 'I did write down these mercies of God ten years ago, and some time I was in mind to have burnt it in the fire, and so destroyed it, because I was ashamed that any should hear of this my sin. But now with better consideration I am contented to shame myself to the world, so that I may bring glory to God … receiving new favours and deliverances from God, I was so far from destroying it, that I could not sleep in quiet till I had written it out fairer, and oh! I could wish it was written in a book, and graven with an iron pen in lead, or in stone for ever to the generations to come'. 'Wallington's Journal', Guildhall Library. Quoted in R. Webb's edition of Wallington's *Historical Notices of Events Occurring Chiefly in the Reign of Charles I* (London: Richard Bentley, 1896), pp. xxvii–xxviii. By contrast, Edward, Lord Herbert's *Life* was, according to Horace Walpole, 'in great danger of being lost to the World'. It was printed by Walpole 1764, and exists in two manuscripts, one in seventeenth-century hand (his secretary Rowland Evans) with corrections in Herbert's own arthritic hand contemporary with the writing of the manuscript, and a derivative one in nearly modern hand. Mario M. Rossi convincingly argues that Herbert wrote it not for the public eye at all but for his own amusement and that of his favourite grandson, Edward. *La Vita, le opere, i tempi di Edoardo Herbert di Chirbury*, 3 vols (Florence, 1947), III, p. 166.

32 *Religio Medici* (1642/43), in *Sir Thomas Browne: The Major Works*, ed. C.A. Patrides (Harmondsworth: Penguin, 1977), pp. 72–3.

33 *The Diary of Ralph Josselin 1616–1683*, ed. Alan Macfarlane (London: Oxford University Press, for the British Academy, Records of Social and Economic History, New Series, III, 1976). Macfarlane notes (Introduction, p. xx) that an earlier version of the diary edited by E. Hockliffe, *The Diary of the Rev. Ralph Josselin, 1616–83* (Camden Society, 3rd series, xv, 1908), reproduces only about a quarter of the original, designating 'many entries of no interest whatever – endless thanks to God for his goodness … prayers, notes about the weather or his sermons, innumerable references to his constant "rheums" and "poses", trivial details of every day life, records of visits to his friends, etc. etc.' (Hockliffe, p. v.) – precisely those things, as Macfarlane stresses, about which we wish to learn.

34 Both Whythorne's and Josselin's responses to disease, illness and death are discussed in Ralph Houlbrooke's comprehensive study *Death, Religion, and Family in England 1480–1750* (Oxford: Clarendon Press, Oxford Studies in Social History, 1998), pp. 70–71.

Chapter 2

Time, Death and Memorialization

Reading the Times

It is a critical commonplace to argue that the deepest 'infrastructure', or 'habitus', of the early modern mind is not economy or society, or even politics or law, but God.[1] While Raleigh's *History of the World*, Clarendon's *Reflections* on the Psalms, or the career and speeches of Oliver Cromwell, are unintelligible without a lived sense of the purposes of God in human affairs, so too are more modest self-representational or autobiographical texts, such as Ralph Josselin's. And God and time form a dense matrix, for time was not ours but God's. The House of Commons was reminded – routinely one might say – by the puritan preacher Stephen Marshall in 1640 that it was nothing but God's instrument: 'the hand of the dial makes not the clock to go', he declared, 'but shows how it doth go'.[2] The Calvinist William Perkins conceptualized the early modern self as 'a double person', arguing that:

> Every person is a double person and under two regiments. In the first regiment I am a person of mine own self, under Christ ... [and must] humble myself, forsake and deny myself ... In the temporal regiment, thou art a person in respect of another. Thou art husband, father ... wife, lord, subject and there thou must do according to thine office. If thou be a father, thou must do the office of a father and rule.[3]

The division of personhood here is rendered in the almost normative early modern opposition between accountability to God and accountability to one's peers, the first expressed through private devotional utterance and prayer, the other through office and function. The appropriate pronoun for the first is the private 'I', and for the second the public 'thou'. Significantly, Perkins assigns the exercise of the familial and public to what he calls 'the temporal regiment' – that is, not to a social so much as a temporal 'space', implying that the 'I', the person he is 'of mine own self', therefore operates in a different, nontemporal modality.

Such a perception is not simply a function of Perkins's Calvinism: the vigorously antipredestinarian Sir Thomas Browne makes the same distinction – with characteristically luminous simplicity – for all Christian subjects: 'therefore, I say, every man hath a double Horoscope, one of his humanity, his birth; another of his Christianity, his baptisme, and from this do I compute or calculate my Nativitie'.[4]

Although early modern life-writings may often slip back and forth between these two dimensions – the private realm of moral self-scrutiny and the public realm of self-advancement – they rarely confuse one with the other. At critical moments in life-experience the distinction – between, that is, the temporal and the timeless – may appear with special clarity, such as, to take two very different instances, the experience of bereavement, especially the death of infants, and the experience of state punishment. The first, so frequent both in life and in the family record of many early modern diaries and journals, is often accompanied by a search for a pattern, and invariably a temporal one, dependent on the recognition of dates and times and calendrical coincidences, that somehow, properly decoded, points to what lies beyond time. The year 1661 may illustrate both examples.

Anne Lady Halkett's reflection 'Upon the death of my deare Son Henry, being 12 of May, 1661' begins: 'What a sad journy hath this beene hether to mee into England [from Dublin] where I expected greatest satisfaction: 1st, in seeing the King and Royall family restored, and then in seeing my relations and friends'. But 'new afflictions' awaited her in London:

> The Lord is pleased … to take away almost the cheefe comforts of my life, which is my deare children, the first as being best beloved, and this as next succeeding, and all to teach mee nott to love the world or any thing that is in itt. I was nott wittnesse of my deare Hary's suffering as I was of his sister's, butt by relation it was a long, lingring sicknese, every day threatning death, and att last it came, to put an end to his mortality just in the night of that day of the weeke (being Sunday) that he first received breath; and had he lived one month longer he had been just three yeare seeing the world and feeling the bitternese of itt.[5]

Lady Halkett, not even present at the death of her son, searches for symmetry and pattern, and hence meaning, grasping at the approximate synchronicity of the day of the week, Sunday, on which her son was both born and died. Similar temporal calculations – following the Psalmist's petition 'teach us to number our days' – occur with persistent regularity in diaries and memorials. Typical is this much earlier account, by her husband, of the death of Elizabeth Wallington:

> This godly, religious and virtuous woman the Mother of those within written twelve children, departed this mortal miserable life on the xx day of November 1603 about five of the clock in the morning, being the Sabbath day. And not long before the Lord took her happy soul unto Himself, she uttered these words, Lord, shall I this day keep my Sabbath with thee? [6]

Chronological arithmetic inhabits the writings of Whythorne or Philip Henry or Ralph Josselin, and indicates an almost instinctive early modern response to a perceived symbolic temporal geometry offering both a calculus and, more importantly perhaps, furnishing the individual with a temporal chart to interpret that pattern. Such gestures are a more workaday counterpart to Sir Thomas Browne's rhapsodic metaphysical meditation on the sepulchral urns found in a field at Walsingham, whose womblike shape prompted him to see our death in our conception, and vice versa – 'the common form with necks was a proper figure, making our last bed like our first; nor much unlike the Urnes of our Nativity'[7] – and who himself managed the perfect temporal symmetry, or circularity, of dying on his birthday.

There were also of course political and coercive lessons to be drawn from contacts – whether in the individual or the state – between events and time's measurement of them. At the Restoration, Philip Henry – like Josselin, a firm believer in special providence – had taken the oath of allegiance but refused reordination (which he regarded as simony), and was thus incapable of preferment. In October 1661, he was allowed to preach a farewell sermon in his Flintshire parish, after which he was a 'silenced minister'. The Uniformity Act took effect on 24 August 1662, and Henry ironically notes that it was 'the day of the year on which I was born ... and also the day of the year on which by law I died' (Old *Dictionary of National Biography*). For Henry, quick to see signs of divine displeasure at the enemies of nonconformity, there was a judgment in the coincidence.

In a public world of intense political agitation, the London of 1661 at which Lady Halkett arrived for the king's restoration had, for at least the last year or so, been vigorously compiling, in newspapers, broadsheets, government 'press releases' and royalist verses, instances of temporal 'coincidences' designed to show, through irony and sarcasm, the workings of providence in the Restoration cause – just as in the earlier years of civil war each side had energetically read the signs of divine favour.[8] They ranged from the stage-managed and spectacular disinterment of the bodies of Cromwell, Ireton and Bradshaw on 30 January 1661, the very day on which Charles was beheaded, to the 'evidences' of providence's mocking temporal signature that brought about the coincidence that Cromwell's death on 8 September 1658, was not only his birthday but also the anniversary of his great but now quite redundant military triumphs at both Dunbar and Worcester. Such state appropriation of the 'meaning' of time and its interpretation was, of course, contested by those, like Thomas Harrison or John Cooke, who were excepted from the Act of Oblivion and interrogated and sentenced to execution as regicides.[9] Their rebuttals to their judges asserted an alternative account of providence's temporal workings and their own relationship to it and appealed to that other 'regiment', as Perkins expressed it, 'of mine own self, under Christ'. They are painfully recorded, among other sources, by Harrison himself, or by the regicide Hugh Peters in his self-memorializing *A Dying Father's Last Legacy to an Onely Child* (London, 1660), or by the disaffected republican autobiographer Edmund Ludlow in his *A Voyce from the Watch Tower*, written abroad and in exile.[10] In the brief liminal period between the death throes of the Commonwealth and the return of Charles Stuart, Ludlow meets a royalist acquaintance and fatalistically observes that, whatever political hands they might play, 'it was twielight (as we call it) with us both: with me it was as that of the evening, when it darkens by reason of the departure of the sunne, but with him as that of the morning, when it vanisheth by reason of its rising' (p. 109). Time and its symbols, it would seem, can be as relative as politics.

While royalist propaganda may have jeered at what was figured as the eccentric individualism of their opponents, the posture of those accused was of course nothing of the kind, in the sense that the regicides and their supporters were simply reinscribing their political defeat as martyrdom in the same way that royalism had earlier in the effusions of *Eikon Basilike* (1649), and with as dense an array of biblical parallelism. But to be genuinely resistant to the dominant ontology of providential control, rather than merely concerned with its manipulation or appropriation, and to proclaim in proud self-advertisement, like Richard Gloucester, 'I am myself alone', is characteristically depicted throughout the period not only as irreligious but as useless, and is ridiculed as such in popularly homiletic or theatrical figures like the over-reacher, the outlawed revenger, or the madman. To the disappointment sometimes of modern discoverers and editors of early modern autobiographical texts, the relentless piety of their subjects is as much a primary defining feature of their self-representations as it is of the vast majority of printed materials to be found on London and provincial bookstalls.[11] And, as the diaries and journals of many of those who, like Edmund Ludlow or Ralph Josselin, lived through the English Revolution indicate, the idea of individual autonomy, it would seem, like the idea of political liberty, emerges most clearly at the point at which it occurs to people that there may be no such thing.

In Time and Out of Time

It is impossible, then, to think of conceptions of the self and time in the period as separable from issues of determinism and autonomy. For early modern subjects time seems not to have been conceived of merely as a relation between events (and thus enabling 'history'), or as a Kantian function of the human consciousness, or as a form of organizational restraint codifying work practices and customs and designed to fulfil needs for predictability and calculability. Rather, it functions as a God-organized enabler of the process of individual sin, repentance and salvation, towards which almost every domestic diary or journal is fundamentally orientated and in terms of which the writing of a 'life', and the life itself, alone gains significance.

However, the most characteristic temporal orientations of modernity, already vigorously at work in the seventeenth century, have, of course, been predominantly towards the control and expansion of capital, commerce and productivity: the development of 'merchant time'. Industrial labour and the pocket watch went hand in hand and, in a story many times told, the creation in the eighteenth century of chronometers precise enough to establish longitude was driven primarily by commercial need. With the exception of the enquiries of physicists like Stephen Hawking or Paul Davies, our own cultural narratives of the human measurement of time invariably lead away, in evolutionary fashion, from liturgical or theological time to the creation of the universally synchronized global economic marketplace, and with it the creation of the consuming 'bourgeois' subject and the modern individualist self. In this history, fourteenth-century Florence has been claimed as unique in its development of 'modern' systems of bookkeeping, insurance and venture capital management, all of which depend upon precise patterns of dating, accounting, and of calculable expectation.[12] But the very exceptional nature of the Florentine city-state in this respect marks the rule that elsewhere timekeeping was not, or not yet, primarily concerned with the investment of capital or the organization of labour but, so it would therefore seem, with something else entirely. One of Ralph Josselin's recurring embarrassments is that his agricultural investments tend to make profits, and his diary reluctantly records a steady accumulation of wealth and property – reluctantly both because of his sense of its incompatibility with his vocation of parish priest, and because of fear of providential reprisals for its undeservedness.

As is also well known, earlier Western discourses on time have in fact been dedicated to the exposure, or elimination, of an *illusio*, that is, to the proposition that time does not, in the most real sense, exist. The dominant Christian view of history (so fully documented by C.A. Patrides[13]) posits a temporal *schema* that 'ends' in an apocalyptic dissolution out of which all things are made new by 'the Alpha and the Omega, the first and the last, the beginning and the end' (Revelation 21, 5; 22, 13). Some philosophical high points in the exploration of timelessness would include St Augustine's speculations on the problem of time and human freedom in relation to God's foreknowledge, countered by Boethius's God who foreknows nothing but, because such a being is timeless, simply knows; or Aquinas's *nunc stans*; or Spenser's Mutability Cantos where sequence and change and decay are subsumed into the paradox of eternal mutability. These views invariably seem to grow from a questioning of the relationship between the human subject and 'God's time', and their exploration is frequently associated with 'autobiographical' situations and contexts: St Augustine defines for Western culture not only the nature of the City of God but in the *Confessions* the nature of autobiographical practice itself; Boethius writes from prison, that most productive site of self-review and self-ordering; the debate with Dame Nature and Spenser's epiphany take place in the poet's own back garden under Arlo Hill in Ireland. Similarly, the temporal as well as spatial trick of Donne's 'We thinke that Christ's crosse and Adam's tree / Stood in one place' (he has made that up) occurs as he represents himself as sick and on his death bed; Sir Thomas Browne's contemplation of the timeless 'metaphysicks of true belief' is part of his own journey of self-exploration ('The world that I regard is my selfe'); the arresting simplicity of Henry Vaughan's 'I saw Eternity the other night, / Like a great ring of pure and endless light' anticipates lost friends 'who are all gone into the world of light!' ('I see them walking in an Air of glory, / Whose light doth trample on my days'); and Milton's motionless and timeless empyrean around the base of which flex, in light and shadow, the various circles of human, angelic and cosmic times, is 'viewed' by an autobiographically self-characterizing poet whose blindness relieves him of the visual evidences of time's progression: 'with the year/ Seasons return, but not to me returns / Day, or the sweet approach of ev'n or morn' (*Paradise Lost*, 3, 41–3). The instinct to read the transient moment against a motionless backdrop of eternity seems endemic in early modern sensibilities. In the compulsorily church-going society of pre-Civil War England reinforcement of such a mode of perception was regularly available to every man, woman and child in the familiar, incantatory, time-collapsing formula concluding the canticles and petitions in the *Book of Common Prayer*: 'As it was in the beginning, is now, and ever shall be: world without end. Amen'.

However many temporal dimensions there may be for the various parts of God's creation and its creatures, there is a fundamental dualism of the two realms of the timeless and the temporal. Giordano Bruno writes (Sir Thomas Browne echoes him): 'Thus ... the divine mind contemplates everything in one altogether simple act at once and without succession, that is, without the difference between past, present and future: to Him all things are present'.[14] Spinoza adds the logical corollary that things can only be as they are for a being who is God: 'in eternity there is no "before" and "after"; for it follows exclusively from the divine perfection that God's decrees cannot be different and could not have been different'.[15] At the same time, neither Bruno nor Spinoza – nor Donne or Milton – would ever deny that temporal succession was a fact of the 'lower' or phenomenal level; it was only on the 'higher' transcendental level of ultimate reality – or of the apocalyptic 'new heaven and new earth" – that time was abolished. In the meantime, time and its measurement on clock faces or in diary entries or in parish records proceeds in accordance with an inevitable sense of forward motion. Isaac Barrow, Professor of Mathematics at Cambridge before Newton, asserts that this sense of motion is not implied by time 'as far as its absolute and intrinsic nature is concerned; not any more than it implies rest', and he explains – proleptically quoting, as it were, Thomas Gray – that 'whether we move or are still, whether we sleep or wake, Time pursues the even tenour of its way'. But, he argues, it is only by means of motion that time is in any way *measurable*.[16]

Using a conceit of winding his watch, the diarist Elias Ashmole displays some varied ways of measuring the forward motion of a journey home and thus the passing of time. At the bottom of a diary page he light-heartedly versifies his 'riding post from London to Bradfield 12 May 1648', counterpointing the inter-activities of bird-song, dance measures, the measures, or *tempi*, of a musical score, his horse's hooves, and the ticking of his watch:

> The Birdes chirpt Tunes, their nimbler wings did play
> Quaver'd Corantes, to shorten the long way.
> The tyme was Tryple, three to one ye hand;
> To their Lavoltes I Gallopt Sarabrand.
> My Horses Leggs Division run till they
> Came to their Stage; [a Semibrieje rest] and hay,
> Where like my Watch I wound, but up ye Spring

The Balance plaied againe, the'unwinding String,
Wheel'd me to my pleas'd Cell.[17]

Ashmole's troping here clearly has little to do with some compulsive need to know what time it is, and everything to do with a sense of the calculation itself – and the rhythmic analogies it provokes – as a source of fascination and delight.

Edward Herbert and Elias Ashmole's watches, with their springs and balances, indicate the availability of rapidly multiplying and increasingly affordable timepieces in the sixteenth and seventeenth centuries, from public and domestic clocks to personal pocket watches.[18] The emblematically instructive dial warning of waste and mortality soon became not death's auditor but life's, a primary economic tool and pragmatic commonplace of social and commercial transaction, whose antique reminders that *Tempus fugit* – time flies – or *Ne quid pereat* – let nothing be lost – become familiar clichés not of the brevity of life or the eternal reckoning but of the need to clinch the deal before the competition. So a question for many early modern writers of 'themselves', both in high art and in more mundane journals and diaries, might be: with what devices, discursive or iconographical, can the linear flow of time, the repeated waves upon the pebbled shore, be contested and what gestures can be made towards that known sense of transcendence? And how, within such flux, and within the inculcated devotional response of submissiveness, can the individual negotiate a space and an identity? Time may well be 'the generall rust of the world' which 'weareth, eateth, consumeth, and perforateth all thynges'[19], including the human body, but as G.F. Waller asserts, 'for most sixteenth-century writers time is … consistently seen as ultimately unreal'.[20] *Ne quid pereat* is the motto painted on the stonework above the outside Wells Cathedral clock, between the two knights who strike the bells with their pikes, and its meaning may be construed by those intended to contemplate it not only as an evident instruction not to waste precious time but also as an affirmation that, despite the verge escapement and trains of pig-fat greased wheels rotating and clunking within, nothing ever *is* lost but resides within the Alpha and Omega of God's eternity.

In many respects, and as most modern critical histories of time and its perception suggest, the early modern period, however loosely defined, is a watershed or transitional period between a patristic and medieval Christian view of time as essentially God's temporary 'invention' for the conduct of human affairs, and the modern conception of time as a measurable physical continuum ordered *by* human societies for the regulation of its affairs. Such changes also affect the ways in which people both orientate and express themselves in relation to them. The rapidity with which the latter kind of measurement and regulation proceeded in the sixteenth and seventeenth centuries clearly did not eliminate or supersede the earlier synthesis but rather complicated and deepened it with urgent personal issues of responsibility, right action, and retribution. From the evidence of the conduct of public and political life, of the imaginative and dramatic literature, and especially of the growing impulse in people to 'chronicle' themselves in first-person verse, in portraits, or in the recording of a life journal or narrative, traffic between the sacred and the secular appears constant and intense. A keen awareness of the 'two regiments', or of two kinds of time that thus render every individual in some sense 'double', is a primary characterizing and informing feature of early modern self-representation, not only where we would expect it in specifically religious, confessional autobiography of the 'chief of sinners' kind [21], but in every sphere in which people endeavoured to depict themselves. Such depiction frequently demonstrates, like Whythorne's, a tension between the putative uniqueness of the self, fostered by Protestant emphasis on individual salvation, on the one hand, and on the other the ordinariness, the homogeneity, of all individuals with respect to the great determinants of providence and time. For early modern subjects too time can mark the sequence of moments that make a life, rendering each individual aware of procession and loss, and inducing both anxiety and hope. It can thus generate another kind of tension by locating the self both in a particular physical time and place and yet in no time and no place. Despite the apparent tyranny of advancing calendar dates and hours o'clock, a characteristic expression of the early modern sense of temporality asserts, and documents, the timelessness not only of *process* but also of the individual self.

Sir Thomas Browne's self-fascinated *Religio Medici* conjures up this sense in a startling trope that is both whimsical and utterly serious: 'I was not only before my selfe, but *Adam*, that is, in the Idea of God ... thus I was dead before I was alive, though my grave be in *England*, my dying place was Paradise, and *Eve* miscarried of mee before she conceiv'd of *Cain*'.[22] In the memory of such a self resides an anticipation of the end of a time-bound world, and this shared and implicit knowledge of that Day of Judgment hovers over all early modern self-depiction, continually monitoring its boundaries, and defining its ultimate reader. As has been suggested, though there are many printed autobiographical texts, much early modern life-writing resides in private manuscripts, some (like Thomas Whythorne's) lost for centuries, and many having no apparent intended reader apart from the writer, and hence no 'self' to be offered and viewed by another, provoking the question, what or who is this text *for*? The question of address and addressee in diaries and journals is often a moot one, and the early modern default position, like that of devotional verse or any confessional utterance, is that they are all in some sense 'overheard by God'. So Browne can suggest possible answers to the question (raised by histories of autobiography) of why, with very few exceptions, early modern life-writing tends to lack that almost genre-defining voice of writer-as-hero or heroine. Firstly, because '[in] my solitary and retired imagination', Browne writes, 'I remember I am not alone, and therefore forget not to contemplate him and his attributes who is ever with mee'; and secondly because '[t]his is the day [i.e. of Judgment] whose memory hath onely power to make us honest in the darke, and to be virtuous without a witnesse'.[23]

Thus far we have looked both at early modern technology and theory of timekeeping, and at some different kinds of *textual* expressions of selfhood in relation to time. A 'self' may be represented and offered to view by means other than textual, of course, and painting one's self or having one's portrait painted would seem to be an ideal way of both representing and conserving the self through history. In early modern self-representation, the reciprocal nexus between inscription and depiction is a significant one: frequently the same motives for self-memorialization and the satisfaction of descendants trigger their production, and the basic tool of each activity, the pencil, is both writing implement and artist's brush (*pinceau*). Autobiographers themselves, like Whythorne in the sixteenth century or Patrick Gordon at the very end of the seventeenth, conceive of writing a life as similar to painting a portrait or self-portrait, Gordon introducing his diary of the years 1635–1699 with the observation that 'it is thought as hard a taske for any man to writt the story of his lyfe, and narrative of his actions, as for ane artist truly to draw his owne picture'.[24] The next section is concerned, firstly, with the analogous selves represented in early modern autobiography and portraiture and their relation to conceptions of time; and, secondly, with the analogous nature of 'narrative' in life-writing and in some kinds of portraiture, and what it may indicate about the early modern self and its depiction in relation to temporal processes.

'All in war with time': The Self and the Portrait

> Wheresoever your life endeth, there is it all.
> > Montaigne, 'That to Philosophize is to Learne how to Dye'[25]

The numerous studies of Tudor and Stuart portraiture by Sir Roy Strong and others seem to indicate that most often it is not so much the self that is represented and conserved in such portraits, but rather the office, function or dynastic authority of the sitter. Thomas Whythorne had his portrait painted as a young man, and again as an older man, and he suggests a range of motives for his preoccupation with this mode of self-representation – motives which complement those of his written autobiography. Whythorne's response to the ephemeral mirror image and the relative permanence of a picture will be discussed later in Chapter 4, but the distinction may be pressed further to emphasize the *autobiographical* dimensions of perceptions of temporality. When visiting again the artist in London who painted his first portrait, Whythorne notes that in his house

> I did see many pictures, as well of those that were much elder than I, as of some such that were of my years, yea, and much younger than I was. The which caused me to think that as some young folks, for that they having a pleasure to behold their beauties and favours, caused their picture to be made, so those that were older than I, although they had no such cause for beauty and favours' sake as many young folk have, did cause their pictures or counterfeits to be painted from time to time to see how time doth alter them.

One interest here is certainly with the ageing process itself. But Whythorne's deeper concern is not with the simple desire to outlive the ravages of time, but with the *nature* of this outliving. In other words, it is not time that concerns Whythorne so much as the kind and quality of self-representation that can be gained in the defeat of time. Both the mirror and the portrait fulfil a moral function, forcing sitters to 'consider with themselves how they ought to alter their conditions, and to pray to God that, as they do draw towards their long home and end in this world, so they may be the more ready to die in such sort as becometh true Christians'.[26] But the portrait has also an intergenerational function. While the mirrored image of the self can be instructive both as an indicator of physical well-being and as an emblematic marker of moral health or decay, Whythorne notes that its image is fleeting. It cannot serve as an instructive medium for future generations. And it is this generational focus that concerns Whythorne at least as much as the theme of instruction itself: that is, the composition of a self not just in the course of a lifetime, but through and in relation to a series of forebears and descendants. Sitters may leave their portraits 'with their friends, especially with their children, if they have any that be young; who, when they do come to years of discretion, though their fathers be dead, yet may they see what manner of favour they had'. (Whythorne speaks here of course as a private 'middling' subject, an itinerant gentleman-musician, rather than as a representative of an aristocratic or political dynasty. He also speaks – though he would not know it at the time of writing – as one who was to die childless.)

Besides simple curiosity about family traits, such a concern with the generations suggests an individual self portrayed as a kind of palimpsest of faces: the two different temporalities occupied by the mirror and the portrait entail not just an ephemeral/permanent contrast, but raise issues of singularity and communality. The composition and expression of self-identity concerns not one life but many, and by holding a number of generations within the same scopic moment an artist and his sitter can provide moral instruction for members of a family: if the depicted fathers 'left a good report of their virtues behind them' their grown-up children should seek to imitate them; but if they were villains, they should 'take heed that they do not follow their ill deeds, but to pray to God for His grace, whereby they may deserve better'.[27] Clearly for Whythorne, the commissioning of a portrait – like the writing of a life – whether of oneself or one's relations is a complex transaction. His focus on the relation of the individual to past and future generations marks 'selfhood' not as a unique or discrete feature, but as a dynamic and even transferable essence. This essence, in Whythorne's terms, is moulded and shaped not just in one lifespan but over several generations. While conscious of individual difference, one is not entirely the 'author' of one's own identity, with or without the help of God: one contributes to it by reading the faces of one's forebears.

If the artist described by Whythorne was able to hold the members of a family together through a contemplation of his canvas, some artists did this not just figuratively but literally, painting them into the canvas so that several generations jostled with each other. Memorial portraits of the period occasionally include groups, such as the six Hispano-Flemish delegates and the five English members of the Somerset House Conference, 1604, painted by an unknown artist[28], all of whom were (quite obviously) at the meeting together. But they sometimes also offer synoptic representations of figures that chronology could never have allowed to be together, thus rendering each individual's temporal location highly problematic. A notable example is found in the two versions by Rowland Lockey of 'Sir Thomas More and his Descendants' (1593), both versions deriving from and extending forward in time an original (1527–28) by Holbein. (The Holbein original has been lost except for an interim drawing.) One of Lockey's paintings is a miniature (24.6 x 29.4 cm), now in the Victoria and Albert Museum, and the other a large (227 x 330 cm, or over seven feet long) canvas in London's National Portrait Gallery (see Fig. 2.1). Portraits like the More family one, commissioned at a time when the family fortunes were sunk in obscurity, may have been influenced by the public, occasional nature of the generational or dynastic portrait. Holbein's 'Whitehall Mural', for example, blends diachronic portraiture and allegory, while 'The Family of Henry VIII: An Allegory of the Tudor Succession', c.1572 and attributed to Lucas de Heer, similarly assembles several generations in what appears as a single temporal space. Lockey's large oil depicts eleven figures variously seated or standing, from Sir John More, Sir Thomas's father, white-haired and in scarlet judge's robes, to their contemporary Elizabethan descendants. In the miniature Sir Thomas More's jester, Henry Patenson, peeps through a curtain revealing a glimpse of Sir Thomas's garden in Chelsea, but he and the garden are omitted in the large canvas. In depicting the family members mingling comfortably in the same room, the painting, with its missals and crucifixes, asserts a family faith and stamps the family's history in the faces of its dead. But it does more than that, for by playing with chronology *and* location in this way, the painter makes those on, or in, the canvas inhabit an 'unreal' world whose simultaneous levels of temporality become a vehicle for self-reflection and self-instruction.

The setting of this large picture is a brown-walled room with a canopied buffet to the left in the background, on which musical instruments, books, silver and flowers can be seen. The walls carry a row of heraldic devices characteristic of dynastic portraits, but two iconographically significant items dominate the background wall space. The first is a portrait within a portrait in which Thomas More's ward, the young Anne Cresacre, may view or, indeed, be viewed by, the picture of her old age. (Anne married More's son John and was mother to the probable commissioner of the paintings in 1593, grandson Thomas More the Younger.) As an older woman in the portrait hanging at the back of the composition, she watches her youthful self and is, perhaps, judged by her own history. The second feature, prominent above the heads of all the family members, is an expensive and clearly state-of-the-art clock which, ironically, is yet quite incapable of telling the time in the picture.[29] Time, then, is not just a matter of minutes and hours. In an imitation of timelessness, the clock's insistence on sequentiality can be manipulated, or even suspended, to furnish a mechanism of self-appraisal and self-recognition in a generational context beyond time or place.

Fig. 2.1   Rowland Lockey, *Sir Thomas More, his Father, his Household and his Descendants,* 222.4 x 330.2 cm, oil on canvas, 1593. National Portrait Gallery, London

Among the correspondences between the motives for the production of portraits and the writing of a life-narrative is the obvious family memorial or, as in the following two examples, the tribute or memorial to a spouse given by a bereaved wife. The self-depiction of the grieving widow contemplating the body of her husband is a memorable feature of Grace, Lady Mildmay's *Autobiography* (c.1617–1620). In 'The Author's Meditation Upon Her Corpse' – 'her' possessively indicating her husband Anthony's, but allowing too for anticipation of her own inevitable decay – Lady Mildmay writes these plangent words, creating an ornamented and self-instructive textual memorial whose language is dominated by liturgical rhythms and echoes of biblical motifs of mortality and resurrection:

> Let me behold my corpse which lieth folden in cerecloths, leaded and coffined here before me yet unburied, and consider: he was as I am, and as he is, I shall be. His candle is put out, his fire is quenched, and he hath made his bed in the dark. The grass is mown, the seed falleth into the earth and shall rise again.

Meditating on the man with whom she lived for almost fifty years, she concludes:

> So long as this my corpse is above the earth, I cannot but think upon him in this manner [i.e. awaiting 'our happy meeting in heaven'], and beseech the Lord to enable me to perform the trust which in his lifetime he reposed in me, to the honour of God, and the comfort of my neighbour, and so rest at the Lord's good pleasure to follow him in my happy end, and blessed departure out of this changeable world to eternal bliss in the everlasting kingdom of heaven.[30]

Her lament conveys a sense both of personal loss and of her social responsibilities as surviving partner. It also records, in formulaic phrases expressive of deep cultural consensus, the contrast between the mutability of this world and the timelessness of heaven. To arrive at 'the everlasting kingdom' involves a temporal journey, an 'ending', a 'departure' and a 'meeting', variously figured in the period in tropes of clocks ticking, of travelling, riding, or – as in Henry King's famous 'Exequy' – of marching:

> But heark! My Pulse like a soft Drum
> Beats my approch, tells *Thee* I come;
> And slow howere my marches be,
> I shall at last sit down by *Thee*. (*Poems*, 1657)

Another early modern tribute of wife to husband, this time a pictorial one, demonstrates that there are further strategies available for recording a sense of personal loss, the fickleness of earthly life, and the nature of an individual life's march or journey. The picture we shall discuss employs the motifs of travel and 'progress' in ways that emphatically register a sense of the eternally present and ineradicable status of every temporal moment, and with it the temporally extended compositeness of every individual. While it is a well-known characteristic of some medieval and Renaissance narrative paintings to tell their story in sequences on the same canvas, rather in the manner of a strip cartoon, a highly unusual – indeed, quite extraordinary – Tudor oil portrait hangs in the National Portrait Gallery, painted by an unknown artist in 1596 on a large panel (74 x 163 cm) (see Fig. 2.2). A relatively small part of this space is occupied by a portrait of the Elizabethan soldier and diplomat Sir Henry Unton (1557?–1596), who died aged about 39 of a fever in France while ambassador to Henri IV. The painting, commissioned by his widow Lady Dorothy, depicts Sir Henry with pen in hand and paper ready as though about to write the story of his life, while the allegorical figures of Fame and Death stand on either side of his head. Anti-clockwise – as we say – from the bottom right-hand corner of the panel are painted scenes of the important events in Unton's life. He is seen as a baby in the arms of his mother; he is a student at Oxford; he is in his study in his home, Wadley House, at Faringdon near Oxford, where he is seen making music, talking with learned divines, presiding with his wife over a banquet, entertained by a masque of Mercury and Diana; he is shown travelling to Venice and Padua, with the Alps in the background; he serves as a soldier in the Netherlands, where he was – is – knighted after the battle of Zutphen; he rides to the town of Coucy La Fère as English ambassador to France; sick with fever he is attended by physicians, but a ship with black mourning sails crosses the Channel bringing his body home to England. His hearse travels towards the Unton family home; the funeral procession of mourners stretches across the lower part of the painting under his portrait and enters All Saints Church, Faringdon, where the funeral service (held on 8 July 1596) is taking place and in front of which lies already, as it were, the recumbent effigy of Unton's monument with his wife kneeling beside it.[31]

Exactly what is so extraordinary about this picture – that is, its (literally) arresting depiction of synchronicity – seems to have been approached only obliquely by art historians, if at all. Sir Roy Strong, who wrote an article in which 'the picture is dealt with exhaustively' – at least as far as its history, allusions, heraldry and social dimensions are concerned – suggests that 'the unique quality of the picture springs perhaps from the character of Unton's widow who seems to have been a woman of strong and remarkable character'.[32] 'Strong' and 'remarkable' are not perhaps very helpful adjectives, yet while the ostensible subject represented in the picture is of course the deceased Sir Henry, there is certainly a sense in which Lady Unton is representing, in both the commissioning of the portrait and her multiple presences in it, not only her husband but *herself*: the panel tells the story of her mortal life, as well as her own mourning and loss. Lorne Campbell offers to sharpen the focus on the picture by suggesting a relation, 'in a general way', between 'this kind of biographical picture' and the narrative cycles of the deeds and lives of princes which existed much earlier. The particular example cited as analogue occurs in Froissart's late fourteenth-century romance *Méliador*, in which one of the heroes paints and presents to his lady a large picture in grisaille on canvas of his own exploits at the Tournament at Tarbonne. As explanatory comment on the Unton portrait this has of course two disadvantages:

Fig. 2.2 Unknown artist, *Sir Henry Unton (1557?–1596)*, 74 x 163.2 cm, oil on panel, 1596.

that the subject of the picture cited is not real but fictional, and, more importantly, that neither party in Froissart's transaction was – even fictionally – dead. No more helpful or relevant is Campbell's linking of the Unton picture with the genre of ex-voto paintings depicting accidents befalling patrons and their miraculous recoveries, in association with images of the saints whose help had been invoked. [33] For Sir Henry, after all, there were no miraculous recoveries, and thus the painting occupies a quite different social and metaphysical space. What such commentary on the Unton painting does not raise is the point that is central to this argument: in the circularity of its narrative, confusing beginnings and endings in the simultaneity of their representation, the painting not only signals the individual's relationship to a double-sided time and space but shows how such a conception of time and the depiction of a self inform and mediate each other. The painting explicitly alludes to the two time-scales of the temporal and the timeless, and indicates one of the many ways in which early modern individuals negotiated simultaneous awareness of these dimensions. As with the gaze in the emblematic mirror, whose suggestiveness was more important than any actual physical reflection, the spectators may read the emblematic purpose of the picture as one that denies, or subsumes, issues of history or chronology, and which also places *them* in an undifferentiated temporal continuum. Further, in its static presence as artifact it also suggests an analogous relation to the material, conserving artifact of the autobiographical manuscript or printed book. The workings of the period's key temporal perspectives, as illustrated in examples of self-representational diary, life-story, or portraiture, suggest a strong sense that – to paraphrase Avogadro's hypothesis – time, like matter, can neither be created nor destroyed. 'Nature' thus instructed Montaigne, as it did Lord Herbert, in the indivisibility of life and death, and with it the orders of time: '*Depart (saith she), out of this world, even as you came into it. The same way you came from death to life, returne without passion or amazement, from life to death: your death is but a peece of the world's order, and but a parcel of the world's life*'. [34] This sense of the existential 'solidarity' of a whole life beyond time is a frequent motif in seventeenth-century treatises on the nature of eternity: W.T.'s *A Discourse of Eternitie* (1633), for instance, defines eternity as 'duration alwaies present' which 'no time can reach'. [35] This sense is famously recorded by Donne in 'The Anniversarie', celebrating like the Unton panel the relationship between husband and wife: 'This, no tomorrow hath, nor yesterday, / Running it never runs from us away, / But truly keepes his first, last, everlasting day'. The lines, though echoing the extravagant hyperbole of those 'houres, dayes, months, which are the rags of time' of 'The Sunne Rising', more soberly capture that sense of the timeless, or time-defying, potentiality even of threatening calendar markers, such as anniversaries, to preserve both individual and communal experience 'unto everlasting life'. Similarly, but in a nonverbal fashion, the Unton portrait pictorially demonstrates a temporal axiom at the heart of many early modern biographical or autobiographical constructions of a life: the perception that an individual life can be both viewed and conserved not only (for purposes of salvation, like the dying thief) as the product of its last term, but also as the sum of all its temporal parts simultaneously.

Notes

1   See Peter Burke, *The Renaissance Sense of the Past*, (London: Arnold, 1969), p. 104; Pierre Bourdieu, *Pascalian Meditations*, trans. Richard Nice (Cambridge: Polity Press, 2000), pp. 208–10.

2   Stephen Marshall, *Sermon preach'd November 1640*, (London, 1645), p. 23.

3   William Perkins, 'A Dialogue of the State of a Christian Man', in *The Work of William Perkins*, ed. Ian Breward (Appleford, England: The Courtenay Library of Reformation Classics, 1970), p. 382; cited by Debora Shuger, 'Life Writing in Seventeenth-Century England', in *Representations of the Self from the Renaissance to Romanticism*, ed. Patrick Coleman, Jayne Lewis and Jill Kowalik (Cambridge: Cambridge University Press, 2000), p. 74.

4   Sir Thomas Browne, *Religio Medici*, in *The Major Works*, ed. C.A. Patrides (Harmondsworth: Penguin, 1977), p. 116.

5   *The Autobiography of Anne Lady Halkett*, ed. John Gough Nichols (Camden Society, 2nd Series 13, 1875), Appendix, pp. 109–10.

6   Nehemiah Wallington's paper, 'A Faithfull Memoriall of my owne Mother that is deceased' drawn up by her husband John Wallington, is reproduced in R. Webb's introduction to Nehemiah Wallington's *Historical Notices of Events Occurring Chiefly in the Reign of Charles I* (London: Richard Bentley, 1896), p. x.

7   *Hydriotaphia: Urne Buriall*, chap. 3, in *Sir Thomas Browne: The Major Works,* ed. Patrides, p. 284.

8   Such chronologically based propaganda may be compared with the equally tendentious 'coincidences', or providential lessons from the calendar, displayed at length in Thomas Beard's *The Theatre of God's Judgments* (London, 1632), particularly on Sabbath breakers; or visited, in William Prynne's *A Divine tragedy lately acted* (London, 1636), upon footballers and Morris dancers. A relentless compilation, from broadsheets, pamphlets, books and diurnals, of such 'notices' of providentially engineered coincidences through the mid-seventeenth century may be found in Nehemiah Wallington's previously cited manuscript *Historical Notices*, ed. R. Webb.

9   See the widely circulated *The Speeches and Prayers of Major General Harrison [et al.]… The Times of their Deaths. Together with Severall occasionall Speeches and Passages in their Imprisonment till they came to the place of Execution* (London, 1660). See also Laura Lunger Knoppers, *Historicizing Milton: Spectacle, Power and Poetry in Restoration England* (Athens and London: University of Georgia Press, 1994), pp. 43–53.

10   Edmund Ludlow, *A Voyce from the Watch Tower Part Five: 1660–1662*, ed. A.B. Worden (Camden 4th series, 1978).

11   In William Jaggard's *Catalogue of English Books* (London, 1619), three quarters of all books listed are religious or moral, and in William London's *Catalogue of the most vendible Books in England* (London, 1657–58), the space given to works of divinity equals that of all other kinds together. For light on the psychology of much early modern self-representational discourse, see John Stachniewski, *The Persecutory Imagination: English Puritanism and the Literature of Religious Despair* (Oxford: Clarendon Press, 1991).

12   There is a debt here to the work of William Robins, of the University of Toronto, and his paper 'Recollecting Risk: Merchant Writing in Late Medieval Florence', *Memory and Commemoration*, Australia and New Zealand Medieval and Early Modern Studies

conference, University of Melbourne, February, 2003. See also Carlo M. Cipolla, *Money in Sixteenth-Century Florence* (Berkeley: University of California Press, 1989).

13 C.A. Patrides, *The Phoenix and the Ladder: The Rise and Decline of the Christian View of History* (Berkeley and Los Angeles: University of California Press, 1964); *'The Grand Design of God': The Literary Form of the Christian View of History* (London: Routledge and Kegan Paul; Toronto: University of Toronto Press, 1972); and the edited volume *Aspects of Time* (Manchester: Manchester University Press; Toronto: Toronto University Press, 1976). For a careful analysis of the historical, theological and philosophical issue of divine timelessness see Alan G. Padgett's *God, Eternity and the Nature of Time* (London: Macmillan, 1992), especially pp. 1–56.

14 Bruno, *Opera latine conscripta*, (Florence, 1889), I.4, pp. 32–3.

15 Spinoza, *Ethics*, trans. W. Hale White, fourth edn (Oxford: Oxford University Press, 1910), I, prop. 33.

16 Isaac Barrow, *Geometrical Lectures* (London, 1735), Lecture 1, p. 35.

17 MS *Ashmole*, 36 fol. 230^{v}; printed in *The Diary and Will of Elias Ashmole*, ed. R.T. Gunther (Oxford: Clarendon Press, 1927), pp. 33–4.

18 See for example Carlo M. Cipolla, *Clocks and Culture 1300–1700* (New York: Walker & Co. 1967); David S. Landes, *Revolution in Time: Clocks and the Making of the Modern World* (Cambridge, Mass. and London: The Belknap Press of Harvard University Press, 1983).

19 John Banister, *The Historie of Man* (London, 1578), sig. Bii^{r}.

20 G.F. Waller, *The Strong Necessity of Time*, p. 25.

21 As for example, in the many autobiographical tracts and manifestos, such as the Catholic Sir Tobie Matthews's conversion narrative (1640), the Calvinist Richard Norwood's *Journal* (1639), sectarian autobiographies like the 'enthusiast' Arise Evans's *An Echo to the Voice from Heaven* (1652), or of course Bunyan's *Grace Abounding* (1666), discussed in Paul Delany's pioneering *British Autobiography in the Seventeenth Century* (London: Routledge and Kegan Paul, 1969), pp. 40–104.

22 Sir Thomas Browne, *Religio Medici*, in *Sir Thomas Browne: the Major Works*, ed. Patrides, p. 132.

23 *Religio Medici*, pp. 72, 119.

24 *The Diary of General Patrick Gordon of Auchleuchries in the Years 1635–1699*, 'Russia Through European Eyes' No.3, Gen. editor A.G. Cross (London: Frank Cass & Co., 1968), p. 3. (Reprint of Spalding Club edition of 1859.)

25 Michel de Montaigne, 'That to Philosophize is to Learne how to Dye', *Montaigne's Essayes*, trans. John Florio (1603), 3 vols. (London: Dent, 1965), I, xix, p. 89.

26 *The Autobiography of Thomas Whythorne*, ed. James M. Osborn, modern spelling edition (London: Oxford University Press, 1962), p. 115. Whythorne's point is reflected in the popular subgenre of 'picture' poems in the period, such as Donne's 'Elegie: His Picture' (*Poems*, 1633), Jonson's 'My Picture left in Scotland' (*Underwoods*, 1641), or Thomas Randolph, 'Upon his Picture' (*Poems*, 1638).

27 Whythorne, *Autobiography*, 1962, pp. 115–16.

28 See Roy Strong, *Tudor & Jacobean Portraits*, 2 vols. (London: Her Majesty's Stationery Office, 1969), I, pp. 351–3; II, plate 680.

29 Roy Strong, I, pp. 345–51; II, plate 679; and *Dynasties: Painting in Tudor and Jacobean England 1530–1630*, ed. Karen Hearn (New York: Rizzoli, 1996) (published by order of the Trustees 1995 for the exhibition at the Tate Gallery, 12 Oct 1995 – 7 Jan 1996). Holbein's sketch for the portrait of Sir Thomas More and his family, 1527, is

reproduced in Norbert Schneider's *The Art of the Portrait: Masterpieces of European Portrait Painting 1420–1670*, trans. Iain Galbraith (Cologne: Benedikt Taschen, 1994), p. 90.

30 The manuscript 'Lady Mildmay's Journal' is in the Northampton Central Library. A modernized and reordered text is printed in Linda Pollock's *With Faith and Physic* (London: Collins and Brown, 1993); excerpts are in Randall Martin's 'The *Autobiography* of Grace, Lady Mildmay', in *Renaissance and Reformation* 18 (1994): 38–82, and in *Women Writers in Renaissance England*, ed. Randall Martin (London: Longman, 1997), pp. 208–27.

31 See Roy Strong, *Tudor & Jacobean Portraits*, 1969, I, pp. 315–19; II, plates 627–33. The article referred to is 'Sir Henry Unton and his Portrait: An Elizabethan Memorial Picture and its History', *Archaeologia*, XCIX (1965): 53–76. The Unton portrait is reproduced in colour in *The National Portrait Gallery Collection*, ed. Susan Foister, Robin Gibson, Malcolm Rogers, and Jacob Simon; introduction by John Hayes (London: NPG Publications, 1988), p. 39; and also more familiarly in the introduction to *The Riverside Shakespeare*, gen. ed. G. Blakemore Evans (Boston: Houghton Mifflin, 1974).

32 Strong, *Tudor & Jacobean Portraits*, I, p. 317.

33 Lorne Campbell, *Renaissance Portraits: European Portrait-Painting in 14th, 15th and 16th Centuries* (New Haven and London: Yale University Press, 1990), p. 53. A nearer – though still very distant – analogy might be found in Theodore de Bry's series of 32 plates for Thomas Lant, 'Funeral Procession of Sir Philip Sidney' (Aldrich Collection, Christ Church, Oxford), reproduced in Katherine Duncan-Jones's *Sir Philip Sidney: Courtier Poet* (New Haven and London: Yale University Press, 1991), pp. 308–39.

34 Montaigne, *Essayes,* trans. John Florio (1603), 1, xix, (Everyman edition, 1965), vol. 1, p. 87.

35 W.T., *A Discourse of Eternitie* (Oxford, 1633), p. 4; pp. 63–4. Cf. William Brent, *A Discourse upon the Nature of Eternitie* (London, 1655), sig. A2r, pp. 13–14.

PART 2
Reflections: Selves and Others

Chapter 3

Looking Out: Travelling Selves

The Profit of Travel

> Travel, in the younger sort, is a part of education, in the elder, a part of experience. He
> that travelleth into a country, before he hath some entrance into the language, goeth to
> school, and not to travel[1]

says Francis Bacon in his essay 'Of Travel'. Bacon's main interest lies in the
benefits of travel for elite young men, and he explains what they should try to see,
from princes' courts to churches and monuments, to city walls, antiquities and
ruins, the training of soldiers, even exercises of horsemanship. Before his journey a
young man should study the languages of the countries that he plans to visit,
consulting books about the itinerary. An accompanying tutor or servant should
already be familiar with the languages and destinations. And, once abroad,

> [l]et him sequester himself, from the company of his countrymen, and diet in such
> places, where there is good company of the nation where he travelleth. Let him, upon his
> removes from one place to another, procure recommendation to some person of quality,
> residing in the place whither he removeth; that he may use his favor, in those things he
> desireth to see or know. Thus he may abridge his travel, with much profit.

Travel, for Bacon, is in other words like the reading of an essay or a book: with the
correct tutelage, one can abridge the experience, extracting its salient features and
returning home all the sooner to apply one's travels to profitable gain. Evidence of
his recent travels should 'appear rather in his discourse than his apparel or gesture;
and in his discourse let him be rather advised in his answers, than forward to tell
stories' (p. 48). By distilling his experience abroad, the young man may put his
travels to good use in the furthering of his career, impressing others with his
sophistication without appearing like an alien or a bore.

One of Thomas Overbury's characters, 'An Affectate Traveller', typifies the
smugness that Bacon warns against: he is 'a speaking fashion; hee hath taken
paines to be ridiculous, and hath seene more then he hath perceived … his *gate*
cryes, *Behold me* … his discourse sounds big, but meanes nothing … [he]
preferreth all Countries before his owne.'[2] Tasteful discretion is the key to
avoiding the scorn this figure incites: 'let it appear that he doth not change his
country manners for those of foreign parts; but only prick in some flowers of that
he hath learned abroad into the customs of his own country' ('Of Travel', p. 48).

Bacon also urges the keeping of a diary (p. 47), which permits the full advantage of *observation*, that blend of perception and thought he prizes in philosophical and scientific works such as the *Novum Organum*:

> It is a strange thing, that in sea voyages, where there is nothing to be see but sky and sea, men should make diaries; but in land-travel, wherein so much is to be observed, for the most part they omit it; as if chance were fitter to be registered than observation. Let diaries therefore be brought in use. ('Of Travel', p. 46)

A diary brings home benefits 'to men's business and bosoms' (*Essays*, Epistle Dedicatory, p. 5), helping to describe, evaluate, and commemorate all that is seen and experienced.

If Bacon's ideal young man treats travel like the reading of a book, to which his diary serves as a personal annotation, Sir Thomas Elyot, in *The Governor*, goes a step further. For Elyot, the ideal journey is conducted *through* a book, sitting in one's comfortable study and reading of others' perils and privations without encountering any of one's own. In the middle of his discussion of training for rulers-to-be, Elyot expresses the 'incredible delight' to be gained from reading about other people's journeys:

> to know the sundry manners and conditions of people, and the variety of their natures, and that in a warm study or parlour, without peril of the sea or danger of long and painful journeys: I cannot tell what more pleasure should happen to a gentle wit, than to behold in his own home everything that within all the world is contained.[3]

At one level his remark conveys the enjoyment that early modern readers could derive from learning about other people, places and customs. More interestingly, Elyot's comment points to the vicariousness of the experience – finding out about exotic others confirms the well-appointed home and the prudence of staying put. Part of this solitary reader's pleasure, then, derives from comparing the conditions in which he reads to those he reads about. The differences mirror personal and social success back to him, reinforcing a humanist ideal of genteel wit recognized and rewarded.

Elyot's views on the pleasures of reading bring to mind John Donne's lovers in 'The Sunne Rising', who imaginatively concentrate the world into their bedroom where they embody all emotions and experiences. But while their shared wonder embraces earthly and cosmic mysteries, absorbing and surpassing all otherness, Elyot's retiring reader 'behold[s] in his own home everything that within all the world is contained'. Far from embracing the wonders of the world, his gaze reduces its variety to curios or ornaments: 'every*thing*' is gathered within his dwelling and knowledge, to behold rather than experience. This brief section of Elyot's famous conduct book captures connections among personal identity, social others, and cultural practices that are being forged anew in the sixteenth century through extensive changes in systems of publishing, travel and their associated activities and institutions – education and literacy; tourism, colonization and trade. In particular, Elyot's words reveal the ways in which reading – and telling tales of other people and places – is a means of affirming one's sense of personal identity. Intertwined with such a social identity is an individual persona, assured in its physical and emotive experience, or seeking such assurance by measuring its own customs and perceptions against those of others. All the better to do this second-hand, where one's appraisal is unlikely to be disturbed by unpleasant and disorienting encounters; and, to this end, it is telling that Elyot ignores the regular descriptions in travel books of conflicts with fellow travellers and compatriots. In the comforts of Elyot's parlour, experience and subjectivity can be mediated at will.

The attitudes represented by Bacon and Elyot are, in a sense, different forms of rhetorical encounter that depend upon each other. The firsthand traveller is both the reader-at-large and the scribbler of diaries. He abridges his experiences in order to put them to use at home, distilling them in his own judiciously modulated accounts. Were this not so, readers like Elyot at home would have no strange lands to read *about*. The effects of travel and travel writing can, however, be far less seamlessly rhetorical, and sometimes more problematic, than either Elyot and Bacon allow. Time and again questions about early modern selves and selfhood are posed when familiar and exotic experiences collide. Moving out of the frame of everyday life discloses its benefits, comforts and limitations for people's ways of thinking and acting. Habitual routines and earnest attitudes are tested by changing circumstances, frequently to be reaffirmed, but on some occasions rejected. The diaries and journals of early modern England reveal contrasts across a full range of contexts, from national and religious institutions to experiences of food and eating, illness and health. In all these situations, the self seems to appear most graphically when encountering a cultural other, be it someone from another land, from an unfamiliar English milieu, or, in some of the most striking cases, the person whom one was *before* one travelled. If in general terms 'early modern representations of [the] self do not emerge in isolation from their material and cultural contexts', then no one depicts this more strikingly than the travel writer, whose textual journeys afford 'a reflection of and on the communal discourses in which they are embedded'.[4] Being removed from familiar material and cultural situations exposes travellers to different ways of living and enables them to reappraise the norms, customs, and people – including themselves – that, for the time being, they have left behind. In this light the summations offered by both Bacon and Elyot are overwhelmingly purposeful. Travel is for them not an act of exploration so much an affirming means of highly rhetorical *interpretation*.

Early modern selves can be changed in all kinds of ways through travel – perhaps improved and educated, but possibly corrupted, ostracized, or killed. Thomas Coryate, the self-promoting traveller and minor celebrity from early seventeenth-century London, includes a formal oration in praise of travel's 'incredible utility' and 'admirable sweetnesse' in the first volume of his *Crudities* (1611).[5] That work's large sales – it was received as the first handbook for continental travel – suggests widespread interest in the claims and details about travel that he provides. Like Bacon and Elyot, he conceives of travel as an interpretive encounter, offering 'all experience of a civill life' (p. 123), and the chance to 'read a new leafe in the booke of nature' (p. 127). Experienced travellers, like Coryate himself, continually grow more pious, worldly wise, and morally strong (p. 131). Travel improves character, and any negative effects – 'pernicious to a Common-weale, and hurtfull to a private life … new manners, new vices, new staines, new diseases' (pp. 144–5) – are attributed more to 'every mans perverse nature and education' than to travel itself (p. 145). And ultimately, earthly travel itself is expertly read as a rehearsal for 'that last and heavenly pilgrimage' (p. 148). In Coryate's excited conception, travel enhances the moral and spiritual aspects of individuals, societies and nations, teaching one how to face the new – and death is the greatest mystery of the unknown – while always remembering oneself and one's comportment.

Writing towards the end of the Enlightenment, Jean-Jacques Rousseau initially confirms a similar course of profitable instruction for early modern journeys, echoing the sentiments of Bacon and Elyot and granting weight to Coryate's hyperbole. Rousseau adds to the ethical and pedagogical baggage that accompanies travel, but in so doing he gradually shifts focus onto the individual traveller and brackets out contact with others. In this reading, travel has become one of the technologies of self-formation, entailing a deep understanding primarily about oneself and only then about relations with others. In Book 5 of *Emile or On Education* (1762), the narrator digresses to consider whether travel is good for young people. It can be, but it must be carried out in particular ways, entailing prerequisites, goals, criteria, and generic skills. For Rousseau, travel comprises a carefully planned curriculum: 'it is not sufficient to roam through various countries. It is necessary to know how to travel … The instruction that one extracts from travel is related to the aim that causes travel to be undertaken.'[6] With aims and knowledge in place, the lessons of travel can help to achieve ethical and educational fulfilment, realizing a potential already there: 'Travel pushes a man toward his natural bent and completes the job of making him good or bad' (p. 455). Through encounters with the unfamiliar, then, he *knows himself*. Once this task is complete, the young man can start to move past solipsism and 'consider himself in his civil relations with his fellow citizens' (p. 455). A well-schooled traveller is ultimately primed to understand the strengths and weaknesses of society and to realize his true individual nature. At the end of his travels, Emile comments, 'The more I examine the work of men in their institutions, the more I see that they make themselves slaves by dint of wanting to be independent and that they use up their freedom in vain efforts to ensure it' (p. 471). To which his mentor responds, liberty lies only 'in the heart of the free man', who bonds himself to 'the eternal laws of nature' (p. 473). At this moment, the traveller seems to break away from others entirely. He passes beyond an emotive attachment to people and places, which would comprise a crucial part of the traveller's self-conception in Laurence Sterne's contemporaneous, hugely successful *A Sentimental Journey through*

France and Italy (1768). The aim of Emile's travels is to get away from others and find life's meaning without them.

In Rousseau's remarks, we can see that travel has moved far from its links to pragmatic early modern ethics as proposed by Bacon, or to the Horatian blend of instruction and delight that Elyot perceives in travel writing. It is being transformed into a mode of phenomenology, of knowing self and other, that will be a central tenet of many Romantic texts and will continue into postmodernity (where, in practical terms, it primarily concerns adventure tourism, while, as topos, it seems increasingly limited to an endless fascination with the task of journeying into oneself). Rousseau's text reveals changes in the ideology of travel and also of the traveller, whose destination has become a place beyond the social but within the self. *Emile* is complicit with these changes, itself a kind of textual odyssey, which draws readers to rethink their social affiliations from 'the heart'. The decisive shift it makes from concerns about the important social and contextual frameworks through which life experiences and identity are formed to the figure of a naturalized individual, whose destination lies within, serves to highlight their role in earlier travel writing. It also underscores the importance of not automatically regarding later preoccupations with freedom, escape, and deep individuality as central to the narratives of early modern travel journals or to the authors' understandings of what is significant about their journeys and the way they relate to and affect their own identities and those of others.

Early modern travel writing repeatedly focuses on the individual's social experiences – his or her contacts and entanglements, be they with the inhabitants of the places being visited, the subject's fellow-travellers, or those back at home to whom the traveller is officially and personally attached. Few early modern travellers ever seem to be entirely alone. Moments of isolation – meditating before a sublime view, musing over companions or loved ones, all familiar topoi from modern books and films on travel – are rarely included or emphasized in the texts. Personal interests and changing emotions are not precluded from such works; instead their significance is located more in the way that travellers manage contact with others than in what they feel and think about the interactions. The representational mode is often dramatic; relationships are for the most part staged events, observed by readers and often retrospectively by the traveller as well. What make the texts especially compelling are not so much authentic accounts of visiting places for the first time or of intimate relations (though at times both kinds of experiences are featured) but rather the complex manoeuvres carried out by the author and other participants, who are not always completely sure of how they are supposed to act or behave towards each other. Placed in more or less new situations – in foreign lands, with companions from various countries or different social groups – the regular strategies for handling interactions often do not seem to be workable or adaptable. In these complications and the anxieties they generate lie some of the more revealing details of the lives and experiences of early modern travellers. The various benefits of travel and travel writing that Bacon, Elyot, Coryate and later Rousseau optimistically promote cannot be guaranteed.

Changing Places, Changing Identities

In recently reviewing the course of western autobiographical writing from the fifteenth to the seventeenth centuries, social historian Peter Burke highlights the impact of three particular developments – the growth of printing, urbanism, and travel. The first relates to the increased availability of autobiographical texts, which encouraged the idea of identity as interesting subject matter for various types of written discourse, from private notebooks to published works. The other two factors are linked to changes in circumstances that sharpened people's feelings of separation from those around them: 'the city, which offers alternative ways of life, encourages a sense of individual choice'; while travel 'encourages self-consciousness by cutting off the individual from his or her community'.[7] Burke offers an overview of the topic, and we might expand the points he makes to suggest that there are different degrees of separation, as well as connection, which affect individual self-consciousness (a point not incompatible with his overall emphasis on 'the variety of Renaissance selves' [pp. 18–19]). In fact, the interplay between the traveller's separations and connections is one of the crucial features of the period's travel journals and diaries. Through depicting these relationships, the texts explore the limits and scope of relations between individuals and social groups. Given the rapid growth in international travel in the sixteenth and seventeenth centuries, mostly driven by trade and politics but often prompted by individual choice, it is possible to recognize travel writing as representing one of that period's major 'generic categories or epistemes of self-identity appropriate to epochal social and cultural contexts'.[8] With the comforts and discomforts it generates and the array of personal and social attitudes it describes, travel offers authors and readers the opportunity to speculate on self-identity from new angles and in novel situations.

Before examining these issues in a number of texts from the period, a helpful contrast can be drawn with a well-known dramatic work that revolves around a sequence of surprising encounters framed by journeys. Like most of his comedies and romances, Shakespeare's early play, *The Comedy of Errors* (c. 1592) is in many ways based on the mishaps and revelations that travel can elicit for locals and visitors. A desperate plea from Antipholus of Syracuse captures the confusion sparked by the arrival of strangers: 'Sure these are but imaginary wiles, / And Lapland sorcerers inhabit here / … we wander in illusions: / Some blessed power deliver us from hence!'[9] At the play's end, the characters depart to 'hear at large discoursed all our fortunes' (V, i, 396): there is strong appreciation that speaking and writing about people's movements is central to a community's sense of how identities and relationships are organized. The finale gestures towards (but does not actually stage) a discursive closure that cannot be realized simply by seeing all the characters together. The mix-ups and repeated attempts to clarify them suggest that whether as a reader, listener or traveller, encounters with others are invariably a kind of encounter with oneself. Though the results cannot be predicted, in comic genres they can almost always be explained.

Antipholus arrives in Ephesus with the upbeat curiosity of a modern-day tourist: 'I'll view the manners of the town, / Peruse the traders, gaze upon the buildings, / And then return and sleep within mine inn' (I, ii, 12–14). Though he assumes that sightseeing will have no impact on his identity, his leisurely plans contain an unsettling potential: 'I will go lose myself, / And wander up and down to view the city' (I, ii, 30–31). The pun on 'lose myself', an indulgent delight or a failure of identity, suggests that self-awareness remains contingent. Rather than always being confirmed, as Thomas Elyot implies, it can lapse through experiencing new places, sights and people, or by confronting the terrors of travel. Master Thomas Dallam, the deliverer of an organ to the Sultan of Turkey on behalf of Queen Elizabeth, records in his diary a related sense of self-risk the morning after a terrible storm – 'In the night we did not only lose the pinnace, the *Lanerett* ... we also lost ourselves' – and all this while the boats were still in the English Channel.[10] In Shakespeare's comic world – a theatre of erring and what you will – self-loss is eventually succeeded by explanation and confirmation of identity and relationships. Journeys are completed as a prelude to dramatic closure, and what might transpire after that is not staged. (*Hamlet* and *Othello* can in part be seen as stories of what happens after the protagonists return from their time away: they begin where and when the other plays end.) But this positive conception of travel's outcomes – one that Bacon also assumes as long as his advice is followed – is often not reproduced in travel journals from the period. These texts are less rigorously prescribed in comic or other generic terms but remain, like many early modern diaries and memoirs, 'particularly open to a series of coterminous and contradictory subject positions'.[11] Positive experience as well as ongoing discord during a trip may lead not to resolution but to drawn-out conflict once a traveller returns. In some cases, the traveller may not survive, leaving instead a record of problems and disputes experienced en route. Self-growth through experiencing new people and places is no sure thing, while the self-assurance with which travellers set out may be jeopardized or overturned.

True and Almost Incredible Reports

Thomas Coryate's claim that earthly travel anticipates a final heavenly journey informs one of the earliest sixteenth-century English travel journals, *The begynnynge and contynuaunce of the Pilgrymage of Sir Richarde Guylforde ... And howe he went with his servaunts and company towards Jherusalem*, published in 1511. Guylforde dies about halfway through the text, five months after departing from Sussex in April 1506, but fortunately after reaching Jerusalem and visiting many of the holy sites in and around the city.[12] The idea of 'contynuance' is thus twofold, as the pious knight's journey doubtless proceeds heavenward, while the diary itself is completed by an unnamed servant. There is no outright admission of the switch of author or any explanation of the cause of death. Indeed, it is surprising to realize that the narrative voice, assumed to be Guylforde's, suddenly starts to report his demise. (It is possible that the servant has been keeping the journal from the start, collaborating with his master or on his behalf.) The group had attended mass at mount Syon, dined with the warden and friars, and been given relics. We are then told that 'mayster Pryor of Gysborogh' had died the previous weekend, and that early in the morning on 7 September 'my M[aster]. Syr Ric. Guylford whom god assoyle disceased ... all the Pylgrymes come to mounte Syon to the buryenge of my sayde Master Guylford where was done by the freres asmoche solemyne seruyce as might be done for hym &c' (fol. xxix). The continuing account of the pilgrimage after Guylford's death and in his name exemplifies the kind of corporate experience that frequently comprises early modern travel. In this travel text, self and social others are not exactly identical, but they are compatible and supportive.

The co-written journal complicates identity in interesting ways. The authorial voices remain closely intertwined though points of contrast gradually do emerge, conveying differences in character and viewpoint. In part, the contrasts can be attributed to the distinct social positions and concerns of the master and servant: the sections composed by Guylforde are less involved with the practical side of the trip and more interested in recording exotic cultural sights and holy places. Different class backgrounds, educations and tastes, all naturalized into a personal voice, can be discerned. At the same time, the link between master and servant, intensified by the former's death, does draw the two perspectives together. The bonds of service and the master's interests shape the servant's outlook and conduct in situations where he might act, speak or write for the other. If not merely a function of the master, the servant is often duty-bound to respond and anticipate that figure's intentions. There is no explicit sign that the servant influences Guylforde's disposition, yet his respectful extension of the journal is testament to the way in which service connects and informs its participants' identities, often through acts of delegated authoring and speech.[13] It also exemplifies the way that the voice of another might enter a diary or journal – not only by taking over the pen but also by virtue of a close relationship in which views are exchanged and shared. The conditions of service and travel accentuate the process by placing each individual, especially in a party of pilgrims, in close, motivated contact.

The diary's communal aspects are reinforced by the pilgrimage's pre-Reformation setting, in which a single faith is followed. In contrast to later travel journals and narratives, the English pilgrims evince no distaste towards the Catholic relics and rituals they observe in most detail in Padua and Venice (fol. iv–v). Guylforde describes the latter as the grandest place 'euer I sawe' (fol. vi); it prompts him to use the first person. He is similarly moved by the church of our Lady in Bethlehem, 'I neuer sawe nor herde of a fayrer lytell churche in all my lyfe' (fol. xxvi). In these instances, he distinguishes his own impression from common opinion as much as from his past experience; yet in doing so he appears to expect that his view will now contribute to what is seen and heard by others. Ardent personal response is valued as it affirms and builds communal perceptions.

After his death, Guylforde's servant continues to use a collective viewpoint to describe the pilgrims' trips to shrines; he explains, 'some of vs visited one place and some an other so that whan we mette eche reported vnto other' (fol. xxxiiii). They share the experiences among themselves and with readers, thereby broadening the pilgrimage's socioreligious significance. No class- or regionally based distinction differentiates the piety of the pilgrims. The author at one point does underscore his own visit to the Sea of Galilee, 'I was thereat and sawe it' (fol. xxxvi). It is as though he continues to marvel that he has actually been there. But mostly he is happy to include 'my vysytation as well as others into this lytell remembraunce' (fol. xxxiiii). Personal experience grows more meaningful by being integrated with the corresponding acts and feelings of others.

In the first part of the diary Guylforde uses the personal pronoun not only to signify a positive reaction to the features of Venice and Cyprus, but also to register a sense of authorial purpose and planning: 'I woll wryte more of this yle at my comynge homwarde as ye shall parceyue [perceive] by the processe of the same' (fol. xi). He doesn't make it back, and his servant alters the plan, offering instead summary details of various Greek islands and noting that 'there wherof is more largely wrytn byfore' (fol. xlix). He does not exhibit the same degree of interest in social institutions shown by Guylforde. Rather, he is prompted to use the first person by a winter squall that batters the pilgrims as they sail back across the Mediterranean: 'it was meruayle [marvellous] to se and with Rayne and hayle more greuously then I haue sene before' (fol. xlix). It is one of a series of bad storms, which are generally recounted from a group perspective: 'we were almoste dryuen vpon the Rok whiche was hydyous and ferefull to loke vpon. ... In somoche euery man made hym redy to almighty god' (fol. xliiii). Desperation can mould people's thoughts alike, and so does relief when they land at Candy to 'grete Joye not oonly for the happy Escape frome the grete daunger that we were late in but also for the lacke and scarseness of vytayllys [victuals] that was in our Galye' (fol. xliiii). The bad weather soon returns and combines with the fear of being attacked by 'the Infidels and extreme enemyes of our Cristen fayth' (fol. l) to draw the pilgrims closer together, at least for a while. Eventually, dangerous conditions and disharmony among the sailors lead the wealthier pilgrims to quit and pay for passage on another ship (fol. lii). Under this kind of pressure, the communal spirit starts to fracture into smaller groupings. Difficulties or threats from outsiders add considerable tension to travel narrative. Less hazardous but frustrating incidents occur earlier at Jaffa, where the pilgrims first disembark and later board their return ship. On both occasions extra payment is extracted: 'with grete diffycultie with moche pacyence and also with large departynge of our money we were delyuerd a borde our Galye' (fol. xli). Guylforde's servant draws extra attention to these concerns in the second section of the journal. In the first part, as might be expected, focus is directed on Jerusalem, and apart from the stay in Venice (whose cultural and religious richness seems to foreshadow the holy city), the narrative hastens to its goal, driven by Guylforde's enthusiasm and anticipation. The return journey is physically slower and more fraught, but perhaps the servant is more preoccupied with matters of practical survival than was the master. Indeed, he closes the text with guarded criticism, emphasizing that it was because they stayed so long at Venice on the outward journey, one of the high points for Guylforde himself, that they hit 'stormy winter wether' on their return (fol. xl). These kinds of changes in narrative perspective, mildly challenging the account in the first part of the journal, hint at a diversity of opinion usually hidden by factors such as a journal's single authorial voice, the demands of service, and the pilgrims' devout camaraderie.

The servant again uses 'I' when the party makes their return across the Alps: 'from the hyght of the Mounte downe to lyuyngborugh I was ramasshed whiche is a right straunge thynge' (fol. lviii).[14] In contrast to Guylforde, who breaks into the first person before an inspiring locale, the servant is moved to do so by an immediate, striking event. A different kind of occasion prompts each author to assert the 'I', suggesting variance between personalities, social interests, and a sense of the suitable occasion for direct self-expression. These contrasts are ones of degree. Overall, *The begynnynge and contynuaunce* is notable for the consistent integration between individual and group perception. The narrative synthesis of people's experiences in Israel and the lightly marked slippage between narrators are testament to the value placed upon sharing and representing experience together. The pre-Reformation tenor of Guylforde's pilgrimage seems to enhance this quality. Yet in terms of autobiographical discourse and theory, what is more striking about the text is the variation it suggests to Philippe Lejeune's musings on autobiography in the third person: 'We do not really know how to get out of the self; that is to say, to represent, equally with our own, a point of view different from our own'.[15] For here we have a text that is 'out of the self', though not in the sense of demarcating another. Lejeune's speculation remains tied to the notion that an individual voice must be discrete. In contrast, the narrators of *The begynnynge and contynuaunce* escape the self by representing points of view *similar* to their own; and they recognize their own points of view only because they are similar to others. In this kind of 'collaborative' autobiography, as Paul John Eakin notes, 'the self's responsibility to the proximate other' is all-important.[16] In one way, Guylforde's text presumes such responsibility in the institution and practice of loyal service and of a common faith. At the same time, the text's integration of the servant and master's viewpoints illustrates the way that many early modern autobiographical works aim at representing 'responsibility' – a combination of obligation and duty to others as well as rapport and dialogue with them, a sense of responding to the other. Many of these works appear to presuppose that without responsibility there is no self or at least no self that can be written about. Yet in some cases, as we will see, responsibility can prove too much for a single person. The pressures it generates might undermine identity. In this regard, early modern travel journals explore the benefits and costs of the self's responsibility to others.

In its un-self-indulgent, communal style, Guylforde's chronicle presents a positive view of an individual's cultural connections. The protagonist's death does not disturb this view; rather, the minimal account of his death helps to emphasize the group's experience. The joy they feel in the holy land and on completing the dangerous journey home rewards and enhances their mutual purpose and commitment. The journal endorses the meaning and value that experience in common gives to an individual life by expanding its singleness and linking it to other people. Not all travel texts represent these effects in such constructive terms. The connections with others that travel necessitates can be problematic, and it is as much to do with the sensibility of the individual traveller as with the complexities of social interaction.

By promoting situations where contact with others is unavoidable, travel writing acts as a 'a major mode of life narrative' that depicts the 'reconstitution of the autobiographical subject in transit and encounter'.[17] In spite of his death, Guylforde's text upholds his identity as a devout pilgrim by fusing voices, his servant's, his own and the pilgrims'. In other texts, however, the effects of 'transit and encounter' can limit or undermine personal representation. The author's expectations are challenged by the increased exposure to opportunity and danger. Risky experiences are often portrayed in early modern travel journals in terms of an '"I" in migration, encounter, conquest, and transformation'.[18] The grand goals sought by these active subjects add focus and aspiration to the narratives they relate. The scale of their undertakings offers the chance to build a great persona, in the mould of culturally celebrated figures like Drake and Raleigh. Yet the realization of identity remains unpredictable, reliant on the adventure's outcome. Many travel journals use a mission or voyage to frame and construct the author's identity only to see complications, mishaps or incompetence undercut his plans and performance. Three levels of narrative develop, one founded on the author's plans and hopes, another based on surprises and disasters that arise, and the third on the increasing self-doubt prompted by these incidents. By analyzing a series of these types of travel journals, all written by figures who are largely unknown today, the early modern awareness of the capability and weakness of identity and experience can be examined. This doubled sense of successful or fragile selfhood is not only a theme for famous dramatic and literary works from the period – Marlowe's *Tamburlaine the Great*, Shakespeare's *Othello*, and Chapman's *Bussy d'Ambois*, for example, all stage the rise and demise of the heroic, questing individual. It also pervades the understanding of the lives of ordinary people who, for a period of time, are propelled out of their regular surroundings into the hazardous world of early modern travel and adventure. The impacts of the experience upon conceptions of themselves are registered in the often fragmented or contradictory journals, diaries and published accounts the travellers produce.

Dangerous Travels

Many of the trips undertaken in the sixteenth and seventeenth centuries, especially those pursued for political and commercial reasons, involve various kinds of risk – from inhospitable climates to disputes between travellers and clashes with local inhabitants. All of these hazards can have a dramatic bearing on the ways in which travel writers represent their own roles on the trip and their relationships with companions. The dangers thrown up by travel offer writers a way to explore the virtues and problems of autonomy and the value of connections between selves and others.

One of the shortest travel diaries published in the seventeenth century is John Dunton's *True Journal of the Sally Fleet with the Proceedings of the Voyage* (1637). Dunton recounts a 1636 mission to the town of Sally (Salé) on the Barbary Coast to gain the release of English and Christian captives along with any other booty that can be snared. He is not a highly reflective diarist, and his main aim is simply to chronicle events in which the group took part. He avoids speculating on political motives and machinations but details the venture's difficulties and successes. Due to poor winds, it takes almost six weeks to leave England, but progress is then swift. English demands are at first rejected by the Sally governor, but by combining with a nearby town, which is already in conflict with Sally, the town is besieged and the prisoners freed. The outcome is testament to the superiority of the fleet and its commanders, the nation and ultimately providence: 'All these good Shippes with the Captives are in safety arrived in England, we give God thankes.'[19] As here, Dunton uses the first-person plural throughout the journal – 'we did see two ships, and wee did give them chase all the day' (p. 12) is another typical example – to consolidate a group perspective of crew and country.

Despite the narrative's straightforward resolution, the author's identity is never fully integrated with the successful mission. The journal itself reveals no division, but the published text also includes a prefatory letter to Lord Vaine, of Charles I's Privy Council, begging help to free Dunton's ten-year old son from slavery in 'Argeire' (Algiers). God's aid must be facilitated by intervention from Vaine and the king. The boy is 'like to be lost for ever, without Gods great mercy and the Kings clemencie, which I hope may be in some measure obtained by your honours meanes, and then your poore suppliant shall be ever bound to pray for you and yours all his dayes' (sig. A2v). The son's enslavement ironically frames the eventual freedom of the Sally captives. The situation compels Dunton to write in an impassioned personal voice. It contrasts with the detached group perspective used through the rest of the journal, and the difference suggests the effort that Dunton makes in suppressing emotion in his compound role as father, author and sailor. Painful personal experience runs counter to the official account. At the same time, in Dunton's conception of paternal identity and duty we glimpse his acceptance of orthodox social hierarchy, comprising God, sovereign and aristocrat, in which he holds a submissive place. Dunton's two voices, in the prefatory letter and the journal, are at once unified and split: they differentiate between personal and professional roles but reveal the subjected position of both within the state.

As the text moves from preface to journal, Dunton might find relief in turning from emotional appeal to dispassionate reporting, submerging his own plight in joint success. Another travel journal from the 1630s similarly explores the way that group experience can alleviate personal suffering. The text belongs to the genre of death-defying ordeals: Edward Pellham's *Gods Power and Providence: Shewed, In the Miraculous Preservation and Deliverance of eight Englishmen, left by mischance in Greenland Anno 1630 nine moneths and twelve dayes* (1631). From the start, Pellham remains aware of a number of formal conventions that he should fulfil. The text opens with a dedication to two aldermen, members of the Muscovia Merchants, the company that funded the voyage. He emphasizes the suffering the group loyally endured: 'The hard adventure my poore selfe and fellowes underwent in your Worships service, is a great deale pleasanter for others to reade, than it was for us to endure' (sig. A2). Their suffering assists not only the company but also the wider society of readers, as it were, preserving them from similar hardship (the very effect that Thomas Elyot appreciated). Commercial and national considerations are uppermost in the dedication, which goes on to claim Greenland for England by dint of the eight men being its first long-term inhabitants (sig. A2v). The text's religious and moral purpose is next addressed. Pellham compares his experience on Greenland to that of some famous Dutch survivors, who in 1596 had been stranded in Nova Zembla. The success of their account 'encouraged mee to publish this of ours'.[20] He then claims that because the Dutch group had better supplies, 'The greater therefore our deliverance, the greater must be Gods glory. And that's the Authors purpose in publishing of it' (sig. A4). With these rather predictable pre-texts complete, the tract soon develops into a graphic account of suffering. The trip's commercial and national motives, 'for the advantage of the Merchants, and the good of the Common-wealth' (p. 2), and the text's religious theme fade before the struggle to survive.

Having been put ashore to find supplies, the eight men are left behind when they fail to rejoin the main party. They know when the fleet is due to return to England and immediately realize their dilemma: 'a thousand sadde imaginations overtooke our perplexed minds, all of us assuredly knowing that a million of miseries would of necessitie ensue, if wee found not the ships' (p. 7). A 'miserable and a pining death' confronts them – no one has survived winter in Greenland before (p. 9). As the account continues, the tone and action oscillate between hopelessness and resilience. Pellham continues to use stylized tropes to depict their plight. The men establish a strict routine of activities and diet and keep a log (the dates of almost all events are routinely noted); their training and experience enable them to mend small boats, build shelters, lamps and some furniture, and kill whatever animals they come across. They battle the conditions and themselves, for despair threatens: 'we began to conceive hope, even out of the depth of despaire ... it pleased God to give us hearts like men, to arme our selves with a resolution to doe our best for the resisting of that monster of Desperation' (p. 12). As winter deepens, the sun disappears for over three months, and from 1 to 20 December there is no natural light. Mental suffering worsens, and Pellham draws on moral-religious allegory: 'tormented in mind with our doubts, our feares, and our griefes; and in our bodies with hunger, cold and wants; that hideous monster of desperation, began now to present his ugliest shape unto us' (p. 23). Their efforts to survive are undercut by depression: 'Thus we did our best to preserve our selves; but all this could not secure us: for wee in oure thoughts, accounted our selves but dead men' (p. 26).

The return of sunlight marks the narrative reversal: animals reappear and can be caught; the men's strength rises; the ice starts to break up and eventually a boat arrives. Pellham records the rescuers' amazement at seeing the survivors (pp. 31–2) – readers gain a fleeting, external view of the long winter's effects on their appearance. Immediately the men try to reconnect, asking 'what newes? and of the state of the Land at home?' (p. 33). Joy at being rescued is soon balanced by their implication in company politics: to save his own reputation the original captain has accused the men of deserting (p. 34). Another context for Pellham's account is thus revealed – to put their side of the story and clear their names. Hence the recurring tone of obligation, to assure everyone of the men's integrity, reiterated a final time on arriving at the Thames, 'to our great joy and comfort, and the Merchants benefite' (pp. 34–5).

Throughout Pellham merges his distress with that of the others and offers little private reflection. No sign of discord among the sailors enters the journal; disagreement and disloyalty seem to exist only in England as certain members of the Company try to protect their interests. Pellham shows no hint of bitterness against his employers. A corporate identity – shared with the stranded men and with the Muscovia Merchants – helps him endure the perils of Greenland and perhaps those of London as well. Pellham's character is thus doubly socialized, and his text underscores the way that a precarious situation can draw out a deep-seated sense of shared selfhood, one that remains suppressed, unrecognized or perhaps rejected in more secure contexts.

Of course, dangerous or stressful circumstances can also foster an individual's separation from others. Under threat, the traveller holds all the more firmly to his own identity. In many travel journals from the period, we witness the authors' struggles to manage their connection to a social group. They ponder whether they are entitled to distance or detach themselves from shared tasks and viewpoints. In these situations, definitions of where personal and group liabilities begin and end grow unclear. For it is not only an ethical question of whether a person should cut themselves adrift from a collective mission – a move that is not always possible in the middle of a voyage – but also a pragmatic one about the short- and long-term benefits and costs of doing so. The risks of either step have to be calculated and re-calculated. The individual must keep playing his part, while evaluating the effects of his actions and whether he needs to change them. In such a predicament, the ties between self and social others are tightened even as the impulse to dissolve them looms larger.

Robert Couerte's *A True and Almost Incredible Report of an Englishman, that ... Trauelled by Land though many unknowne Kingdomes, and great Cities* (1612) provides a gripping example of how the social and physical hazards over a long journey can both threaten and reinforce a sense of individual identity. This double effect is neatly captured in Couerte's dedication to the Early of Salisbury. The 'tedious and dangerous Trauels' have produced a weary but resilient figure: 'I haue here exprest no more then I haue directly seen, and to my great sufferance and difficultie proved'.[21] In an epistle to the reader, Couerte also echoes Elyot's recognition of readerly comfort. Its effect here, however, is to underwrite the reality of the author's gruelling experience; he offers 'a true report of my dangerous Trauels, which will ... be as pleasing to thee in reading, as they were painefull to me in suffering' (sig. A4v). The author's persona has been forged through the labour of travel.

From departure, Couerte's voyage around Africa and on to India for the East Indian Merchants is dogged by problems. The ship makes a number of false starts before favourable winds enable it to get away, but after having travelled south for a while it proves difficult to get new supplies. The governor of one of the main towns on the Canary Islands mistrusts the sailors and will not sell them provisions. Couerte in turn denounces them as 'subtil and currish people' (p. 3). Replenishing the stocks of food and water continues to be a problem. What other people eat and whether they provide the crew with decent supplies become major themes in the way Couerte characterizes them: 'the Ethiopians are by nature very brutish or beastly people, especially in their feeding' – they eat offal and old flesh (p. 5). In contrast, the people of Gomora 'seeme to bee ciuill, kinde, and true hearted to strangers' (p. 8). At this stage of the journey, Couerte's focus remains on the new people and countries that the English encounter; he adopts an unmarked group perspective – the 'Englishman' in the title – that will recur throughout the *Report*. Yet as it continues, that point of view is gradually complicated. The trials they confront produce tensions and disagreements among the crew. Couerte grows detached from some of his mates and commanders, and as his travels unfold he refers to them less frequently and focuses more and more on his own fate. He retains a sense of Englishness, often as a touchstone for observations of places and people; yet along with that generic position a particularized view starts to emerge. As new incidents test his endurance, patience and health, Couerte's life gains solidity and presence for the reader. It is not marked by ethical or emotional confessions, but the number of testing events builds distinctiveness from others – a self as the accumulation of trial and observation.

Couerte's identity comes across quite sharply when he criticizes his companions. One of the ship's boys confesses to a 'foule and detestable sinne committed amongst vs', for which he is judged and executed (p. 19). Four members of the crew, 'being foure murderous and bad minded men' (p. 21) are tried and executed for murdering the master of the pinnace: 'he was knockt in the head with a Mallet hammer' (p. 21). Couerte also grows increasingly critical of the ship's 'wilfull Master' (p. 23), especially after he refuses to hire a local pilot, the ship runs aground and sinks, and the crew is forced to evacuate, losing cargo and provisions. In these remarks we hear personal opinion but not an individualized, reflective moral judgment. Couerte wants to state not explain his views; he seems to assume that readers will accept his account.

After the ship is sunk in September 1609, Couerte travels mainly on land. He provides often-sketchy details of the Indian cities and towns through which he

passes. He meets the great Mogol at Agro (Agra) and presents him with a golden
whistle, before heading back with four other Englishmen across Persia and Arabia
to Aleppo and Tripoli, from where he sails for England. By this time he is 'very
weake, with long and extreame trauell' (p. 65). He conceives his travels as pain
and suffering and blames 'the follies and ouersight' of the ship's master, Phillip de
Groue, 'a Flemming, and an Arch-villaine', whom he finally accuses of being 'a
detestable buggerer' (p. 68). Couerte is immensely relieved to land in England:
'For to mee, all the Nations and kingdoms, that in this my travels I passed by and
saw ... seemed nothing comparable to it' (p. 67). By the end of the *Report*, Couerte
is thus represented by contrasting character effects: he reclaims his local identity as
a loyal servant to King James, the Privy Council and the company of the East
Indian Merchants, but the range of exotic experience and duress over three years,
from 1608 to 1611, distinguishes him from compatriots and readers.

Some years ago, Paul Delany maintained that autobiographers such as Couerte
revealed 'an inability to come to terms with their own selfhood'.[22] He added that
they were unable to capture 'the personality' of the strangers they encountered and
instead focused on topography in an unreflective way (pp. 116–17). From
Couerte's *Report*, we can understand why Delany would make such claims: there
are no instances of introspection or ethical judgment. Moments of detailed
description can reveal an interest in different customs – such as the religious
practices of the Bannians, 'a strange people in their beliefe ... fond superstition,
and abhominable Idolatry' (p. 27), or the burning of widows among the
Pythagoreans in India (p. 35). Memories of hardship occasionally prompt a bitter
exclamation that captures personal and physical feelings – at one point they have
'no better water' to drink 'then was almost halfe Cow pisse' (p. 45); as they wait to
join a trade convoy in the city of Parra, the narrator mentions 'my self being also
sicke there' (p. 51). Yet Couerte attempts no analysis of what his experience might
mean for him or how it relates to the rest of his life. Indeed, he shuns grand
intentions, describing his report in the dedication as a 'rude ... discourse' whose
value for readers lies in its 'faithfull discouery'. Its key message is to affirm his
preserver's 'miraculous power, in safeguarding me beyond mine owne hope or
mans Imagination'. Couerte offers a tale of 'hard and painefull Pilgrimage', keyed
to the moral, religious, national and commercial interests of Jacobean England. In
this regard, his work's significance is not fundamentally different from modern
travel autobiographies, which are also guided by cultural expectations about what
will be observed and how it will affect the traveller. Though Couerte's journal does
not delve deeply into the mind's passions, it responds to areas of social curiosity
about many features of other countries and peoples with whom English contact
was increasing.

A True and Almost Incredible Report thus illustrates the functions of life
writing in a wider cultural dialogue. It can be linked to the reconception of
autobiographical discourse that Jerome Bruner proposes: 'while autobiography
exists, as it were, in the private intentions of the autobiographer, it also exists for
its public interpretive uses, as part of a general and perpetual conversation about

life possibilities'.[23] In travel journals like Couerte's, 'private intentions' are rarely prominent; they are coordinated to assumptions about social life at home. Such assumptions do not go unquestioned, but exceptions tend to derive either from foreign customs or from the corrupt conduct of the traveller's companions. The usual focus is on topics such as religion, social order, food and health, the layout of towns and cities and geography, issues which combine to portray social and personal life in broad terms. In reporting on these aspects of other countries, travel journals are not avoiding significant aspects of personal life. Instead, they are enabling authors' and readers' shared understanding of possibilities for living, built up over daily experience of familiar customs and habits, to be considered and usually supported. Though the possibility of norms being reappraised or even challenged is never entirely absent from the texts, in most cases, even disturbing accounts produce a salutary effect – as Thomas Elyot felt, the trials and tribulations of others reaffirm familiar customs.

Thomas Dallam, Queen Elizabeth's organ-builder, provides another revealing case of the way in which personal experience is coordinated with public understandings of individual duties and obligations towards country and sovereign. His world is abruptly transformed when he is ordered to deliver an organ to the sultan of Turkey (Dallam is chosen since he can ensure that the organ works properly after arrival). An apparent newcomer to life on shipboard, Dallam seems to enjoy the company of the sailors, drinking heavily with them in Deal while they await favourable winds. (There is a stark contrast with Richard Madox, whose negative shipboard experiences are discussed below.) Despite the dangers posed by stormy weather and a brief encounter with a French man-of-war, Dallam remains enthusiastic about life at sea. He is thrilled at seeing schools of porpoises and pods of whales, impressed by coastal cities and fortifications in Spain, and amazed by the profusion of goods in the market at Algiers, their first port of call. On the Greek island of Zante and at his urging, Dallam and a few of his mates climb a prominent hill to enjoy the view. He mixes with the locals they encounter on the climb, exchanging various tokens for food and drink. As they sail past Turkey, Dallam organizes for himself and others to be rowed to the spot where Jonas was cast out of the whale's belly. When a party of Turks boards the ship, Dallam plays the virginals to their applause. This episode exemplifies his enthusiasm about travel: he eagerly participates in all the experiences on offer.

As the journey ventures further east things become more complex. Some of the men are taken prisoner and payment has to be made to release them; the captain blames Dallam and others for getting into danger. Relations with Turkish ships start to grow fraught – the English are expected to provide lavish gifts to show their good will. Supplies run low and they cannot afford to replenish stocks completely. On arrival in Constantinople, Dallam must repair the organ, which has deteriorated in the hold. He retains his optimism, marvelling at the royal seraglio, and after he installs and plays the organ he is again feted. At the formal presentation to the sultan, Dallam, garbed in green silk, accompanies the English ambassador. He is summoned to play and is staggered by the pomp that surrounds the Grand Signor: 'the figure of him was nothing in comparison of the train that stood behind him, the sight whereof did make me almost to think that I was in another world ... I stood dazzling my eyes with looking upon his people which stood behind him, the which was 400 persons in number' (p. 56). He is also extremely anxious; at one point the sultan rises to watch him play more closely, 'I thought he had been drawing his sword to cut off my head' (p. 57). Dallam is rewarded with gold and is 'not a little joyful of my good success' (p. 57). However, his achievement complicates matters. The sultan wants him to stay, promising two concubines to compensate for the family Dallam pretends to have back in England; he is enticed by jewels and a glimpse inside the harem. The ambassador advises him not to refuse but to 'be merry with them' so he will not be forced to remain (p. 58). When Dallam's ship is about to leave, he is forced to disembark. Is the ambassador playing a double game – trying to please the sultan while only pretending to protect him? Dallam stays in the seraglio and on one occasion barely misses being executed for stumbling into the sultan's presence. He falls ill but is at last allowed to start the return trip. Various adventures take place – quarantined in a lazaretto, tempted by a mermaid's song, attacked by Spanish men-of-war – before the ship finally gets home.

Dallam relates a positive story: the opulence of the sultan's palace far surpasses that of the Elizabethan court, and the voyage across the Mediterranean is filled with memorable experiences. Underneath these events is the veiled sphere of international diplomacy, in which Dallam is a tiny player whose role for a time assumes unexpected prominence. Who knows what negotiations might be progressed or held back by the sultan's reception of the queen's gift? His wide-eyed enjoyment of his importance conveys the excitement of exotic worlds, but his travels see him shift between the stability offered by known contexts and the unpredictable opportunities, or risks, created by new ones. For a time, Dallam foresees another self that he might become – in residence at the sultan's court, perhaps like Captain Hawkins, one of Robert Couerte's companions who, by remaining at Agra and being royally treated, nevertheless abruptly exits the traveller's discourse and the familiar world: 'this is asmuch as I can say concerning him' (*True and Almost Incredible Report*, p. 42). When these kinds of choices or changes arise for the English travellers, the restricted theatre of their usual actions and its dependence on a set of insular life choices come into view. Perhaps writers such as Couerte and Dallam are for the moment restlessly aware of those limits before accepting the reassurance held out by the homewards trip.

The traveller from the period who writes most eagerly about plunging into other worlds is Thomas Coryate. Spurred on by the success of his travels in Europe and the sales of *Crudities*, Coryate ventures to 'the Court of the Great Mogul' in India, from where he greets his English friends with a compendium of letters and narratives written in 1615 and published a year later.[24] As noted earlier, Coryate uses his travels to reinvent himself as a celebrity: 'Thomas Coryate, Travailer *For the English wits, and the good of this Kingdom*: To all his inferiour Countreymen, Greeting' reads the title page. Unlike the other travellers whose journals have been discussed, Coryate does not set off on a mission, task or pilgrimage; the trip itself and an unparalleled reputation are his goals: 'in breeding me, [Somerset] hath produced such a traueller, as dooth for the diuersitie of the Countries he hath seene, and the multiplicitie of his obseruations, farre (I beleeue) out-strippe anie other whatsoeuer' (p. 5). Coryate travels in order to write and build an illustrious character. The *Greeting* exemplifies the way in which for all his exposure to other places and people, even the keenest traveller never loses sight of his local community and position in it.

Coryate died on the journey, but before setting off he had returned to his birthplace of Odcombe, where he pronounced a valedictory address and presented his walking shoes to the town. (They were hung up in the local church and remained there till the early 1700s.) His final trip, from Somerset to Asmere and beyond, thus retraces his life through the world:

> such is my insatiable greedinesse of seeing strange countries: which exercise is indeede the very Queene of all the pleasures in the world, that I haue determined (if God shall say Amen) to spend full seauen yeares more, to the end to make my voyage answerable for the time to the trauels of Vlysses; & then with vnspeable ioy to reuisite my Country. (pp. 6–7)

In a letter to Master L. W., Coryate recounts his fifteen-month journey from Jerusalem to India. He passed through cities and rivers known from biblical and classical times. Now he links his character in the journal to the western canon, invoking Ulysses as a literary and personal ideal. On the trip to India, Coryate is struck by the 'goodly city of *Lahore* ... one of the largest Cities in the whole vniuerse' (p. 13) and by 'the famous Riuer *Indus*, which is as broad againe as our *Thames* at *London*, and hath his originall out of the Mountaine *Caucasus*, so much ennobled by the ancient both Poets and Historiographers, *Greeke* & *Latin*' (p. 14). He goes on to describe the Mogul himself and the 'verie spacious' extent of 'his Dominion' (p. 21), which surpasses the mighty Turkish empire in size, land quality and revenues (pp. 22–3). Many of the sights at the Mogul's court are beyond compare: unicorns, 'the strangest beasts of the world', and elephant fights, 'the brauest spectacle in the worlde' (p. 25). With an eye on his own publicity, Coryate rides on one of the Mogul's elephants: 'determining one day (by gods leaue) to haue my picture expressed in my next Booke, sitting vpon an Elephant' (p. 26). In self-satisfied tones typical of many travellers, as if proving their canny worldliness, he highlights how little he spent on food during his 'ten moneths trauels betwixt *Aleppo* and the *Moguls* Court, but three pounds sterling, yet fared reasonable well euerie daie; victuals beeing so cheape in some Countries where I trauelled' (pp. 28–9), and what good health he has kept: 'I do enjoy at this time as pancraticall and athleticall a health as euer I did in my life: & so haue done euer since I came out of England, sauing for three dayes in *Constantinople*' (p. 31). In another letter, Coryate describes the lavish gifts presented to the Mogul by other potentates, including 'one of the richest presents that I haue heard to be sent to any Prince in al my life time' – two elephants adorned in gold, 'the whole, a hundred thousand pounds sterling' (pp. 31–2). He seems to have entered a magical realm, becoming a fantastic figure himself. These details are followed by Coryate's wishes to be remembered to relatives, friends and acquaintances in London and Somerset, including such notables as Jonson, Donne and Inigo Jones. His self-image might now be a match for theirs, and he closes this letter with *A Distich to the Traueller*, which imagines the impressed response of his famous addressees: 'All our choise wits, all, see, thou has engrost: / The doubt yet rests, if they or thou haue most' (p. 47). The final message is addressed to his mother: he apologizes for planning to be away for a further four years but lists a dazzling set of cities and sites through which he wants to pass, including the sepulchre of Tamburlaine and Mount Ararat, where Noah's ark came to rest (p. 51). To this most caring reader, Coryate claims to have 'performed such a notable voyage of *Asia* the greater, with purchase of great riches of experience, as I doubt whether any English man this hundred yeares haue done the like' (p. 49).

In his amusing, effusive way, Coryate maps the local and foreign social networks across which a traveller's identity is shaped. He welcomes the individualized role that travel creates through separation from family and regular companions, and limited rapport with new acquaintance. At the same time, Coryate is aware that his character as traveller depends on the reception he gains at home and abroad. He practises a style of identity-production that concentrates on self-presentation and on convincing others to recognize and confirm his appeal. The texts he puts together aim to distinguish his personality from readers while positioning them to accept his idealized view of Thomas Coryate – to think like him while acknowledging they cannot be him. Coryate is a self-consciously 'affectate traveller', to recall Thomas Overbury's stereotype. He flouts Bacon's advice to travellers on returning, tactfully and energetically trying to build admiration for his exploits. Through this ebullient self-commemoration, Coryate imagines the traveller's celebrity as a perfect version of the self's eminent relation to others in early modern society.

The texts written by Guylforde, Pellham, Dallam, Dunton, Couerte and Coryate aim to reconcile the traveller's self-focus with the interests of their English readers. Where Guylforde invites readers imaginatively to join the pilgrimage, Dallam and Coryate encourage them to emulate their enjoyment of the journeys. Pellham, Dunton and Couerte use a mixed address to impress the official groups on whose behalf they set out and to captivate a wider readership with tales of hardship, endurance and derring-do. Publication of these works ensures that, at the least, they offer a balanced account of their travels to maintain the support of social superiors and patrons. Doubts about the journeys' motives and outcomes find their way into most of the texts but yield to a pragmatic emphasis on (qualified) success. Responsibility to the audience – in terms of service and respect, or in terms of wanting them to appreciate the full scope of the experience – is once again a primary consideration for all of the authors.

When turning to travel journals from the period that were unpublished, we find much greater ambivalence about the effects of travel. The institutional planning and political results of expeditions are open to criticism in a way not possible, or advisable, in the published works. Most notably, the impact of travel on the author's personality and responsibility to others is explored in candid, reflective detail. The focus in these works moves between the writers' encounters with the inhabitants of new lands, their association with travelling companions and acquaintances at home, and their efforts at understanding the implications of these meetings for their own lives. The journals recount positive and antagonistic contacts with others along with periods of relative isolation, when the travellers reassess their actions and attitudes. The ways that they think about their roles and relationships are continuously affected by the changing situations in which they find themselves. The complex mix of contexts and contacts turns these journals into ongoing dialogues between self and others. Distance and alienation rather than affinity and celebrity are often the dominant motifs.

A striking example is provided by Richard Norwood (1590–1675), who worked for a number of years as a surveyor in the Bermudas and played an important role in 'planting' the islands. His *Description of the Sommer Islands, Once Called the Bermudas* links mathematical and geographical expertise with full commitment to the future of Protestant England. It represents his work from 1613 to 1617 as central to profitable colonization, 'to diuide the Countrey, and to Assigne to each Adventurer his shares or portion of land'; for only then can the land begin 'to receiue a convenient disposition, forme, and order, and to become indeede a Plantation'.[25] Norwood concludes that 'the planting of them [the Bermudas and Virginia] must needes adde much to the strength, prosperitie and glory of this Kingdome … and in all tend to the glory of God' (p. xc), exemplifying the way in which mapping and surveying in the period often invoke a doubled 'imputation of spatial mastery and/or social aggrandizement'.[26] This acute sense of space and place reverberates through Norwood's own journal, which recounts life, career and religious conversion. The jingoistic blurring of location, national and religious destiny in the *Description* is adapted to a personal account.

The journal starts as a disciplined spiritual exercise. Norwood withdraws to a solitary place and time, seeking to recall his whole life and treatment by God. In order to avoid forgetting particular incidents, he tells us that he set aside almost every Saturday afternoon during 1639 to compose the journal. The process is one of deliberate self-reckoning, cognizant of the necessary demands of time and situation; Norwood wants an audience to be fully aware of the pains he has taken. His efforts are further emphasized by the numerous signs of Norwood's revisions – crossed-out and rewritten passages, additional marginal comments, and so forth. The journal is something he worked on, reassessing its impact and value, oscillating between the roles of author and reader. The ordered approach to composing the journal is complicated by the pressures of self-portrayal. How candid should he be? Uncertainty is manifest in some heavily edited sections concerning Norwood's sexuality. He wants both to inscribe and to efface some of the things he has done and desired. Thus in blotted but partly legible lines,

Norwood describes how as an apprentice in London and elsewhere, 'the corruption of my heart showed itself abundantly [in lust, as touching the maid at my Aunt Edwards, the maid at Billing ... wantonness with my master's daughter ... also in the ... sin, in apparelling, etc., also] in vanity of mind's and self-conceitedness' (p. 17). The tension between the blotted details and the sentence's morally sound, edited conclusion replays the conflict of desire and self-restraint that Norwood experienced on these occasions. An incidental reference to his marriage – more as time-marker than as a celebration of union, 'I took a chamber at Mr. P ... where I continued above four years till I married' (p. 104) – suggests that it has not helped resolve his conflicts. In contrast to that brief allusion, a number of references to beloved male companions and bedfellows are developed, from his early school friend, Adolphus Speed, whom Norwood envied and 'yet ... loved ... very well' (p. 11), to his 'loving friend', the ship's gunner, en route to the Caribbean (p. 41), to various servants and acquaintances with whom he must later sleep to calm himself while undergoing frightening satanic visitations (pp. 93–104). Love for other men is normalized and does not seem to trigger spiritual or moral dilemmas. Indeed, as suggested below, without this kind of intimacy (perhaps even with it), Norwood remains in a state of unremitting spiritual and personal anxiety.

As a child and youth, Norwood lives in various towns before commencing an apprenticeship. Village life is viewed retrospectively as 'fruitless and dissolute' (p. 6), and young men's amusements are dismissed. He repeatedly opposes his enjoyment of acting and attending the theatre to an ability to respond to God's word. The conflict is first divulged when at the age of fifteen Norwood is living in Stony Stratford: 'I acted a woman's part in a stage play. I was so much affected with that practice that had not the Lord prevented it I should have chosen it before any other course of life' (p. 6). Acting in plays and reading romances again distract Norwood 'from the word of God' when he is an apprentice in the capital (p. 17). Years later, after returning to London from the Caribbean, he avidly frequents the theatre, 'Yea, so far was I affected with these lying vanities that I began to make a play and had written a good part of it' (p. 42). Repeatedly through his life, Norwood's participation in popular culture, especially that afforded by the metropolis, is portrayed as disrupting his spirit. The allures of place and company thwart the obligation to self-scrutiny and knowledge. Even at an early age, Norwood indicates, praise from others on account of his godly ways is to be distrusted: 'I thought it no small matter to be beloved of God, but I doubted much whether that were so or how they could know it was so. Besides, I knew myself to be worse than they took me to be' (p. 7). Incessant self-concern grants little credibility to others' perceptions.

Throughout his life and travels Norwood grapples with the pressures of responsibility, in the tensions among the imperatives of solitude, of communing with self and God, and of socializing with others. The journal itself is produced as an exercise in isolation, and, in retrospect at least, Norwood frequently dissociates himself from his peer group, even if at the time he 'esteem[ed] them the noblest sparks and the bravest men of all others' (p. 14). As a young man travelling in

Europe, he depicts himself as often being alone, though such periods are usually succeeded by his teaming up with one or more compatriots: in the Low Countries he encounters a group of English soldiers who, like Ancient Pistol, are bent on robbing other travellers (p. 20), while 'from Basel into Italy, I was accompanied with an Englishman whose name was Thomas' (p. 23). Clearly, Norwood is not averse to being alone, but his isolation is always framed by contact with others. On one striking occasion while in the Caribbean, he is forced to weigh up the value of solitude as against companionship. Due to a plague of rats, the settlement has suffered a 'great want of victuals' (p. 53), and having built himself a skiff Norwood decides to sail from the main settlement 'to get some palmetto berries for relief' (p. 54). His servant, Giles Marsh, is unwilling to go along and Norwood sets off alone. He picks the berries but, having stopped for the night on an uninhabited island, finds that the northeast winds prevent him from leaving:

> This five days seemed to me the most tedious and miserable time that I ever underwent in all my life ... yet till then I never seemed to understand what misery was; yet I had victuals sufficient, only I seemed as banished from human society and knew not how long it might last. Yet at other times I was apt to retire myself much from company, but at this time I thought it one of the greatest punishments in the world, yea, I thought it was one of the greatest punishments in hell, and the sense and apprehension of it made me to think of hell as of hell indeed, a condition most miserable ... but now I thought I would rather suffer anything than be deprived of human society. (pp. 54–5)

At last, the wind changes, but it is a perilous journey and the skiff starts to fall apart: 'I conceived I had and did grievously tempt God in going so desperately in such a boat as was scarce worthy to adventure a dog in' (p. 55). Finally, he gets back, 'The Lord was pleased accordingly to bring me safely home' (p. 55). Norwood's anguish while stuck on the island forces him to ponder his sense of responsibility to others. Though completely alone, he does not fear for his life; instead he is surprised to realize that he misses company as much as he does. Norwood finds that his usual preference for solitude is based on an unspoken awareness that people remain at hand and that he can return to them when he chooses. He is more reliant on others than he had recognized and cannot abide total or enforced isolation.

Norwood's ambivalence about company and solitude rebounds upon him with disturbing force after he returns to London. The conflict between self-possession and ill feeling towards others implodes. He endures a kind of spiritual-psychological breakdown, estranged from other people but feeling that he is constantly accompanied by 'the presence of Satan in soul and body' (p. 93). Writing 24 years after this crisis, which, he feels, was largely caused by 'spiritual pride' (p. 107), Norwood believes that he has never fully recovered, comparing himself to a savagely beaten man: 'Surely a man though he might recover and live, yet it's like it would be but a feeble life, and ... [he] would never be his own man again' (p. 105). He starts to find what respite and recovery he can through interpersonal contact: 'I began to perceive I had too much neglected outward helps and comforts' (p. 103). He often sleeps with male companions and recalls the serene grace extended towards him at that time by his cousin's dying wife.

Norwood's journal depicts the limits of identity that the individual traveller can reach in the early modern period. Independence and self-reliance, the virtues to which in later eras many travellers and adventurers sincerely aspire, are seen as feeding a kind of spiritual egotism, which cuts him off from other people as well as from God. A committed participant in England's colonial ventures, an 'I' posed in encounter and conquest, Norwood finds that the ideological and cultural confidence with which he could map the Bermudas and Virginia and predict their lucrative prospects does not direct his own future. Even though he only ever recounts how he acts for himself, to his bewilderment he remains responsible to and reliant on others. Confidence and expertise as a surveyor not only of lands but also of others and himself (along with authorship of a number of mathematical and related studies and his standard work of navigation, *The Seaman's Practice*, 1637) cannot guarantee self-stability. His identity fragments between cultural roles and personal experience. In capturing this conflict so vividly, Norwood's journal illustrates an important issue about representational practices in sixteenth- and seventeenth-century life-writing.

The critics Smith and Watson note that in some early modern texts, 'the autobiographical subject objectifies himself as an actor in the world and records the externalisation of his character, showing how the subject becomes a subject of history'.[27] In making this point they seek to denaturalize the image of an individual autobiographer, writing with full consciousness and perception of self, which is often presupposed in some autobiographical criticism, especially that focused on texts from later periods. They contest claims or suppositions that 'the autobiography has to give that unique truth of life as it is seen from the inside';[28] if the self is 'not known except privately and intuitively', then 'what the autobiographer knows, of course, or what he experiences, is all from within'.[29] Materialist and new historicist influences on autobiographical theory are not the first attempts to complicate ideas of the immanent subject. In the 1960s, John N. Morris noted that one of the chief effects of seventeenth-century spiritual autobiography, a genre that could include Norwood's journal, was to set up '[t]he ambiguous relationship between inner and outer life, sometimes issuing in an outright opposition between self and society, [which] has been a principal preoccupation of post-eighteenth-century minds'.[30] Some years later, Janet Varner Gunn suggested that a long line of autobiographical theory from Descartes to the twentieth century has aimed to achieve a 'provisional act of unsituating the self from the world transformed into a condition of the self's authentic nature'.[31] She implies that the 'situated self' remains an equally important critical concept for understanding autobiographical discourse. Perceptions of the cultural contingency of 'the isolate uniqueness that nearly everyone agrees to be the primary quality and condition of the individual and his experience' have a longer critical history than is sometimes suspected.[32]

When read in relation to the *Description of the Sommer Islands*, Norwood's journal uneasily straddles these two strains in autobiographical discourse, which distinguish between social and individual notions of character. It captures, in Eakin's terms, 'an unresolved tension between relational and autonomous modes of identity'.[33] Norwood recounts his journeys and actions in the world, his part in early modern England's colonial project, and his involvement in London society. Yet a conscious place and role in that famous social history are unable to fulfil his sense of character. He tries to turn inward to discover a spiritual identity but instead discovers 'satanic' traces of encounters, desires, and other figures from his past. He is unable to realize a complete or discrete self, what he calls 'his own man'; and the failed attempt creates greater anxiety. As a result, he returns to others for moral and physical solidarity, and with their aid he feels able to connect to the other, his God, who provides him with a sense of self-stability: 'it was much to my loss and had been to my utter overthrow if the Lord had not supported me' (p. 109). Though conscious of his part in the history of English expansion and colonization, Norwood is also the subject of a personal and social history that he cannot fully conceive. In part he is caught up in a paradigm shift between externalization and internalization of character, between responsibility to the other and to the self, which unfolds during the sixteenth century and beyond. Perhaps in less grand terms, he struggles to reconcile the different demands on his personality that derive from the religious, professional, personal, sexual, and other situations and relations in which he is involved. Neither an outwardly focused social character nor an inwardly reflective one can wholly explain his sense of identity to himself. The text finishes with a withdrawal from an autonomous quest for self-insight; it is superseded by a sequence of requests to God for greater knowledge. Within the journal's limits, Norwood finds that commitment to making such requests and awaiting a response must be enough to satisfy a sense of who he is.

Norwood lived on for another thirty-five years after composing his journal. He returned to Bermuda and ran a school. He completed a number of surveys there and in England, and published three more books: one on spiritual matters, one on civil and political strife in the 1640s, and the third on his 'doctrine of triangles'. He died and was buried at Bermuda in October 1675. The 1639–40 journal in no way pretends to give a full account of his life. Instead it is written at a crucial period when he feels the need to review his past and how God has 'dealt with' him (p. 3). It is a partial autobiography but one that does reach a point of closure in the author's spiritual compliance. The pressures of responsibility to others are overcome through submission. And though we cannot know if his requests were answered, the intimate need to write about his life seems to have passed.

The tensions between autobiographical closure and responsibility to self and others amid the changing circumstances posed by travel lie at the centre of the diary of Richard Madox, the last work to be considered in depth in this chapter. Madox's diary, which was mostly written in 1582, is a richly detailed text that draws together all the issues of self-representation raised in the travel journals discussed so far. Prior to the voyage, Madox was a Fellow of All Souls College and University Proctor at Oxford. The Earl of Leicester, then the University Chancellor, appointed him chaplain of the first English trading mission aiming to reach Cathay. Largely on account of the greedy incompetent master, Edward Fenton, selfishly hoping to emulate Francis Drake, the boats only got as far as Brazil. The entries Madox makes record the gradual disintegration of the voyage and of his own health. The journal stops in late December 1582. Madox died on 27 February 1583, and the two ships returned to England a few months later. Madox's journal is both a personal and an official text: he was the authorized registrar for the expedition, and along with the master's log and that of other senior officers, Madox's journal was always going to be scrutinized by the likes of Leicester, Francis Walsingham, Drake, and the masters of Muscovy House, all of whom had initiated and sponsored the voyage. There are considerable social and political demands on what he writes, in addition to the moral-religious earnestness Madox feels as chaplain. His efforts to negotiate these pressures, along with his need from time to time to vent emotion and frustration, make the journal an absorbingly hybrid text, which shows the pervasive intertwining of personal and social discourses that is the mark of much early modern life-writing.

The journal is prefaced with a list of years and dates, which more than anything suggests the author's confidence that he is on a path to somewhere. The chronology synthesizes cosmic and personal history: it starts with 'Founding of the World 5544 [BC]', continues through 'Study at Oxford 25 Jan. 1567' and 'Proficiency in logic 1571 Nov.', and concludes with admission to the 'Proctorship 1 April 1581'.[34] This last detail, with the prominent future it hints at, is less than two years before Madox's death. The journal proper commences a couple of months before the expedition leaves England. The earliest entries convey a strong sense of assurance amid a very familiar world. Geographically, they span Oxford, the towns where his family lives, and London. These are trips into the known. He recounts a visit to 'Wollerhanton' (Wolverhampton), during which his sister has a baby girl, whom Madox christens (pp. 71–2). He dines with various old acquaintances, and emotionally farewells his two brothers (p. 73). Through January and February 1582 he does the social rounds at Oxford, ceremoniously resigning various roles and duties, along with prized belongings, to different colleagues. He feels confident and in touch with the world – after a boozy dinner, Madox and friends discuss 'philosophy by a question of fansy where they herd me attentyvely' (p. 77); he reports news of political and military losses in the Low Countries (pp. 82–3); and in response to a claim that he has dealt rather shamefully with a 'collector', Madox 'did answer him [his accuser] home and yet with charity' (p. 87). He seems to be widely respected.

At the same time, Madox is starting to move among more diverse, challenging circles. He appears before Drake and the master of Muscovy House, aligning himself quickly with their outlooks: 'I sought not gayn but was glad to serve my cuntrey or ther honorable house or my lord and therfor would refer my self to them which knew better than my self what was fit for me' (p. 77). They are the words of one who has been trained, disciplined, and thus far rewarded by a system of service and patronage. Self-knowledge is subject to social influence. In addition, Madox's sphere of acquaintance radically changes. He leaves a world of fellows and tutors for one of sailors and speculators: 'M. Fenton our general made a great dynner at the Popes Head for al the captons and Muscovie merchants wher we wer about 30 or more' (p. 100). As the ship awaits favourable conditions so it can depart, he begins to experience physical discomfort from seasickness and moral disquiet over the crew's conduct, especially after they are allowed to return to shore when the boats cannot leave. In regard to the former he can resolve 'to bear yt with a good corage til by acqueyntance you become famylier with the heaving and setting of the ship' (p. 110); but he never comes to grips with the latter. Madox's social world has irrevocably altered, and his diary alternates between frustration and dejection as he records the relations he now must share with others.

Madox's new situation exemplifies the way in which moral and social differences between people in their home communities accompany them on their travels. Indeed, such differences may grow to be of great consequence in the intense relationships into which travellers are often forced. There is far less social space to escape one's companions, while the new locations and circumstances that arise can render irrelevant the ways of dealing with those whom one would usually have sought to avoid. Necessity breeds new kinds of social relationships among travel companions. Part of the interest, and relief, for readers back at home lies in hearing how members of these unconventional groupings are able to deal with each other. In some situations Madox can identify with all his shipmates; he then uses a generic 'we' to talk about their responses; at other times, the first-person plural is more selective, drawing together fellow officers, or constituting a small group only of Madox's moral peers. He identifies a few close colleagues – before they finally leave England 'I supt ther and lay with M. Wil Barnes ... a very honest yong gentilman and sober. He gave me a fayr fringed handkercheffe to remember hym and so I shold althoe I had receved nothing' (p. 129). After a while, he finds that he and the other chaplain, Walker, are often the only ones trying to ensure that the expedition proceeds legally. They insist vehemently to Fenton that the crew should not be permitted to steal from other ships (pp. 196–7). Madox preaches against doing so but finds the crew 'wer al withowt pytty set upon the spoyl' (pp. 143–4). Indeed, if another ship flies a Spanish flag they affirm 'that we cold not do God better service than to spoyl the Spaniard both of lyfe and goodes' (p. 144); (later Madox wryly reveals that those who urged such action panicked when they encountered a small Portuguese boat [p. 168]). Continued opposition to piracy results in a conspiracy against Madox, or so Walker tells him; Madox concedes, 'I perceived my self in some suspition as one condemning other of presumption' (p. 203). Nevertheless, he retains his sense of righteousness.

Madox is on a steep social learning curve. At the beginning he is rather shocked when fellow chaplain Walker tells him 'how his wife and he wer parted by consent althoe not dyvorsed'; Madox adds in cipher, 'He told me of many that he had ocupid' (p. 132). The moral affront pales in significance as the voyage continues; as noted, Walker becomes one of his few confidants. Shipboard life is harsh: not only do a number of sailors die but, to Madox at least, the atmosphere is hostile. Early on he is surprised that while he lets the ship musicians use his storage chest, 'I cold se none do so els but my self' (p. 129). Later he feels compelled to intercede in the punishment for stealing dealt out to a ship boy, 'I begd his pardon' (p. 144); he intervenes in a similar case some months later. The deaths of sailors by drowning and fever give him nightmares: 'God by merciful to us that lyve. He is the fyfth whom we have throen overboord' (p. 158). After the pilots mistake an island they were heading for, Madox prays again for God's guidance, 'our pilote, our master, our leader, and al, than shal we not err' (p. 161). He feels adrift, anxiously dependent on people whose skills and principles he cannot fully trust or comprehend.

The ill-omened ship and Madox's continued sickness produce disorienting dreams and 'strange visions', such as that of the pope in residence at Oxford (p. 155). Most disconcerting and complicated is the inevitable entanglement in shipboard politics and rivalries. Madox notes that there is much quarrelling among the officers as soon as the voyage is properly under way from 2 June. After two months, by mid-August, he mockingly characterizes Fenton as 'our little king ... that fearsome commander and popular tribune' (p. 169). By 10 September sarcasm turns to disgust, 'is this the way to rule free people?' (p. 182). Later he caustically records Fenton's attempt to buy his support with a gift and vows not to be swayed (p. 216). Fenton soon accuses Madox of treachery, yet he declares his innocence (p. 227). He finds it increasingly difficult to advise Fenton to act ethically. By December all senior members of the crew are concerned about their 'return into England with such infamy' if no treasure is found (p. 265). Madox too is dismayed at the prospect of the voyage's failure, but he remains adamantly opposed to piracy. Antipathy towards Fenton is equalled by contempt for the crew at large. Early on, Madox pities a few individuals, such as 'Old Robert Parkyns of Ratclif', who dies in mid-June (p. 145). Increasingly, he is appalled by the greed and violence. He is totally unable to ignore or adapt to the sailors' subculture. They drink too much and do not respect his counsel. The soldiers mistrust everyone (p. 186), and the sailors are 'rapacious and greedy' (p. 255). Late in the voyage his frustrations erupt, 'what the wit of a sailor would know, dull, obtuse and, what is worse and almost common to all of this class, rash and stubborn and intolerant of all instruction and learning' (p. 234). The others seem to regard him as presumptuous, yet he shrugs it off, 'fynding my self utterly cleer and having my whole trust in God I was myry and pleasant' (p. 203). The little community contains all the tensions of English society, brought to a head by the demands of unusual settings and experiences, the dull routine of shipboard life, and the constant pressure to make a commercial profit. Enforced coexistence compresses the social and interpersonal conflicts of different backgrounds and outlooks.

Three months after departure, in response to what has been happening, Madox starts to record axioms on human nature: 'It is a remarkable thing how eager we are for fame that is most delusive and how much we thirst to acquire wealth and that too quickly, but we avoid dangers and toil' (p. 182); 'In adventures of discovery seldom any man bringeth publique good to his own lyfe, more seldom with his own gayne but never yf he be careful ether of lyf or gayne' (p. 187). Clearly he derives a kind of solace from his ability to present such observations. They suggest the continuity and value of his Oxford experience. He gains similar pleasure from contemplating scenes from various Roman plays and implying analogies between the characters and various men on ship (pp. 195–6). These exercises are totally mismatched with his current situation and companions. There is no shared interest in sober reflection. Instead, Madox is under continuous pressure to divulge the content of his diary, especially as it becomes more obvious that the venture is going to fail. The second section of the diary begins in mid-September, around three months after departure. Madox is now aware that different accounts of what has happened will ultimately be presented and that he needs to be covered: 'When I perceaved that dyvers made notes of our viage and I had nothing but what remayneth in memory to tel when I come home, I purposed hencforward to keep a breef remembrance of those things that shal happen of any moment' (p. 189). To safeguard his position, he proposes to write in code and cipher. The journal is maintained as part of an impending dispute in which Madox is thoroughly implicated, notwithstanding his conviction that 'I had born an honest and friendly hart to al men, espetialy to the general' (p. 203). None of his recollections can now afford to be tranquil; their account aims, as do many autobiographical texts, 'to win redress',[35] though in this case Madox is also trying to anticipate any accusations that might be made against him. In November the vice-admiral approaches him and asks whether he is keeping a diary: 'he persuades me that it can be safely secreted with him, for before our return they will all be carefully searched. I denied it absolutely since as I was sickly before, I could not keep one, afterwards I wholly neglected to do it. He says the councillors will expect it of me' (p. 226). No longer able to trust anyone's motives, he is forced to deny the journal's existence. Doing so enhances its importance for Madox but also increases the pressure on him. As the days and weeks pass, Fenton and others all insist that he reveal the diary that they know he must be keeping. In the face of inducements, Madox clings to his sense of right action: 'although that truth for me is certain that he who receives a favour sells his liberty, I vowed, howsoever this matter turns out, to cater to the vices or passions of no one more than is meet' (p. 216). The journal signifies a hidden space in which Madox can try to work through complex, possibly dangerous situations, explaining and planning his actions. It warily addresses future situations as much as it records events that have already occurred. Further, Madox's diary inscribes, as Nussbaum suggests more generally, discursive contingencies, 'a private working out of what cannot and is not ready to be published; it may explore positions in discourses not suitable for public scrutiny'.[36] It provides room to plan conduct and conversations in anticipation of exchanges likely to take place.

As we would expect in a chaplain's diary, Madox includes prayer and dialogue with God. Yet the pressure and rivalry of Elizabethan society penetrate such moments. At the venture's beginning, Madox is told that the likes of the Earl of Leicester and Francis Walsingham regard him highly. He writes in response:

> I pray God grant me his grace and favour *that* the effect and yssue of my lyfe be somwhat answerable to the expectation of thes good noble men and gentilmen, for as the God of heaven whom I serve and wil do for ever hath kyndled in ther harts a certayn hope of me withowt my desert so I trust his bownty will bestoe upon mee his spetial blessyngs that I be not altogether left unto my self or to my own wyt and so overthroe all, but I trust that the Lord who hath kept me from youth up will keep me to the end. (p. 115)

In orthodox terms, Madox withdraws responsibility for actions that he nonetheless considers his own. He submits himself to God just as a bright civic future is foretold. Distance from the immediate patronage of powerful figures provides Madox with the space for solemn but wishful thinking about the future. The ambiguous mix of effacement and assertion, 'not altogether left unto my self', exemplifies the extent to which deference, to social superiors and to God, is internalized and interwoven with personal motivation. As the voyage grows increasingly acrimonious, Madox trusts that guidance from above will help him manage his conduct and relations: 'in respect to those who are my companions in this voyage, I shall strive with the approval of the Holy Ghost to prove as worthy as possible' (p. 216). His hopes come to nothing; the growing antagonism between crew members precludes rapprochement. In one of his final entries, written while, like many on board, he is quite ill, Madox turns to one of the officers, Mr Parker, who is extremely anxious about the voyage's consequences: 'I pitied the man; indeed he is very jelos of his reputation but hath not in him to mayntayn it' (p. 265). It is a displaced self-portrait; for the emulous rivalry that determined much of aristocratic and courtly male culture in the Elizabethan period has been drastically increased by the closed world in which all these figures find themselves. Madox's diary is a record of its impact on a relatively ingenuous newcomer. He seeks the status and identity that seem to be presented to him, only to find that the offer intensifies the rivalry with fatal force.

As was the case in Couerte's *Incredible Report*, supplies often figure as a contentious issue in Madox's diary, especially when the crew wishes to land and replenish stocks, while the master, Fenton, wants to push on to win fortune and dominion. The sailors frequently catch different species of birds and fish, and Madox tries them all, comparing the flavour and texture to foods eaten in England, reinforcing and testing the limits of familiar tastes. At one point, months into the voyage, on a tiny island off the Brazilian coast, Madox and two others catch and roast some birds: 'although we ate them without bread or salt or drink, nothing ever seemed to me to have tasted more delicious' (p. 248). Whether the delight is absolute or relative to the privations thus far endured is not clear. Either way, the tone stands out – unequivocal enjoyment, all the more striking because at this point in his journal Madox is increasingly using irony, codes, and ciphers, as relations between members of the voyage are fast deteriorating. For a moment those pressures seem forgotten. The entry captures the spontaneous pleasure that food can produce, and readers seem to draw close to the author's immediate experience, without the traces of animosity and secrecy that seem to impinge on most of his other remarks.

A similar effect emerges in the diary when Madox writes of his health, beginning with an ineffective purgation before setting sail and then his early seasickness, 'Rumatique I was and exceeding costyve, and troubled with hartburning which be appendixes of the sea' (p. 143). His costiveness keeps up through the voyage, and he laments that after he and others had eaten an exotic white plum, 'dyvers sayd they purged greatly but with some of us they wroght no alleviation' (p. 175). The reader glimpses an individual regimen of self-inspection, cross-checked with the apparent well-being of others. Madox's last comments on his health report continuing sickness: 'When I realised that my blood was boiling with excessive heat I prevailed upon our physician to open the vein in my left arm and let out 10 ounces of blood, but myn arm hath byn stif ther ever syth' (p. 212). Illness ties him to others: 'Almost all of us in the whole fleet are afflicted with violent headaches'; but it also distinguishes him, since others do find respite but he none: 'Many gain some relief by bloodletting' (p. 261). We do not read of visits from shipmates as he slowly dies, though earlier he had included details of visiting his fellow chaplain, Walker: 'We found the man weak and prepared to die, however, we discovered great signs of health' (p. 231). The journal does not record Madox's decline; the chaplain does not depict an elaborate art of dying that reaffirms faith and providence. His end is simply foreshadowed by the abrupt end of the diary, two months before his death occurred on 27 February 1583. The crew's reaction to his death is not known, but his last effort to conceal the diary was obviously effective.

For all its vivid descriptions of exotic foods, foreign peoples and locations, and more than any of the other travel autobiographies we have considered, Madox's journal exemplifies the key feature of such texts: the most interesting effects of personal identity emerge in the tensions and differences that the subjects experience with their compatriots, both those who have stayed at home and those who accompany the authors on the trip. The kinds of accusations levelled at Edward Pellham and Robert Couerte are likely to have enveloped Richard Madox if he had survived. As Francis Bacon observes, the traveller's homecoming can be highly sensitive – physical separation never terminates relationships but it can conceal or cloud how and why they might be changing. In various ways, what all of these authors find is that no matter how far they travel they never get away from their original communities. In fact, in some ways they find themselves more tightly and complexly circumscribed than ever.

In this light, the travel diaries and journals probe the unpredictable borders between personal identity and group relations. By virtue of leaving behind regular social routines and contexts, the traveller becomes a marked man, doubly subject to new and old acquaintance. The reliance on and contact with people that early modern travel requires can make the traveller an object of scrutiny. Differences in ethical outlook and class and educational backgrounds, which could usually be negotiated more or less comfortably, encroach forcefully upon his experience, either directly in the relationships with companions or through apprehensions of what those at home will make of his journey. While group experience on land or sea can provide security, friendship and intimacy, it can also be frustrating and threatening. Unity in the face of external or foreign dangers might quickly unravel; solidarity might give way to individual manoeuvring for power, profit or survival. The premises of the travellers' identities are gradually exposed, often to be reinforced, but sometimes to be confronted or subverted.

Through travellers' attempts to retain and promote their identities and perspectives amid familiar parties and recognized factions, as much as before unimagined sights, people and conditions, we can discern the cultural and self encounters which fashion and divide early modern individuals. Unlike a modern-day counterpart – who, in freedom from the familiar, seeks contact with a genuine identity, the urge to self-realization through travel that Rousseau proclaims in *Emile* – an early modern traveller rarely acknowledges the possibility that a voyage might change his self-conception. He passes into alien settings fortified by a sense of defined social roles and obligations. The most he expects is that travel will affect his place in the world, hopefully for the better. Yet time and again the people he meets and re-meets, with their varied manners, motives and conduct, test personal and social structures of identity that were felt and lived as intrinsically integrated. The journals and diaries that we can still read record their authors' responses to these challenges.

This Travelling Age

In the reader's preface that begins his *Itinerary Containing His Ten Yeeres Travell* (1617), Fynes Moryson apologizes for the 'barrenness' of explaining exchange rates and the like, all of which he has 'inserted only for the vse of vnexperienced Trauellers passing those waies … who shall desire to view forraign kingdomes'.[37] Moryson suggests that sophisticated readers would already have visited these countries and might not even need to read his book. He had first set off 25 years earlier, 'out of my innated desire to gaine experience by trauelling into forraigne parts' (p. 1). He provides detail about the cost of food, lodging and transportation, and he also comments on the inconvenience posed by fellow travellers and local residents: though costing more, it is preferable to ride from Stode to Hamburg than sail, for 'the annoyance of base companions will easily offend one that is anything nice' (p. 3); steadfastness is necessary when sharing a coach in Frankfurt – 'I coming first … tooke the most commodious seat, which these my worthy companions (forsooth) tooke in ill part, yet neither their murmuring nor rude speeches could make yeeld the place to them' (p. 37); thick skin helps with accommodation in Holland – 'he intreated a gentleman of Friesland to admit me partner of his bed, but I hearing the gentleman condition with him about the cleannesse of my body and linen, for very scorne would not trouble his worship, but chose rather to lie vpon a bench' (p. 43); and tenacity is the best way to counter

Copenhagen's residents – 'the common people, as if they had neuer seene a stranger before, shouted at mee after a barbarous fashion; among which people were many mariners, which are commonly more rude in such occasions, and in all conuersation' (p. 57). The disquiet Moryson seems to inspire in those around him does nothing to shake his self-image; in fact it seems to reaffirm his cultural and personal confidence. He never doubts his superiority to these various European nationals and assumes that experienced English readers and travellers will acknowledge his viewpoint.

In a similar way, in his 1660 *Memoirs* of travels through Europe, Sir John Reresby declines to offer elaborate descriptions of the layout and buildings of cities he visited. For Paris, 'in this travelling age, most men's experience can give a better account of';[38] and for Venice, it seems preferable 'Not to trouble the reader with a long description of a city so exactly done by others' (p. 54). Reresby makes the point that in the year of Charles II's restoration, the English travel journal is a thoroughly familiar genre. Its purposes and structure are understood, its conventions widely recognized. Reresby smoothly fulfils the form, providing, like Moryson and Coryate before him, details of distances, travel and accommodation costs, major institutions and buildings, and sharp summaries, aimed to tickle English sensibilities, of the qualities of each nation's people. A loyal supporter of the monarchy, Reresby is pleased to affirm his upper-class character against those with whom, from time to time, he must travel, as on one particular trip to Blois, 'a day's journey distance from Orleans in a passage-boat, with some French men and women, who, by singing, to make the journey more pleasant (some of them having good voices) made it less so; infecting the air at the same time with wafts of garlic (a great food in that country, with bread) that it more nauseated the smell than gratified the ear' (pp. 21–2). In this droll syntax and observations, we hear an urbane resistance to foreign, popular culture and the reassertion of a particular kind of Englishness, whose fortunes for the time being have waned. Reresby explains that his motives for travelling in the mid 1650s are symptomatic of a generation's reaction to the social-political tide and the advent of the commonwealth: 'to live there appeared worse than banishment; which caused most of our youth (especially such whose families had adhered to the late king) to travel; amongst others myself' (p. 1). The situation at home can also affect how one must proceed overseas: in Brussels, Reresby pretends to be a Frenchman, 'for had it been known in England that I passed through Flanders, where the King of England, then was, it had afforded colour enough to Oliver [Cromwell] to sequester my estate' (p. 127). The upper lip is wittily but firmly set. Fifty or so years earlier, on various occasions Moryson also felt obliged to disguise himself, sometimes as a local to avoid being robbed in northern Germany (pp. 37–8), or as a Dutchman in Spanish-ruled Milan, to evade arrest on account of England's involvement in the ongoing war in the Netherlands (p. 155).

In their textual efforts to personify the elite young man on the move – the figure whose welfare so interested Bacon – Moryson and Reresby underscore the way in which the travel diary seeks to authorize the journey's final stage: the return of the self, enhanced, perhaps, by acquaintance with unfamiliar habits and accomplishments, but still substantively the same. In representing their authors' continual adjustment to the people and places they visit, the travel journals we have examined capture an important aspect of early modern identity – that while social and personal traits remain on the move, never quite arriving at their expected destination, the sense of oneself – of who one is in society – seeks to remain static and, indeed, to appear unchanged by travel at all. Moreover, and notwithstanding the unsettled social and political climates of Tudor and Stuart England, one senses in many descriptive features – the revulsion at foreign garlic, for example (or the prideful rejection of foreigners who suggest that one's English self might not be clean), and the myriad of sensibilities so confidently shared with those at home – an almost audible sigh of gratification for the fact that one is English. (As Thomas Nashe affirmed, any English traveller is an unfortunate one.) It is this juxtaposition of the transitional with the possibilities of being 'other than oneself' that links the early modern traveller – looking outward – with the subject of the next chapter who peers anxiously inward at his or her metaphysical mirror or looking glass. When observing Europe and the great globe, travellers are bolstered by stout conceptions of the lands they will return to; and yet the very concern about returning home with an unchanged demeanour bears its own measure of acknowledgement that things might indeed be internally changed (even if this acknowledgement is implicit, like the anxious straightening of garments on re-entering a room). As we turn to the subject of mirrors, the activity of observation and reflection becomes more self-consciously personal. Abounding with reflections that display moral and metaphysical lessons for self-comportment, the mirrors we encounter in literary texts are also, as we shall see, fascinatingly multiple and their images precarious.

Notes

1   Francis Bacon, *Essays or Counsels–Civil and Moral* (1625), Harvard Classics, ed. Charles W. Eliot (New York: Collier, 1969), p. 46.
2   Sir Thomas Overbury, *Characters, or Wittie descriptions of the properties of sundry Persons*, in *The 'Conceited Newes' of Sir Thomas Overbury and His Friends*, ed. James E. Savage (Gainesville: Scholars' Facsimiles and Reprints, 1968), pp. 79–80.
3   Sir Thomas Elyot, *The Book Named the Governor* (1531), ed. S.E. Lehmberg (London: Dent, 1970), p. 35.
4   Patrick Coleman, 'Introduction: Life-Writing and the Legitimation of the Modern Self', in *Representations of the Self from the Renaissance to Romanticism*, ed. Patrick Coleman, Jayne Lewis and Jill Kowalik (Cambridge: Cambridge University Press, 2000), p. 11.
5   Thomas Coryate, *Coryate's Crudities*, 2 vols. (Glasgow: James MacLehose, 1905), 1, p. 123.

6 Jean-Jacques Rousseau, *Emile or On Education*, trans. Allan Bloom (New York: Basic, 1979), pp. 452–4.

7 Peter Burke, 'Representations of the Self from Petrarch to Descartes', in *Rewriting the Self: Histories from the Renaissance to the Present*, ed. Roy Porter (London: Routledge, 1997), p. 22.

8 Michael Mascuch, *Origins of the Individualist Self: Autobiography and Self-Identity in England, 1591–1791* (Cambridge: Polity, 1997), p. 18.

9 *The Comedy of Errors*, in *The Riverside Shakespeare*, gen. ed. G. Blakemore Evans (Boston: Houghton Mifflin, 1974), IV, iii, 10–11, 43–4. All references to Shakespeare's work here are to this edition.

10 Quoted in J. Theodore Bent, 'Master Dallam's Mission', *The Antiquary* 18 (1888): 6. Further references to Dallam's diary are to the summary and quotations in this article.

11 Felicity A. Nussbaum, 'Toward Conceptualizing Diary', in *Studies in Autobiography*, ed. James Olney (New York: Oxford University Press, 1988), p. 129.

12 *The begynnynge and contynuaunce of the Pilgrymage of Sir Richarde Guylforde ... And howe he went with his servaunts and company towards Jherusalem* (London: 1511), fol. xxix.

13 Jonathan Goldberg discusses the role of the secretary's writing on behalf of the master in *Writing Matter: From the Hands of the English Renaissance* (Stanford: Stanford University Press, 1990).

14 'Ramasshed' meaning 'tobogganned'; the *Oxford English Dictionary* cites this same sentence from Guylforde's text.

15 Philippe Lejeune, 'Autobiography in the Third Person', in *On Autobiography*, trans. Katherine Leary (Minneapolis: University of Minnesota Press, 1989), p. 45.

16 Paul John Eakin, *How Our Lives Become Stories: Making Selves* (Ithaca: Cornell University Press, 1999), p. 178.

17 Sidonie Smith and Julia Watson, *Reading Autobiography: A Guide for Interpreting Life Narratives* (Minneapolis: University of Minnesota Press, 2001), p. 150.

18 Smith and Watson, *Reading Autobiography*, p. 90.

19 Iohn Dvnton [John Dunton], *A True Journal of the Sally Fleet with the Proceedings of the Voyage* (London: 1637), p. 26.

20 Edward Pellham, *Gods Power and Providence: Shewed, In the Miraculous Preservation and Deliverance of eight Englishmen, left by mischance in Greenland Anno 1630 nine moneths and twelve dayes* (London: 1631), sig. A3.

21 Robert Couerte, *A True and Almost Incredible Report of an Englishman, that ... Trauelled by Land through many unknowne Kingdomes, and Great Cities* (London: 1612), sig. A3v and sig. A4r.

22 Paul Delany, *British Autobiography in the Seventeenth Century* (London: Routledge & Kegan Paul, 1969), p. 108.

23 Jerome Bruner, 'The Autobiographical Process', in *The Culture of Autobiography: Constructions of Self-Representation*, ed. Robert Folkenflik (Stanford: Stanford University Press, 1993), p. 41.

24 Thomas Coryate, *Greeting from the Court of the Great Mogul* (1616; Amsterdam and New York: Da Capo, 1968).

25 Richard Norwood, *The Description of the Sommer Ilands* [sic]*, Once Called the Bermudas*, in *The Journal of Richard Norwood, Surveyor of Bermuda* (New York:

Scholars' Facsimiles and Reprints, 1945), p. lxxvi. *The Description* is reprinted from John Speed's *A Prospect of the Most Famous Parts of the World* (London: 1631). References to Norwood's journal are also to this edition (1945); quoted sections that are included in square brackets (as presented in the edition) had been crossed out or rewritten in the journal.

26 John Gillies, 'Introduction: Elizabethan Drama and Cartographizations of Space', in *Playing the Globe: Genre and Geography in English Renaissance Drama*, ed. John Gillies and Virginia Mason Vaughan (Madison: Fairleigh Dickinson University Press, 1998), p. 36.

27 Smith and Watson, *Reading Autobiography*, p. 88.

28 Roy Pascal, *Design and Truth in Autobiography* (London: Routledge & Kegan Paul, 1960), p. 195.

29 James Olney, *Metaphors of Self: The Meaning of Autobiography* (Princeton: Princeton University Press, 1972), pp. 23, 35.

30 John N. Morris, *Versions of the Self* (New York: Basic, 1966), p. 34. On Norwood's journal as a kind of spiritual autobiography, see Delany, *British Autobiography* pp. 60–62.

31 Janet Varner Gunn, *Autobiography: Toward a Poetics of Experience* (Philadelphia: University of Pennsylvania Press, 1982), p. 7.

32 Olney, *Metaphors*, pp. 20–21.

33 Eakin, *How Our Lives*, p. 181.

34 *An Elizabethan in 1582: The Diary of Richard Madox, Fellow of All Souls*, ed. Elizabeth Story Donno (London: Hakluyt Society, 1978), p. 70.

35 John Sturrock, *The Language of Autobiography: Studies in the First Person Singular* (Cambridge: Cambridge University Press, 1993), p. 49.

36 Nussbaum, 'Conceptualizing Diary', p. 134.

37 Fynes Moryson, *An Itinerary Written by Fynes Moryson, Gent. Containing His Ten Yeers Travell thorow Twelve Dominions* (London: 1617).

38 Sir John Reresby, *The Memoirs and Travels of Sir John Reresby*, ed. Albert Ivatt (London: K. Paul, Trench, Trubner, 1904), p. 8.

Chapter 4

Framing a Reflected Self:
Language and the Mirror

Without perspective nothing can be done well or properly in the manner of painting and drawing. The painter who relies only on practice and the eye, without any intellect, is no more than a mirror which copies slavishly everything in front of it.

Leonardo da Vinci[1]

The mirror that invites Leonardo da Vinci's disparaging glance is in his view flat and unyielding, a device of mimicry that contributes to a painting nothing of an artist's perspicacity.[2] Da Vinci's reference above provides just one of the many mirror contexts that help connote the complex realm of early modern individuality. In positing the mirror purely as an artistic device, however, his is one of the rare viewpoints that does not bring into play its dazzling array of keys to social self-production. For people across Europe, reflection underscored instructional self-*recognition*, a premodern sense of structured social identity that could be renewed, recalled or striven toward. And in tension with such concepts and practices of self-representation, the mirror also challenged these familiar lines of identity through a range of shifting philosophical and corporeal boundaries. It is this tension that renders it useful to our study of autobiographical identity in early modern England.

Connections between mirrors, autobiography and self-representation flourished in the early modern period through an abundance of artistic tropes. Attempts to historicize and record the proliferation of mirror references have inspired such elaborately detailed studies as Herbert Grabes's *The Mutable Glass* and Jenijoy Labelle's *Herself Beheld: the Literature of the Looking Glass*.[3] Yet while poetry and drama declared the 'looking glasse' to be a place 'indeed / Wherein a man a History may read,'[4] mirrors did not consistently feature as part of nonliterary discourse about the self. Indeed, given the mirror's importance to early modern writings, it is remarkable that there are very few descriptions of even brief physical encounters with the glass, though is safe to assume that most 'autobiographical' writers – Richard Rogers, Bishop Hall, Margaret Hoby, Grace Mildmay, John Worthington, Elias Ashmole, to name just a few – were of the class of person to have access to a mirror in which they could check their appearances at will. Our argument is not that those who had access to mirrors were disinclined to observe themselves; but rather that they had very different notions of what such observation meant, and how it might be conceived of and recorded. The fact that few writers commented on their actual physical appearances suggests that, at least for the purpose of writing, the cast of a complexion, for example, or one's eye, girth, or other physical markings, served less to distinguish an individual than a social self;[5] and that this distinction plays itself out within the iconography of mirrors in fascinating and complicated ways.

Bringing the Mirror to the Masses: Sermons and the Theatre

Signals of moral development or direction, standards of ideal conduct, and reflections of sins such as vanity and worldliness – these were the values associated with the early modern mirror. From portentous reminders to oneself in the course of a running diary, as in the preacher Richard Rogers's 'endeavour to see one year thus passed, that it may be a glass to me hereafter'[6], to more self-consciously literary endeavours, mirrors were imbued with multiple meanings, ornamenting language as conspicuously as the large, framed glass artifacts themselves enriched upper-class family homes – or, more accurately, the homes of those with upper-class aspirations. There were, however, many thousands of citizens who did not have such mirrors or such homes, and who lacked the means, and perhaps the leisure and education, to sit around reading literary works, let alone writing them. For these many and varied people, literary mirrors touched their lives by way of two main vehicles: sermons and the theatre.

Preachers and dramatists competed fiercely for patronage from audiences of all classes, ranks and levels of literacy. Puritan clergy and their supporters made their sermons highly theatrical,[7] while also repeatedly attacking the theatre; and the theatres, for their part, drew heavily on biblical tropes to touch on the temporal and eternal dimensions of the self.[8] Important to note here is that both church and theatre were replete with references to mirrors and self-reflection. 'For if any be a hearer of the word, and not a doer, he is like unto a man beholding his natural face in a glass: For he beholdeth himself, and goeth his way, and straightway forgetteth what manner of man he was', proclaims James's epistle (1. 22–24). While James urges man to recover himself, St Paul uses the glass mirror to depict the very image of man's divinely bestowed understanding of God's image: 'But we all, with open face beholding in a glass the glory of the Lord, are changed into the same image from glory to glory, even as by the Spirit of the Lord' (2 Corinthians 3.18). The dramatist and poet Fulke Greville draws on St Paul's image in depicting the soul as it leaves the body: 'To see it selfe in that eternal Glasse, / Where time doth end.'[9] We might counterpoise with this cerebral mirror the image of man's earth-boundedness as depicted in *The Homily on the Misery of Mankind*: 'Heere (as it were in a glasse) wee may learne to know our selues to be but ground, earth, and ashes, and that to earth and ashes we shall returne'.[10]

The image of earthly human frailty finds a secular parallel in Ben Jonson's mirror, which exposes 'the time's deformity / Anatomised in every nerve, and sinew, / With constant courage, and contempt of fear'.[11] The idea of death as the mirror that makes man suddenly 'to know himself' is further developed in Aemilia Lanyer's dramatic poem, *Salve Deus Rex Judaeorum*, where it is woven into a context comparing glass mirrors to their metal counterparts. As we shall see later in this chapter, many people of the early modern period were fascinated by the difference between the shadowy, imperfect reflection offered by conventional metal mirrors, and the sharper, more 'real' reflection to which glass mirrors gave them access. Lanyer's conceit pairs man's earthly gaze with the 'dym steele' of a metal mirror, in contrast to the 'spotlesse truth' offered by God's 'chrystall' glass.[12] This draws on the image from St Paul that pulls together the now and then – the temporal and the eternal spheres – in juxtaposing the darkness of the bronze mirror, in which one could capture only a dim reflection of one's face, with God's clear glass: 'For now we see through a glass, darkly; but then face to face: now I know in part; but then shall I know even as also I am known'.[13]

These were the kinds of conceits through which congregations at sermons, and audiences in public spaces, were acquainted with the verbally brocaded image of the mirror. Poetic and liturgical mirrors will turn up elsewhere in this chapter, reiterating the importance of its illustrative associations. Reflection and mirroring, tropes of the self *par excellence* for recent literary and cinematic works, had a very different resonance for early modern English lives. In a culture that rarely encouraged expressions of interiority – and which, indeed, hardly had a language for it – the mirror served as a stylized and complex vehicle for speculation about religion, mortality, eternity, and, through this, the social and philosophical dimensions of identity. Beginning with a discussion of the making of the mirror and its social impact in the sixteenth century, we will describe its relationship – complicated, often obliquely articulated – to the rhetoric of selfhood in early modern England.

How Mirrors were Made

Glass mirrors date back to the third century A.D. in Egypt, Gaul, Asia Minor and Germany. These mirrors were very small, one to three inches in diameter, and the quality of reflection was poor. For many centuries, then, metal mirrors of steel, silver and gold were preferred until a technique was found for producing long, flat, thin glass, and artisans devised a way of spreading hot metal onto glass without causing breakage.[14] The term 'mirror' referred to metal mirrors as well as to 'water mirrors', crystal mirrors and mirrors of glass, while 'looking glass' (or, less commonly, 'seeing glass') designated mirrors made of glass compound.[15] By the end of the twelfth century looking glasses were revived, adopted first in Germany and Italy, and gradually reaching England.[16] A mixture of antimony and lead was heated two or three times. Molten resin was poured into the mixture, which was blown by means of a pipe into a spherical bowl with a hole in it. The bowl was shaken so that the mixture would spread around the inner wall, and the leftover liquid was drained out of the opening. The bowl was then left to stand until the amalgam had cooled and hardened, when it was cut in half to make two convex mirrors. Convex mirrors were not new, of course – classical metal mirrors were all slightly convex – but for both Renaissance artists fascinated by perspective and for ordinary people such mirrors provided a novel way of distorting the face.

In sixteenth-century Venice the production of glass mirrors became an important industry, and techniques for making mirrors were significantly refined. The round bowls used as moulds for convex mirrors were by the middle of the century replaced by glass cylinders that could be leveled out to make flat mirrors. The reverse side of a mirror was covered with an amalgam of tin and mercury, in the production of which a sheet of tinfoil was set on a table. On top of the foil the glassmakers poured pure mercury, and over that they placed a sheet of paper. Before it hardened, the glass, cut and flattened from the cylindrical mould, was lowered onto the paper. The artificers subsequently removed the piece of paper so that the glass would touch the surface of the mercury. They weighted the glass down to allow the excess mercury to seep out, leaving a thin layer that would bind itself to the tin, forming a backing. A month later a piece of metal was attached to this backing, and the resulting glass mirror gave a very good reflection.[17]

Because this process pushed the technology of the day to its limits, large glass mirrors were very difficult to make, and thus neither cheap nor readily accessible.[18] In mid-seventeenth-century Venice a silver-framed looking glass, 115 by 65 cm, cost 8000 pounds, while a Raphael painting, itself a prized acquisition, cost 3000 pounds.[19] Sabine Melchior-Bonnet suggests that on the continent, at least, the procurement of large mirrors was linked to a person's lifestyle and craving for aristocratic connections more than to the availability of personal resources.[20] And if John Aubrey's description of Francis Bacon's house at Gorhambry is anything to go by, in England as well the looking glass was a mark (and, indeed, an enhancement) of grandeur:

> The upper part of the uppermost dore on the east side, had inserted into it a large looking-glasse, with which the stranger was very gratefully deceived, for (after he had been entertained a pretty while, with the prospects of the ponds, walks, and countrey, which this dore faced) when you were about to returne into the roome, one would have sworn *primo intuitu,* that he had beheld another Prospect through the howse: for, as soon as the stranger was landed on the balconie, the conserge that shewed the howse would shutt the dore to putt this fallacy on him with the Looking-glasse.[21]

The looking glass was built into Bacon's house to enhance the illusion of grandeur. Already handsome in its fittings and proportions, Bacon's house seems all the more splendid to the unsuspecting newcomer because the servant has been instructed to quickly shut the door, 'put[ting] the fallacy on him with the Looking-glasse'. The visual trick wrought by the looking glass thereby augments the awe of the spectator and the self-importance of the master of the house.

Quite predictably, mirrors were less important for those classes whose labour was not linked to their sense of display or of personal etiquette. Regional inventories provide pertinent examples, such as that of the parish of Darlington, a northern market town.[22] Only two of the testators – both wealthier members of the town – bequeathed looking glasses. The looking glass left by Mary Throckmorton must not have been of the smallest size, given that it was valued, along with sundry small items, at six shillings;[23] another left by Mary Lascelles was valued at only one shilling and sixpence.[24] A set of twelve small glasses left by Anthony Dennis was valued at less than two shillings.[25] Given that a bed was valued at between two and six shillings,[26] a mare and foal with saddle and bridle cost four shillings,[27] a set of linen sheets could fetch anything between five and thirteen shillings,[28] and five bushels of wheat and rye were valued at sixteen shillings,[29] these looking glasses and small glass mirrors were not beyond the means of country people.[30] Notwithstanding the affordability of small mirrors, however, they do not appear to have been considered particularly necessary or desirable, or the reflections they offered worth remarking on.

The case was quite different for courtesans who used mirrors for their toiletry, and Cathy Santore[31] and Sara Pennell have demonstrated the mirror's importance both in crafting a toilette and in helping to define the intimacy of a dressing room.[32] The popularity of mirrors for upper-class women drew a predictable slough of invective from conduct writers like Richard Braithwaite, who noted the increased use of makeup along with the rise of the glass:

> What a serious intercourse or sociable dialogue is between an amorous Mistresse and her Looking-glasse! The point or pendant of her feather wags out of a due posture; her Cheeke wants her true tincture; her captious Glasse presents to her quicke eyes one error or other, which drives her into a monstrous distemper. Pride leaves no time for prayer. This is her CLOSET FOR LADIES, where she sits and accommodates her selfe to *Fashion*, which is the period of her content, while purer objects are had in contempt. This is not the way to make Privacy your mindes melody. [33]

Striking here is the contrast between the serious self-scrutiny that could be afforded by private moments before the mirror, and the frivolous distraction into worldly pride and vanity that is the natural path for 'amorous Mistresses'. Instead of a window into the soul, Braithwaite sees the glass as blocking a woman's sensitivity to her soul, distracting her with pride, vain contentments and 'monstrous distemper'. The closet for ladies, then, seals a woman within a realm of vain fancies.

Small, mass-produced glass mirrors were used by those at court, available first in Venice and later, by the middle of the sixteenth century, spreading to England as well as other parts of Europe. Worn decoratively at the waist by women and in the cap by men, these were an essential aid to personal grooming.[34] Castiglione's conduct manual, *The Book of the Courtier*, widely read in English court circles, offered praise for the courtier who showed 'a meticulous regard for … personal appearance'.[35] But Castiglione also added a caution in view of the rising fascination with this newly industrialized means of reflection, criticizing those rather excessive individuals who carried 'a mirror in the fold of [their] cap[s] and a comb in [their] sleeve[s] ... walking through the streets always followed by a page with a brush and sponge'.[36] Similarly, Mary Tattle-well (an 'author' possibly both collaborative and male) describes an effeminate suitor as 'a dainty purfum'd carpet Captaine, a powdred Potentate, a painted Periwig frizled, frounced, Geometricall curious Glas-gazer, a comb'd, curl'd and curried Commander, a resolute profest Chacer or hunter of fashions, and a most stiffe, printed, bristled, beardstarche'.[37] The iconography of mirrors, then, was capable of revealing an unseemly concern with one's social persona.

Because the system of patronage and coterie culture at work in the upper classes effectively nurtured poets, dramatists and visual artists, the circulation of the small glass amongst such people can offer a plausible explanation for the burgeoning interest in the mirror as a literary motif of self-scrutiny. But what exactly *was* the shape staring back at the beholder from an often shadowy, imperfect glass, and what did it have to do with notions of selfhood and individuality?[38] Such a question involves a whole range of subtle social issues that help address the complex realm of autobiographical selfhood.

Mirrors and the Artists' Marketplace

> Sin of self-love possesseth all mine eye,
> And all my soul, and all my every part;
> And for this sin there is no remedy,
> It is so grounded inward in my heart.
> Methinks no face so gracious is as mine,
> No shape so true, no truth of such account,
> And for my self mine own worth do define
> As I all other in all worths surmount..
> But when my glass shows me myself indeed,
> Beaten and chopp'd with tann'd antiquity,
> Mine own self-love quite contrary I read;
> Self so self-loving were iniquity.
>   'Tis thee (myself) that for myself I praise,
>   Painting my age with beauty of thy days.

Revelling in his self-conceit, Shakespeare's poet of Sonnet 62 peers into the looking glass, stopping short at the image of 'myself indeed, / Beaten and chopp'd with tann'd antiquity'.[39] His looking glass reveals the unsettling disparity between the face he imagines he has and the face he owns. He ruefully recalls the alacrity with which he first approached the mirror, expecting there to individuate himself from other, less worthy lovers:

> Methinks no face so gracious is as mine,
> No shape so true, no truth of such account,

And for my self mine own worth do define
As I all other in all worths surmount.

In his glass he sees reflected not his superior worth but his ordinariness, his own mortality, and a foolhardiness that links him 'indivisibly' to a 'tanned antiquity' of other lovers. The poet's trip to the mirror is thus a salutary one. No longer spry and self-loving, in a quasi-Neoplatonic gesture he soberly offers to replace his own image altogether with that of the lover he had hoped to woo.

Or so it seems. We would argue that this ritual gesture of temperance involves a complicated process in which the poet assembles an intricate set of counter-images that challenge the conceit of self-reflection. Firstly, it is not his physical reflection that the poet finds striking – it is the 'sin' of 'self-love' that engrosses him, possessing 'all mine eye, / And all my soul, and all my every part'. His reflection in the mirror is in these terms more moral than corporeal. Secondly, in availing the poet of a private moment of spiritual chastisement, the mirror effectively becomes a form of spiritual soliloquy, a way of talking with God. Through these images of reflection, therefore, the mirror takes on the task of spiritual instruction. Somewhat perversely, however, while the poet modestly recoils at the reflection of his foolish vanity, it is still the *mirror* that permits him to gloat: through the conceit of reflection he argues for two of the most important Aristotelian virtues, humility and magnanimity. In one refracted image, the sonnet itself effectively takes on the shape of a literary convex mirror, simultaneously collapsing the poet's words into a history of *vanitas* while also parading his merits.

Shakespeare's complicated system of reflections in Sonnet 62 invokes a speaking self that does all sorts of things in front of the mirror. It preens, self-castigates, peeps modestly from behind self-deprecating images, and even offers to absent itself altogether. The rhetoric of reflection communicates various spiritual and worldly attributes within the givens and obscurities of the spoken word. But *is* the poet's self a rhetorical one, and, if so, to what extent? Does the trope of reflection serve to display an individuated self or to mediate it as a social function? The pioneering work published by Stephen Greenblatt in 1981[40] laid the ground for two subsequent decades of critics who have speculated on autobiographical self-representation in the early modern period.[41] Two researchers – Debora Shuger and Sabine Melchiori-Bonnet – have made the mirror the focus of substantial contributions to this debate.

Debora Shuger argues that mirrors in early modern English artistic practice – writings, paintings, woodcuts and the like – describe not a reflexive self-consciousness that might be seen to herald the birth of modern subjectivity but, in fact, the reverse.[42] She suggests that while representations of mirrors reflected many things, they almost never revealed, or even purported to display, an individuated self (p. 22). Mirrors were instruments of correction; Platonically angled, upward-tilted emblems intended to reflect paradigms of virtue; remembrances of mortality; and cruel reminders that sins such as vanity must be punished. (They functioned, indeed, as all of the symbols toward which

Shakespeare gestures in sonnet 62.) On this basis Shuger argues convincingly that far from a Burkhardtian exemplar of the birth of individual, the early modern mirror was the mark of a culture that was yet to have a place, and a vocabulary for, the kind of 'I' with which we are now so familiar.

Shuger suggests that while people four centuries ago would not have hesitated to use an available mirror to remove spinach from their teeth, the mirror as trope has a special function. Rather than a preemptive sign of our own postindustrial individuality, she sees it as in fact the opposite. It designates a self that lacks 'reflexivity, self-consciousness, and individuation, and hence differs fundamentally from what we usually think of as the modern self' (p. 35). Shuger's early modern subject is not uninterested in the connection between the reflected self and the cosmos: indeed, the mirror is a highly emblematic means of exploring the boundaries and the complexities of this relationship. But she sees the mirror motif itself as profoundly medieval in representing a self that 'is not identical to oneself but *like* it – a significantly similar other prior to about 1660'. It reflects 'those whom one will or does resemble' rather than oneself (p. 37).

Highly formalized and emblematically rich, the rhetoric of reflection in the early modern period thus enabled complex forms of dialogue. Its iconographic formality lent itself particularly well to writers of advice material for women. Alice Sutcliffe's *Religious Meditations*, for example, begins with a formal instruction to use her book as an educative mirror:

> Would'st thou (fraile Reader) thy true Nature see?
> Behold this Glasse of thy Mortality.
> Digest the precepts of this pious Booke,
> Thou canst not in a nobler mirrour looke.
> Though sad it seeme, and may loose mirth destroy.[43]

In a more combative context, writers like Constantia Munda and Ester Sowerman make use of the mirror to respond to Joseph Swetnam's rantings against women. Munda accuses Swetnam of 'seek[ing] applause / By rayling and reviling to deprave / The mirrour of Creation, to out-brave / Even heaven it selfe with folly,[44] while the pseudonymous Sowerman deploys the literary mirror to disseminate the image of 'that blessed mother,' the counter-image to Swetnam's whore, the 'mirrour of al woman-hood, the Virgin *Marie*.'[45] The advice material for women prepared by male conduct writers is more conventionally admonitory, using mirrors as edifying devices of spiritual appreciation and beautification. In advising young women on the ideal composition of their spiritual selves, Thomas Salter links the earthly to the eternal realm while also deftly distinguishing the two in terms of 'real' importance.

> In my imagemente there is nothing more meete, especially for yong Maidens, then a Mirrhor, therin to see and beholde how to order their dooyng, I meane not a Christall Mirrhor, made by handie Arte, by whiche Maidens now adaies, dooe onely take delight

daiely to tricke and trim their tresses, standying tootyng twoo howers by the Clocke, looking now on this side, now on that, least any thing should bee lacking needefull to further Pride, not suffering so muche as a hare to hang out of order, no I meane no suche Mirror, but the Mirrhor I meane is made of an other maner of matter, and is of muche more worthe then any Christall Mirrhor, for as the one teacheth how to attire the outwarde bodie, so the other guideth to garnishe the inwarde mynde, and maketh it meete for vertue.[46]

Richard Hyrde likewise says of 'good lernynge,' that it 'sheweth the ymage and wayes of good lyvynge evyn right as a myrrour sheweth the symylitude and proporcion of the body'.[47]

Another conduct writer, Barnabe Rich, urges women to turn their mirrors inward so as to 'grope the concience': 'Yet by this Glasse me thus composed, it is not to view any exterior part of the body, but first to grope the conscience, and then by a diligent observation to survey the interior part of the soule: And as I have not fashioned any smooth resemblance whereby to flatter, so I have not forged any deformities thereby to slander'.[48] Rich also reminds women to use their beauty not for temporal indulgence, but as a salutary reminder of the divine: 'This externall beautie of the body, so much esteemed of amongst women, when they behold it in a Glasse, it should stirre them up a farre off to display the [majesty] of the Creator, and from thence should passé with the wings of their cogitations to the contemplations of the highest *Faire*, which is the invisible beautie of the Almighty God, from whence as a *Fountaine*, all smaller *Rivers* derive their beauties' (p. 229). While Rich attributes a woman's earthly beauty to divine reflection, the dramatist John Ford has Giovanni use it to boldly celebrate a beauty that surpasses art, and even the hand that makes all nature: 'If you would see a beauty more exact / Than art can counterfeit or nature frame / Look in your glass, and there behold your own'.[49] And in the rambling ballad of the Countess Clarissa that languishes anonymously in the papers of the British Library, beauty is itself an instrument, and an object, of spiritual amplification: 'In books she sees the mirrour of her minde / In a mirrour she her beauties booke doth finde, / Her forehead title is not small and pent, / Like to some narrow matters argumente'.[50]

Such implications of inward and outward graces (and of eternal and physical dimensions) are not, however, always the happy provenance of the mirror, as Shakespeare suggests in Sonnet 77. Rather than the inward graces, Shakespeare's 'glas' reveals 'how thy beauties wear' in the inevitable progression toward death. And, on a less sanguine note again, Elizabeth Grymeston's *A Sinner's Glasse* posits the very fact of mortality as an invitation to corruption: man's 'eies and eares' are portrayed as 'open gates to send in loades of sinne into our minde'.[51]

In all of these contexts, mirrors serve a highly social and gestural function. In context with the ritual instructiveness of such images, it is useful to consider Sabine Melchior-Bonnet's booklength study, *The Mirror: A History*. Like Debora Shuger, Melchior-Bonnet argues for the mirror's symbolic representation of selfhood. Though the early modern mirror was 'a tool of precision and control in the teaching and enforcement of civility', it was 'not yet an instrument of individual rights even if it allowed the possibility of a solitary interaction with the self. The feeling of selfhood that the mirror awakened was a conflictual one of modesty or shame, consciousness of the body and of one's appearance under the watchful eye of another' (pp. 139–40). Importantly, however, Melchior-Bonnet argues that the mirror offers more than a means of understanding one's dimensions through the formal outlines of emblematic images. She stresses the mirror's capacity for fracture and internal distance. Although the medieval universe was 'closed, circular, and susceptible to being deciphered,' early modern thinkers no longer assumed 'a structured universe by which one could rise from an inferior sphere to a superior one'. The mirror, once used as a reflection of God's perfection in man's imperfect being, now 'impose[d] distance and separation within a formerly closed system' (p. 119).

And what exactly *was* this distance and separation? The terms convey the corporeal and eternal dimensions of selfhood, the perfection of eternal life which existed always as a promise within the smallest corporeal affairs. In terms of this topos the man who sees himself in God sees a reflection of God's power, and in rendering a physical, sensory reflection of God in his own image he enters 'a new experience of subjectivity'. It is in this way – the incarnation of the atemporal within the sensory – that painters like Jan Van Eyck are moved to use the mirror image, depicting themselves at the heart of a painting to convey a sense of distance, as well as intimate self-reflection. By portraying 'himself in the form of a miniscule silhouette in the divine eye-mirror, precisely at the vanishing-point of the painting,' Melchior-Bonnet claims that the painter signifies the importance of the infinite within the present moment. In other words, the invisible is made present within the visible. The mirror thus 'lends itself to self-examination and interior dialogue. The eye-mirror of the humanist presents a new way of looking at the world, but it continues to situate itself at the core of a system of correspondences and analogies akin to the medieval mirror'.[52] For example, in *Self-Portrait in a Convex Mirror*, Parmigianino represents himself in a convex mirror on a specially prepared convex panel. Distorted by the panel, the face has a hint of caricature, turned slightly to the side, the eyes hooded and world-weary, the cheeks full and somewhat pompous-looking in a young person. The hands, distorted also by the convex panel, are enormous, the tapered fingers draped quietly in front of the body. This distortion mirrors the salient features of the artist as he sees himself – his perception of himself as disenchanted with the world; as inward and contemplative, his face refusing to meet our gaze head-on; and as a man whose hands, the instruments of his art, find themselves oddly disproportionate not just to the room in which the painter is seated, but to the canvas itself. Parmigianino's canvas, with its distorting mirror, draws us into his privately skeptical realm even while it tempts us out toward the light depicted in the far left-hand corner (see Fig. 4.1).

In these terms, then, the mirror offers a fascinating convergence of the physical and the iconic, the emblematic and the instructive, in depicting early modern selfhood. But what is arresting about these images is that while they are instructive, they are very often not simply, nor singularly, so. Mirrors root the seeing self in the realm of premodern consciousness, while gesturing toward spaces and hidden depths within the self. As an artistic function, the mirror offers not just a flat, stable reflection of, for instance, mortality, or *vanitas*, but something else as well: in a conflation of refracted images, it invites (and facilitates, through its variety of emblematic associations) a sense of movement, shifting from a physical function to a compound of often contradictory speculations. Real as well as figurative, then, the mirror's *physical* function spins the act of reflection into a series of epistemological uncertainties, so that it serves in itself as a trope of transition, as a way of glimpsing the eternal within the temporal. Within the language of mirrors are embedded multiple reverberations, echoes, twists and contortions, physiological and cosmological speculations. This may explain why, despite the art of flat mirror-making that signals such advancement in perspective, many actual and verbal mirrors are still described as convex: conveying more than one individuated image, they reflect a range of speculations about the place of the 'I' in a world marked by enormous changes in cartography, the shape of the earth, and the shape of the universe itself.[53] And in 'reflecting' the radical instability of the 'I', the mirror posits the *specular* as the means of social speculation.

Fig. 4.1   Francesco Mazzola Parmigianino, *Self-Portrait in a Convex Mirror*, c.1523–1524. Kuntshistorisches Museum, Vienna

Speculations in Selfhood: Shakespeare and Others

Perfectly suited to such speculation were the poems that proliferated at the time, positing the mirror as an emblem of both the known and the intangible. Milton's *Paradise Lost* affords a resonant example. Coming upon a 'smooth lake', Eve stoops down to see a 'shape within the wat'ry gleam / Bending to look on me'. Starting in bewilderment, she finds that 'it started back',[54] suggesting less an image of self-love than a childlike enchantment with a new companion (as distinct from the kind of modern Lacanian child for whom the mirror marks a trajectory toward individuation).[55] And for Philip Sidney, reflections open out the concept of truth to a state of inference and uncertainty, distorting it in the very same moment that they purport to make it known: if a writer's feigning 'made David as in a glass see his own filthiness',[56] yet at times poetry is tellingly illuminated by the 'unflattering glass of reason'.[57] Sir William Davenant echoes this view in his preface to *Gondibert*, mistrusting the 'perfect glass of Nature' by which a heroic poem 'gives us a familiar and easie view of our selves'. It is 'sometimes with the Eye of Envie, which enlarges objects like a multiplying glass', that we behold heroic figures. We think them 'immense as *Whales*, the motion of whose vast bodies can in a peacefull calm trouble the Ocean till it boyl'. In Denham's *Coopers Hill* (1642), the poet writes:

> The streame is so transparent, pure, and cleare,
> That had the selfe-enamourd youth gaz'd here,
> So fatally deceiv'd he had not beene,
> While he the bottome, not his face had seene.

Unbeguiled by the water the poet describes, the youth can yet stumble on a natural stream and meet his demise. What almost *is* a mirror is also almost *not*, the two images interweaving in a nexus of mortality, hubris and spiritual immaturity. And Donne's 'The Good Morrow' invokes the mirror to radically question the very nature of what is real. If the act of reflection reveals the face of another, and this face reveals the heart, then these two reflected selves form a sphere that displays the unity of the cosmos:

> My face in thine eye, thine in mine appears,
> And true plain hearts do in the faces rest;
> Where can we find two better hemispheres,
> Without sharp North, without declining West?[58]

Donne's hemispheres – the reflective gazes exchanged between two lovers – represent the 'reality' that emerges from their union, while also alluding to the convex physical shape of the eye. If the eye is itself a convex mirror, then the question is left gaping from Donne's poem: does the eye distort a 'real' physical world, or is this physical world itself merely the *creation* of the eye, subject to the twists and tricks of perception? What the mirror shows is both familiar and unsettling, reassuringly symbolic as well as cosmologically unstable.

Shakespeare, in Sonnet 24, uses a mirror to explore the ambiguity that lies at the heart of adoration and displacement: the face of the adored becomes the site of a self at once familiar and unfathomable, at once functional and obscure. The presence of both subject and object is challenged by the reciprocal reflections that mark acts of social exchange. In a tightly woven but discordant movement from quatrain to quatrain, the sonnet plays on the process of reading a series of changing reflections:

> Mine eye hath play'd the painter and hath stell'd
> Thy beauty's form in table of my heart;
> My body is the frame wherein 'tis held,
> And perspective it is the painter's art.
> For through the painter must you see his skill,
> To find where your true image pictured lies;
> Which in my bosom's shop is hanging still,
> That hath his windows glazed with thine eyes.
> Now see what good turns eyes for eyes have done:
> Mine eyes have drawn thy shape, and thine for me
> Are windows to my breast, where-through the sun
> Delights to peep, to gaze therein on thee;
> Yet eyes this cunning want to grace their art;
> They draw but what they see, know not the heart.

In the first quatrain the poet describes himself as painting his subject's beauty. The poet is also the willing frame for this beauty, holding it in 'perspective' in his body. The word 'perspective' anticipates the second quatrain, in which he explains why his art can reflect the subject more truly than any other means: it is through his 'skill' that he captures the subject's image, hanging it safely within his own 'bosom'. In the second quatrain this act of mirroring also captures the attention of his subject, for s/he must look into the poet in order to appreciate the skilful reflection of her/himself. The third quatrain plays on the reciprocity of mirroring. With the subject happily focused on her/his own reflection, the poet is himself free to feast on his subject's eyes; and in so doing he sees his own reflected self, which has become the willing storehouse of his loved one's image. In the act of imaging this beauty, therefore, the poet most truly sees himself as a representational form, that is, as known *and* displaced by his own gaze. And in the final couplet the poet pauses with a 'yet,' as he realizes the implications of this representation. He knows himself by looking at another; but he cannot see into his subject's heart. It is impossible, therefore, to see himself truly through reflection.

For Shakespeare, then, language offers a (slippery and undependable) means of distilling and mirroring reality. Shakespeare returns again and again to the subject of language, what it seeks and what it continually displaces: the truth about motive, the truth about treachery, the truth about truth itself. Consider Edgar's anatomically framed response to the death of the servant Oswald in *King Lear*. Searching through the dead servant's pockets to discover a letter he has left for Edmund, Edgar excuses his own breach of courtesy by noting that the alternative is a savage breach of the law: 'Leave, gentle wax; and, manners, blame us not. / To know our enemies' minds, we'ld rip their hearts; / Their papers, is more lawful. (*Reads the letter*)' (IV, vi, 259–61). In a stunning physical conceit (and with uncharacteristic irony), Edgar opens the letter, exposing its words as a lawful, though bad-mannered, alternative to ripping open his enemies' bodies to reflect the corruption at their hearts.[59]

Perhaps nowhere is the ambiguity of the mirror more tellingly expressed than at the end of *King Lear*, when the old King tells his servant: 'Lend me a looking glass' (V, iii, 262.) This request draws on the famously iconic image in *Richard II*, in which the deposed king calls for a glass: 'Give me that glass, and therein will I read. / No deeper wrinkles yet? Hath sorrow struck / So many blows upon this face of mine, / And made no deeper wounds?'[60] Finding that the 'objective' reality of the mirror fails to manifest his broken self, Richard smashes the glass, using his own imagination to reflect the fragility of his fate: 'For there it is, crack'd in an hundred shivers. / Mark … How soon my sorrow hath destroy'd my face' (IV, i, 289–91). Richard is all too aware of the discrepancy between what the glass gives us and who we think we are, and of the impossibility of matching the one with the other except through the whims of imagination. But such is not the case with the later ex-king, the elderly and ailing one who indeed mirrors his predecessor in a tragically ironic trope of transition. In *King Lear's* final scene, Lear's eager request for the looking glass is intimately invested with his aspiration and despair; yet the pace of his last speeches is such that perhaps there is never time for the mirror to be brought to him.[61] Regardless of whether or not he gets to put the glass to Cordelia's lips, Lear knows that while he looks for life, he must yet howl out its absence to the men of stones (V, iii, 262–3). For the audience, the surface of Lear's mirror – whether actual or imagined – thus suggests a terrible irony: no matter how he may look to it to reflect the objective 'truth' of Cordelia's breathing, in the end the glass displaces his gaze, transforming it into the *subjective* force of his own wishing. This wishing is only as substantial, and as mutable, as his words: and words themselves are like the vacant depths of a glass, bodying forth shapes that are gone in an instant.

Outside the Frame? Mirrors in Tracts and Journals

Ideals of good conduct and unflattering admonishments of frail humanity – these are the hallmarks of the mirror, while in juxtaposing closure with internal distance and separation, the shape of the eternal is shadowed within the physical, suggesting intense speculation about the nature and manifestation of identity. But what of the texts outside liturgical and artistic tropes, the journals, essays and tracts that make up the bulk of early modern written artifacts? Do they offer alternative concepts for the form and function of reflection, or are those images they afford no less formal and emblematic?

'It is Death alone that can suddenly make man to know himself,' advises the adroit Elizabethan courtier, soldier, philosopher and explorer Sir Walter Raleigh in an archetypal gesture toward eternity. Death

> tells the proud and insolent that they are but abjects, and humbles them at the instant; makes them cry, complain, and repent, yea, even to hate their forepassed happiness. He takes the account of the rich, and proves him a beggar, a naked beggar, which hath interest in nothing but in the gravel that fills his mouth. He holds a glass before the eyes of the most beautiful, and makes them see therein their deformity and rottenness, and they acknowledge it.[62]

For Raleigh, Death is the grim reaper who comes to claim those debts accumulated in Man's time on earth. Tilted less to view the devastation wrought by secular pleasures and more toward the healing grace of God, the anonymously authored tract, 'The Sicke Man's Comfort' offers this advice:

> When we have laid all this [our sins] to the sicke man's charge, and in the Law as in a Mirrour wee have set before his eyes to behold his judgement and sentence of condemnation: when we perceive him wounded and pearced to the heart with sorowe, we must them laye to his wound some asswaging medicine, and do as Masons do when they hewe their stone; first they give grete blowes with their hammer, and make gret peaces fall off, and then they poolish it over with a plaine, that the strokes are no more seen: so must we do, after we have handled the sick patient roughly, and thrust him downe to hel by the rigorous threats of the lawes: we must comfort him, and fetche him againe by the sweete amiable promises of the Gospel, to the end that the sowplenes of this oyle may asswage the nipping sharpnes of the law. (p. 61)[63]

The mirror motif pleads an understanding of God's judgment and the law, positioning the mirror as a conventional Protestant means of self-improvement in the eyes of God. And in an echo of St Paul's 'through a glass darkly' image, we see that in the end it is God who recognizes the truth of which man himself can see merely the reflection; and it is only God who can unify the broken body in embracing the soul.

More complicated and arresting is the figure of Thomas Whythorne, who describes a 'self' represented by both mirrors and portraits. Visiting in London the artist who has painted several portraits of him, Whythorne notices many other portraits about the painter's house of sitters, young and old, and speculates that people 'cause their pictures … to be painted from time to time to see how time doth alter them'.

> But now, peradventure, you would say that they may see themselves when they will in a looking-glass. To the which I do say that the glass showeth but the disposition of the face for the time present, and not as it was in time past. Also it showeth the face the

contrary way, that is to say, that which seemeth to be the right side of the face is the left side in deed; and so likewise that which seemeth to be the left side is the right. And also the perfection of the face that is seen in a glass doth remain in the memory of the beholder little longer than he is of beholding the same. For so soon as he looketh off from the glass he forgetteth the disposition and grace of his face.[64]

Because the mirror offers no capacity for historical reflection, for Whythorne it leaves a trace of mutability. It is simply a temporal reflection of a face whose aspect is all too fleeting, progressively marked by life's vicissitudes. A portrait, on the other hand, offers the opportunity to imprint one's face permanently on the world, so that in looking at a canvas one can contemplate one's history. The mirror's limitations are compounded by its distortion of left and right, and by the fact that having looked in a mirror, one forgets immediately the shape of one's face. Is a glass reflection itself, then, really worth anything at all beyond the inaccuracy of ephemeral representations?

In Michel de Montaigne's view it is indeed worth having because it enables him to speculate on the immediacy of his physical self and its relationship to being and seeming. 'My looking glasse doth not amaze me,' he claims as he looks into his glass, noting a degeneration in 'my face and eyes' so severe that 'I often move my friends to pitty, ere I feele the cause of it'. '... [E]ven in my youth,' he continues,

it hath divers times befaln me, so to put-on a dusky looke, a wan colour, a troubled behaviour and of ill presage, without any great accident; so that the Physitions perceiving no inward cause to answer this outward alteration, ascribed the same to the secret minde or some concealed passion, which inwardly gnawed and consumed me. They were deceived: were my body directly by me, as is my minde, we should march a little more at our ease. ... I am of the opinion, that this her temperature hath often raised my body from his fallings: he is often suppressed, whereas she, if not lasciviously wanton, at least in quiet and reposed estate. I had a quartan ague which held me foure or five months, and had altogether disvisaged and altered my countenance, yet my mind held ever out, not onely peaceably but pleasantly.[65]

Montaigne's reflected face, he feels, bears little congruence with his mind. If his face could only be governed in the disciplined way that his mind is, it would not have a scurvy hue; but faces, he suggests, do not always match the rude health of souls. Hence while he acknowledges the flatness of reflection – the sense that an image *means* something, that one's complexion can signify a physical or emotional state – Montaigne is also intrigued by the possibility it offers for shifting asymmetries. The self that gazes back at him is sceptical, signifying a whole range of things and nothing entirely, and, indeed, questioning the consonance between mind and body that was later to be crystallized as Cartesian dualism.

While Montaigne accepts, and marvels at, the asymmetry between body and soul as signified by the glass, many mortals are unhappily beguiled by it, unaware of their own distortions. It takes the provision of wise counsel – a tutor, or a friend

– to conjoin subjective perception with reality. And in his letter to Mr. Newton, tutor to the prince, Bishop Joseph Hall makes this point:

> How happy a service shall you do to this whole world of ours, if you shall still settle in that princely mind a true apprehension of himself… break those false glasses that would present him a face not his own: to applaud plain truth, and bend his brows upon excessive praises! [66]

Sir Francis Bacon assigns to a friend this important duty of accurate reflection:

> … observing our faults in others is sometimes improper for our case; but the best receipt (best, I say, to work, and best to take) is the admonition of a friend. It is a strange thing to behold what gross errors and extreme absurdities many (especially of the greater sort) do commit, for want of a friend to tell them of them, to the great damage both of their fame and fortune: for, as St. James saith, they are as men, that look sometimes into a glass, and presently forget their own shape and favour. [67]

Bacon offers two kinds of glass. One, the physical image in the mirror, is closed and static, promoting a self-regarding gaze in which, quite ironically, one loses sight of oneself. This physical mirror prompts the author to speculate on a second kind of reflection, in which the glass of friendship counters vain self-engrossment. A friend observes and defines one's passage through the world, in the process warding off the absurdities of pride and willful blindness. In *The Booke of the Governor*, Sir Thomas Elyot also writes of selves that act as glasses, though his trope of reflection is more conventionally hierarchical (as is, indeed, Bacon's in his essay, 'Of Praise').[68] In Elyot's view the 'excellent' self should be elevated through 'the glasse of authority', enlightening those of 'inferior understanding'. This reflected self is not *simply* superior, however: the act of elevation enables it to 'se and also be seene'. Its 'excellent witte' measures the movement of those beneath it at the same time as it confirms its own superiority.

In both instances above, static physical images invoke their own limitations while promoting a kind of roving spiritual speculation. In other words, the 'thisness' of the physical mirror provokes the writer to speculate on what the material mirror cannot reveal – aspects of selfhood that can only emerge in one's passage through, and beyond, the mirror and thus the world. Even then, these images may be shadowy and half-realized, depending on friendship to impose form and definition. Robert Devereux, second earl of Essex, describes a similar speculation on the capacity of friendship to reflect, and define, aspects of the soul that may elude the physical mirror: 'He that thinkes he hath, or wisheth to have, an excellent face, noe sooner is tould of any spott or uncomelines in his countenaunce then he hyes to shew himself to a glasse, that the glasse may shew againe his true likenes unto him.' On one level we might entertain a compellingly familiar image of the earl, like someone today in a restaurant bathroom, anxiously checking his face in the glass to compare corporeal reality with report. But the word 'again' is arresting. It suggests that no matter what sores or spots may visit the complexion, the mirror will take the observer back to some other, 'truer' visage. This could be an act of repetition that restores a familiar unblemished state; or it could be an act of idealization that 'restores' an ideal, Platonically inflected beauty. There is a strong sense, then, of the mirror as something unfixed, of a multivalent image that encourages, and allows for, transition. In revealing the physical spot on the face, the mirror also offers a likeness that is implicitly retrospective or ideal, or both. Thus the earl goes on to say that the mirror can accurately reveal *both* the blemish and a state of perfection; and that, likewise, a true friend can recall one to a spiritual countenance unblemished by present sin, or (as here) to a political countenance unblemished by sedition:

> The same curiositye moves me, that desire to have a fayre minde, to shew the true face and state of my minde to my true freind, that he like a true glasse (without injury or flattery) may tell me whether nature or accident have sett soe fowle a blemish in it as my accusers pretend. I am charged that either in affection or opinion, or both, I preferre warr before peace, and soe consequently that all my actions, counsells and endeavours doe tend to keepe the state of England in contynuall warrs, espetially att this tyme when some peace may be had and I only impugne it.[69]

Ever the courtier alert to the slightest imperfections in his outward mien, the earl is accustomed to checking his physical appearance in the glass. But in its literary manifestation, the mirror holds this physical image in the very moment of transforming it into a series of speculations. The truth-telling capacities of the (literal and figurative) glass are counterpoised with the false images reflected back on the earl by those who assess his body as part of a wider social organism. In this relatively simple passage, Essex nonetheless presents a kaleidoscope of mirrors, countering each perspective with a series of others: the physical mirror in which the subject looks at himself; the truthful gaze of the friend who faithfully mirrors back to him his physical imperfections; the friend's simultaneous capacity to serve as a mirror for his moral self-correction; the reflection of this moral countenance in the speaker's outward mien; and the sullying (and implicitly inaccurate) reflection thrown back at the speaker by the eyes of the world. In enabling the very function of self-scrutiny, these multiple reflections also imply the subjection of any image thus garnered to the vagaries of perception, both private and public.

Essex's mirror motif makes a fascinating comparison with an anonymous description of his father, Walter Devereux, who had called for a mirror at his deathbed 22 years earlier. In this description the looking glass functions as a nexus for the first earl's literal and metaphoric gaze:

> This daye in the morninge about six of the clocke he called for his looking glasse and, looking in it, he asked of us, why do yow thinck that I looke in the glas? It is not for pride, but I hadd almost forgottest my favor and I looke in the glas that I might carie the remembraunce of my countenance with me that I shall apeare with before my Lord Jhesus Christ.[70]

The mirror indeed 'reflects' not the elderly earl's 'favour,' which he has 'almost forgot' anyway, but that same passage from the apostle James' epistle alluded to by Whythorne and Bacon and others: 'For if any be a hearer of the word, and not a doer, he is like a man beholding his natural face in a glass: For he beholdeth himself and goeth his way, and straightway forgetteth what manner of man he was' (James, 1. 23–24). And Devereux's reliance on the biblical premise itself evokes a mass of associations. Suggesting an image of the elderly earl prudently composing himself in his final hours to meet his Maker, its biblical echo implies that he is so at one with God's Word that he does not *know* himself apart from this Word.[71] It is likely that the representation of the earl has been carefully composed by posthumous report, marking out the lines of his spiritual passage toward his maker. Whatever the source of authorship, however, the mirror motif provides a complex, reverberative system of unstable reflections for the earl. Compounding the literal word of God with a vigilant sense of worldly *sprezzatura*, he perfectly mirrors the biblical figure who gives over his self to God and is content to see himself only through reflection; and in comporting himself under his final duress in a manner ideally suited to a man about to meet his maker, he maintains the grace of the ideal courtier.

Aside from the multiple levels of mirroring offered by its biblical connotations, the passage has a deeper relationship to self-fashioning in an existential sense. In the very act of peering into a glass, the dying man suggests a self that he does not know. Its favour is 'almost forgot'. Perhaps he has indeed moved beyond this physical self to a state of tranquility; or perhaps his self-image is so fractured and uncertain that he cannot 'know' it if it is not staring back at him. A further point of interest is provided by the way in which the mirror affords both father and son – Walter and Robert Devereux – a means of self-scrutiny that combines intimacy and display. In this shared trope they afford their own generational form of 'mirroring.' For both earls, mirrors provoke speculation, challenging the reality of the very physical images they define. They suggest the multiplicity of perspectives from which a self can be known, and the diversity of functions that it serves.

Further abstractions on reflection are offered by Descartes and Sir Thomas Browne. For Descartes, while the corporeal is *known* through its reflection in the mind's eye, the 'things' cannot be confused with their reflections: 'physical things, the images of which are formed in my thought and which the senses themselves explore, are much more distinctly known than the unknown me who is outside the scope of the imagination'.[72] While the body is anatomically divisible, moreover, the soul (for Descartes, synonymous with the mind) is not:

> we can understand the body only as divisible whereas, in contrast, we can understand the mind only as indivisible. Nor can we conceive of half a mind, as we can of even the smallest body. Thus their natures are recognized as being not only distinct but even in some sense opposites.[73]

Browne, in his 1642 meditation *Religio Medici*, also uses the mirror motif to identify the relationship between body and soul, contending that earthly knowledge is transmitted to the angels through mirroring: 'If they have that intuitive knowledge, whereby, as in reflection, they behold the thoughts of one another, I cannot peremptorily deny but they know a great part of ours'. Browne goes on to use a triple negative to argue for the 'inorganic' nature of the soul – 'Nor truely, can I peremptorily deny, that the soule ... [is] inorganicall' – suggesting as evidence the fact that the products of bestial acts are not merely beasts, but have also 'an impression and tincture of reason in as high a measure'. 'Sense', the property of animals and humans, is organic; but the 'soul', belonging to humans alone, is not an organ. The body speaks to both the corporeal sameness and the ineffable *difference* between man and beast: 'for in the braine, which wee tearme the seate of reason, there is not anything of moment more than I can discover in the cranie of a beast ... Thus we are men, and we know not how'.[74] And if 'we know not how' we are men, then perhaps, as he contends above, we come closest to an understanding of our humanness through the *reflection* that is 'intuitive'.

The images of the mirror in the writings cited above offer little that departs from the mirrors used in fictional and visual art described earlier. The first person discussions of Montaigne, Bacon, Elyot and Browne, for example, do not offer a more private (and thus more straightforwardly Burkhardtian) engagement with the glass, an engagement that might mark a difference from the function of the artistic mirror; rather, mirrors in these discursive passages are similarly emblematic and instructive, similarly gestural and potentially multifaceted. Whether it be to suggest mutability or moral instruction, to magnify faults or display ideals of virtue – or, perhaps, to play on various of these functions – the mirror appears to be as carefully and pragmatically modeled in tracts, meditations and occasional papers as it is in sonnets, plays and paintings.

So what, then, might we conclude about the early modern literary mirror? Its most important function, we believe, was to draw on, and to delineate, the relationship between the corporeal and the eternal: a relationship that was, after all, the crucial one for early modern minds. The shadow of the eternal was shaped always within earthly affairs, and few emblems suggest this more aptly than the mirror. At all times and everywhere God's image was to be found: not always at the forefront of a temporal activity, God was nonetheless a part of it, like a ghostly reflection in a piece of glass or metal. And if the mirror perfectly encapsulated the *presence* of the eternal in the temporal, it also signaled the distance between earth and heaven, man's mind and that of his Maker. This affords another reason to dwell finally on the words 'through a glass darkly:' they designate the shadow of man's *inadequate* comprehension, as well as the sheer effort and focus of this comprehension itself. In early modern writings the image of the mirror helps us to reflect on, and beyond, the reified abstractions of rhetoric, allowing us to rethink and explore the terms and conditions of what is termed 'autobiographical' discourse across the many different modes of life-writing.

Notes

1   Leonardo da Vinci, <http://codesign.scu.edu/arth12/text_davinci.html>.
2   In an altogether different kind of instruction, Leonardo da Vinci, offering advice to a painters, instructs them to 'keep [their] mind[s] as clear as the surface of a mirror, which assumes colours as various as those of the different objects'. 'On the artist's temperament and good working habits' in Alessandro Vezzosi, *Leonardo da Vinci: The Mind of the Renaissance* (New York: Discoveries, 1997), p. 136
3   See Herbert Grabes. *The Mutable Glass: Mirror Imaging in Titles and Texts of the Middle Ages and the English Renaissance* (Cambridge: Cambridge University Press 1982), and Jenijoy La Belle, *Herself Beheld: The Literature of the Looking Glass*, (Ithaca: Cornell University Press, 1988).
4   Anon. *A Pleasant Comedie, called Wily Begvilde: Spectrum* (London: Clement Knight, 1606). Internet reference: <http://www.shef.ac.uk/~tdrg/Texts/60tq79wb.htm>.
5   The point is not that the mirror did not offer a form of introspection, as argued, for example, by Alan Macfarlane and Gerry Martin in *Glass, A World History* (Chicago: University of Chicago Press, 2002), but rather that it did not facilitate this as a part of everyday self-scrutiny.
6   Richard Rogers, *Two Puritan Diaries, By Richard Rogers and Samuel Ward*, ed. with an introduction by M.M. Knappen (1933), (Gloucester, Mass.: P. Smith, 1966), p. 96.
7   Consider, for example, one of the most famous sermons of the seventeenth century, Thomas Adams's *The White Devill*, which was published in 1613 and reached five editions by 1621. In the preface to the 1615 edition, Adams cites the claim that the sermon is too theatrical: 'It is excepted that I am too merry in describing some vice. Indeed, such is their ridiculous nature, that their best conviction is derision; ... Others say, I am otherwhere too satirically bitter. It is partly confessed.' *The White Devill: Or, the Hypocrite Uncased* (London: Printed by N. Bradwood for Ralph Mab, 1613).
8   Consider, for example, William Prynne's *Histriomastix*, 1632 (see *Shakespeare's Theatre: a Sourcebook*, ed. Tanya Pollard [Oxford: Blackwell, 2004]), a 1006-page diatribe against the theatre, masques and entertainment generally. His labeling of women as 'notorious whores' was said to be an attack on Queen Henrietta Maria, who was at the time appearing in a play at court. He was forced to appear before the Star Chamber, and eventually had both ears removed and was branded 'SL' (Seditious Libeller') on both cheeks.
9   *Sonnets from Caelica*, 87, pub. 1633. Richard S. Sylvester, ed., *The Anchor Anthology of Sixteenth-Century Verse* (Garden City: Anchor Press/Doubleday, 1974).
10 The *Homily* was a part of Protestant liturgical services. In 1542 the Church authorized Thomas Cranmer's suggestion that a book of homilies should be compiled. The twelve of the first book, including the Homily on the Misery of Mankind, were edited by Cranmer and published in 1547.
11 *Everyman Out of His Humour. The Complete Plays of Ben Jonson*, ed. G.A. Wilkes, vol. I (Oxford: Clarendon Press, 1981), pp. 275–411, 'After the Second Sounding', lines 120–22.
12 Looke in this Mirrour of a worthy Mind,
    Where some of your faire Virtues will appeare;
    Though all it is impossible to find,
    Unlesse my Glasse were chrystall, or more cleare:

Which is dym steele, yet full of spotlesse truth,
And for one looke from your faire eyes it su'th. (Lanyer, *Salve Deus Rex Judaeorum*.)
Brown University Women Writers Project, first electronic edition, 2001.
<http://www.wwp.brown.edu/encoding/research/NASSR/WWP.html>.   Source   copy
owned by Huntington Library, shelfmark 62139. STC 15227.5.

13 In the King James translation of the Bible, this famous mirror image in 1 Corinthians
    13. 12 neatly offsets the highly polished brass mirrors of Greek times (the esoptron,
    made of fine polished metal) with the image of perfect self-perspective offered by
    God's mirror: 'Now I know in part; but then shall I know even as also I am known'.

14 Sabine Melchior-Bonnet, *The Mirror: A History*, trans. Katharine H. Jewett (New York:
    Routledge, 2001), pp. 112–13. Melchior-Bonnet gives an extensive account of the
    history of mirror making, as well as the iconographic functions of the mirror throughout
    the centuries.

15 See Grabes, pp. 70–74.

16 Grabes, p. 71.

17 For a detailed description of the making of mirrors in Venice, see S.N. Popova, 'Istoria
    Zerkal' (History of Mirrors), *Voprosy Istorii* (USSR), (1982) 5: 184–8. Please note: this
    article is not available in English translation.

18 See Popova above, pp. 186–7; Herbert Grabes, pp. 70–93; and Melchior-Bonnet, p. 30.

19 Melchior-Bonnet, p. 30. Note that Popova, in her paper, puts the pricing very
    differently: the mirror at 68000 lira, the Raphael painting at 3000 lira (roughly one
    twenty-second of the price).

20 Melchior-Bonnet, p. 29.

21 John Aubrey, *Brief Lives and Other Selected Writings*, ed. Anthony Powell (New York,
    Charles Scribner's Sons, 1949), p. 195.

22 *Darlington Wills and Inventories 1600–1625*, ed. J.A. Atkinson et al. (Newcastle-Upon-
    Tyne: Athenaeum Press, 1993).

23 Mary Throckmorton, 1620, *Darlington Wills*, p. 172.

24 Mary Lascelles, 1616, *Darlington Wills*, p. 152.

25 Dennis 1611, *Darlington Wills*, p. 112.

26 Compare Mary Lassells, 1616, *Darlington Wills*, p. 154, with Mary Throckmorton,
    1620, *Darlington Wills*, p. 172.

27 Thomas Robinson, 1612, *Darlington Wills*, p. 121.

28 Compare Cuthbert Corneforth (41), 1616, *Darlington Wills*, p. 148, with Mary
    Throckmorton (48), p. 172.

29 John Corker, *Darlington Wills*, p. 164.

30 It is interesting that English inventories right into the late seventeenth century list
    looking glasses as a commonly inventoried possession specific to the gentry and the
    lower echelons of the upper classes. For more on this subject, see Lorna Weatherill, 'A
    possession of one's own: Women and consumer behaviour in England, 1160–1740',
    Journal of British Studies 1986 25(2): 131–56.

31 Cathy Santore, 'The Tools of Venus', *Renaissance Studies* (Oxford), 1997, 11 (3): 179–
    93.

32 For example, Pennell says of the early modern bedchamber that it was 'at once a
    "venue" for intimacy and for social gathering (at times of lying-in, death, and illness),
    and the objects amassed to decorate it spoke not only to their owners, but to those privy

to such bedside social encounters'. 'Consumption and Consumerism in Early Modern England', *The Historical Journal* 42, 2 (1999): 555. See also Melchior-Bonnet, p. 28.

33 Richard Braithwaite, 'The English Gentlewoman', in the facsimile collection *Conduct Literature for Women*, 6 vols, ed. William St. Clair and Irmgard Maasen (London: Pickering and Chatto, 2000), vol. 6, 15.

34 See Grabes, p. 71 and Melchior-Bonnet, p. 23.

35 First published in Italy in 1528, the popularity of *Il Cortegiano* (*The Courtier*) meant that it was translated into 20 different European languages in the sixteenth century alone.

36 Baldassare Castiglione, *The Book of the Courtier*, trans. Thomas Hoby. (Harmondsworth: Penguin, 1967), p. 68.

37 'The Woman's Sharp Revenge: Or an answer to Sir Seldome Sober that writ those railing pamphelets called the Juniper and Crabtree Lectures, & c. Being a sound Reply and full confutation of those Bookes: with an Apology in this case for the defence of us women.' Performed by Mary Tattle-well, and Joane Hit-him-home, Spinsters. 1640. Bodleian Library, STC 23706. p. 67

38 Mirrors were often stained and opaque because they were silvered with lead, or because of the addition of manganese oxide which gave a dirty yellow color. Manganese oxide also produced air bubbles. Melchior-Bonnet, pp. 13–17.

39 All references here to Shakespeare's works are from *The Riverside Shakespeare*, general ed. G. Blakemore Evans (Boston: Houghton Mifflin, 1974).

40 Stephen Greenblatt, *Renaissance Self-Fashioning: From More to Shakespeare* (Chicago, University of Chicago Press, 1981).

41 See Introduction.

42 Shuger, 'The "I" of the Beholder: Renaissance Mirrors and the Reflexive Mind', *Renaissance Culture and the Everyday*, ed. Patricia Fumerton and Simon Hunt (Philadelphia: Pennsylvania University Press, 1999), p. 21.

43 Alice Sutcliffe (Woodhouse), *Meditations of Man's Mortality* (1634), Brown University Women Writers Project first electronic edition, 2002. <http://www.wwp.brown.edu/encoding/research/NASSR/WWP.html>. Source copy owned by British Library, shelfmark: 4412.aa.54.

44 Constantia Munda, *The Worming of a Mad Dog* (1617), Brown University Women Writers Project first electronic edition, 2002. Source copy owned by Folger Shakespeare Library, STC 18257.

45 Ester Sowerman, *Esther Hath Hang'd Haman* (1617), Brown University Women Writers Project first electronic edition, 2002. Source copy owned by Henry E. Huntington Library. Shelfmark: 69499.

46 Thomas Salter. 'A mirrhor mete for all mothers, matrons, and maidens, intituled the mirrhor of modestie'. [1579], *Conduct Literature for Women, 1500–1640*, ed. William St Clair and Irmgard Maasen, 6 vols (London: Pickering and Chatto, 2000), vol. 5, pp. 13–14.

47 See his dedicatory letter prefacing *A Devout Treatise Upon the Pater Noster* translated by Margaret Roper from Desiderius Erasmus. Hyrde's dedicatory letter is written to Frances, daughter of Margaret Roper (the oldest daughter of Sir Thomas More, who translated Erasmus's exposition of the Lord's Prayer). Hyrde's letter is entitled 'Richard Hyrde unto the moost studious and virtuous yonge mayde Fraunces. S. sendeth gretynge

and well to fare'. Cited Brown University Women Writers Project. Available on-line at http://www.wwp.brown.edu.

48 'The Excellenciy of Good Women' and 'My Ladies Looking Glasse', *Conduct Literature for Women*, vol. 4, p. 216.

49 John Ford, *'Tis Pity She's a Whore*, ed. Derek Roper (London: Methuen, 1975), Act I, scene 2, 205–7.

50 'Upon the Countesse of Carlisle sitting by a Glasse, and reading in a book'. British Library Harl: 6918 f16.

51 Elizabeth Grymeston, *A Sinner's Glasse* (London, 1604).

52 Melchior-Bonnet, pp. 126–7. She suggests, furthermore, that the mirror 'hardly reveals any kind of iconic reality, distorting the "real" with which it identifies itself. It no longer hides a secret – the secret is henceforth in the mind that perceives and recognizes the resemblance' (p. 131).

53 It is useful to look at John Gillies's *Shakespeare and the Geography of Difference*, (Cambridge: Cambridge University Press, 1994), which describes early modern cartographic discourse as informed by an ancient classic geographical tradition as well as contemporary colonial enterprises.

54 *Paradise Lost*, Eve's reply, Book IV, 457–69 (New York, Signet, 1982).

55 Lacan writes of the young child who first sees himself reflected: 'This jubilant assumption of his specular image by the child at the infans stage, still sunk in his motor incapacity and nursing dependence, would seem to exhibit in an exemplary situation the symbolic matrix in which the I is precipitated in a primordial form, before it is objectified in the dialectic of identification with the other, and before language restores to it, in the universal, its function as subject'. Jacques Lacan, 'The Mirror Stage as Formative of the Function of the I as Revealed in Psychoanalytic Theory' (1949), in *Ecrits – A Selection* (London: Tavistock Publications, 1977).

56 Sir Philip Sidney, *The Defence of Poesy*, ed. Katherine Duncan-Jones (Oxford: Clarendon Press, 1989), p. 228.

57 *The Defence of Poesy*, pp. 212–50.

58 *John Donne: Poems*, ed. John Carey (Oxford: Clarendon Press, 1990), pp. 89–90.

59 In contexts of punishment for treason ripping open of a body was indeed lawful. Accounts like Holinshed's suggest that treason had its own special punishment much more severe than that for murder. Traitors were drawn to the gallows on hurdles (they were not permitted to walk). They were hanged and then cut down alive, their entrails and genitals burnt before their faces, heads cut off, and their bodies quartered. By cutting up the body in this way the authorities supposedly exposed to the traitor his false heart (women were not subjected to quartering, although their breasts could be amputated.) See Albert Hartshorne, *Hanging in Chains* (New York: Cassell, 1891), pp. 46–8); George Ryley Scott, in *The History of Torture throughout the Ages* (London, T Werner Laurie, 1940) p. 92); and, for accounts of the executions of the regicides in 1660, see Laura L. Knoppers, *Historicizing Milton: Spectacle, Power and Poetry in Restoration England* (Athens and London: University of Georgia Press, 1994).

60 *Richard II*, IV, i, 276–9.

61 By this is meant that while Lear asks for a glass, there is no evidence that there is time for it to be actually brought to him. If a glass is brought on-stage, he may hold it up in the hope that his daughter's breath will 'mist' it. But the 'feather' to which he refers can only be made to stir through the anxious breath of the father who leans over his

daughter, willing her to offer signs of life. This stirring offers its own reflexive image of the will of the father displacing itself into the life he wills into his daughter's dead body.

62 1614. Quoted from *The Norton Anthology of English Literature*, ed. M.H. Abrams (general editor), and Stephen Greenblatt (associate general editor) (New York and London: Norton, 2000), vol.1, p. 888.

63 Elizabeth of Bridgewater writes similarly in her eulogy for her infant daughter: 'though her soul is singing Alelujahs, yet is her sweet body here, seized on by worms, and turned to dust till the great day shall come when all appeare united both body and soule, before the judgement of God'. British Library 236, sig. 121r.

64 From *The Autobiography of Thomas Whythorne*, Modern Spelling Edition, ed. James M. Osborn (London, Oxford University Press, 1962), p. 115.

65 Michel de Montaigne, *Essays of Montaigne*, ed. W.E. Henley, trans. John Florio. 3 vols (New York: Dent, 1967), 'Of Experience', vol. 3, pp. 369–70.

66 *The Works of the Right Reverend Joseph Hall*, ed. Philip Wynter, 10 vols (Oxford: Oxford University Press, 1863), Epistle IV: 'Of gratulation for the hopes of our prince, with an advising appreciation', vol. 1, pp. 137–8.

67 *Bacon's Essays* (fifth edition), ed. Richard Whately (London: John W. Parker and Son, 1860), p. 304.

68 Bacon, *Essays*, pp. 552–3.

69 Robert Devereux, second earl of Essex, *Apologie:* preface from Public Record Office, State Papers 12/269/71, fols. 101r–125v. Scribal copy, with marginned heading: 'An apologie of the earle of Essex against those who falsely & maliciously taxe him to be thonely hinderer of the peace & quyet of this kingdome, written to Mr Anthony Bacon' (1598).

70 An account of the death of Walter Devereux, 1st Earl of Essex, in Dublin, Sept. 1576. British Library, Harleian Ms 293, fols. 115r–20r.

71 This is a conventional spiritual trope, as suggested, for example, by Mary Rich: 'thoughts of eternity were so much on my mind, indeed it was no wonder to me that I appeared so much altered … for I was so much changed to myself that I hardly knew myself, and could say with that converted person, I am not I'. Mary Palgrave, *Saintly Lives: Mary Rich, Countess of Warwick* (London: Dent, 1901), p. 163.

72 René Descartes, *Meditations and Other Metaphysical Writings*, Second Meditation: 'The Nature of the Human Mind; and that it is better known than the Body', trans. Desmond M. Clarke (New York: Penguin, 1998), p. 27.

73 Descartes, *Meditations*, p. 14.

74 *Sir Thomas Browne: The Major Works*, ed. C.A. Patrides (Harmondsworth: Penguin, 1977), *Religio Medici*, Sect. 33, p. 102; Sect. 36, p. 106; Sect. 36, p. 107.

PART 3
The Self at War:
Military Diaries and Journals

Chapter 5

The Expedition to Cadiz, 1625

The Duke of Buckingham's ambitious but disastrous expedition to Cadiz in 1625 is recorded in three very different 'autobiographical' journals by three individuals who each had a deep personal interest in the expedition and in how to represent themselves in relation to it. The first is *The Voyage to Cadiz in 1625. Being a Journal Written by John Glanville, Secretary to the Lord Admiral of the Fleet (Sir E. Cecil), Afterwards Sir John Glanville, Speaker of the Parliament, &c., &c.*, first printed by the Camden Society in 1883.[1] This is the record of the expedition by its official Secretary, apparently offering a purely factual journal of the voyage and minutes of the councils of war 'holden abord the Anne Royall'. The second is a self-justifying account by the beleaguered Lord Admiral of the Fleet himself, *A Journall, and Relation of the action, which by his Majesties commandement Edward Lord Cecyl, Baron of Putney, and Vicount of Wimbledon, Admirall, and Lieutenant Generall of his Majestys forces, did undertake upon the coast of Spaine, 1625.*[2] And the third, in a quite different populist idiom, is a rare printed book of 1626 narratively entitled *Three to One: Being, An English-Spanish Combat, performed by a* Westerne *Gentleman, of* Tavystoke *in* Devon shire, *with an English Quarter-Staffe, against Three* Spanish *Rapiers and Poniards, at* Sherries *in* Spaine, *The fifteeene day of November, 1625. In the Presence of Dukes, Condes, Marquesses, and other Great Dons of* Spaine, *being the Counsell of Warre. The Author of this Booke, and Actor in this Encounter,* Richard Peeeke.[3] The documents and manuscripts in the Calendar of State Papers Domestic contain several other records of the Cadiz expedition, including letters from various commanders on the voyage, mostly of complaint at its mismanagement. But the three texts chosen here – one a transcript of an original document, the others short printed quarto books – vividly illustrate the authorial stresses of recording personal experiences in a dangerously shifting public arena in which the writers are always accountable. Their written records they know will be the subject of intense scrutiny. These texts thus occupy a position at the furthest remove from those diaries or journals for which no obvious or apparent reader seems to exist. They reside firmly in the public and political world that generates and shapes them. In each of them too, in different ways and with different effects, the writers reveal – or conceal – themselves and their motives in discourses that, while conforming to the rhetorical and generic expectations of their readers, exhibit an urgent need both to organize 'facts' to their own advantage and to invent for themselves a voice to meet the personal, political and social requirements of the moment.

'It concerneth much your honour'

King James I notoriously showed little interest in martial matters of any kind, preferring hunting and the role of Rex Pacificus, European peacemaker, which he actively adopted after 1603. In recent years commentators have treated his bookish pacifism with some sympathy, but at the time there were insinuations of physical cowardice, and growing restlessness concerning the perception of impotence attached to England's military decline. According to Sir William Trumbull, English ambassador in Brussels, a view widely held in the Spanish Netherlands was that under James the English were 'effeminate, unable to endure the fatigations and travails of war; delicate, well-fed, given to tobacco, wine, strong drink, feather-beds; undisciplined, unarmed, unfurnished of money and munitions'.[4] There were great hopes for the Cadiz expedition, driven by the Duke of Buckingham following the pacific James's death in early 1625, and supported by the new king Charles. Parliament and crown expected to make fat profits but also expressed a desire to restore England's maritime power and reputation. In the event the expedition achieved neither. Followed shortly by Buckingham's even more disastrous Ile de Rhé expedition, it confirmed amply enough the views and prejudices of critics, and the three journals to be considered each participate, in their variously peevish, bewildered, or chest-beating wrong-footedness, in the sense of failure generated by the voyage and its associated gestures of shame and defiance.

Briefly, the expedition to the Spanish coast, masterminded by Buckingham to harass Spain and to loot the Spanish Plate Fleet returning from America and the West Indies, was put in the charge of his friend Sir Edward Cecil as lord marshal and general of the sea and land forces – though Buckingham himself had supreme command. A substantial 'fleet of ships may be employed, accompanied with ten thousand land soldiers', Buckingham wrote to Cecil in early May, 1625, and told him to choose officers who were 'covetous to measure gold by their hats, and other spoils by ships' lading'.[5] Despite ruthless conscription and vast borrowing and expenditure, the preparations for the ships and army assembled at Plymouth were plagued with corruption, delays and discontents – long years of peace had left the Navy Commissioners and the victualling and ordnance offices quite unprepared for the organization of such a massive operation.[6] Buckingham, persuaded to withdraw from personal command, handed the expedition over to Cecil and travelled to Plymouth to hasten him on his way. The king too reviewed the troops and Fleet, was easily impressed, and raised Cecil to the peerage as Viscount Wimbledon. The Fleet finally consisted of 14 King's ships, 30 merchant ships and over forty Newcastle colliers, conveying 10,000 soldiers and 5,000 seamen. Cecil was assisted in command by a council of war, from which he was required to take advice. The council included Robert, earl of Essex as Vice-Admiral (and who later led the parliamentary forces in the first years of the Civil War) and the captains and colonels of the expeditionary force, among them several of Buckingham's kinsmen. Cecil's orders were to destroy the king of Spain's shipping and, if possible, take possession of some port on the Spanish coast – San Lucar was suggested, but the choice was left to him and the council of war. He was also ordered to look out for the Plate Fleet, in the hope that by its capture he could both cripple the Spanish war effort and recoup the very considerable costs of the expedition.

With some misgivings, Cecil took the Fleet out of harbour on 5 October, only to return again the next day: he thought – prophetically as it appears in the narrative – the time of year too late, the Fleet vulnerable to dispersal by storms, and the soldiers, 'being raw men and by nature more sickly, even in summer, than any nation in the world', vulnerable to illness.[7] Sir John Coke, Buckingham's naval adviser, already driven to distraction by the many problems of the Fleet that were referred to him, wrote immediately to Cecil warning him that 'it concerneth much your honour to suspect those that give advice to lose time or which pretend the safety of the ships to frustrate the voyage', that 'the wars require hazard', and urging him to admit no further delay. Cecil replied that he would make all haste[8], and 'the 8. of Octob. Being Saterday wee set sayle about 3 of the clocke in the afternoone with a wind at north north east'.[9]

Buckingham's scheme was not without its critics, and opposition from some quarters was vigorous.[10] But it was agreed by many that something had to be done to improve the Navy's ability to counter frequent coastal piracy and to secure the defence of England. At the Oxford session of Parliament in 1625, John Glanville, MP for Plymouth and one of the burgesses of the city, may have satirically declared that 'the King's ships do nothing, going up and down feasting in every good port'[11], yet he was unlikely to be a supporter of such an extravagant Spanish adventure as Buckingham's. Indeed, Glanville was an energetic opponent of the crown in Parliament, and in return for his outspoken criticisms of 'the expense of the kingdom' (that is, the debts of both James and Charles) he was appointed Secretary to the Fleet – presumably as a punishment, to keep him out of Parliament for the duration, and to give him a firsthand opportunity to see how royal and national debt may be heroically redressed. Glanville's reluctant journal, *The Voyage to Cadiz*, sticks strictly to the facts, complex and murky though they were: having recorded himself as Secretary, he uses the first person ('I' did this and that, etc.) but only to authenticate his office and his presence at the deliberations of the voyage. Except in the journal's final sentence ('But I was prevented by a long and dangerous sicknes, which alsoe is the cause that I can give noe further accompt of this voyage' [p. 122]) there are no 'personal' accounts, asides, insertions or opinions of any kind; his preferred locutions are 'it was agreed' or 'it was thought by some', etc. Part of Buckingham's 'Instructions' to Cecil was that he should keep a 'daily Journal', by his Secretary, of all occurrences of the voyage and keep him regularly informed. Thus, Glanville's account is the discharge of a duty, and consists chiefly of a log of the voyage and minutes of the councils of war, consultations, and other meetings held aboard Cecil's flagship the *Anne Royall*. Two energetically self-representational features, however, frame the journal's textual detachment and taciturnity.

The first is that prior to the expedition's departure Glanville had drawn up a document seeking to be released from his appointment as Secretary: 'Mr. Glanvills reasons against his beinge imployed for a Secretary at Warre'.[12] Though in the third person, it is here rather than in the journal that Glanville truly speaks for himself. His first reason to be excused is that 'Hee is a mere Lawyer, unqualified for h'imployment of a Secretary: his handwriting is so bad that hardly any but his owne Clarke canne reade itt, who should not be acquainted with all things that may occurr in such a service'. He pleads that he has rent to pay on his house in Chancery Lane and the expenses of his legal practice; he has many clients whose cases he cannot abandon or redistribute at short notice; he has public, legal and business responsibilities he cannot desert without 'much prejudice ... to very manie'; and his carefully built up practice over twenty two years will disintegrate and his clients go elsewhere so that 'he shal never be able to recontinue them againe'. Further, he has a wife and six children dependent on him, 'dispersed into 4 gen'rall counties, with severall frendes in Hertfordshire, Bedfordshire, Gloucestershire and Devonshire, during his sicknes, and hee cannot in his straight and upon so short warninge, setle his affaires for such a journie'. His mother, 'an aged lady, who relies much upon his Counsell and resort, will become herby much weakened and disconsolate'. This may at times read like an over-ingenious schoolboy plea to be excused games, but along with the rabble conscripted to man the Fleet and the soldiery, Granville seeks to project himself as an equally raw and press-ganged levy. He protests that his 'cominge to Plymouth att this tyme was only to attend y[e] service of his Recordershippe there, to assist the Maior and his brethren to entertaine his Maiestie', implying that he was, like many others, compulsorily impressed into this venture and unfairly entrapped. Despite their 'villainously bad' handwriting, Granville's pleas were disregarded. Aboard the *Anne Royall* he does his reluctant and minimal duty, until the general sickness that overwhelmed the returning stragglers from the expedition forces him to abandon his scribal post.

The second framing feature of Glanville's journal follows the ignominious failure of the Cadiz expedition. No Spanish ships at Cadiz were taken or burned, no Spanish port was either secured or sacked, and no treasure ships were captured. Unable even to stay on the coast to keep up a blockade, Cecil's fleet, its ships battered and leaking and its crews incapacitated by sickness and death, limped back into whatever Irish or English harbours could be found. And Glanville, careful and apparently detached note-taker of all that was said and done on the voyage, himself took an active part, with the earl of Essex and others, in bringing charges of gross misconduct against Cecil, and in May 1626 vigorously urged the impeachment of Buckingham.[13]

The *Journall* of Sir Edward Cecil, Lord Admiral of the Fleet, is an altogether more complexly stressed and fractured document in whose very title – 'which [action] by his Majesties commandement Edward Lord Cecyl ... did undertake' – lies already a familiar seed of time-serving self-justification. Like Glanville's account, it too is framed by a prior commission and an aftermath: in the letter of

May, 1625, Buckingham reminded Cecil that 'I have put into your hands the first infinite trust and pawn of my goodwill that ever I had in my power to bestow', and Cecil replied in fulsome terms that he would not let him down.[14] With the clear evidence of both the expedition's and Cecil's costly failure, public indignation fell chiefly on Buckingham, though Cecil too was liable to severe censure. Despite charges being laid, no evidence was taken, and the favour of Buckingham and Cecil's denials of personal incompetence assured an acquittal. It is in the *Journall* that Cecil, drawing heavily but selectively upon the account by the expedition's Secretary, recounts the difficulties of the enterprise as he saw them, and represents himself as doing the best that was possible in chaotic circumstances. He knew very well what was at stake: the expedition, unsuccessful though it was, had committed the king to an act of war against Spain, and Buckingham's future and Cecil's own reputation were at hazard. Everyone was disheartened by the missed opportunities and failures at Cadiz: Sir William St Leger, member of the council of war, wrote to the Lord Admiral conceding that 'our men are no men, but beasts',

> but the truth is, more might have been done. But the action is too great for our abilities, of which I am so much ashamed that I wish I may never live to see my sovereign nor Your Excellency's face again … God send you hereafter a better account of your future employments than you are like to have of this.[15]

The dead weight of Buckingham's 'infinite trust', the rebuke of Coke warning that the whole expedition 'concerneth much your honour', and the tart advice that 'wars require hazard' (that is, risk-taking and daring, not caution and mere prudence), visibly trouble Cecil as he tries to assemble a reasonable account of himself and his actions. His narration is designed to show that whatever could have been done was done, and he dwells constantly on the problems of command, the frictions between sailors and soldiers, the harassments of negligent or insubordinate officers. Defective ships, disobedient commanders, wretched rations, and inadequate intelligence, besides the predations of sickness and the ravages of wind and storm, entirely explain, in Cecil's account, the voyage's failure to secure its objectives. But although Cecil works hard for detachment and clarity, his writing is traversed by fault-lines of self-excuse and self-justification. Anger, frustration, indictments of the stupidity or the self-seeking of others, and moments of sheer incomprehension and bewilderment – ('I know not how it happened') (p. 19) – break through the narration to make his *Journall* as inadvertently self-revealing as a dramatic monologue by Browning.

Cecil reports that two days out at sea he called a council 'for the settling of instructions for a Sea-fight', giving himself opportunity to cite verbatim at the outset of the *Journall* the relevant articles of his orders, whose lack of clarity about the overall command of the Admiral and the lawfulness of individual initiative was to cause much confusion (p. 1). Cecil then describes how, barely four days into the voyage, a storm destroyed all the Fleet's longboats, two ketches were lost, the Fleet dispersed, 'many ships were in danger almost to despaire', and '138 Landmen, 37 Sea-men' were 'lost in the wracke'. The *Anne Royall*'s mainmast almost rolled overboard and she was threatened by both literal and figurative loose cannons: 'two of her greatest peeces of 5000 weight a peece broke loose in the Gunners roome', Cecil complaining that 'the danger was partly by the negligence of the Officers, that did not see carefully to the fitting of these things while we lay in Harbour' (p. 2). This theme of others' negligence runs throughout the *Journall*, along with complaints that his orders were frequently either ignored or disobeyed. He invites readers to check his narrative against his orders, and to note that everyone had the same order: recovering from the storm, 'Now we began to make ready for extraordinary fight, and gave the same order to those that were with me, and the rest, as by my generall instructions under my hand may appeare' (p. 3). Ten days out Cecil says he 'gave especiall order to all the Captains, and Masters present, to keepe more neare together, and to haile their Admirall every morning reproving their former negligence, and misorder in that kinde', and he carefully records in the *Journall* a copy of those orders, together with their final command that 'all officers peruse their other Articles every day that they might be expert in them' (p. 4). Since the rest of the narration would seem to indicate that the former negligence and misorder in that kind continued unabated, it is clear why Cecil is so anxious to record his instructions so precisely.

On 20 October and having survived the storm, it was decided to anchor off St Mary Port at the entrance of Cadiz Bay while the Lord Admiral and council thought what to do next. Their three great ambitions were to secure a land base on the Spanish coast, to destroy as much enemy shipping as possible, and to capture the returning Plate Fleet. Attacking Cadiz itself was not an option since official intelligence described it as heavily fortified. Two days later Cecil held another council of war. Glanville records that some members wanted an immediate assault on Cadiz, for they had received a report – which was in fact correct – that the town was at that moment poorly defended and short of provisions (*The Voyage*, pp. 41–2). Cecil records none of this in his own *Journall*, but only that he gave orders to enter the Bay of Cadiz and that, 'not knowing what ships might be there', every ship should clear its decks for action (p. 7). The objective agreed by the council of war on 22 October was, according to Cecil, to establish a secure harbour at Port Royal further into the Bay, and to take Fort Puntal, which guarded its approach. The scaling ladders loaded aboard the ships at Plymouth could not be located until it was too late to use them, grenades could not be located at all, and many ships reported the 'wetting and spoiling of of greate quantities of Gunpowder and match' (Glanville, p. 27). Although items provided by the Ordnance Office included ten brass siege guns and ten field pieces along with their carriages, shot and powder, there is no evidence that any of the heavy ordnance was ever unloaded let alone used in battle – probably because of a shortage of longboats.[16] But after much loss and confusion a party was landed under the command of Sir John Burroughs, and Puntal (entirely fortuitously as it happened) waved white handkerchiefs in surrender. It is only much later in the *Journall* that Cecil dismisses any 'design of Cadiz, for that it was delivered to his Majestie before we went, that it was extraordinary fortified, (as we found it when we came to viewe it)' (p. 14). What Cecil says he saw of Cadiz, from horseback three or four miles off and after their attack on Puntal, engaged his reputation as a professional soldier: 'I have been so long at the wars, that I dare undertake, that they who thinke that *Cadiz* was to be taken' (with an obvious glance back at members who had urged an immediate assault) 'cannot tell how to come to it without Cannon, if there were none but women in it' (p. 17). Cecil must maintain at all costs that, every other prize having slipped away, the prize of Cadiz was never, from the beginning, a possibility anyway. He records, in a rather cleverly orchestrated moment, how he gathered the colonels together to let them know that 'if any out of his experience could think there were any way for us to undertake the Town of *Cadiz*, it would be a great honor to us, & a service acceptable to our King & State'. With mock-melancholy and a glum sort of satisfaction he continues: 'When I propounded this, we were all on horsback standing round in a ring; but I found not one man of that opinion, that it was seazable' (p . 17).

A major reason, however, why Cadiz was not 'seazable' had nothing to do with its defences and everything to do with the incapacity of the expeditionary forces – a fact Cecil is naturally at pains to play down. Cecil decided to 'land some companies to secure Sir *John Burgh*' on the peninsular (but, he adds, 'with no design of Cadiz'), and in the haste and confusion of these operations most of the men, like Burrough's own, were landed without food or water. The shrillness of Cecil's language seems desperate to secure the fact that it was not his fault:

> I was much troubled at some of the Officers, that the soldiers with Sir *John Burgh* had not carried bisket in their Snapsackes, being that I gave a generall order to the Sergeant Major Generall, that when any soldier should land they should bring victuals with them, for that the Snapsackes were ordained for nothing els; as I did keepe mine owne order my selfe, for that all my voluntary Gentlemen and servants did carry their victuals in Snapsackes, yea, not so much as my Chaplin but carried his Snapsack. (p. 15)

But worse was to follow. As the weather suddenly turned very hot and exhausted soldiers complained of thirst, they came across some deserted farmhouses, which contained great vats of wine, and Cecil – contradicting instructions he had originally issued – gave permission for the casks to be broached. The result was entirely predictable. This is Secretary Glanville's account:

> The worser sort set on the rest, and grew to demand more wine, in such disorder and with such violence that they contemned all command … not respecting my Lord Lieutenant himself … No words of exhortation, no blows of correction, would restrain them, but breaking with violence into the rooms where the wines were, crying out that they were King Charles's men and fought for him, caring for no man else, they claimed all the wine as their own … The whole army, except only the commanders, was all drunken and in one common confusion, some of them shooting at one another amongst themselves. (*The Voyage*, pp. 59–60)

Confirming Glanville's record of complete anarchy, Sir William St Leger told Buckingham that a mere 500 of the enemy 'would have cut all our throats. And there was no hope to see things in a better condition, for our men were subject to no command. Such dissolute wretches the earth never brought forth'.[17] Not surprisingly, Cecil's record has quite different details and emphases, minimizing the seriousness of the episode, exonerating himself while slyly implicating others (including St Leger), and making no reference to any breakdown in command.

> Within two miles of the Bridge, the Souldiers began to cry, they had neither meate nor drinke, and the day they marched was a very hot day. Heere I rode before to quarter the Armie, and to discover the avenues and passages; and as I came backe, one came to me, and told me, that there was some wine in a Cellar, and that if it were delivered out in order, it would serve to refresh the Souldiers that wanted both bread and drinke. But little did I thinke that all the Country was full of wine; and knowing of no more than one Cellar, I gave order, that every Regiment should have a proportion of wine, which I did see delivered with mine own eyes.

Military order and efficiency mark Cecil's version, together with an attempt at pleading good sense. There are no farmhouses, only the cellars of the fort; thus the wine is part of Spanish victualling, and to be drunk or destroyed anyway. Behind his narration, however, lurks the knowledge of disaster and fear of other's reports as he continues:

> If every Officer had seene it as well distributed as they were directed, it would have done them good, not harme. But when other Magazines were discovered, (for the provision for the West-Indies was there) there was no keeping of the Souldiers from it; but the best way we could devise, was to stave it, and let the wine run out; which Sir *William* Saint *Leger*, the Sergeant Major Generall, bestowed some time about. But when this was done, the Souldiers neverthelesse would drinke it in the sand and dirty places. (p. 16)

With a drunken army (a 'disorder', as Cecil admits) there was no question of an assault on anything or anyone, yet Cecil's account ignores this incapacity and indicates instead other good reasons for withdrawing, such as their lack still of food and water, the ease with which they could be cut off, and above all by those defences of Cadiz. It is at this point that Cecil rides ahead to view the ditches, bulwarks and town walls of Cadiz, and stage-manages his gloomy consultation with his colonels confirming its impregnability. No mention is made of an entire army too drunk to move.

What may seem at first in Cecil a pedantic fussiness about who had what orders from whom grows in intensity to become one of the crucial issues of the expedition. A large part of his 'explanation' for what went wrong centres on the wilfulness or laziness of others. At one point, having written to Essex and his squadron to make all haste and hoist all his sails, he complains that 'I must confesse they went the most untowardly that ever I did see men, for they did not hoyse up all their sayles as they were commanded'. At such moments Cecil depicts himself yelling and shouting: 'I followed as fast as I could, and cryed out to them to hoyse their sayles & advaunce', but even this hands-on leadership has little effect; 'some of them increased theire sayles, but not much'. Clearly angry and baffled, Cecil conducts an inquiry:

> But I could never learne by all the Seamen in my shippe to know those shippes that were so backward and when I did inquire, every man excused himselfe saying it was not he, and our businesse grew so hott that I could not immediately inquire after it any further not knowing the shippes one from another. (pp. 7–8)

Like an outmanoeuvred schoolmaster interrogating pupils, Cecil seems here quite unaware of (or unwilling to acknowledge) his own ineffectiveness and lack of authority. When he shows once more how he tried to lead by example this too goes horribly wrong. When ships' masters claimed that the water in the Bay of Cadiz was too shallow for further progress (it turned out they were quite right – most of 'the Kings shipps' subsequently ran aground), he describes how he took a barge 'and went from shippe to shippe, crying out to them to advance to *Puntall* for shame, and upon paine of their lives'. 'Finding some of them not very hastie', he goes to Essex's ship to enlist support, but 'I did not see many make haste'. Thoroughly exasperated, he explains to the reader that, despite having given 'as strict a command as I could devise', 'I saw no other way to bring them up but by example' (p. 11). Having given them this example of courage, leadership and hazard in war, Cecil then has to record the unpalatable fact that his heroics merely brought them within helpless range of Fort Puntal's guns and 'as soone as we came nigh the fort they shotte our shippe twice together thorough and thorough the very midst of her within a foote at least of the water and mist no shippe they shott at, and kild as many commaunders of ours besides soldiers as we killed in all of theirs' (pp. 11–12). For reasons of this kind the *Journall* makes both painful and, depending on one's detachment, hilarious reading, with Cecil – a far from adept practitioner of what is now known in political language as 'spin' – attempting both to tell the truth (that is, to conform to other public records of the expedition) and to show himself in as good a light as possible. At times he resorts to a grimly ironic humour to demonstrate his own grimly ironic situation. Earlier Cecil had asked his naval captains for their view of the two forts making up the Bay's defences, and 'they told me that 20 Colliers with some of the Dutch would beate them to dust before morning' (p. 9). With his ships, including his own flagship, holed, many men killed, and having bombarded the fort with everything they had, Cecil writes: 'The fort of *Puntall* that I was told would be beaten to dust in a night did receave 1700 shott and not one stone removed out of his place' (p. 12). At another point, when the Fleet is once more out at sea, Cecil seems intent on ensuring that Sir Michael Gere (a thorn in Cecil's side throughout the voyage) is depicted as insubordinate and unstable. Cecil here – as so often in the *Journall*, and in particular with regard to the Earl of Essex's entrepreneurial activities – is quite explicitly alluding to scores that he knows are being settled in London. Gere, 'who had been wanting 5 dayes, came to us, who went wilfully from us without leave; and when his Master told him of it, hee beate him with a Cudgell, which is against all discipline and reason, his Master having had better command before, than ever he had' (p. 23).

Much time is misspent on the voyage chasing the Fleet's own tail, a circumstance that clearly renders Cecil both furious and impotent. 'Wednesday the 19.[October] in the morning wee were in the height of the Cape [of St Vincent], and discovered 11. sayle of ships, which we chased, thinking they had beene enemie, but they proved to bee of our owne, being the Vice-Admirall my Lord of *Essex*' (pp. 4–5). After the abortive attempt to secure a land base and with the Fleet again at sea, cruising up and down in hope of encountering the Plate ships, Cecil records that on 'Munday the 7 [November] we discovered 9 or 10 saile of Ships to the leeward, we bore up, and found them to be of our own Fleet, who had carelessly lost company, which as now, so divers times before, had occasioned us to chase our owne men, whereby our course was much hindred' (p. 22) – and this 'notwithstanding I had sundry times before strictly commanded the Captaines and Masters to stay better by the Fleet, which they observed not; I did again charge them once more to observe their directions that were prescribed them' (p. 21). To his evident chagrin and frustration, Cecil seems to be constantly issuing orders of which no one takes the slightest notice. On Sunday 30 October, just after the Fleet had left the Bay of Cadiz, a (probably deliberately) laconic entry records that, in squally conditions and with a contrary wind, 'this day we had 4 ships in chase, but could not fetch them up' (p. 20). Cecil may have fudged the date somewhat (other sources suggest it was 1 November when ships making their way to Cadiz were sighted), and may be smudging the trail, but what they had in fact seen, it was later to emerge, was part of the Spanish fleet bringing silver from the New World. The fleet's capture would, even at this late stage, have turned disaster into a triumph. But the opportunity slipped away over the horizon. Ironically, it was not until more than a week later that Cecil notes that 'This day [Thursday 10 November] I gave the Captaines their instructions, if we met with the West-India fleet, how to dispose and order themselves' (p. 23). In the meantime, the Fleet continued where it could to give chase to unidentified shipping, with familiar results: 'Thursday the 17, the wind north west, faire weather. Wee gave chase to some ships that were farre a head of us, whom we found to be my Lord of *Essex* and some of his squadron, whom wee had not seene in many dayes before' (p. 24).

Cecil's own attempts at appropriate self-disposal and self-ordering are apparent throughout the *Journall*, which seethes with barely repressed resentment, indignation and anxiety. The Lord Admiral had never previously had command at sea and was totally ignorant of naval affairs – an acknowledged incapacity that haunts his narrative. In discussions at Plymouth, when the king was present, experienced seamen had suggested San Lucar as a place that could be captured without too much opposition. But when Cecil called a council at sea on 20 October the naval experts, markedly less gung-ho, now delivered their opinion that 'the Haven of S. Lucas is so barred, as it is hard and dangerous, both for the going in, and comming out, especially for ships of burden as his Majesties are'. Obviously exasperated, Cecil writes: 'Then I demanded both of the Sea Captaines & Masters why they could not speake of these difficulties before his Majestie'. Their irritating reply, that it is one thing to be ashore and 'farre off' and another 'being upon the place', leaves Cecil at a loss, 'so that I could say no more to them, being as I was no great Seaman, and that I was strictly tide to their advice that did professe the Sea' (pp. 5–6). It is a dilemma in which Cecil frequently finds himself. After yet another misidentification – by himself this time – of the number of vessels at sea, Cecil admits that it 'shewes the difference of men practised at Sea, and of them that are not', and he confesses, 'I was much troubled hereat' (p. 10). At six in the morning he wakes up Lord Denbigh to remind him that 'you are no ould Seaman', and telling him to 'gather all the Seaman together that are of the counsell & others' in order to take the best advice possible, 'according to my instructions, to give preheminence to Seamen in Sea businesse, and unto Landmen in land affaires' (pp. 13–14). Constantly dependent too on his own instructions, Cecil has to second-guess what naval opinion might be: 'I hastened this preparation … that our ships might speedily put into execution what course soever the Seamen should resolve upon' (p. 14). Often he has to be content with a possibly specious or insolent technical answer he cannot contest, as when he sends to know of a captain 'what he had done touching the firing of the Enemies ships; and that it seemed very strange to mee, that the exploit which was so easie was not done. He sent me word, that the reason why he went no sooner, was because of the wind and tyde' (p. 18).

It has been argued in defence of the Cadiz expedition that its failure was not simply Stuart inexperience or bungling but the result of problems of logistics and command inherent in such complex operations. In the retrospectively glorious days of Queen Elizabeth, Drake and his fellow commanders had set sail in 1589 with an even greater force of 150 ships and 18,000 men to attack Lisbon, but were defeated by the same combination of maverick captains, supply failures, poor intelligence, sickness and inexperience that affected Cecil.[18] But in Cecil's *Journall* we have peculiar access to a mind anxious to negotiate those difficulties discursively and in competition with other less sympathetic accounts. The *Journall* seeks to project its author as, at the very least, well intentioned in the midst of confusion and disaster, and responsibly aware of what inquests will follow. Barely afloat in leaky ships, the scattered forces made their individual ways back to England: Cecil brought the *Anne Royall* to harbour in Kinsale, Ireland, 'with 160 sicke men in my ship, 130 cast overboord, with a leak of above 6 foot water in the hould', and he cannot refrain from adding, as criticism of the Navy and for the information of his judges, 'she was so old and so decayed a ship' (p. 27). While the battered flagship is in Kinsale undergoing repairs, Cecil hears of a final, crushing irony: a Dutch ship comes in from Lisbon and the crew, 'who had served the Spaniard, did certainely affirme, that they saw divers letters from *Cadiz*, that the [Plate] Fleet came in, 4 daies after our comming out of *Cadiz* Bay' (p. 28). While arguing that the sickness afflicting the men was the 'heavy hand [of God] upon us' (p. 21), Cecil finally reflects on the what-ifs and the might-have-beens of the whole expedition:

> So that if any of the 3 accidents had hapned that follow, we had bin Masters of the Spanish Fleet. The first is, If the Councell had condiscended to me to have kept *Puntall* for 14 daies. The second, If the wind had not changed as it did. The last, If the Plate fleet had kept the course they ever have done these 40 yeeres; for they had no manner of newes of us, and had then come amongst us; and if we had stayed in the Bay, they had done the like. But man proposeth, and God determines. (p. 29)

Cecil's catalogue includes a vindication of himself and his judgment ('If the Councell had condiscended'), a helpless shrug at the unpredictability of North Atlantic winter weather and the inability of *anyone* to respond to such infuriatingly novel behaviour by the Spanish fleet. On the brink of more and infinitely multiplying 'ifs' ('and if we had stayed in the Bay'), Cecil consigns the problem, and his part in it, to the inscrutable will of God as his best and only defence.

In a sense, it worked. Cecil's efforts to clear himself of personal incompetence successfully wafted him through the shoals of public censure to emerge after all as a substantial military figure, despite Sir William St Leger's prediction and his own continuing indistinctions and failures. In a familiar paradox of public life, the more wretched the record the higher the promotion: the old *Dictionary of National Biography* suggests that Wimbledon's few successes and many failures did not prevent him being regarded 'as an heroic leader of armies', and its author quotes from a letter (clearly currying favour with someone) by Sir Kenelm Digby (January 1636–37):

> England is happy in producing persons who do actions which after ages take for romances; witness King Arthur and Cadwallader of ancient time, and the valiant and ingenious peer, the Lord Wimbledon, whose epistle exceeds anything ever done by so victorious a general of armies, or so provident a governor of towns.

A destiny in the company of Cadwallader and Arthur is probably not what Cecil dreamed of as he constructed his self-excusing portrait of a survivor of disasters at sea anxious to avoid the political fall-out. But whatever Digby's motives in the letter, England appeared to have a need for heroes, wherever they might be found. Amerigo Salvetti, the Florentine resident in London, had noted that while the Cadiz expedition was under way people were boasting that the great days of Elizabeth had come again – a mood of elation cruelly punctured by the news of failure, and giving way to cynicism, bitterness and despair.[19] In the gloomy aftermath, with clouds of ill-will hanging over Westminster, Whitehall and especially Buckingham's York House, and with apparent confirmation of the effeminate, feather-bedded and drunken character of England's military, a canny printer and an extrovert and flamboyantly patriotic former seaman got together to produce the third item in this trilogy, Richard Peake's (or Pike's) *Three to One*, a text which also bears the distinct marks of a maritime salvage operation.

The Pike and the Pen

Pike's autobiographical narrative (and we know virtually nothing more about him than is contained in this text) is addressed to his 'Loving Countrymen', but is prefaced by a dedicatory epistle 'To the Kings Most Excellent Majestie' which clearly suggests that the heroic Pike had already had an audience with Charles:

> As your Majesty hath bene gratiously pleased, both to let your poore Soldier and Subject, behold your Royall Person, and to heare him speake in his rude Language; So, if your Majesty, vouchsafe to cast a Princely Eye on these his unhandsome Papers; New Sun-beames shall spread over him, and put a Quickning Soule into that Bosome, which otherwise must want Life, for want of your Comfort.

It may be speculated that Whitehall, at least, saw in Pike's story a much needed antidote to the bad publicity following the failure of Buckingham's expedition and may well have encouraged its writing and printing. For less courtly readers, Pike offers his credentials, entreating (or warning) them not 'to stagger in your Opinions of my performance, sithence I am ready with my life to Justify what I set downe'. Implicitly claiming kinship with Drake and Raleigh and other Elizabethan sea-dogs, Pike asserts he is 'a *Westerne Man, Devonshire* my Countrey, and *Tavestoke* my place of Habitation'. (John Glanville, the Cadiz expedition's record keeper and fierce critic, was also a Tavistock man.) Pike characterizes himself as a simple truth-teller, that familiar early modern figure, literary, theatrical and social, of the robust plain-speaker:

> I know not what the Court of a King meanes, nor what the fine Phrases of silken Courtiers are: A good Shippe I know, and a poore Cabbin, and the Language of a Cannon: And therefore, as my Breeding has bin Rough, (scorning Delicacy:) And my Present Being consisteth altogether upon the Soldier, (blunt, plaine, and unpolished;) so must my Writings be, proceeding from fingers fitter for the Pike then the Pen: And so (kinde Countreymen) I pray receave them.

And he adds: 'Neither ought you to expect better from me, because I am but the Chronicler of my owne Story'. (B[r])[20]

The story that unfolds is indeed an extraordinary one. The narrative begins with Pike's enthusiastic joining up in Plymouth (in contrast to the reality of forced conscriptions): he hears 'the Drumbe beating up for a New Expedition, in which many Noble Gentlemen, and Heroicall Spirits, were to venture their Honors, Lives, and Fortunes', and, he says, 'Cables could not hold me' from going. He is assigned to a Navy ship, the *Convertine,* under Captain Thomas Portar, and part of the Earl of Essex's troublesome squadron. (The ship is mentioned several times in Cecil's *Journall.*) Pike describes the siege of Fort Puntal, celebrating manly valour, resourcefulness and heroism under fire. With no mention of Cecil or his mismanagement in getting them into this vulnerable position, Pike describes how they

> came up so close to the Castle, as possibly Men in such a danger either could, or durst adventure, and there fought bravely: The Castle bestowing upon us a hotte salutation (and well becomming our approach) with Bullets; whose first Shot killed three of our Men, passing through and through our Shippe, the second killd foure, and the third two more at least, with great spoile and battery to our Shippe: The last Shotte flying so close by Captaine *Portar*, that with the winde of the Bullet, his very Hands had almost lost the Sence of feeling, being struck into a suddaine numbnesse.

But despite torn shrouds and tackle and a constant enemy barrage, the expeditionary force heroically won through, at one point expertly landing 'shotte into the mouth of *Spanish* Cannon, where it sticketh fast, and putteth that Roarer to silence', while Pike adds, 'I, for my part (without vaine glory be it spoken) discharging at this time, some threescore and ten Shotte, as they recounted to me who charged my Peeces for me' (B-B²). Pike goes on to knock out single handedly a Spanish gun emplacement, and his hurts and bruises ('though they were neither many, nor dangerous') are rewarded with gifts of money from 'many Gentlemen in our Shippe'. With the fort subdued, Essex landed a regiment close by (Sir John Burrough's men), and according to Pike the sight of them caused 'many of those within the Castle (to the number of six score) to run away; wee pursuing them with showtes, hollawings, and lowed noises, and now and then a Piece of Ordnance overtooke some of the *Spanish Hares*, and stayed them from running farder' (B³).

At this point the Fleet made for Port Royal while the land forces occupied the peninsular between Puntal and Cadiz, with Pike ('for I was no Land-Soldier') on board his ship. But he makes it his task to remind readers of the demonic character of the enemy and of the indignities suffered by those heroic English soldiers:

> In going up [to a bridge] some of our Men were unfortunately and unmanly surprised, and before they knew their owne danger, had there their Throates cutte; Some having their Braines beaten out with the stockes of Muskets; others, their Noses slic'd off; whilst some Heads were spurned up & downe the Streets like Footballs, and some Eares worne in scorne in *Spanish* Hattes.

In case this is thought to be mere report, Pike adds, 'when I was in prison in *Cales* [Cadiz], (whether [whither] some of these *Spanish Picaroes* were brought in for flying from the Castle,) I was an eye witnesse, of *English* Mens Eares worn in that despightfull manner' (B³ ff.).

With the land forces having marched out of sight and the ships waiting for wind, Pike ventures ashore, like others that day, in search of food and water. He comes across some Englishmen carrying oranges and lemons back to their ship, and goes in search of fruit himself, encountering on the way three dead countrymen and one badly wounded. 'I then resolved (and was about it) for Christian Charities sake; and for Countries sake, to have carried him on my back to our Shippes, farre off though they lay', when he is surprised by a Spanish horseman ('whose Name as afterward I was informed, was *Don Juan of Cales*, a Knight') and a fight ensues in which Pike (naturally) gets the better of the horseman and has him on his knees begging for mercy. About to spare the Spanish knight his life and to send him home on foot, Pike suddenly finds himself surrounded by fourteen Spanish musketeers. Once he is captured and his hands tied, the knight, says Pike, 'most basely' cut him 'through the Face from Eare to Eare' and he is 'led in Triumph, into the Towne of *Cales*'.

It is here that Pike's distinctive adventure begins. Nothing heroic or celebratory could be related about the further progress of the expedition proper, which sailed off shortly after into disaster: Pike is captured by the Spanish on Monday 24 October, and notes, 'the Fleete departed the Friday following, from *Cales*, at the same time when I was there a prisoner'. (C^{2r} Cf. Cecil, *Journall*, p. 20). He has no ill will towards his commanders for leaving him:

> Yet, thus honestly was I used by my worthy Friend Captaine *Portar*; He above my deserving, complayning, that he feared he had lost such a Man: My Lord Generall (by the solicitation of Master *John Glanvile*, Secretary to the Fleete) sent three Men on Shore, to enquire in *Cales* for me, and to offer (if I were taken) any reasonable Ransome; But the Towne, thinking me a better Prize then (indeede) I was, denyed me and would not part from me. (C^2)

(Not unexpectedly, Cecil's *Journall* records nothing about such lost or abandoned men or negotiations of ransom.) Pike runs a gauntlet of abuse and stabs from halberds as he is led through the streets of Cadiz to prison, where he is confined for 18 days and his wounds tended so that he can be interrogated ('I was … so wounded in my Face and Jawes, that I could hardly speake'). Understanding that he is to be moved to Jerez and fearing he will be 'put to Tortures', Pike requests a young English fellow prisoner, incarcerated for debt, to be his representative, 'thinking there was no way with me but one; (That I must be sent packing to my long home)'. What Pike commissions, with its projection of a stoic, heroic, patriotic, defiantly Protestant, family orientated and dutiful subject of the king, is a self-portrait far removed from those ambitiously acquisitive men, 'covetous to

measure gold by their hats' privately recommended by Buckingham as ideal subjects for this venture of spoil and looting.

> Countrey-man, what my Name is, our Partnership in Misery hath made you know; And with it, know that I am a *Devonshire* man borne, and *Tavestock* the place of my once abiding. I beseech you, if God ever send you Liberty, and that you saile into *England*, take that Countrey in your way; Commend me to my Wife and Children, made wretched by me, an infortunate Father, and Husband: Tell them, and my Friends, (I intreate you for Gods cause) that if I be (as I suspect I shall be) put to Death in *Sherris*, I will dye a Christian Soldier, no way, I hope, dishonouring my King, Countrey, or the Justice of my Cause, or my Religion. (C^2-C^{3r})

In the event, of course, Pike survives – and much more. In his narrative the Spanish appear as an unpredictable mixture of barbarian and humanitarian, demonic and civilized, cruel and courteous. He is indeed conveyed to prison in Jerez, where two Irish friars are sent to confess him, 'for tomorrow', they tell him, 'you must dye'. Pike, roundly rejecting their offer, seizes the opportunity to educate these 'Spirituall Ghostly Fathers' in the Protestant faith. He also notes that the commander of Fort Puntal, Don Francisco Bustamente, 'was brought in, Prisoner for his Life; because he delivered up the Castle; but whether he dyed for it, or no, I cannot tell'. Pike himself is brought to trial, accompanied by 'two Drumbes, and a hundred Shotte', before 'three Dukes, foure Condes, or Earles, four Marquesses, besides other great Persons'. The first matter to be dealt with is the encounter with Don Juan and, on hearing evidence from both sides, Pike is commended and the Spanish knight is publicly rebuked for cowardice and baseness. (As with other incidents in Pike's story, this moment echoes Elizabethan and Jacobean theatre, and closely resembles Philip of Spain's sentencing of a cowardly Spaniard who had basely killed an Englishman in Thomas Heywood's popular Spanish Armada play *If You Know Not Me, You Know No Body*.[21]) There follows the more serious business of the interrogation, the gathering of military and political intelligence. Skilfully and courteously, Pike tells them (through the Irish friars as interpreters) no more than they probably already know, or that he wants them to think, about English shipping, ordnance and defences. It is clearly important that the text should avoid any hint that an indiscretion by Pike may have affected the success of the venture, but its cunning narrator is quite prepared to explain to the Spanish why Cecil's forces did this or that – or, of course, did not. When asked why, 'in all this Bravery of the Fleete', they did not take Cadiz as well as Puntal, Pike replies: 'The Lord Generall might easily have taken *Cales*, for he had neere a thousand Scaling Ladders to set up, and a thousand Men to loose; but he was loath to rob an Almeshouse, having a better Market to go to: *Cales*, I told them, was held Poore, Unmand, and Unmunitioned'. The Duke of Medina, taking the bait, asks him what better market. 'I told him, *Genoa*, or *Lisbone*, and as I heard, there was instantly, upon this, an Army of six thousand Soldiers sent to *Lisbone*' (D[r]).

As in the depiction of his capture and humiliation at Cadiz, with its subdued subtext of Christ's sufferings, so in the court at Jerez the common people 'who encompass me round' (the phrasing is biblical) jeer and mock and offer 'scornes, and bitter jestes … throwne upon our Nation'. Pike bites his lip and lets them 'runne on in their Revilings'. The same jeering, its sophisticated banter more witty but more threatening, is offered by the aristocrats and officers, and Pike seeks to hold his own in an ominously jocular debate about English hens and Spanish pullets. His stout defence, in this alien and hostile arena, of England and Englishness, provokes a dare from the Duke of Medina ('with a brow halfe angry') to fight with one of these Spanish pullets. Pike's shackles are removed and the floor is cleared for combat, rapier and dagger the weapons. A Spanish champion, Signior Tiago, presents himself. 'When wee had played some reasonable good time,' Pike writes, 'I disarmed him thus'. And he describes in exact detail the manoeuvres that up-ended his opponent. He delivers the weapons to the dukes, and is asked if he dare fight against another. Pike seeks to be excused, but is very aware of the perilous position he is now in – a peril which, of course, serves only to emphasize his own courage: 'For, to my selfe I too well knew, that the *Spaniard* is Haughty, Impatient of the least affront; And when he receives but a Touch of any Dishonor, Disgrace, or Blemish, (especially in his owne Countrey, and from an *English* Man,) his Revenge is implacable, mortall, and bloudy' (D^2).

What follows in Pike's narrative is both a jingoistic, defiant celebration of English grit and heroism, and also a tribute to Spanish generosity of spirit in their acknowledgment of true valour. Having no real choice, Pike fights again, armed only with the shaft of a halberd – as close as he can get to his own favourite weapon, the quarter-staff. But this time three Spaniards armed with rapiers confront him. Pike notes that he is not, at least, going to die basely ('For Three to kill One, had bin to Mee no Dishonour'), and with these thoughts he falls to it. The rudely spoken Pike depicts his heroic isolation, like Samson among the Philistines, or Daniel in the den of lions, with a highly dramatic and patterned rhetoric:

> The Rapier Men traverst their ground, I, mine; Dangerous Thrusts were put in, and with dangerous hazard avoided: Showtes ecchoed to Heaven, to encourage the *Spaniards*; Not a shoute, nor Hand, to hearten the poore *English* Man; Onely, Heaven I had in mine Eye, the Honor of my Countrey in my Heart, my Fame at the Stake, my Life on the narrow Bridge, and Death both before me and behind me.

Pike kills one Spaniard, and disarms the other two, 'causing the One of them to fly into the Armie of Soldiers then present, and the Other for refuge fled behind a Bench'. Opening the moral of the tale and defining the political purpose of its writing and publication, Pike declares: 'I hope, if the braving *Spaniards* set upon *England* (as they threaten), we shall every One of us, give the repulse to more then Three' (D^3).

Unable to see how it would be possible to escape from the murmurings and threats against him, Pike records the prompt intervention of the Duke of Medina, who grants him protection and proclaims that none, on pain of death, should meddle with this heroic Englishman. He is showered with money and gifts, including, says Pike, 'a long *Spanish* Russet Cloake I now weare, which he [the Marquesse of Alquenezes] tooke from one of his Mens backs'. He is entertained by the Marquess, is sent to the king in Madrid ('where I was lodged in the most sumptuous Bedde that ever I beheld'), is given Spanish lace shirts, a gold chain, 'and two Jewels for my Wife, and other pretty Thinges for my Children'. The king grants Pike his freedom and a hundred pistoles for his expenses, and Richard Pike, the scourge and cynosure of the Spanish, returns to England, landing at Fowey on St George's Day, 23 April 1626.

He brought with him, besides his Spanish treasure, a challenge to the Duke of Buckingham, entrusted to him by the brother-in-law of Spain's chief minister, the

Conde d'Olivares. (Buckingham and Olivares were old enemies since the Spanish marriage negotiations of 1623, wrecked, according to Buckingham, by 'the foolery of the Conde of Olivares'.[22] Buckingham was also a notorious womanizer, and was said to have made advances to the Countess of Olivares, hence perhaps the interest of the brother-in-law.[23]) Pike delivered the challenge in London on 18 May 1626 [24], and it was not, of course, the only challenge that Buckingham was to face. That same year he was impeached by Parliament (but survived), and two years later he was dead, assassinated by John Felton, a melancholy puritan 'fanatic', to the acclamation of almost the entire nation. Richard Pike, model of that stalwart, honest Englishman and antithesis to everything that Buckingham, in the popular imagination at least, stood for, was also, like Felton, commemorated in verse, in an 18-stanza poem 'Written by a Friend' concluding *Three to One*, and later in the century in a broadside ballad entitled 'A Panegyric Poem, or Tavestock's Encomium':

> Search whether can be found again the like
> For noble prowess to our Tav'stock's Pike,
> In whose renown'd never-dying name
> Live England's honour and the Spaniard's shame.[25]

Pike's adventures quickly made it to the popular stage in *Dicke of Devonshire, a tragi-Comedy*, almost certainly written by Thomas Heywood.[26] The play expands the action into five acts through the addition of a (largely unconnected) romantic subplot, but in the main plot Pike's own narrative – which so closely resembles in any case the confrontations and gestures of patriotic adventure plays – is faithfully followed. Implicitly in the autobiographical text and quite explicitly in the play, with its opening speeches harking back to the glory days of Elizabeth, a salvage operation is under way to restore English confidence despite the wreckage of Buckingham and Cecil's traumatic misadventure.

Pike is a perfect example of a man constructing himself and his attributes *out of* the materials furnished by popular theatre and Elizabethan fiction. The text's primary purposes, in a climate of national depression, are clearly and cheerfully propagandist and patriotic, and Pike's adventure play narrative – even though it bears the autobiographical marker of author-as-hero – is hardly revelatory of a truly individual person as we would understand him today. It has the generic marks of the narrator as nongenteel and nonmetropolitan hero, strong of arm, biblically literate, of unshakable royalist and Protestant convictions, and (like Raleigh himself) with a proudly provincial accent. An important element in Pike's appeal to readers and to playgoers, as too in the general response to Felton's action, was the relatively low social class of these heroes, the 'ordinary' Englishman who, though doggedly loyal to king and country, will not be bullied or deceived by 'great ones'. And their identities as figures of sanity and integrity are exactly congruent with their *generic* identities as lower-middle-class English patriots, and are insisted on by acts of self-representational inscription: in case Felton was cut down immediately and his motives misunderstood, he stitched into the lining of his hat a paper asserting a role identical to that so colourfully exhibited and dramatized by Pike: 'that man is cowardly, base and deserveth not the name of gentleman or soldier, that is not willing to sacrifice his life for the honour of his God, his King and his country'.[27] But it was, of course, a generic identity that was to be cruelly tested and dismantled in the years that lay ahead.

*   *   *

We have seen in each of these 'Cadiz texts' the ways in which their authors conceive of themselves in relation to their representative roles and offices, and how the texts they produce are determined, generically and in their constructions of a speaking, or writing, 'self', by the functions they see those texts as serving. His professional and personal life disrupted by the war, the lawyer Glanville's routine precision gathers together what he realizes will become evidence for use in court, and traces of his true motives lie outside his deliberately impersonalized text. Cecil, on the contrary, puts himself, as commander of the Fleet, in the centre of the frame – a frame which he knows to be at once judicial, political and personal – justifying his actions by reproving those of others, and appealing wherever possible to forces beyond the control of any man. The vista of the expedition and its trajectory is, in narrative form, wholly constrained by the self-important self-presentation of the narrator, who uses it only to exemplify both his mastery of the situation and his bad luck. He tells us nothing directly of his interior feelings, his deep anxieties or his fears of failure, but his attempt to build a portrait of the ever-judicious general nevertheless keeps collapsing behind him. Pike's text conforms exactly to Thomas Heywood's formula for successful popular theatre, where the action should be, like *Dick of Devonshire*, 'lively and well-spirited'. 'What English blood,' asks Heywood, 'seeing the person of any bold Englishman presented, and doth not hug his fame, and hunnye at his valour [?] … What coward, to see his countrymen valiant, would not be ashamed of his own cowardice?'[28] It is to even more urgent issues of valour, shame and cowardice in the diary and journal narratives of those caught up, some 20 years later, in the English civil wars that we shall now turn.

Notes

1   The title adds: 'Never before printed. From Sir John Eliot's MSS at Port Eliot'. Ed. Rev. Alexander B. Grosart (Camden Society, New Series XXXII, 1883).

2   London (?): Elliot's Court Press (?), 1626. A facsimile is published by Da Capo Press, Amsterdam & London: Theatrum Orbis Terrarum Ltd., 1968.

3   The surname, here "Peeeke", is also recorded as Peeke, Peake, and Pike. The book (36 pp.) was printed in London by Augustine Matthewes for J[ohn] T[rundle], 1626. Its running title is *Three to One; Being, An English-Spanish Combat*. Quotations are from the copy in the Henry E. Huntington Library.

4   Trumbull, in Public Records Office, State Papers Flanders, SP 77, 18. p. 164v. See

Roger Lockyer, *Buckingham: The Life and Political Career of George Villiers, First Duke of Buckingham 1592–1628* (Longman: London & New York, 1981), p. 251. Sir John Oglander, after praising Elizabeth as 'one of the noblest, most generous, bravest princes that ever England had', notes that 'King James the First of England was the most cowardly man that ever I knew. He could not endure a soldier or to see men drilled, to hear of war was death to him'. *A Royalist's Notebook: The Commonplace Book of Sir John Oglander Kt. Of Nunwell (1585–1655)*, transcribed and ed. Francis Bamford (London: Constable, 1936), pp. 192–3.

5   Lockyer, p. 250.

6   On the equipping of the expedition see Richard W. Stewart, 'Arms and Expeditions: The Ordnance Office and the assaults on Cadiz (1625) and the Isle of Rhé (1627)', in *War and Government in Britain, 1598–1650*, ed. Mark Charles Fissel (Manchester: Manchester University Press, 1991), pp. 112–32.

7   Charles Dalton, *The Life and Times of General Sir Edward Cecil, Viscount Wimbledon*, 2 vols. (London, 1885), II. p. 142; Public Record Office, State Papers Domestic of the Reign of Charles I, SP 16, 11. p. 22.

8   State Papers Domestic 16, 7. 9, 29. Lockyer, p. 275.

9   Cecil, *A Journall And Relation of the action ... upon the Coast of Spaine, 1625*, p. 3.

10   Lockyer, pp. 262–7.

11   SPD 16, 28. P .10; Lockyer, pp. 270–71.

12   'Glanville Records', Public Record Office, reproduced in Grosart, pp. vi–vii.

13   For Glanville's contribution to Parliament's articles of impeachment against Buckingham, see Lockyer, pp. 321–2.

14   Lockyer, p. 250.

15   Dalton, II, pp. 201–2. Historians have repeated St Leger's gloomy judgement: M. Oppenheim's *A History of the Administration of the Royal Navy ... 1509–1660*, introd. K.R. Andrews (Aldershot: Temple Smith, 1988, reprint of London, 1896), p. 221, calls the venture 'the low watermark of English seamanship', and Geoffrey Regan's *Someone Has Blundered: A Historical Survey of Military Incompetence* (London: Batsford, 1987), gives a prominent place to the Cadiz expedition, pp. 147–65.

16   Public Record Office WO 55/1681. The Irish peer Henry, Viscount of Valentia, Master of the Ordnance on the expedition, is not recorded as having ever had anything to do with the actual deployment of ordnance but was energetic in dispute over flags and precedence in the fleet chain of command. See Stewart, p. 130, n. 13.

17   Dalton, II, p. 200.

18   Lockyer, p. 284.

19   Lockyer, p. 281.

20   The Huntington Library text is unpaginated except for lettering the gathers A–E.

21   In *The Dramatic Works of Thomas Heywood*, 6 vols (New York: Russell & Russell, 1964, reprint of 1874 edition), vol. 1, pp. 224–5.

22   See Lockyer, pp. 140–48, 163.

23   Lockyer, p. 153.

24   Thomas Birch (d. 1766), *The Court and Times of Charles I*, 2 vols (London: Henry Colburn, 1849), vol. 1, p. 104.

25   Reprinted in Mrs Bray's *Borders of the Tamar and the Tavy*, vol. 1, n.d., p. 241. (See also old *DNB*.)

26   First printed from the Egerton MS 1994 by A.H. Bullen, *Collection of Old English Plays* (London, 1883), vol. 2, pp. 1–99. Bullen tentatively assigns the piece to Heywood;

Arthur Melville Clark convincingly argues that this 'remarkably competent play' is definitely Heywood's work. See Clark's *Thomas Heywood: Playwright and Miscellanist* (Oxford: Basil Blackwell, 1931), Appendix II, pp. 276–86. The play is not listed in Andrew Gurr's *The Shakespearean Stage 1574–1642*, 3rd edition (Cambridge: Cambridge University Press, 1993).

27 Lockyer, pp. 458–9. A facsimile engraving of Felton's paper is printed in C.J. Smith, *Historical and Literary Curiosities* (London, 1840).

28 Heywood, *Apology for Actors*, 1612, in E.K. Chambers, *The Elizabethan Stage*, 4 vols (Oxford: Clarendon Press, 1923), vol. 4, p. 251.

Chapter 6

Besieged Cities: The Civil War

Cities and Selves under Siege

When Innogen, in *Cymbeline*, rejects Cloten, 'whose love suit', she says, 'hath been to me / As fearful as a siege' (III, iv, 132–3), or when Donne writes of himself as 'a usurpt towne' (*Holy Sonnets* XIV), these images of siege and battery would, for the vast majority of English readers who were not travelled professional soldiers, have been just that: images. Until the violent eruptions of the Civil War, siege warfare was what happened elsewhere in Europe, at Boulogne, Juliers, Cadiz, or Salé on the Barbary Coast, or at La Rochelle, and no English city or town had experienced a siege in living memory. While the most memorable military encounters of the Great Civil War took place in literal battle*fields* – Marston Moor, Edgehill, Hopton Heath, or Roundway Down – the most prolonged and destructive operations were carried out in and around cities in the form of siege warfare. Many English cities were besieged – Hull, Newark, York, Chester, Bristol, Plymouth, Gloucester – some – Exeter or Lichfield for instance – changing hands as successful besiegers were themselves besieged.

There is a very full literature on the sieges of the Civil War from military historians concentrating more or less exclusively on ordnance and gunners, earthworks and defences, mining and breaching by sappers, supply lines, logistics and so on.[1] But our question is directed rather to the effects of the besieging of English towns and cities on the English psyche, both collectively and individually. Here evidence is to be found not in the numerous records of purely operational procedures and ambitions nor in financial accounts of siege defences but in the diaries, journals and narratives of individuals caught up, both as participants and victims, in this peculiarly intimate form of aggression. Pastures, livestock, gardens, public buildings and private homes, were invaded and desecrated, the aggression rendered the more destructive and bewildering in that it was inflicted by the English people (for the most part) upon each other.

In the many recent analyses of the defining character of early modern selfhood much emphasis is placed on the identity and delineation of the self in terms of notions of office, social function and position, of collective membership of guild or profession or religious community (as in 'the body of Christ' of church or churches), and by marital and family bonds.[2] So what happens to the psyche when physical forces threaten to tear such identifiers apart? Identity is also very tellingly constructed by its relationship with the county, city or town of birth and family residence, especially in relatively static populations of limited mobility – when a town or community is threatened one's self-identity is critically in a state of disarray or arrest. Richard Helgerson has shown that the sixteenth and seventeenth centuries were the age of both rural and urban chorography, a mode of writing descriptive of the physical landmarks, fields, streets, public buildings and local histories of particular regions.[3] Such chorographical attentiveness to locality and community is associated, Helgerson argues, with forms of national identity that implicitly tie subjects to the land – to place broadly conceived – as much as to the monarch or, indeed, to Parliament. The wholesale fracturing of these markers by which individuals understood their selfhood could only induce traumas beyond and greater than the nominal 'causes' (complex though they were) of the Civil Wars. What – to be specific – is the impact on the *mentalité* of a city's inhabitants when they and the corporate life that structures and identifies them are attacked, dismembered, and occupied by military and ideological forces that demand their allegiance or submission – or, as in several towns and cities, when they are besieged again and reoccupied by rival forces?

One response, as Jonathan Sawday has argued and illustrated, lies in a diagnosis and discourse of madness. During the Parliamentarian army's occupation of London in August 1647, a pamphlet appeared claiming to represent 'above 12 millions of well-affected (before so ill-distracted) people of all sorts, Ages, Sexes, and Sises'. *Englands Mad Petition* (one of many such documents, as Sawday indicates, which have come down to us from this period) is drafted in the form of an address to Parliament, and argues, in Swiftian fashion, for the prompt enlargement of lunatic asylums in 'the cities of *London* and *Westminster*, with other cities, Towns, and Boroughs, throughout the kingdom', in order to accommodate the national madhouse into which England had been transformed by civil war. Primary examples of individual and national 'lunacie' are the denial and dismantling of natural affiliations derived from family relationships, local allegiances and a sense of neighbourhood: the ties of 'Proximity, Consanguinity, Affinity, Alliance, Christianity, Vicinity, or Naturall Affections' have all been destroyed, replaced by 'an (almost) universall lunacie and apostasie'.[4] Just as the individual, provoked to divide itself by melancholy or insanity, may in a moment of rebellion against the unified authority of the self, commit self-murder, so the unity and integrity of the nation may be destroyed by dividing itself against itself in 'intestine war' – and this latter, intestine war, may crucially affect the former, the unified authority of the self.

Nehemiah Wallington, in his handwritten *Historical Notices of Events Occurring Chiefly in the Reign of Charles 1*, tirelessly compiled reports and eye-witness accounts of royalist atrocities upon entering besieged cities: '*Exeter*, that famous city in the west, having for the space of three months defended themselves against the proud enemy', finally admit the royalist troops, who are 'more like tigers, or savage beasts, than humane men', says Wallington. (The comparison with wild animals is a recurring marker in these texts of a descent from full personhood and autonomy.) As they flagrantly 'swagger, roar, swear, and domineer, plundering, pillaging or doing any other kind of wrong' the townspeople are 'in such a miserable condition that they are even terrified to the death'.[5] Most of the military most of the time are drunk. At Cirencester, taken by royalists, the male inhabitants are either killed or carted to prison in Oxford prior to looting and pillaging. At the siege of Bristol 'these wild Cavaliering Rebels' break all their articles of peace and fall 'to plundering, pillaging, robbing, stealing, cutting, and slashing, as if they never had been brought up to any other practice' (2. pp. 175–7). The Londoner Wallington is a deeply committed puritan and parliamentarian for whom demonizing royalist armies and commanders was a routine rhetoric, but even he allows for the possibility that the invading troops, controlled by alcohol and avarice, are out of composition with their ordinary selves, '*as if* they had never been brought up to any other practice'. Even royalist diarists like Sir John Oglander and Henry Townshend, describing the war around Worcester, went so far as to acknowledge that parliamentarian soldiers were better regulated than royalists, whose looting invariably seemed to go unpunished. Townshend describes the looting and ravages of the royalist soldiers (especially Irish soldiery) at the siege of Worcester and prays that 'all good Christians may insert into their Litany. From the plundering of soldiers, their Insolency, Cruelty, Atheism, Blasphemy and Rule over us, *Libera nos Domine*' (p. 129).[6] Townshend also describes a characteristic Cavalier sortie at the siege of Worcester:

This morn about 5 of the clock Capt. Hodgkins, also called "Wicked Will" for his desperateness and valour, sallied out with 16 horse in a medley humour of drink into the enemy's Court of guard at St John's, shot one, and all came off safe, yet he so loaded with drink and top heavy that he fell twice by the way, and was carried over the Severn in a boat half asleep (p. 126).

Here civic unrest and anarchy is fascinatingly personalized, and the consequence of deranging oneself by drink recorded by Townshend in what appears to be a mixture of disgust at its irresponsibility and admiration at its indifference.

From royalists less clear-eyed than Townshend come frequent ridicule of the vulgarity and meanness of the men in the parliamentary armies and their names: according to Cowley, the colonels and majors of the parliamentarian army were nothing more than a riff-raff of tailors, butchers, dyers, tanners and sailors, fanatically zealous and hypocritically pious, socially and morally inferior, and a corrupting solecism both in the textual world of epic romance that he was constructing in his poem on the Civil War: 'What should I here their Great Ones Names reherse? / Low, wretched Names, unfit for noble Verse?' (*The Civil War*, III. 383–4)[7], and in the body politic of the nation. In similar vein John Taylor, the royalist 'water poet', published in 1642 his popular woodcuts depicting images of an upside-down world (horses whipping carts, rats chasing cats) which he called *Mad Fashions*, claiming that the depiction of such emblems 'plainly doth declare / This Land (Quite out of Order) out of Square'.[8]

From soldiers in uniform and in the field (rather than civilian commentators or poets) the diaries and journals that survive tend to be frustratingly factual and laconic, documenting a company's marches and quarterings, and receipt and disbursements of pay. 'Evaluative' or personal comments are usually about food, drink and weather. Captain Samuel Birch, for example, notes 'an extreamity of wet and foul wether and want of provisions ... A miserable time for the soldiers as I have seene at any time'. His diary entries are filled with nights spent in leaky barns 'quite without victualls, or any reliefe after a hard march', broken by the unexpected piece of good fortune: 'Before day or breakfast wee march't this morning away towards Cockermouth, which the enemy had close besieged, but hearing of our comeing, went hastily away, leaving their great gunne and some victualls behind, which the garrison seised'.[9] Captain Richard Atkyns gives a vivid account of the dangers of siege warfare, inflected with a lamentation over its waste:

> 'Twould grive one's heart, to see men drop like ripe fruit in a strong wind, and never see their enemy; for they had made loopholes through the walls, that they had the full bodies of their assailants for their mark, as they came down a plain field: but the assailants saw nothing to shoot at but mud walls, and must hit them in the eye, or lose their shot.[10]

Shooting the enemy in the eye may yet be easier than looking him in the eye. The 20-year-old Richard Symonds, in his *Diary of the Marches and Moovings of his Maties Royall Army, Himselfe being personally present*, coldly observes some captured parliamentarians:

> They all, except here and there an officer, (and seriously I saw not above three or four that looked like a gentleman), were stricken with such a dismal feare, that ... [they] presst all of a heape like sheep, though not so innocent. So durty and dejected as was rare to see. None of them, except some few of their officers, that did looke any of us in the face.[11]

The inability to look each other in the face is a subtle acknowledgement of a sense of personal derangement and inauthenticity. Parliamentarian moral outrage at the impiety and inhumanity of the enemy, royalist social outrage at the impropriety and arrogance of its enemy, a disgruntled and unpredictable military on both sides, and a universal distrust and fear of soldiers and their 'Rule over us', were all equally symptoms of a national insanity – an abandonment of the ideal order of national government and of self-government. Thus, like self-alienated individuals unable to contemplate their own fractured gaze in a mirror, even the soldiers cannot bear to look each other in the face.

Another frequent response to the 'maddest mad rebellion, / That ever story told' (as John Taylor also put it)[12], was one of pacific retreat – into Marvell's 'Garden of repose', or into one's own household and private life, or, like the irenic Lord Herbert of Cherbury, to retreat from London to one's castle in the Welsh marches. But the therapy of Marvell's garden only works by 'annihilating all that's made', while Richard Lovelace's 'The Snail', protectively within its own 'self curl'd', dies in its own tomb and dissolves in 'jelly', and, in political language less figurative but no less brutal, Lord Herbert is forced to yield up his castle to besieging parliamentarians to save his library from incineration. But for most inhabitants of English towns and cities the options for retreat were extremely limited anyway, and for very large numbers of citizens the primary experience of the Civil War was one of living in a city under siege and, by analogy, of living with a self under siege.

The focus here will be on the textual detritus, as it were, chiefly from two besieged cities, Gloucester and Exeter. The narratives and diaries, written by individuals within these cities, emphasize both in their textuality and in their recording of the voices of the participants, the crucial role of language in the conduct of these struggles. As is commonly observed in war, the first casualty is language: summonses and responses between besiegers and the besieged – the formal traffic between the parties – reveal a slippery rhetorical landscape of courtesies and goodwill mixed with threats, lies and deceit. Letters written to friends elsewhere convey the peculiar misery of civil war for individuals and families, and diurnal narratives catch the fear and disorientation which arbitrary military power induced in 'ordinary' citizens.

Summonses and Responses

The verbal pathways of demands to surrender and refusals to do so followed well-worn routes: from the besieging forces, boasts of superior fire power, the imminent arrival of massive reinforcements, conciliatory terms and conditions of surrender, and a plea to think of the welfare of the entrapped populace; from the besieged, defiance and resolution, and a dismissive critique of the terms of surrender. Tones of voice could vary between more-in-sorrow-than-in-anger, mock-humble politeness, hissing disdain, or rhetorical filibustering. For example, on 10 August 1643 heralds read out Charles's proclamation for the city of Gloucester to surrender, offering conciliatory terms 'out of our tender compassion to the city' but also dire warnings should they refuse and the city be taken by assault. After keeping the heralds waiting for four hours Sergeant Major Pudsey, accompanied by bookseller, councillor and future sheriff Tobias Jordan – representing military and civil authority in the city – returned a defiant reply which set the siege operations in motion. The text itself offered a 'humble answer' which claimed loyalty and obedience to the king but only as his orders were presented through Parliament. According to royalist historian Clarendon, Pudsey and Jordan were men of 'lean, pale, sharp and bad visages' whose weasel words were delivered 'without any circumstance of duty or good manner, in a pert, shrill, undismayed accent', revealing Clarendon's deep conviction that what was most at stake here was decent breeding, appropriate respect, and proper etiquette.[13] John Dorney, town clerk of Gloucester, put it differently, clearly perceiving the linguistic and

rhetorical dimension of siege warfare. His *A Briefe and exact Diurnall* of the siege
of Gloucester begins:

> After the unexpected surrender of Bristoll, the City of Gloucester was assaulted with
> several Letters, Messages, and such verbal solicitations, by divers in the Kings Army of
> no meane quality, thereby pretending our good, and expressions of their love and care of
> us, but really intending their own sinister ends and our destruction.[14]

Dornay sustains this sensitivity to games of language as he describes an attack by
the royalist Welsh regiment:

> The Welshmen ... had now at last gotten the heart to advance as far as the Towne Ham,
> where placing themselves in a ditch, they played upon our maides and workmen that
> were fetching turffs out of the little meade, but our great Gunne at the pen speaking
> some harsh language to them, frighted them away, bereaving some of their owne native
> language (p. 11).

In this satirical account, and employing the familiar 'device' of the speaking
cannon issuing irresistible words of truth, the cowardly non-English-speaking and
mercenary Welsh are so verbally assaulted they are unable to recall that primary
marker of both their community and their individual selfhood, their native tongue.

The exchanges at Exeter – initially held by Parliament, then by the royalists and
besieged by Parliament – between Sir John Berkley and Sir Thomas Fairfax in
January 1646 illustrate a more subtle level of discourse. Fairfax advises Berkley to
surrender, lists the terms and conditions, and warns Berkley not to delude 'those
poore people' with imaginary hopes of rescue by the king's army. Berkley tersely
replies, and points out the ambiguities and loopholes in the conditions of surrender.
Matters then become more heated and more personal. Fairfax replies that Berkley
has set 'too low an esteem upon those Propositions which are made to the Officers
and Gentlemen', that he does 'a little reflect on the Honour of the Parliament and
my own', and that he, Fairfax, shrugs off 'your low opinion ... of my
recommendation' and 'the smallness of my merit'. But Fairfax suggests to Berkley
that

> As I had power to give you a summons, so I believe it lyes also in my power to give
> souldiers souldierly conditions, and thus you have a Reply to all, because ... you
> mentioned Duty and Conscience, and forgot in your Answer (that which seemes to me
> as incumbent upon both, as any thing you have said) to wit, a due care of the Inhabitants
> of that poor and miserable place you are in, made so by fireing of so many of their
> Habitations, and those heavy pressures wherewith they have been so long burthened,
> and now the exposing them to the deprivation of their lives, and that little estate that is
> left them, that I say you should speak of conscience, and forget; this seemes very strange
> to mee. That your eyes may be opened, and they best provided for, is the wishe of, Your
> Servant, Fairfax.[15]

Such combinations of military threats, cynical derision, personal sniping, sarcasm, humanitarian and moral one-upmanship, as well as hard-headed pragmatism, mark most negotiations over the disposition of many English citizens' lives, property, and their selves. The potential of 'diplomatic' language, disposed to persuade and coerce, or, if unsuccessful, to vilify and shame, precisely replicates the role of the 'umpire' conscience in the individual, and is equally liable to corruption and abuse.

Letters from the War Zones

From the siege of Gloucester two letters survive written by the 22-year-old Henry Spencer, Earl of Sunderland, to his pregnant wife at home. Spencer describes the tedium of life in the trenches, where he is 'more solitary than ever I was in my life', and his commentary on the war around him is of the kind usually glossed by historians (especially perhaps military historians) as showing – as if there were some other side – the 'human side' of war. Certainly Lord Spencer's solitariness is largely the product of the fact that he is quartered in one of the 'little private cottages' of which this country, he says, is full, and where it is difficult to entertain or be entertained. (More lowly ranks, including the Welsh, are sleeping under hedges.) And his failure to mount up on this particular day is because, as he confesses to his wife, 'I have got such an angry pimple, or rather a kind of small bile, in such a place, that as I cannot ride without pain, so I cannot with modesty make a more particular description'. He contemplates the preparations for an imminent assault:

> Our gallery will be finished within this day or two, and then we shall soon dispatch our mine, and them with it. Many of the soldiers are confident that we shall have the town within this four days, which I extremely long for, not that I am weary of the siege; for really, though we suffer many inconveniences, yet I am not ill pleased at this variety, so directly opposite to one another, as the being in the trenches with so much good company, together with the noise and tinta-marre of guns and drums, the horrid spectacles and hideous cries of dead and hurt men, is to the solitariness of my quarter.[16]

Spencer compares public and private, military and domestic, interior and interactive worlds (as he does throughout the letter), but here his syntax is oddly confused, as if he is consoling himself with the fact that the camaraderie of the trenches and the prospect of blowing up the citizens of Gloucester will be a welcome relief from boredom but that it is probably not appropriate to say so.

Among the several letters and other documents from the sieges of 1642–43 at Exeter, many give rousing accounts of heroic resistance, with the usual scorn of the enemy's drunken sentries, anecdotes of humiliating surprisal of sleeping malignants, miraculous escapes from shot or grenadoes clearly directed by God to miss their mark, and of soldiers 'incompassed like wild beasts (whose nature they resemble)'.[17] But Lieutenant Hyworde writes more compassionately to his friend in

London, 2 January 1643, pointing up the difference between a battlefield and this kind of assault on civilian populations. He relates how he rode around at three in the morning to check on his sentries when an enemy pistol went off by accident, unleashing into the night a volley of carbine fire from the sentries, so that

> in a quarter of an houre the city was in a posture of defence, onely the cryes of women and children did so trouble us, that I professe I had rather oppose an enemy in the field, though with some disadvantage, then to endure that torment in a city most strongly fortified.[18]

A pamphlet entitled *Strange, true, and lamentable Newes from Exceter, And other parts of the Western countreyes* (London, 1643) rehearses the sufferings of the people under military rule and in the madness of the destruction of crops, livestock, orchards, houses and individuals, and its title page carries a woodcut of a kneeling, praying woman, her hair reaching down her back, simultaneously representing the county of Devonshire (the legend beneath her), the women of Devon, and an individual and particular suffering woman. From her mouth, affirming a patient providentialism, issue words from the afflictions of Job: 'Have pity upon me, Have pity upon me, O my friends, for the hand of God hath touched me' (see Fig. 6.1).

Siege Narratives

Most of the textual material surviving from Civil War sieges is the work of military commanders, propagandists, and members of the city or town elites. Only very rarely do we hear the voices of relatively humble or 'ordinary' people who had lived through the events described, and who recorded some of the effects of civic unrest on their sense of who and what they were. In an unusual manuscript document from the siege of Exeter valuable insight is given into the behaviour – ignoring ideology and difference – of people whose ties of relatedness and community defy arbitrary and invasive expressions of 'authority', and in which the authentic voices of Exeter women are reproduced, apparently verbatim. The manuscript relates the story of Dr John Whynell, minister of the church of St John's Bow, who refused to take a parliamentarian oath and was punished by the Roundhead authorities. He was taken before Lord Stamford, who 'gave him sharp reperamands and ordred hee shud be hanged [ther was a galos on Estgate on purpose to hang such as they disliked *(marginal note)*]' which the Doctor desired might not be till hee had been tried'. Stamford brusquely answered that 'hee had had Tryall enough', and Whynell is banished and dumped outside the city gates; orders are given to plunder his house, and 'it shud be death [to] whoever shud releve him or take him in'. His neighbours immediately 'secured all that was valeable over gardens backwards for him', and at night he was taken in by 'old Mrs Mathews, Mrs Burnell's grand mother' who 'said to him shee knew how twas with him but hee shud not lye in the streets but shee would entertaine him; hee was very unwilling shee shud run such a hasard but shee said shee did not care and made him come in that night'.

Fig. 6.1   Title page: *Strange, true, and lamentable Newes from Exceter, And other parts of the Western countryes*, **London, 1643**

In the meantime Dr Whynell's pregnant wife, trying to locate her husband, finds herself also locked out of the city. She is brutally interrogated by Major Baxster who 'held a musket to her brest [shee was big with child (*marginal note)*] telling her shee shud be shot if shee attemted to come in'. But Mrs Whynell later persuades some authorities to allow her to draw up a petition for her husband, and she is advised to take it to the Mayor who 'shud do what hee wood'. The hearing is vividly recorded as follows:

One Mr Clarke was Mayor, an honist king's man and her frend, who was willing to grant it and was seconded by Alderman Crosing: but Alderman White stood up and protested if it was so hee wood never more apeare thare: on which Mrs Weynell desired to know why hee was against the Doctor that had been old frends; and he said hee was a man that did more mischife than a littell armey and besides hee was against the Cause; so the Mayor called her aside [and told her] hee durst not press it for twas in thare power to serve him as they had the doctor but shee shud come another day on which My Lord Stamford wood be thare, which shee did but hee was not in Court but sent his secretery who sayed Doctor Weynell was limb of Anty-Christ for hee preached up sedition and was for popery and refused the oth, Ergo, hee was a limb of the Anty-Christ and Mrs Weynell tould him if that was all the proufe hee could bring, Ergo, hee was a fooll; this set the whole Court in to such a laughter as made him rune out.

This traumatic episode concluded happily for the Whynells though it did not of course for many others. The royalist attacks on the city 'grew so warme that the bullets came throw the curtens and was like to have murdred them'. Mrs Whynell's maid 'tooke up as many as shee could car[ri]e in her apron' and took them to Stamford who, realizing well enough the city could no longer hold out, 'tould the maid her Maister and Mistress might go whare they wood for securerety', so they joined the king's army at Heavitree and 'in a littell time the Ceety was taken and they returned to thare house'.[19]

The Exeter text here describes how antagonisms between citizens and military, and between the citizens themselves, are exacerbated in the claustrophobic confines of a besieged city. Insubordination, disobedience and even mutiny against the possibly temporary authority of occupiers, conducted sometimes with malicious glee, are an inevitable part of the experience of usurpation and siege. They are also frequently encountered among the soldiers themselves. Among those conscripted into parliamentarian or royalist armies as foot soldiers to execute their officers' commands there are frequent rumbles of discontent and even mutinies. Lord Spencer's resentment at being billeted in a cottage has its reverse image in the antagonism between officers and men expressed by private soldiers, complaining that common soldiers 'go very poor and thin in habit' and have a 'Dogs life hungry meales, Long marches, and hard Lodgings', while officers were well paid and comfortable. A voice purporting to speak for the common soldier complains that

it is not unknowne unto you what perills and danger we have under you duiring the whole warre, how we that are private souldiers are they who fought and conquered the Kingdome and yet our officers they have reaped the honor and profitt of all our enterprises and sufferings … they have been recompensed and rewarded and we continue still in our old condition of want and misery, and if we have gotten but a red coat which is a fools Livery we have thought our selves sufficiently rewarded and recompensed.[20]

The Souldiers Demand of 1649 appeals to 'all my fellow souldiers I meane especially the foot', and, resentfully conscious of the gap between ideology and actuality, asks 'whether we are not used more like beasts than men, like slaves than Christians and whether we that fight for the freedome and Liberty of the Subject are not the men that are most subjected to thralldome and slavery, having lost that our selves which we seek and laboure to obtain for others'.[21]

Such disillusionment issues finally in a deliberate collective forgetting (an Act of Oblivion) that the Great Rebellion, with its triumphs and defeats, its paradoxes and hypocrisies, ever happened. The desire for oblivion, for a national erasure of the memory of the 'loss of blood' of the Civil Wars, is a striking characteristic of the aftermath of the conflict. It has, for instance, been noted in an investigation of the scores of petitions for the relief of poor and maimed soldiers following the Act of 1662 how many of the ex-royalist officers and men scripted their petitions in such a way as to avoid unduly dignifying the recent conflict or asserting any ideological basis for it: their opponents are rarely called 'parliamentarians', scarcely ever even 'rebels', but simply 'the enemy' – that is, merely those designated as opponents. Major battles such as Edgehill, Marston Moor or Naseby are hardly alluded to and indeed the epic word 'battle' itself is scarcely ever employed to dignify events remembered, one supposes, only as messy and inglorious bloodbaths. The conflicts of 1642–51 are most usually referred to as 'the late Rebellious times', 'the late unhappy war' or 'the Troubles', at least one veteran feelingly referring to 'the late unnaturall and *un*civill warrs'. One memorializing ex-Cavalier went through his diary after the Restoration, crossing out the term 'rebels' and replacing it with 'parliamentarians' – though whether as an act of reconciliation or as an attempt at historical neutrality and distance is hard to say.[22]

The experience of dislocation, disinheritance and dispossession through war, civil or otherwise, is a universal one, from the Homeric epics to twentieth- and twenty-first-century examples too numerous and familiar to rehearse. We have tried to give some account here of what civic invasion and unrest meant to mid-seventeenth-century English communities and individuals and how it was expressed – in terms of madness, drunkenness, moral anarchy, the abandonment of right judgment, and the dismemberment both of social relations and the self – by those who experienced its effects and who wrote about it. The royalist captain Richard Atkyns, confused by defeat, and lousy with filthy bandages and suppurating wounds, wrote in his diary in 1643 (though innocent of what future scholars might want do with it) a sentence that resonates with the issues we are exploring here: 'I could not tell what to do with *my selfe*'.[23]

Notes

1 E.g., Peter Young and Wilfred Emberton, *Sieges of the Great Civil War, 1642–1646* (London: Bell & Hyman, 1978); Christopher Duffy, *Siege Warfare: The Fortress in the Early Modern World, 1494–1660* (London: Routledge and Kegan Paul, 1979); Mark P. Donnelly and Daniel Diehl, *Siege: Castles at War* (Dallas, Tex.: Taylor Pub. Co., 1998).

2 E.g., in many of the studies in collections such as: *Representations of the Self from the Renaissance to Romanticism*, ed. Patrick Coleman, Jayne Lewis and Jill Kowalik (Cambridge: Cambridge University Press, 2000); *Betraying Our Selves: Forms of Self-Representation in Early Modern English Texts*, ed. Henk Draghsta, Sheila Ottway and Helen Wilcox (London: Macmillan; New York: St. Martin's, 2000); *Early Modern Autobiography: Theories, Genres, Practices*, ed. Ronald Bedford, Lloyd Davis and Philippa Kelly (Ann Arbor: University of Michigan Press, 2006).

3 Richard Helgerson, *Forms of Nationhood: The Elizabethan Writing of England* (Chicago: University of Chicago Press, 1992), pp. 105–47.

4 Jonathan Sawday, '"Mysteriously divided": Civil War, Madness and the Divided Self', in *Literature and the English Civil War*, ed. Thomas Healy and Jonathan Sawday (Cambridge: Cambridge University Press, 1990), pp. 127–43. The anonymous *Englands Mad Petition* (London, 1647) is in British Library, Thomason Tracts, E.404 (30).

5 Nehemiah Wallington, *Historical Notices*, ed. R. Webb, 2 vols (London: Richard Bentley, 1869), 2. pp. 174–5.

6 Sir John Oglander, *A Royalist's Notebook*, ed. F. Bamford (London: Constable, 1936), pp. 117–19; *The Diary of Henry Townshend ... 1640–1663*, ed. J.W. Willis Bund (Worcestershire Historical Society, 1915–20), vol. 1, p. 139. See also Donald Pennington, 'The War and the People', in *Reactions to the English Civil War, 1642–1649*, ed. John Morrill (London: Macmillan, 1982), pp. 115–35.

7 *Abraham Cowley, Poetry and Prose*, ed. L.C. Martin (Oxford: Clarendon Press, 1949).

8 John Taylor, *Mad Fashions, Old Fashions, All out of Fashions* (London, 1642). Sawday, p. 129.

9 'A true and perfect account of the receipts and disbursements of Captaine Samuel Birch', May 15 1648 – April 2 1650. Historical Manuscripts Commission, series 29. vol. 3 (London: HMSO, 1891–1931), pp. 174, 177.

10 Atkyns, diary entry for 25 April 1643, *The Vindication of Richard Atkyns Esquire* (1669), ed. Peter Young, in *Military Memoirs: The Civil War* (London: Longmans, 1967).

11 Symonds, Add.MSS BL, 17062. Edited by Charles Edward Long as *Diary of the Marches of the Royal Army during the Great Civil War, kept by Richard Symonds* (London: Camden Society, MDCCCLIX).

12 John Taylor, *Mad Verse, Sad Verse, Glad Verse, and Bad Verse* (London, n.d.), BL, Thomason Tracts, E.46 (i3). Quoted in Sawday, p. 129.

13 Malcolm Atkin and Wayne Laughlin, *Gloucester and the Civil War: A City Under Siege* (Stroud, Glos.: Alan Sutton), pp. 47–8; Edward Hyde, 1st Earl of Clarendon, *History of the Rebellion and Civil Wars in England*, ed. W.D. Macray (Oxford, 1888), vol. VII, pp. 297–8.

14 John Dorney, *A Briefe and exact Diurnall, Containing the most materiall and Remarkeable passages that happened in the late well formed Siege laid before the City of Gloucester* (London, 1643), p. 1.

15 Fairfax's first letter, BL; TT, E.320.18; 'Perfect Occurrences of Parliament', 30 January

to 6 February 1646; Berkley's reply, BL; TT, E.320.21; 'Special and Remarkable Passages', 30 January to 6 February 1646; Fairfax's response, BL; TT, E.320.22; 'Mercurius Veridicus', 25 January to 1 February 1646. The correspondence is reproduced in Mark Stoyle, *The Civil War Defences of Exeter and the Great Parliamentary Siege of 1645–46* (Exeter: Exeter Museums Archaeological Field Unit, 1990).

16 Letters first printed in 1819 in T.D. Fosbrooke, *An Original History of the City of Gloucester* (Gloucester, 1819; reprinted 1986). The letters are also reproduced in Atkin and Laughlin, *Gloucester and the Civil War*, pp. 171–2.

17 E.g., 'True and Joyfull Newes from Exeter', November 1642, BL, TT. E.128 (11); printed in Mark Stoyle, *Documentary Evidence for the Civil War Defences of Exeter, 1642–43* (Exeter: Exeter Archaeology, 1992), pp. 53–5.

18 'A Famous Victory Obtained before the city of Exeter', BL, TT. E.84 (24); Stoyle, *Documentary Evidence*, p. 57.

19 Bodleian Library, J. Walker MSS, C.2, ff.252-252v. Reproduced for the first time in Stoyle, *Documentary Evidence*, pp. 60–61.

20 'Pay provision and good accomadation for the privat Soldiers' (in manuscript), BL E.537 (8).

21 *The Souldiers Demand* (Bristol, 1649), BL E.555 (29). The above quotations are cited from Brian Manning's 'Military *Coup d'Etat* and Army Mutinies in England, 1648–1649', in *Men, Women and War*, ed. T.G. Fraser and Keith Jeffery (Dublin: The Lilliput Press, 1993), pp. 28–55.

22 Charles Carlton, *Going to the Wars: The Experience of the British Civil Wars 1638–1654* (London: Routledge, 1992), p. 346.

23 Richard Atkyns, *Vindication*, p. 26.

PART 4
Women and Life-Writing

Chapter 7

A Gendered Genre: Autobiographical Writings by Three Early Modern Women

'My father could not abide to see a woman unstable or light in her carriage, to hold her head one way and her hands another and her feet a third way, her eyes tossing about in every place and the features of her face disfigured by evil countenances,' writes Lady Grace Mildmay in the later life autobiography that she wills to her grandchildren (1617). 'But he liked a woman well graced with a constant and settled countenance and good behaviour throughout her whole parts, which presenteth unto all men a good hope of an established mind and virtuous disposition to be in her.'[1] Thus emerges an impeccable image of Grace Mildmay herself, a seventeenth-century English gentlewoman with exemplary physical and social containment – perfectly ordered, nothing out of place, all of her features and gestures suggesting a composite harmony.[2] In a patriarchal society – one in which many woman read but did not write, and in which a woman's writings were sometimes managed by a male editorial hand[3] – Lady Grace's voice is strong, bolstered by the confidence that she is writing for the glory of God. Repeatedly seeking for her words to be 'approved', she turns first to God – 'This book of mine is the consolation of my soul, the joy of my heart and the stability of my mind, as they are approved by the word of God' (p. 25) – and then to her descendants: '[T]here is nothing [which] hath happened unto me in the course of my life ... but the like may fall out to some other, wherein my comforts and remedies may be approved unto them as they have been unto me' (p. 25).

Anticipating at every turn her temporal and divine audiences, Lady Grace's autobiography bears the constant weight of biblical allusions and instructional purposes, so that any search for psychological inwardness, in consequence – for a sense of *who* she was as an individual – yields little more than a patchwork of formalized commonplaces. To simply call such discourse 'autobiography' or 'life-writing' raises intriguing and complicated questions. What motivates this gentlewoman, at an advanced age, to record the events of her life? What does she intend her readers to see? Strained by the freight of worldly and eternal concerns, how do her words reveal, or conceal, elements that we might deem 'autobiographical'? And a larger question hovers over these particulars: how might this private, upper-class gentlewoman speak, if at all, to the category, 'early modern Englishwoman'?

People's lives are, and always have been, subject to interpretation through conjecture. This is even more the case with the lives of early modern women because of their culturally encoded silence.[4] In the effort to tease out the socially quieted voices of women living four hundred years or so ago, approaches have been made from many different places, including the liberties and permissions granted by gendered identity[5] and, more specifically, by gendered writing, which, in devotional contexts, associates supplication with a conventionally feminine narrative stance;[6] analyses of the socially constructed meanings of women's deaths;[7] discussions of childbirth,[8] work[9] and literacy,[10] as well as attempts to discern a voice amongst the many women who could neither read nor write.

Amidst the huge wealth of material by early modern women that could possibly direct our attention, and an even more dizzying variety of possible critical perspectives, this chapter takes as its main subject a rather modest selection consisting of three well-known female diarists: Lady Grace Mildmay, Lady Margaret Hoby and Lady Anne Clifford[11], in the discussion of whose writings we will reflect on the lives of many other women's life-writings in order to expand or elaborate on points of analysis. At face value the primary focus on Mildmay, Clifford and Hoby might seem quite conservative, given that these great ladies have already been abundantly written about, and that they were all three women of similar class: all manifestly had sufficient literary skills and leisure to write about themselves, while Hoby and Clifford were in fact cousins.[12] We have chosen these three women largely *because* they form a nexus of established critical interest (and, indeed, in the case of Mildmay we have used Linda Pollock's skillfully edited selection of her writings rather than the more unwieldy original facsimile that is less familiar to scholars). Our purpose is not to uncover new, un-talked-about women about whom to write, but rather to examine new possibilities for writings widely acknowledged as exemplary artifacts from the period. In Mildmay's case we will refer to the conduct literature – highly formulaic, instructional and narrowly focused – from which she took guidance, examining her writings against the established 'godlie' template for ethical self-regulation. Contemporary seventeenth-century conduct literature can thereby serve as a kind of palimpsest that enables us to contemplate 'self-representation' in terms of the strict moral, educational, generational and social guidelines that Mildmay sets for herself. The running diaries left by Lady Margaret Hoby and Lady Anne Clifford make fascinating studies against the backdrop of Lady Grace's autobiography, enabling us to juxtapose various forms of life-writing (memoir, running diary, secular diary, and so on) and the modes of spiritual and secular composition they employed in the commitment of 'self' to paper.

In short, we could say that if Mildmay's autobiography is driven by the will for a composite, strictly structured harmony between the world she is soon to leave and the eternal realm toward which her attention is directed, Lady Margaret Hoby's diary measures her struggle toward this harmony, which remains, day by day, an aspiration yet to be satisfactorily accomplished. Lady Margaret meticulously details her daily deeds, the record of which calibrates her relationship with God. While Lady Grace's retrospective memoir continually reiterates her worthiness before God, Lady Margaret's running diary provides an anxious daily reckoning. Looking further to the diaries of Lady Anne Clifford, her entries share certain aspects of both the retrospective memoir and the running diary: her record runs from year to year, although in her last years she peppers her daily remarks with retrospections of earlier events, with an eye to their coincidental (and monumental) significance.

A discussion principally directed toward these three diarists will allow us to address a variety of relationships between words and self-identity. Why these women chose the literary forms they did; how they refer to themselves, colouring their writings with active and passive constructions; how they envisaged temporal and eternal existence; what elements of godliness defined aspiring selfhood in an unavoidably temporal mode of expression; and what aspects of their lives they thought worth recording: such are the features that define how, and in what ways, they approached the notion of self-identity and individuation. We are thus able to find out more about how these women derived, and expressed, autobiographical expressions of themselves as individuals, as well as how the many other women who emerge in the course of our discussion might be portrayed beside (and before, and behind) them.

Invoking a Blueprint

'There is nothing that hath so much power to poison the world as the press,' says Joseph Hall, Bishop of Norwich,

> which is able, in one day's warning, to scatter an heresy over the whole face of the earth. In the times of our forefathers, when every page and line was to pass the leisure and pains of a single pen, books were geason [scarce] and, if offensive, could not so easily light into many hands to work a speedy mischief. Error, that could but creep then, doth now fly, and in a moment cuts the air of several regions... we have reasons to rue the inconveniences that have followed upon the abuses of this so beneficial a practice. For, as all men are apt to write their own fancies, so they have, by this means [of print], had the opportunity to divulge their conceits to all eyes and ears: whence it hath come to pass, that those monstrous opinions, which had been fit only to be condemned to perpetual darkness, have at once both visited and infected the public light ... Never age or nation hath had more cause to cry out of this mischief than this age of ours.[13]

Written in 1640, Hall's words give shape to the fears that grew along with the expansion of print culture. Acknowledging in all men the impulse for some kind of life-writing or self-expression ('all men are apt to write their own fancies'), he sees the press as turning such fancies from private self-gratification to devilish proliferation. Important for this discussion is firstly the acknowledgement of private life-writing as an impulse and a practice; and secondly the counsel not to cancel out such fancies, but to curb their distribution. These fancies are, Hall ruefully acknowledges, an unfortunate part of human nature, and should be designated to darkness as to a latrine – it is only when aired that they spread infection. Against the judicious singularity of his forefathers' careful pens, therefore, Hall counterbalances the 'mischief[s]' wrought by those who facilitate easy distribution; to the former he ascribes the word of God, while to the latter he attributes the spread of 'monstrous opinions'.

Lady Grace's autobiography contributes to the war about words that accelerates, in the early seventeenth century, toward Hall's gloomy conclusions. The autobiography follows in the tradition of 'godlie' books, developed amongst Puritan gatekeepers as a counterweight to the corrupting influence of secular publications. As increasing numbers of women – many of whom could read even if they did not write – had access to printed matter, such 'godlie' books were designed to confirm right conduct as well as right relations between husbands and wives, parents and children, masters and servants, matrons and maids.[14] The main focus of instruction was the 'weake sexe' of womankind, which required firm direction.[15] 'I would haue her if she reade,' says Thomas Salter, 'to reade no other bookes but suche as bee written by godlie fathers, to our instruction and soules healthe, and not suche lasciuious Songes, filthie Ballades, and undecent bookes as be moste commonly now a daies sette to sale, to the greate infection of youth' (p. 39). The words of such fathers were divine instruments, able to 'delight' women *and* to 'pricke and incite their hartes, to follow vertue, and haue vice in horror and disdaine, yea their mindes ... wilbe come noble and magnanimous thereby' (p. 23). Lady Grace's intention is in concert with these opinions: she desires that 'whosoever readeth them [her words] may make good use of them, especially seeing they shall find every point of doctrine confirmed and approved by the scriptures' (p. 24).

Against the proliferation of idle words, then, Lady Grace adds her own trenchant voice, avowing the indisputable word of God. '[B]ooks of idle plays' she sees as 'fruitless and unprofitable matter which will pervert and carry the mind from all goodness and is an introduction to all evil' (p. 24). At the outset of her autobiography she declares that she will never 'receive any doctrine from men which proceedeth not from God according to the truth of his word in all sanctity and true holiness' (p. 23). Words provide a direct connection between God's will and earthly acts; and the task of humankind is to defend them against abuse and misapprehension. It is to this purpose that her own words are dedicated; and she describes her clear intention to map 'the best course to set ourselves in from the beginning to the end of our lives', alluding to the need to understand, and to be obedient to, the laws of God and 'the chronicles of the land' (p. 23).

Continuing in line with the slew of advice literature that painted poor conduct as the result of weak (female) wills, idleness and bad company[16], Lady Grace counsels careful guidance from the ground upward. On the topic of the raising of children she writes:

it cometh to pass too often and too universally that the minds of children are tainted and corrupted, even from their infancy, and made capable of every lewd and evil conversation and are made impudent and bold without all shame ... Many gentlemen and their wives are desirous to place their sons and daughters in honourable services; ...but they take no care to furnish their minds with true religion and virtue and other good parts fit for such preferment. (p. 25)

Only after briskly laying out the groundwork for childhood education in general does Lady Grace introduce her particular childhood self, and she mentions it not for its rendering of a specific set of circumstances (as one might expect, for example, of a memoir written today), but for its illustration of general precepts for childraising. She first mentions her much-loved governess, who instructed herself and her sisters as to the proprieties of mind and spirit:

I had experience of a gentlewoman ... brought up by my mother from her childhood, whom afterwards she trusted to be governor over her own children ... she made good use of all things that ever she did read, see, or hear and observed all companies that ever she came in, good or bad, so that she could give a right answer and true judgment of most things and give wise counsel upon any occasion. (pp. 25–6)

The description of her governess's excellent work in preparing herself and her two sisters for adulthood (though one of her two sisters died before reaching maturity) falls strictly in line with the counsel meted out by various conduct authors of the time: the avoidance of evil or unproductive company, the severe judgment of husbands and wives who show 'impudent behaviour one towards another' (p. 27), and the development of skills in needlework, singing and the like.[17] She then moves on to a description of her father's dictates for behaviour. Her father, Sir Henry Sherrington – who served as sheriff of Wiltshire from 1566 to 1567 and was knighted by Queen Elizabeth in 1574 – had 'a diligent eye over us, observing us in all our words and actions' (p. 30). He was seen by Lady Grace 'with his own hands ... [to] scourge a young man naked from the girdle upwards, with fresh rods, for making but a show and countenance of a saucy and irreverent behaviour towards us his children' (p. 28). Sir Henry's attention to the spiritual propriety of his children's upbringing was matched by that of his wife, all of whose counsels have been 'laid up in my mind, almost these fifty years' (p. 29). Every morning, Lady Grace recalls, her mother 'would withdraw herself alone and spend an hour in meditation and prayers to God, with her face all blubbered with tears' (p. 29). Such tears, her mother believed, 'did never break the beauty of a woman', and she instructed her daughters to reserve them for this purpose alone: 'she counselled me never to weep but for my sins' (p. 29).

The Meaning of Time Past

Recalling the means by which, in writing his diary, Thomas Whythorne lays out an ongoing dialogue between himself, his ancestors and his descendants, Lady Grace deftly inserts her own advent into her narrative, building the picture of her youthful self as the product of excellent principles and precepts. Lady Grace's autobiography attests to the value of 'familiar talk and communication' with her children and grandchildren, affirming her desire – as with the portrait of the gentleman-tutor Thomas Whythorne discussed in Chapter 1, in which the self is assembled in terms of moral and social generalities – to pass on to her descendants the meaning gleaned from her own life, 'I being dead, as if I were alive' (p. 24). However, the apparent purposes and motivations of Whythorne and Lady Grace Mildmay in this respect are very different. In Whythorne's text, familiar biblical phrases accumulate with items of communally agreed secular wisdom to convey a deep-seated understanding of identity as providentially disposed; and yet all of these commonplaces serve an immediate struggle to bridge the gap between his socially determined role as tutor and his ambitions to be a gentleman. In the interest of gentrification he has his portrait painted more than once over several years, expressing the general curiosity of those who 'did cause their pictures or counterfeits to be painted from time to time to see how time doth alter them'.[18] He also notes the importance of portraits for descendants who, 'though their fathers be dead, yet may they see what manner of favour they had' (p. 115). Whythorne's interest in his altered reflection is symptomatic of his fervent concern with his own potential for social mobility. Within a socially and theologically determined realm whose temporal paradigms are imprinted on every individual, he struggles with the identity he has inherited, seeking to measure its very nature and the extent of his own autonomy.

Everywhere in Whythorne's autobiography we can sense a measure of uneasy self-scrutiny: in his attentiveness to the marks of temporal life upon his face, for example; in his noticing of the temporal effect of certain actions ('from time to time,' 'for the time present'); and in his curiosity about how his descendants will view him after he is dead. His interest in an autobiographical self, then, could be seen as a somewhat *restless* acquiescence in the 'larger plot', the predicated temporal backdrop that marks the passage of individuals toward that place that has no need to mark the time. Lady Grace Mildmay's purpose in writing an autobiography is almost exactly the other way around. The larger framework of the generational continuum to which she constantly alludes provides a justification for her own life-writing, as well as a reassuring blueprint to which she willingly defers in piecing together the details of her narrative. Her attention is directed not toward these details, but toward the blueprint itself. '[T]he Lady le Despencer, hath endowed you with her ancient and noble blood,' she writes to her granddaughter, Mildmay Fane. 'Preserve that blood unspotted evermore as she hath done, chaste and upright in all her virtuous conversation from her youth unto her old age' (p. 43). Such is Lady Grace's own purpose: justifying her memoir through her duty to memorialize the venerable conduct of her ancestors and to pass down their counsel to her descendants, she records her own life as a commendable part of this God-fearing lineage. And in the very ordinariness of her reflections, strung together as they are through biblical allusions and the sage commonplaces that she draws from the conduct literature of her time, she reflects the entire lineage of worthy individuals within its proper larger picture, which is 'a testimony of the love and presence of God', a God who will 'be with them forever and increase and multiply the gifts of his holy spirit in them'. Her memoir thus provides a means of ordering both the retrospective and proleptic dimensions of her life, documenting 'the perfection of a good life in this world and everlasting blessedness in the kingdom of heaven' (p. 24).

If we compare Lady Grace's project to Whythorne's, then, there is a marked difference in emphasis. His writing emerges as often whimsical and self-reflexive: he assesses his own reflection as the record of clean living, for example, and, at various points, looks back on his experiences as having prompted acts of creativity ('wherefore to ease my heart I wrote as followeth'; 'whereupon I made this sonnet following'). Like a curator at the door of a museum, in contrast, Lady Grace introduces us to her life, proffering her age and experience as the correct vantage point for examining its value. Framed by the wisdom of her antecedents, her time on earth, she suggests, aptly illustrates the precepts for ideal conduct. And here resides the paradox of Lady Grace's spiritual journey. Those who have gone before her are revered pillars at the forefront of her narrative, models of rectitude to be admired and imitated; yet while they constitute her gauge, her guides, and her community, they are *also* forever part of that frail humanity beyond which she strives to rise in a biblically paraphrastic conversation with God that is both personal and paradigmatic: 'What have I gained by the troubles of my whole life, even that which I have learned: (that is to say) to put no confidence in man nor in any child of man, nor in any earthly things which are all changeable and uncertain … [T]here is no truth in them' (p. 39). Constantly underscored by passages from the Bible, her narrative seems to insist that the record of her life – and of all lives past and future – remains ultimately with God, and that to record her life at all is not just a temporal event but an eternal one.

It is this understanding of the eternal within the temporal that grants plausibility to an account that appears, at times, willfully misrepresentational. As we will see in the section following, the author practices a willful concealment or 'alternative construction' of events because it is the *template* of the past that is essential to her own literary self-expression, requiring all who visit its pages to accept the conditions of the time-honoured model on which she draws. And this is a strong mark of early modern Protestant women's life-stories – those written by them and on their behalf – in which the self-assertion permitted by the narrative form necessitates self-effacement, a constantly remarked-upon subjection to God's design that becomes, in effect, the 'statement' of selfhood.[19]

In this respect, a classic companion to Lady Grace might be provided by the *Examinations* left by Anne Askew, edited and 'elucidated' by John Bale (see note 3), three quarters of a century before Lady Grace herself wrote. The *Examinations* leave a record of a female martyr who was tried, sentenced and put to death for her religious convictions in the reign of Henry VIII. In response to doctrinal inquisition, Askew suggests that as a mere woman she has no business in offering responses. While women should reflect prevailing male opinion, she argues, it is not the business of a woman to reflect *upon* this opinion: 'I told him I was but a woman and knew not the course of scoles'. In so doing Askew mobilizes the constraints of femininity – expectations of silence and obedience – in attempting to escape patriarchal jurisdiction.[20] (Bale supplements this argument in his belief that God inspired Anne Askew to resist her Catholic aggressors through the fact that woman's weakness make them fertile sites for the workings of His grace.)

While Askew's *Examinations* provide a more extreme example of a woman's 'statement' of strength as embedded in inculturated inferiority, more conventionally aligned to the life of Lady Grace is that of the 'godly, religious and virtuous' Elizabeth Wallington, a woman who did not write her own life-story, but who, after her holy death in November 1603, was described by her husband as

> very loving and obedient to her parents, loving and kind to her husband, very tender hearted to her children, much affecting the sincere preachers of God's Word, loving all that were godly, much misliking the wicked and profane. She was a pattern of sobriety unto many; very seldom was seen abroad, except at church; when others recreated themselves on holidays and other times, she would take her needlework and say, 'here is my recreation'. She was of fine inventions for drawing works, and other choice works, and many a fine and neat piece of work hath she soon dispatched, she would so apply [to] it; besides a very good judgment in setting out works in colours, either for birds or flowers. God had given her a pregnant wit and an excellent memory. She was very rife and perfect in all the stories of the Bible, likewise in all the stories of the Martyrs, and could readily turn to them; she was also perfect and well seen in the English Chronicles, and in the Descents of the Kings of England. She lived in holy wedlock with the Husband of her youth twenty years wanting but four days.

> These are the glories of a worthy praise,
> Which of this virtuous woman now are read,
>   In honour of her life and latter days,
>   To number her among the blessed dead.[21]

Elizabeth Wallington's qualities are considered worthy of itemization by her husband – and of preservation by her son, Nehemiah Wallington, in a document entitled, 'A Faithfull Memoriall of my owne Mother that is deceased' – not because of their particulars (which are, after all, thoroughly conventional in their laudability), but because of their conformity to precepts of female godliness, restraint and obedience. As with Lady Grace's account of herself, in the account of Elizabeth Wallington rendered by her husband the female self is styled as an imprint of God's will, and the narrative account delivers her life back into the hands of its maker.

The Gendering of Spiritual Identity

The imprint of God's will in such representations is complicated by gender, however. For both male and female autobiographers of the time, spiritual identity depicts a feminized union between body and soul. This union is fundamental to the understanding of gender, and, indeed, to the gendering of religious understanding. Firstly, the privacy of devotion is seen as commensurate with woman's 'natural' private space, the home, and the attitude of supplication with her 'naturally' gendered piety.[22] 'My beloved is as a bundle of myrrh unto me, he shall lie between my breasts,' says Lady Grace, echoing the Song of Solomon.[23] 'His mouth is as sweet things and he is wholly delectable' (p. 79).[24] 'Oh, let my wellbeloved lay his left hand under my head and with his right hand let him embrace me' (p.75).[25] The sexualization of devotional language grants to women a certain power: their 'naturally' passive role and demeanour serves as a model for mortals who seek unity with God.[26] Thus we see men, as well as women, expressing themselves as wedded to God with the lavish adoration of a corporeal lover. Henry Constable asks, 'Give me then purity instead of power, / And let my soul, made chaste, pass for a maid.'[27] Male devotional poetry of this period – in Donne, George Herbert, Herrick, Crashaw – is deeply and famously informed by a willing displacement of gender. Confirming the feminization of Donne's 'Batter my heart' sonnet, Bishop Joseph Hall, quoting Matthew 5.6, 'Blessed are they which hunger and thirst after righteousness: for they shall be filled', praises the God who 'ravishest my soul' (p. 547), while in a more domestic context Richard Rogers writes of the premarital years in which 'sighes and plaints' to God 'were more sweet to me than hony', lamenting, since his marriage, the loss of time and space for communing with God.[28] God is encountered as an implicitly masculine lover, adored by all scribes, masculine and feminine.

But if on the one hand femininity provides a natural posture for devotion, on the other hand God's lineage is structured on a gendered hierarchy. Seventeenth-century women's writings are marked by adoration for God, *as well as* for God-in-man. From the heavens, God rules over everything; but on earth, man is the arbiter of God's will unless he is drawn by earthly lusts from his native judgment. Learning from man 'with silence, and all subjection' is a woman's earthly place, says Lady Grace in her autobiography. 'Let not a woman teach,' she writes, paraphrasing St Paul to Timothy (1 Timothy 2.11–12), 'neither usurp authority over the man, but be in silence' (p .45). Men's good opinion, indeed, signals her seriousness and virtue: 'I was ever beloved of all good men, and conversed most with them, and that was the gracious gift of God who also kept all wicked company from me' (p. 39). In this she is joined by a chorus of 'godlie' voices supported by Pauline authority. Man's 'superioritie and authoritie' is derived directly from God, says William Gouge, for example,[29] the true husband upon whom a woman's first 'hopes and desires' are fixed, and 'the sweet Bridegroom' of a woman's soul.

Early in her manuscript, Lady Grace offers a description of the two key men in her life. She begins with a lengthy description of Sir Walter Mildmay, her husband's father: his excellence in grace, humility and fidelity to the Queen, and his 'unspotted carriage' within his family (p. 32). This, and the 'extraordinary love and favour' that he showed toward herself in her 'tender youth', frames the noticeably low-key introduction of her marriage: from Sir Walter's proposition, to his son's (Sir Anthony's) unwillingness to enter into marriage, to his father's promises of financial rewards, to Sir Anthony's capitulation, it takes exactly six sentences for Lady Grace to document her difficult pathway toward marriage. This pathway is striking not just for its brevity, but also for the author's seeming unwillingness to inflect her narrative with any judgments or conclusions: Lady Grace simply recalls waiting while Sir Walter cajoles and bribes his son. After the wedding is completed, however, she finds herself living not on the substantial sums of money he has promised along with the gift of 'a posie in my wedding ring ... "Let thy faith remain inviolate"' (p. 33), but as a penniless member of his household. While it was common among the aristocracy for a newly married couple to live as guests of the groom's parents for a few months or even a few years, Lady Grace – living, with her husband, on a combined allowance of 130 pounds per year to cover their clothing as well as the cost of personal servants and other household needs – was kept in this situation for the next twenty years. Her husband remained at large for at least half of each year.

It is disconcerting to read Lady Grace's description of these events, less because of the events themselves than because of the manner in which she depicts them. She pays no attention to Sir Walter's breach of promise beyond the simple mention of it; nor does she express puzzlement at having had to establish herself largely alone in his house. These are merely difficulties to be overcome by her dutiful regard: to her husband she expresses a commonplace scriptural loyalty ('I carried always that reverent respect towards him,' [p. 41]), while Sir Walter is recalled as a man of 'clear judgment and true grounded discerning of whatever he spake of' (p. 31). Her wonderment is directed at the dexterity with which her husband manages to travel so extensively on the meagre allowance given by his father. Any exercise of ethical, or even social, judgment is overlaid by gratitude toward the divine providence that has guided her husband's choices in adversity: 'But God who can make a little go far put into his mind to remember, a time to spare and a time to spend, which he did observe in all his expenses, wherein God reserved a blessing for the future times' (p. 33).

In depicting the complications of her marital situation, Lady Grace neatly triangulates her relationship to God, husband and father-in-law. Her marriage is couched in the typical terms articulated in the Bible[30]: 'the husband is the wive's head, even as Christ is the head of the church and the son is the saviour of his body. Therefore as the church is in subjection unto Christ, even so let the wives be to their husbands in every thing' (p. 44). Of her husband, Sir Anthony, she notes more particularly that 'I have observed an extraordinary favour of God toward him divers ways wherein appeared the love, mercy and protection of God over him' (p. 41). Yet the success of her particular domestic situation requires that God be invested in the head of her household as well.[31] Despite her father-in-law's parsimony, therefore, she says, 'I thought myself in the house of God all the time of my abode with my father-in-law, for that no evil company was permitted to resort to his house nor to appear in his presence, whereby I was preserved from the sight or hearing of evil' (p. 34).

Lady Grace's interpretation of her home life is fascinating for the way in which she manages to contrive a devotional frame for her 'self' and its 'life'. It is clear that the story of her life is not motivated by familiar modern-day sensibilities, the interest of which is likely to be, for example, in the revelation of her own, or her husband's, or her father-in-law's, psychology. Rather, her struggle is to match the events and relationships in her life to the proportions of godly living. And it is this feature – the way in which she subordinates a highly neglectful situation (an absent husband, a shallow and mean-minded father-in-law) to the requirements of her spiritual journey – that permits some access to *who* Lady Grace is. As we suggested in the introduction to this chapter, she sees herself as first and foremost an exemplary Christian figure, and wishes to contribute this fact to an ongoing communication with future generations. To this end, the all too evident shortcomings of the Mildmay men are remarked upon, but not puzzled over, because their function is representational rather than revelatory. While Lady Grace declares the primacy of both men in her life, they have only a figurative connection to the consummate narrative of her relationship with God. 'The goodness of the Lord ... hath ever followed me so from time to time ... [and] is worthy to be remembered of me and all that discerned of me, from one generation to another,' she says, adding to the generational mix an ancient strain of Psalm 100. 5: 'For the Lord is good; his mercy is everlasting; and his truth endureth to all generations' (p. 85). Her childhood reminiscences are also enfolded into this pattern. Her father's beating of the servant who displays 'saucy and irreverent' behaviour, for example, is of interest not for what it reveals about her father, but for the model it provides of a godly upbringing. The origins and ends of devout conduct she wishes future generations to heed lie in the conviction that, from infancy, it is God who is at the centre of all things, and that 'the greatest love in earthly parents is but hatred in comparison of the love of God to his children' (p. 34).

Spiritual Identity and Double Time

In narrating the events of her life in this way, Lady Grace links her identity to the awareness of 'double time' that was described in Part One. The various events of her temporal life are mentioned as points of absorption into the reality that *matters*: the union with God that goes beyond time. This is the reality that she derives through her own lineage, and that she, in turn, bequeaths to her descendants. Indeed, *not* to bequeath it would be a mark of gross spiritual failure. Lady Grace's material life, it should be noted, is very much taken up with financial matters: the shortfall in the funds promised by Sir Walter and the paltry inheritance that Sir

Anthony receives from him; the expectation of inheritance from her own father, broken at the very last moment by his rewriting of his will under the persuasions of her sister; the recovery of the original will, the battle with her sister to have this former will validated, and the getting together of a dowry for her daughter, which is complicated by the parsimony of her deceased father and father-in-law. In all of this, however, the devoutness of her path remains central. She is the servant, and the supplicant, of God, patiently expecting the bounty that runs through, and beyond, the events of this world, and discerning in the apparent arbitrariness of temporal life an enduring divine wisdom. Having been taught from her childhood days to 'look for troubles, which appertaineth to all the children of God' (p. 28), she sees adversity as an opportunity, given by God, to be resourceful: 'There was never any thing more blessed unto me in this life than mine afflictions and trials which were never greater than God enabled me to bear' (p. 39). Keeping this in mind, her gift of a dowry to her daughter without any care for her own straitened means provides evidence of faith in 'the abundance of God's blessing' (p. 36). And she sees her blessings as many: 'as I gave myself wholly into God ... so he received me graciously and preserved me in safety and diverted and prospered me' (p. 34).

God's blessing is thus given not only 'ever', but everywhere, in the life depicted by Lady Grace (p. 72). 'For whensoever we receive this holy sacrament of our Lord Jesus Christ his blessed body and blood, worthily, faithfully and according to his holy institution; the fountains of the gardens are broken unto us, the well of living waters floweth out unto us and the springs of Lebanon runneth swiftly unto us throughout all our parts; from our head unto our feet, so that no part is left unwashed or unrefreshed' (p. 77). Here she paraphrases the Song of Solomon (4. 15–16) to express the organic, and highly sexualized, union between God's eternal life and her own mortal body. The point about this – and about practically every other of her quotations cited here – is that she expresses her spirituality in terms of constant textual pastiche, pasting it together from the archives of her spiritual education, and echoing the Hebrew erotic poem as an allegory of Christ's relationship to the Christian soul. Distinctively derivative, imitative and allusive, her prose strains after quasi-biblical authenticity through the layering of linguistic analogy.

But if this (borrowed) language can merge body and soul, it can also effect a radical splitting between them; and this rupture is, for Lady Grace, a hazard of corporeal existence, in which the beating of 'my heart' is 'the original of all the desires and evil carriage of my mortal body' (p. 74). Her autobiography, derivative as it is, continually reminds us of the strain of this division: 'Oh, my stubborn and crooked heart, weaker and much worse than my corrupt and sinful flesh' (p. 74). In the record of her life the division is, in a sense, 'healed' by the author's constant reminder to herself of the eternal meaning that underscores temporal affairs. Describing her solicitousness towards relatives and servants and their ungrateful plotting against her, for example, she understands that they 'rendered me evil for good' (p. 86)). Their injustice, and the suffering woman's righteousness, are already anticipated by, and resolved within, her integrative narrative: its devotional blueprint gives her a 'natural' claim to the role of suffering, righteous being as chosen by God. And God, quite unsurprisingly, 'turned his loving countenance towards me' (p. 37).

Lady Grace's autobiography can in this sense be seen as a means of knitting up the inexplicable, the erratic, or the inexcusable, within the seamless horizon of eternal justice. Again and again, in addressing the double dimensions of her existence, she draws on the generational continuum that connects her life in the world to her life beyond it. Her 'unspotted garment' is a state of innocence, preserved against the evils of the world: 'I spent the best part of my youth in solitariness, shunning all opportunities to run into company least I might be enticed and drawn away by some evil suggestions to stain mine unspotted garment and so be robbed of mine innocency' (p. 34). This image recalls the 'chaste and upright' bearing of her 'unspotted' forbear, Lady Despencer, as well as the 'unspotted carriage' of Sir Walter Mildmay: 'the Lord so led and carried me in all my ways and preserved mine innocency so unspotted' (p. 38). And in her typically Protestant caution about the insinuating presence of evil, she joins a wider epistolary movement by women whose purpose in writing letters to their descendants was to endorse the path of spirituality and to bolster them against the workings of the devil.[32] In this context it is noticeable that notwithstanding her criticisms of the 'Papists' who 'worship their false god and set him up in their hearts' (p. 90), Lady Grace's insistence on the immaculate brings to mind Catholic beliefs and symbology. This was not uncommon for Protestant women, who, despite rebuking the robes and idolatry that they associated with the Catholic faith, still often perpetuated the use of Catholic rituals – the status of sacred virginity, for example – to express their piety.[33] (Here we might pause to contemplate the subject of our discussion against the backdrop of her ancestors in a perspective that may not be readily available to herself. Despite her reliance on the legacy afforded by her unspotted ancestors, Lady Grace might be more thoroughly imbued with intergenerational imprints – those of her Catholic ancestors – than she apparently understands or could readily acknowledge.)

In appreciating Lady Grace's relationship to the temporal and the eternal – and, more specifically, her insistence upon integrating the temporal *within* the larger frame of the eternal – we can see a striking parallel between the 'materials' of metaphor and corporeality. The unspotted spiritual apparel of herself and her ancestors – her insistence upon a clean and unadorned spirituality – are consonant with her physical bearing. Of women's dress she echoes 1 Peter 3. 3–4 in a conspicuous conjunction of corporeal and spiritual quiet composure: 'a meek and quiet spirit … For even after this manner in time past did the holy women who trusted in God attire themselves and were subject to their husbands' (p. 44). She also cites the advice of her mother, Lady Sherrington, who 'said that she could give me jewels and pearl and costly apparel. But she would not until I were furnished with virtue in my mind and decked inwardly and willed me first to seek the kingdom of God' (p. 28). In recruiting her generational continuum to assist in preserving the unspotted chastity of body and soul, Lady Grace follows those conduct writers who deplored the stereotype of worldly women, prone 'idlely and wanto[n]ly to gad abrod' (Becon, in St Clair and Maasen, p. 281), 'scorn[ing] to be closed vp in any obscure place' (Rich, 4. p. 249), and whose garish clothing and makeup flouts their husbands' gravity (Gouge, 5. p. 115). 'It is the guise of ... harlots to prancke and pricke up themselves to inueigle men's affections,' says Snawsel's well-spoken character Eulalie, whereas 'honest and religious matrons, we are neat inough, if we be cleanly, and can please our husbands' (Snawsel, 4. p. 117). In response to these stereotypes, Lady Grace suggests that a woman's apparel, like her mind, must be modest and subordinate to her husband, and, echoing her mother, she quotes approvingly from 1 Timothy 2. 9–10, 'let women array themselves in comely apparel with shamefastness and modesty, not with braided hair or gold or pearl or costly apparel, but (as becometh women that profess the fear of God) with good works' (p. 45).

It is perhaps entirely predictable that women like Lady Grace are inclined to define themselves counter to the stereotype of the woman who dresses with attention to detail and gads about town. Her interest is not in examining what is *in* the world, but in looking beyond it through the long-sighted lenses. Claiming little interest in getting herself up for the outside world, it is somewhat ironic that she does indeed 'get herself up' just as meticulously for the masculine spiritual judge who takes great notice of her studious asceticism. Advice books of the period are embellished again and again with the image of bodily asceticism as God's mirror. Dorothy Leigh says for example in *The Mothers Blessing* (1616),

> for who so is truly chaste, is free from idlenesse and from all vaine delights, full of humility, and all good Christian vertues: who so is chaste, is not giuen to pride in apparel, nor any vanity, but is alwaies either reading, meditating, or practising some good thing which she hath learned in the Scripture. (*Women's Writing in Stuart England*, p. 27)

'The vnchaste woman', she adds, 'is proud, and always decking her selfe with vanity ... but also so much wickednesse' (p. 27). She likens such women to 'strumpets and whores, who for couetousnesse sake sell their soules and bodies, and make themselues such filthie vessels in this earth, that it is most loathsome to thinke of'. They 'bragge as well of their jewels and costly apparel that the world bestoweth upon them' (p. 50). In an advice book to her unborn child, Elizabeth Jocelin laments the fact that such women are praised before those of true merit: 'you will heare a well drest woman ... more commended than a wise or honest, or religious woman' (St Clair and Maasen, 5. pp. 355–6).[34] Asceticism, for Mildmay, Leigh and Jocelin, exists as a visible, and necessary, sign of rectitude. For such women themselves, dressing and acting with modesty signals the (modest) expectation of their own understandings. 'Let wives submit themselves unto their husbands as unto the lord,' Lady Grace recites from the epistles, 'as the church is in subjection unto Christ, even so let the wives be to the husbands in every thing' (p. 44). She praises 'time past' when 'the holy women which trusted in God attire[d] themselves and were subject to their husbands' (p. 44). Through this understanding of God's will as mediated on earth, they express themselves and, indeed, justify their thoughts as 'worth' expressing.

'God had placed me in this house': The Meaning of Domestic Life

Historians and literary critics have devoted a good deal of attention to the nature and scope of women's occupation in Lady Grace's times.[35] This subject was also heavily debated by her contemporaries, with several writers dramatizing debates about upper class women's entitlement to expansive social roles. Sir Thomas Elyot's Platonic dialogue, *The Defence of Good Women* (1545), reflects the wish of humanists to promote women's capacity for virtuous action, and to suggest that the compass of such action should not be confined to the home.[36] Nicholas Breton's *The Praise of Virtuous Ladies* (1580) offers a more light-hearted, and highly rhetorical, defence of women's sense and virtue; while Robert Snawsel's *A Looking-glasse for married folks* (1610) dramatizes a debate between various women about the ideal extent of their social and domestic roles.[37] In arguing for the benefits of women's learning, Richard Hyrde examines the various reasons against it, countering each negative with a positive: 'I never heard tell nor read of any woman well learned that ever was (as plenteous as evil tongues be) spotted or infamed as vicious. But on the other side, many by their learning taken such increase of goodness that many may bear them witness of their virtue'.[38] Jane Anger's 'Protection for Women' (1589)[39] argues strongly for women's right to action and self-government. And the debate about women's capacities and capabilities is staged not only in pamphlets and conduct manuals, but also in journals and commonplace books left to descendants. William Dethick, for example, leaves us this diary note:

> God hath created a woman, to be an helper to man, and made hir of his fleshe and bone, therefore above all mortale things is she to be honored, no less than Man, having in hir, all [pure extollments] as may be founde in Man viz fortitude ... [the capacity] to distinguishe good from evill. God hath also given to woman, and man, indifferently, knowledge of his miraculous workes, [and they] both, doe glorifye his name. Yea by Women, men are honored, and may not be [divorced] from them ... Adam was composed of earthe, or claye: But Eve was made of a man's rib ... And honoring the vertue of ffortitude (no more commended in Man) by great and good examples, it may be proved, that woman['s virtue should be] extolled, no lesse than Man. The magnanimity of Minerva, Mother to Apollo, appeared in manye bloodye battalls.[40]

No matter how trenchant the arguments for women's independence, however, it remained that men, in the main, mistrusted women's capacity for prudent judgment. 'He who lets his wife go to every feast and his horse drinke at every water, shall have neither good wife nor goode horse,' facetiously wrote Sir Francis Fane, husband to Lady Grace's daughter Mary, in a commonplace manuscript now lodged at the Folger Library.[41] Thomas Burton notoriously linked the thinking gentlewoman to an increased susceptibility to mental defect and depression: 'For seldom should you see an hired servant, a poor handmaid, though ancient, that is kept hard to her work and bodily labour, a coarse country wench troubled in this kind'.[42] Excellence in housewifery – not simply 'the art of keeping house as a wife' but also the art of house-management – was a means by which to usefully evaluate women of varying ranks and occupations.[43] And the writers of advice books – even if they avoided accusations of madness, or the extremes of Joseph Swetnam's misogynistic *The arraignment of lewde, idle, froward and unconstant women*[44] (first published in 1615 as a response to Anger's 'Protection for Women') – did much to entrench this view about women's domestic suitability and accountability. According to Heinrich Bullinger, for example, the honest woman should never 'go eny where without her husbandes knowledge and leaue' or 'take upon her anye farre iourney. And yf hir husband be gone forth or be not at home, let hir holde hirselfe as a wedow and lyue quiet'.[45] In his *Catechisme* Thomas Becon exhorts women 'continually to remain at home in their house, diligentlye and vertuously occupied, except urgent, waighty and necessary causes compell her to go forth, as to go unto the church, to pray or to hear the worde of God, to help with sick neighbors or to … go to the market to bie things necessary for her houshold'.[46] Thomas Salter counsels 'a Maiden, beyng become wife, by the instruction and teachying of her prudent Mistres,' to 'be sufficient to gouerne a houshold and familie discretely' (5. p. 39). Patrick Hannay says: 'It befits not Man for to imbrace / Domesticke charge, so its not Womans place / For to be busied with affairs abroad: / For that weake sexe, it is too great a load' (4. p. 376). And Richard Braithwaite urges women, where possible, not to venture out at all: 'for divers maine respects, a custome very irregular and undecent, that *Women* should frequent places of *Publike* resort, as Stage-playes, Wakes, solemne Feasts, and the like.'[47]

Lady Grace's autobiography complies firmly with the outlines of such manuals: 'God had placed me in this house, and if I found no comfort here, I would never seek it out of this house and this was my certain resolution' (p. 34). All of her activities in the home – her morning studies in divinity, her singing ('I … practiced my voice in singing of psalms and in making my prayers to God and confessing my sins' [p. 35]), her drawing and needlework ('I found in myself that God wrought with me in all' [p. 35]) – are illustrated as acts of piety. Prominent amongst her worthy household acts is her medical practice. Despite the disdain expressed by (predictably male) physicians for those 'inauthentical' women whose claims to medical knowledge amounted to 'dangerous whisperings about the sick',[48] administering 'physick' within the limits of womanly skill was seen as an important aspect of a housewife's training. In his tract, *The English Housewife*, Gervase Markham, who, in early 1615, published one of the most comprehensive guides for women's household instruction, recommends for housewives 'a physical kind of knowledge; how to administer many wholesome receipts or medicines' to household members and (for the gentry) to servants and field workers. 'The depths and secrets of this most excellent art of physic,' he adds, 'is far beyond the capacity of the most skillful woman, as lodging only in the breast of the learned professors; yet that our housewife may from them receive some ordinary rules and medicines which may avail for the benefit of her family is ... no derogation to that worthy art.'[49] It was acceptable for a woman to learn some physic from her father, as in the case of Mary Trye, for example.[50] And during her lifetime Lady Grace acquired a good deal of medical knowledge. Having read, in her youth, 'Dr Turner's herbal and in Bartholomew Vigoe' [a work of surgery] (p. 26), she records her own medical contributions as a form of praise for God, who has given humankind 'precious gums for medicine' as well as the 'wisdom and knowledge to use them' (p. 84). But unlike some of her contemporaries who developed similar skills and interests – Anne Harcourt and Margaret Hoby, for instance – Lady Grace did not go out to treat the sick. Rather, all her work was done within the home, under the strict guidance of the medical experts with whom she corresponded. Her memoirs evidence no disapprobation from them, nor from any other men (including God), in response to her use of medical knowledge: 'every day I spent some time in the herbal and books of physic and in ministering to one or other by the directions of the best physicians of mine acquaintance, and ever God gave a blessing thereunto' (p. 35).

Domestic Spirituality in the Life of Lady Margaret Hoby

'I thinke there is not a woman so unlovely, nor so unnurtured, but if she doth bring a large portion in her purse, she shall have a husband,' writes Barnabe Rich with brutal bluntness.[51] A woman's domestic value was, of course, linked inextricably to her financial assets: once married, all of her financial assets went to her husband. (Indeed, it was not unknown for women of especially high rank to give their names and ranks to their husbands in order to ensure his legal right to their property.) Lady Margaret Hoby, a wealthy young woman from Yorkshire gentry, had a very 'large portion in her purse,' and attracted many suitors each time she was left a widow.

While Hoby's lifespan (1570–1633) partially intersected with that of Lady Grace Mildmay, her diary was written largely in the Elizabethan period. Unlike Mildmay, who wrote her journal in 1617 near the end of her life, Hoby began writing a diary at the age of 29, three years after marrying her third husband.[52] Her first husband was Walter Devereux, brother to Robert, earl of Essex, and son of Walter Devereux (these two relatives are discussed in the chapter on mirrors, Chapter Four of this volume), and her second was Thomas Sidney, brother to the poet Sir Philip Sidney. Thomas Hoby, her third husband, was a tiny, opinionated man, litigious and given to falling out with the neighbouring gentry. He was less appealing than her first two husbands, who came from glamorous, powerful families. But whether or not Lady Margaret herself 'liked' her husband – or whether, perhaps, she married him to succumb to family pressure to protect her wealth[53] – is never a point of interest or inquiry in her running diary. The character of Thomas Hoby remains impenetrable as his wife plods through hundreds of notations about praying and seeking the advice of her chaplain, Master Rhodes, the even tone of her daily devotions and good deeds broken only by anxiety about not being devout enough:

> after the sarmone ended, I Came home, where I did little good but talked of many maters.. with Mrs. Ormston, with whom I read a whill of the Bible: and after I returned in to my hart, examenid my selfe, and Craued pardon for my severall ommitions and Comitions: the Lord stringten me with his grace that I may sinne no more in the Like sort, amen: then I went to supper, after to the repetition and prers, and so to bed. (2 October, 1599, *Diary*, p. 27)

Any small slice of Hoby's diary will yield many entries about her marital life: 'I brak my fast with Mr Hoby' (25 July 1600, p. 101); 'I walked about with Mr Hoby amonge workmen' (29 July 1600, p. 102); 'I talked with my husband'; 'I talked with Mr Hoby of sunderie thinges' (29 July 1600, p. 102); 'I dined with Mr Hoby and so kept him Companie all the day' (1 August 1600, pp. 102–3). The frequency of references to her husband serves only to highlight how *little* these references tell us about him, or of the complexion of the conversations and activities shared by husband and wife. Some very few entries, such as those of 18 July and 19 July 1600, invite a small measure of interpretation. On 18 July Lady Margaret records having come 'to publeck praers and, after, to priuat, wher I please the lord to touch my hart with such sorow, for some offence Cometted, that I hope the lord, for his sonne sake, hath pardoned it accordinge to his promise' (p. 99). The next day 'After priuat praier I wrett an answer to a demand Mr Hoby had giuen me ouer night' (p. 99). Why Hoby should have written to her husband, who lives in the same house, invites us to speculate on some degree of ill-feeling between them, linking, perhaps, the 'offence' noted on 18 July to a demand that her husband has obviously written her overnight, and to which she responds in kind. But equally, estrangement may not be the case, and it seems, indeed, only temporary if at all, since on 23 July Hoby describes having 'talked with Mr Hoby of the sall of linton,' (p. 100) and, two entries later, of having 'brak my fast with Mr Hoby' (25 July, p. 101).

The opacity of Lady Margaret's diary begs the question of how, from such full information about her doings and scant information about her thoughts, we might glean a sense of *who* she was as an individual. Almost the whole of the very first entry (Thursday 9 August 1599) is torn away from the manuscript, but the remainder of this entry is quite telling: 'day was deadnes in praier, and my greatest offence was want of sorow for the same: the Lord of his mercie increase true and fervent mourninge vnto god that he neuer take his spiritt from me amen amen' (p. 3). The 'amen, amen' conveys a self-imposed pressure, marking a sharp difference from Grace Mildmay's rhetorical composure. Mildmay spells out the boundaries and justifications of ideal female self-expression, learning, subjection and dress, in a tone that is both authoritative and inclusive: acknowledging herself not 'trained up in university learning' (p. 25), she nonetheless speaks for a whole community of antecedents, peers and descendants, announcing 'the best course to set *our*selves in', 'whereby *we* may the better judge' (p. 23), and so on. All of those to whom she speaks are united in a dynastic community under the watchful eyes of the God who is the ultimate audience. Lady Margaret Hoby's narrative voice is, in contrast, less inclusive, more personal and tentative, without actually saying anything particularly probing about her person.

As we move further into Hoby's diary, it is her sense of anxious self-scrutiny for the purpose of spiritual cleanliness – the sense that every little action matters, and that something is at stake in remembering it rightly – that animates the banal, repetitive events, imbuing them with them a presence that we might deem 'individual'. On Friday 10 August, for example, she dutifully records the times at which she eats, maintains the household, attends her husband, and prays, ending with 'much Comfort' that implies a sigh of relief: 'imediately after [supper] praer and Lector, for the diligent attencion of which the Lord did heare my praier by remouing all wanderinges which vse to hvrt me so that I receiued much Comfort, I went to bed' (p. 3). Each day tests anew her devotion to God, and all of her actions are either a trial of her devoutness ('I went to awiffe in trauill of child, about whom I was busey tell 1 a Cloke, about which time, She being deliuered and I hauing praised god, returned home and betook my selfe to priuat praier'[Wednesday 15 August, 1599, p. 6]), or a punishment for transgression ('I arose, haueinge release of my sickness, according to the wonted kindnes of the Lord, who, after he had Let me se how I had offended … with a gentle corriction let me feele he was reconsiled To me' [Friday 17 August 1599, p. 7]). Her entries serve as a check to her Puritan conscience, a prod to greater acts of piety, and a mark of her relief when a day is lived sufficiently well. Whereas Lady Grace's autobiography follows the blueprint of a spiritual prototype – so that its pages delineate the figure of piety that will be passed down through the ages – Lady Margaret's diary documents the struggle through which, from day to day, she conceives of her relationship with God.

Being childless herself, Lady Margaret seems unconcerned with passing her diary down to anyone else. Neither does she need to define her place within a history of god-fearing ancestors: although she refers often to walking and talking with her mother, she does not sketch her upbringing, nor the pedagogical influences upon her life. In the pages of her diary is represented her ongoing struggle to communicate with God more fully in her prayers, thoughts, relationships and actions. Hers is not (as with Lady Grace) a piety that *proves* her worth before God, but a piety that *seeks* worthiness in God's eyes. Lady Margaret's scrupulous notation of her doings and 'priuat examinations' permits her to remain ever vigilant in assessing her checks and balances as she lives in pursuit of virtue and right living. We might think for a moment of Milton's great poem *Paradise Lost*, published a little more than fifty years on, in which temptation gives flesh to its characters, making the blood run in their veins. For Lady

Margaret, the infrequent temptations she encounters are simply the reminders that God issues to the body in the service of the spirit: 'the lord hath freed me a long time from any temptation grious [grievous], though the body haue benn a little Justly punished,' she notes, for example, on Thursday 22 June, 1600 (p. 84). She begs God's grace 'to rissist and ouer Come' temptation (Sunday 26 August 1599, p. 10) and vows that 'how so euer Iustly god hath suffered satan to afflicte my mind, yet my hope is that my redeemer will bringe my soule out of troubles, that it may praise his name: and so I will waite w[ith] patience for deliuerence' (Monday 6 May 1602, p. 180).

And it is the service of the spirit that links Lady Margaret with the double time that recurs thematically in our study, the relationship between the temporal – the ongoing progression from event to event – and the timeless. Her days are spent in those activities – public and private devotion, writing, reading, talking with the chaplain, Mr Rhodes, discussing sermons with her friends, dressing the wounds of sick workmen and counseling the servants – that mark an onward temporal progression whose resolution lies within the 'real' truth of heavenly transcendence. Thus a day that diverts from this path is grievously wasted: 'I praied, and then walked with a stranger with whom I hard litle good talke, and therfore the time, as ill bestowed, I greeued for' (Wednesday 9 August 1600, p. 97). In terms of the spiritual clock by which Lady Hoby lives, the catalogue of minor and repetitive events that litters her diary becomes more than trivial, and, indeed, of utmost significance: it is a measure of her spirit's constant movement, which, like the ticking of a physical clock, moves always, and minutely, in relationship to some larger purpose beyond time itself. Wasted time means dishonour to God, and she begs him to 'redeeme time' (Thursday 6 September 1599, p. 15). She also understands, and expects, punishment for neglected devotions: 'After priuat praers I went about the house, an then eate my breakfast: then I walked to the church with Mr Hoby: after that I wrougt a litle, and neclected my custom of praier, for which, as for many other sinnes, it pleased the Lord to punishe me with an Inward assalte' (Monday 10 September 1599, p. 16).

In regulating her life to the meter of eternity, Lady Margaret does not renounce her body, but, indeed, makes it a focus by which she monitors her spiritual life. Her bodily ills, recorded with detailed attention on various days, have both an immediate temporal impact and a larger spiritual meaning. As frequently as Lady Margaret is ill, just as frequently is her spirit in need of adjustment: 'having supped, I was at publeck praers very sicke: the Lord pardon the sinne for which I was so punished, it beinge the will of god often to punishe one sinne with another, for I had Litle proffet by that praier, by reasone of my sicknes' (Wednesday 19 September 1599, p. 20). Physicians, like Dr Brewer and Dr Lister, are people she frequently consults, while she herself acquires some medical training. But despite the immediate provocation of a bodily ailment, she manages never to lose sight of its larger meaning. Physicians are no more than God's instruments in the wider significance of all temporal ills: 'it is the Lord, and not the phisision, who both ordaines the medesine for our health and orders the the ministering of it for the good of his children, closinge and vnclosinge the Iudgments of men at his pleasure: therefore let euerie one phisision and pactente Call Vpon the Lord for a blessinge' (Friday 31 August 1599, p. 13).

Lady Margaret devotes a good deal of attention to others' ailments as well as her own. Many mornings are spent dressing wounds on hands and legs, various trips are made to attend women in childbirth, and, on one occasion, she is asked to slice open a child who is born without an anal passage:

> this day, in the afternone, I had had a child brought to se that was borne at Silpho, one Talliour sonne, who had no fundement, and had no passage for excrementes but att the Mouth: I was earnestly intreated to Cutt the place to se if any passhage Could be made, but, althought I Cutt deepe and seearched, there was none to be found. (Wednesday 26 August 1601, p. 161)

As with Lady Grace, Lady Margaret's service to the body is also a service rendered to God, and this is one of the principal ways in which she supports those members of the lower classes with whom she comes into contact. The other is, of course, in spiritual guidance, which she renders with the ingrained superiority of her own class and station: 'after, I reed of the bible, and walked alone, and then went into the kicthine, wher Mr Rhodes and my selfe had som speach with the poore and Ignorant of … som princeples of religion' (Wednesday 22 August 1599, p. 9); '[I] did pray with Mr Rhodes: then I did read a while to my workwemen' (Friday 3 November 1599, p. 34).

Prominent in her diary is the fear of the plague, which spread wildly in 1603, a year distinguished by the political and social uncertainty that marked the transition between the death of Queen Elizabeth and the accession of King James. 'We hard that the plauge was spred in whitbye, and that ther died at London :3200: a week,' she writes on 4 September 1603 (p. 191). On the 8th of September she writes of having visited her mother and returned to her home at Hackness,

> wher we hard that one in the towne, hauinge binne in Hardwoodall at Mr. Busshills house whouse childrine were Come from whitbie was fallen sicke wt :3: of his children more :vpon which, fearing the worst, we Returned the same night to Newton againe, wher we remaine vntill god shall please, in mercie, to deall wt vs. (p. 192)

Whereas Lady Grace has the vantage of hindsight to organize and cohere the details of her life, Lady Margaret writes in the midst of uncertainty, not knowing how best to escape the plague that is closing its jaws around her rural community. While Lady Grace's narrative seeks to present her experience as an entirely fit for the divine, therefore, Lady Margaret's words tell of her urgent quest to deepen and clarify her connection to God, that He might show his mercy by saving her from the plague. On the 27th of September she tells of the safety of her home and her fear of contamination from elsewhere, her narrative pushing her onward to greater acts of devotional exercise in what she describes as a thirst for God's pleasure:

'thes day we hard from Hacknes that all there was well, But that the sicknes was freared to be at Roben Hood bay, not farr off: I Continewe my accustomed exercises but my increasinges in goodes waies is not as I thirst for' (p. 193). Striving for God's pleasure, she seeks thereby to have surety of peace in the life to come and to be spared, in the temporal life, the ravages of illness.

The diary, understandably, conveys a story in the process of unfolding – the diarist tells of her fears, but does not yet know their outcome. 'This day we had Mr farfaxe and his wiffe, Mr Skatey, Mrs Netelton, at dinner with vs,' she writes on 15 November 1603. 'We sawe the printed pater [paper] of those that died at and about London this sommer, which were :31967: from July to October' (15 November 1603, p. 197). She lives in fear and dread, seeking ever more profoundly to please her God and to be granted His mercy. Unlike Lady Grace, who writes confidently of the cumulative significance of events in her life, Lady Margaret always fears for the worst and hardly dares hope for the best.

As Lady Margaret's diary progresses toward its latter stages, its intensity diminishes, and it becomes less a record of her conversation with God and more a record of household and financial matters, of comings and goings, and of contacts with the outside world, including a lengthy litigation initiated by her husband against a neighbour who abused the Hobys' hospitality.[54] Indeed, in April 1605 Lady Margaret notices with distress the degeneration of her journal from its original private covenant with God:

> at Night I thought to writt my daies Iournee as before, becaus, in the readinge over some of my former spent time, I funde some profitt might be made of that Course from which, thorow two much neccligence, I had a Longe time dissisted. [B]ut they are vnworthye of godes benefittes and especiall faoures that Can finde no time to make a thankfull recorde of them. (1 April 1605, pp. 210–11)

But this resolve does not restore the journal to its former spiritual intensity, and by June 1605 it peters out altogether. While nothing is known of her after this time, the annotator of her diary notes that Francis Bacon calls her 'the best Lady that ever any knight in the world inioyed' (p. 221), and she seems to have been beloved of her servants as well as the many young people who visited her home at Hackness.

When considering what Lady Margaret's writings can tell us about her private self, her diary, in its most intensely devout stages, projects the intensity of her daily struggle to grow closer to God, and the frustrations of being human. We might speculate on why a wealthy young woman, in the early years of a society-driven marriage, might begin a spiritual diary. Perhaps she was one of the many people inspired, as Elaine McKay suggests, by the literary endeavours of friends and relatives.[55] The alternative reasons that might occur to a reader some four hundred years later – grief for a former, more glamorous love-match, perhaps, or disappointment in one's new situation[56], or a sense of isolation, even a casual suggestion from her husband or her mother – are all plausible. But beyond the deep-seated striving for communion with God – a striving that Lady Margaret renewed daily in the pages of her diary – our quest to know her mind and purposes *better* through her writings turns up, in effect, how much we *cannot* hope to know. Any reason we deduce for her sudden wish to document her relationship with God, and for the change in the complexion of her diary as the years roll on, is purely in the realm of conjecture and likely, perhaps, to be anachronistic.[57]

In comparing the diary mode with that of autobiography, Dean Ebner makes the important point that an autobiography is a 'life-review' in which an individual undertakes to examine a personal life history. A diary, in contrast, generally purports to record a life in progress.[58] Elaine McKay concludes on this basis that as readers we do not expect the same level of retrospective analysis in a diary that we do in an autobiography. In following Grace Mildmay's autobiography with the diary of Margaret Hoby, we can recognize the difference between the autobiography's tendency toward a retrospective mapping of one's experiences as against the diary's running record of events, while also appreciating Linda Pollock's argument that a diary is not simply a spontaneous outpouring of events as they are lived. Diarists have their own way of sorting experiences in accordance with their purposes and preoccupations, so that while a diary may not have the composite shape to be found in a late-life retrospection, it can indeed be quite as formally encoded.[59]

Between a Diary and a Retrospective: Anne Clifford's Days

If we evaluate the secular and spiritual aspirations described by Lady Grace Mildmay and Lady Margaret Hoby, we see a particular correlation in that God is front and centre of both life-writings: Lady Grace rounds up days and years within the thrust of an ongoing narrative that firmly establishes the temporal (adversities, triumphs, celebrations and practices) as an ongoing exercise in the service of God; while in recording her everyday routines, Lady Margaret Hoby portrays a continual, and continually unresolved, act of self-examination in which she struggles to make her temporal life worthy of her divine Maker. In contrast to these two manuscripts, the diaries of Lady Anne Clifford, cousin to Margaret Hoby, have an unashamedly secular interest. Even in her clear and pleasurable description of her appearance, we sense in Clifford's writings a worldly attention that distinguishes her from Grace Mildmay's devout sense of communal purpose and Lady Margaret's anxious self-denial. Of her childhood Lady Anne says, 'I was verie happie in my first Constitution, both in my mynd and Bodye. Both for internall and externall Endowments, for never was there Childe more equallie resembleing both Father and Mother than myself'.[60] Notwithstanding the pleasing concord of the physical parts bestowed by her parents, there was great marital discord between them, and following her father's death, Lady Anne embarked on a long battle to win the inherited lands bequeathed by him to her uncle but due to her by law. This battle forms the thread that weaves its way through a myriad of routine events: '*January 1617:* Upon the 28th at this time I wore a plain green flannel gown that *William Punn* made me, and my yellow taffety waistcoat' (p. 52). 'Upon the 30th Mr *Amherst* the Preacher came hither to see me with whom I had much talk. He told me that now they began to think at *London* that I had done well in not referring this business to the King and that everybody said God had a hand in it' (p. 52); '*June 1617:* The 3rd: Mr. *Heardson* came hither in the morning and told me that many did condemn me for standing out so in this business, so on the other side many did command me in regard that I have done that which is both just and honourable. This night went I into a bath' (p. 70); '*February 1619, the 2nd*: That day I made pancakes with my women in the Great Chamber. The 10th Wat. Coniston began to read St. Austin of the City of God to me, and I received a letter from Mr. Davis with another enclosed in it of *Ralph Conniston*, whereby I perceived things went in *Westmoreland* as I would have them' (p. 87). (The Clifford estates covered most of the county of Westmoreland.)

Clifford's diary is not devoid of spirituality, and, indeed, she herself was a devout Christian, constantly aware of her God who evaluated all things temporal and who would, in the end, be the force to right all wrongs. But her narrative steers the reader not toward the spiritual sum of her life (as with Mildmay's autobiography) nor toward an evaluation of daily thoughts and actions in terms of their spiritual merit (as with Hoby). Rather, God remains, for Clifford, an image of solace when temporal events run awry ('I kneeled down to my prayers and desired GOD to send a good end to these troublesome businesses' (7 February 1617, p. 54), and, quite often, of remorseful recognition that the troublesome affairs of the world have dwarfed those of the soul: 'my Lord and I had much talk of and persuaded me to these businesses ... All this Lent I eat flesh and observed no day but Good Friday' (16 and 19 April 1617, p. 64).

Emerging as they do over more than one volume, Lady Anne's diaries blend various kinds of retrospection. The first, the 'Knole Diary', exists now as an eighteenth-century transcript of a diary that originated at the time of Lady Anne's first marriage to Richard Sackville, earl of Dorset. Covering the years 1603–1619, the Knole Diary begins in 1609, the year of her first marriage to Sackville. As a 19-year-old bride, Lady Anne gives a retrospective account of Queen Elizabeth's death, which occurred in 1603 when the author was 13. By 1609 the question of her inheritance was already in dispute, and her beginning of a narrative at that particular time was very likely inspired by her need to keep records of all transactions, both financial (in terms of accounts) and social (in light of her entry into marriage). She thus began a system of record keeping that was to last throughout her very long life.

From a portrait of Queen Elizabeth's death, and various descriptions of herself and her mother as she recalls them six years later, Lady Anne jumps, in the next excerpt of the Knole Diary, to 1616. While all of the entries are written in retrospect ('All the time I stayed in the Country I was sometimes merry and sometimes sad, as I had news from *London* ... Upon the 8th day of February I came to *London* ... Upon Monday the 12th my Lord *Rous* was married ... Upon the 14th, my Lord supped at the Globe' [p. 18]), it is difficult to determine whether they were made at different points in the year, or, indeed, all at once at the end of the year. Given the accuracy of the dates, it is quite certain that this diary must have been compiled from various notations made by Lady Anne as the days and months progressed; and the frequent footnotes supplementing her notations suggest that she added various points of interest in later years as she reread her diaries. The Knole diary covers 1617, skips 1618, and ends on the 31st of December 1619. Existing only as a transcript, this diary is almost certainly incomplete, both within the years that are documented, and in the entire year (1618) that is omitted from the notations for 1616–1619. We have no way of knowing, therefore, how far the hand of the transcriber took away from, or supplemented, that of Lady Anne herself. Over the rest of her life Lady Anne prepared the notes – either in her own hand or in the hands of those who transcribed her thoughts – from which she later compiled what she called her Great Books. The original notes or transcriptions are lost, but the later transcriptions (the Great Books) cover the period from 1620 until the death of her second husband in 1649, and from 1650 until the end of her life. These last are called the Kendall Diaries.

Lady Anne's parents, Lady Russell and George Clifford, had much estrangement during their marriage; and at one point, when the king was at Grafton, Lady Anne records the fact that although her mother was present, she was 'not held as mistress of the house, by reason of the difference between my Lord and her, which was grown to a great height' (p. 10). Lady Anne's two marriages were also disastrous, fraught with spousal conflict concerning her right to inherit her father's lands. She provides numerous examples of Dorset's neglect ('in the morning my Lord went to *Penshurst* but would not suffer me to go with him although my Lord and Lady *Lisle* sent a man on purpose to desire me to come' (August 1617, p. 75); his profligate carousing with others, including the wayward king ('My Lord went often to the Court abroad and on Twelfth Eve lost 400 pieces playing with the King' (January 1619, p. 84); and his constant greedy pressuring of his wife to give up her inheritance in exchange for a settlement that could replenish his depleted coffers. But such entries are contradicted by her summation of his life, in which (like Lady Grace in her eulogy to her dead husband) she praises Dorset. Acknowledging him 'extremely chollerick by nature which was increased the more by the Office of Lord Chamberlain to the King, which he held many years,' she also calls him 'one of the greatest men of his time in England in all respects'. (Clifford ed., *The Kendal Diary*, 1650–1675, pp. 105–6.)

There were six years between Dorset's death and Lady Anne's second marriage to Philip Herbert, earl of Pembroke and Montgomery, undertaken a year after her first daughter, Margaret, was married. A violent, self-seeking and much loathed man, Herbert lived with Anne only a few years before leaving her in the country in preference for a life at court. He tried hard to compel Anne to agree to betroth her second daughter, Isabella, to his own son (the issue of his first marriage), his motivation being the 5000 pounds to be settled on her marriage. But Lady Anne maintained that a second child should be able to choose her own husband, and, moreover, that a husband should not be in command of his wife's wealth. 'I lived in those my Lordes great families as the Rver Rhone runnes through the lake of Geneva, without mingling anie part of its streams with that Lake,' she says in the Knole diary of her own marital life (*The Diaries*, Clifford ed., p. 94). She maintains a righteous commitment to establishing independence for herself and her daughters.

The very last months of Lady Anne's life are documented quite narrowly, transcribed by servants who were instructed to note down when, for example, on 22 February she pared her nails, had her head shaved and took a bath in water that had been used for boiling beef and bran, 18 December 1675 being the last time that she had cleaned herself in this manner. (*The Diaries*, Clifford ed., p. 256) The entries in this section blend the account-keeping of a lifetime with Lady Anne's predilection for coincidence, which she sees as inspired by providence: each entry marks not only what she does on the recorded day, but also the memory that is providentially evoked by each of these activities. 'The 24th day. I remembered how this day was 60 years [since] my first Lord & I, after I had been to see Warwick Castle and Church, went out of the Inne there' (*The Diaries*, Clifford ed., p. 257); 'The 5th day, being Sunday, I remembered how this night 52 years [ago] was the last night that ever I lay in Great Dorset House' (*The Diaries*, Clifford ed., p. 261). In this way Lady Anne balances the immediacy of her late life experiences with a sense of their historical placement. Bearing in mind the significance of her life within her cumulative family lineage, she gives to events a monumental significance within a providential design.

The Great Picture

With her eye ever on her place in history, in the last thirty years of her life as she managed her vast estates, Lady Anne restored many buildings and monuments, using the initials 'AP', that drew on the Pembroke name bequeathed to her by her second husband. Perhaps her most famous project was the 'Great Picture', a huge triptych – eight feet tall and four feet wide in each of its panels – that she commissioned in 1646 at the age of 56. While the artist's attribution is unclear, it was probably painted by Jan van Belcamp (see Fig. 7.1). The triptych provides a spatial manifestation of Lady Anne's wish to perpetuate her family destiny, and it depicts what she sees as the important moments of her life. On the left-hand panel stands Lady Anne as a 15-year-old girl, the age at which her father died and at which she should have inherited his estate. Framed in the upper corners, to left and right, are her tutor, the poet Samuel Daniel, and her governess, Mrs. Anne Taylor. Lady Anne is shown with her lute, as well as the books she evidently studied with Daniel and Taylor: among them the Bible, Augustine's *City of God*, John Downame's *Christian Warfare*, Camden's *Britannia*, Daniel's prose *Chronicle of*

Fig. 7.1   Jan van Belkamp, Lady Anne Clifford's Great Painting, 1646. Reproduced courtesy of Abbot Hall

England, Abraham Ortelius's *Map of the World*, Ovid's *Metamorphoses*, Castiglione's *Courtier*, Montaigne's *Essays*, Cervantes's *Don Quixote*, Chaucer's and Spenser's works, and Sidney's *Arcadia*.

In the middle panel of the Great Picture stand Lady Anne's brothers, Robert and Francis, who died in childhood, and her parents, George Clifford and Lady Margaret Russell. Looking out at the viewer, both parents gesture toward their young sons, who also look outward rather than toward either parent. Under his velvet coat the earl wears the special suit of armour that he commissioned on his appointment as Queen's Champion. Behind the family group are four more portraits, representing Anne's four aunts, all of whom are frequently mentioned in her diaries. Bordering the central panel are the nearly forty coats of arms borne by Anne's antecedents over the centuries. On the right-hand panel stands Lady Anne at age 56, the year in which she commissioned the painting. The dog clawing at her leg symbolizes her loyalty to her husbands, framed above her and now deceased. The shelves above them are littered with books, the considerable disarray of which (unlike those in the left hand panel, stacked in quiet repose) indicates constant current use. These are works of religion, moral philosophy, history, and recent literature. They include the Bible, Henry More's *Map of Mortality*, Bishop Henry King's Sermons, Donne's Sermons, Plutarch's *Morals* and *Lives*, Guiccardini's *History* in French translation, Henry Wotton's *Book of Architecture*, Donne's *Poems*, Jonson's *Works*, and Herbert's *The Temple*. The conspicuous presence of the much used books in the panel recalls her reference in her diaries to 'Good books and virtuous thoughts' as the means by which she has sustained her independence during both her marriages, blending secular resolve with the truth of God's providence: 'I gave myself wholly to Retyredness as much as I could, in both those great families, and made good bookes and vertuous thoughts my companions' (*The Diaries*, Clifford ed., p. 94). The paper she touches on the table may represent her own writings: a diary, biographies of members of her family, an autobiography, family histories, and the sea chronicles of her father. In this panel Lady Anne rests alone and secure, having safely buried both troublesome husbands and feeling now able to look back in quiet satisfaction at her family lineage. Finally in possession of her lands, she is free, in secure old age, to devote herself to running her estates.

The Great Picture has an interesting and instructive relationship to Clifford's diaries. The diaries abound with descriptions of both husbands' violent tempers, her struggle to persuade the king that she should not give up her inheritance; gossip that is reported to her, both in favour of, and against, her claim to property; trips she makes to advance her claim; banishments from London and the court; as well as a myriad of details concerning her daily routines, her entertainments, the effects on her health of overeating, stress and smallpox. In the diaries we see time unfold, as Lady Anne progresses through her various occupations and preoccupations, culminating in the series of entries that brings the past into the present by recalling other events that took place on various days of a current year. As she interweaves with reminiscences her final records of daily activities, the timeline that has flowed through the diaries finally folds back upon itself. In the triptych, however, time is managed in a different and more formal way. It is collapsed into three distinct periods: her childhood (in which her brothers, and not she, are depicted), her girlhood at the brink of legal inheritance, and her satisfied old age. Each of the three tableaux 'tells' a story that is ostensibly quite simple. In the middle panel, the vignette of the parents and two sons depicts a normative portrait of aristocratic childhood to which, if we know the content of the diaries, we can add layers of loss and disappointment (the death of the two sons) as well as marital estrangement. To the left, the portrait of a girl framed by governess and tutor suggests a properly styled youth in which Lady Anne ingests an understanding of books and of women's wisdom. Supplementary to this tableau is the battle that was launched in Lady Anne's 15th year, the year that she was first denied her rightful inheritance. And in the panel to the right we see her framed by the two dead husbands, with the emblem of loyalty prominent about her person, her casually arranged books suggesting a freedom of mind and frequency of scholarly contemplation.

Time, with its vagaries, its disappointments and triumphs, is thus condensed, within the triptych, into moments of artful simplicity. The portrait serves as an intensely secular, and intensely spiritual, emblem of how Lady Anne wishes herself to be remembered: as the fitting descendant of a grand, learned family and the bearer of this grandeur into forthcoming generations. Locking into place an image of how things *seem*, the Great Picture's canvas is challenged by the diaries to articulate the complicated detail of how things *are*. And yet 'seeming' and 'being' do not (as they customarily do today) bear clearly identifiable definitions of 'pretend' or 'real' selves. Rather, the opposite is true. Lady Anne has not commissioned the painting to whitewash her narrative history: her purpose is instead quite similar to that of Lady Grace in writing her autobiography. She wishes to display her family's worth to God and to viewers, both living and in the future. Her intention, then, is not to construct a 'fake' self that denies her history, but to distill this history to its most important elements, those elements that link her identity to parents, siblings, tutors, and, eventually, to her descendants, all manifested in the eyes of God.

What Words Mean

This chapter concludes by asking the rather broad question: whose writings, of the three diarists we have examined, provide more access to the author's life and thoughts, access to who the writer *is* as an individual? Grace Mildmay emerges as a clearly delineated figure, providing a stout narrative encasement in which to preserve the piety of herself and her family. She might be seen to reveal her Protestant devotion, as well as her sense, as her life draws to a close, of the subordination of temporal concerns to the providential pattern of eternity. But in the process there emerge intriguing questions about her identity. Given that her marriage occurred 50 years before her diary was written, do her late life reminiscences efface the emotions she might have entertained at the time of, for example, her marriage to a man whose main goal was to be absent from home, as well as her subjection to the caprices of a parsimonious father, a treacherous sister and a deceptive father-in-law? If Lady Grace's autobiography is to be taken at face value, these adverse events afford opportunities for her to grow closer to God. But how did she respond to the injustices at the time, and how did she express her responses in words and actions? These are questions that leak out of a memoir's compressed chronology, questions to which answers might never be found, or to which answers might sometimes be pieced together from the written records of others who knew the writer. The few letters written to Lady Grace by servants and doctors reflect little more than the class boundaries that mark communications of the time, so that the civilities of 'your humble servant', and so on, forbid any genuine opinion of her person. And the epitaph written for Lady Grace by her daughter, Lady Mary Fane, simply repeats for the mother the kind of descriptions that she has herself afforded others: 'Here also lieth Grace Lady Mildmay ... she was most devout, unspottedly chaste maid, wife and widow' (*With Faith and Physic*, p. 21).

In comparison with Lady Grace's authoritatively delineated manuscript, and in particular with Anne Clifford's colourful account of the various stages of her life, when reading Lady Margaret Hoby's diary we might (as has been suggested in our discussion of her) be struck by a certain blandness. Because Hoby's text functions as an examination of her conscience before God, we find no attempt on her part to make a cumulative assessment of her domestic life, her activities, her meetings with the preacher, her meals, her likes and dislikes, beyond the manner in which any one of these might, on a certain day, bring her closer to God, or draw her further away from Him. Hers is a reckoning prepared for herself and God, not for her descendants. And yet, conversely, her submission to the minutiae of daily activity is counterpoised by a sense of the eternity that weighs upon her. All immediacy of sensory impression, as well as of temporal enjoyment, is subordinated to an assessment of the eternal light that looms over each activity. It is, perhaps, precisely *within* Lady Margaret's struggle to reconcile the temporal and the eternal worlds that we experience something of the person she was. Individuality, as we know it, we will not find – but what does in fact emerge is a sense of personal intention, as well as a caution, a patience, an endlessly anxious scrutiny of the events of her everyday life in view of their eternal significance. The more harmoniously integrated her domestic activities, the closer she comes to concord between the temporal dimensions of her life and the ever present eternal meanings that push hard up against it.

In assessing how these women's life-writings take shape and what they mean – what they say about their authors' lives, how they might relate to the term, 'individuality' – we can note that all three writers claim an inclusiveness that is common to many diaries of this period. They write of the will to be included rather than to be extraordinary; the will to establish oneself as a functional and worthy part of a community. Lady Grace and Lady Anne focus on illustrating themselves in context with their ancestry: the former establishes a lineage of God-fearing ancestors, while the latter describes a complex social and financial life that adds depth and complexity to the Great Picture's overt harmony between the secular and the spiritual attributes of learning as passed down through her family. Lady Margaret describes a secluded family life through which she calibrates a personal and agonistic conversation with God. 'Self', for these three writers, is always composite, never separate: and the realization of selfhood is the understanding of how fully to inhabit – whether through prayer, through rightful inheritance of property, or through rightful expression of virtue – the place that one is born to. Indeed, none of these features is incompatible with the others: Lady Anne's secularity, for instance, is quite in tune with her sense of herself as a Christian. These writers' expressions of 'selfhood' are instead a matter of emphasis, since none of them sees herself as rising beyond what she is by birth equipped to possess.

Notes

1   *With Faith and Physic: the Life of a Tudor Gentlewoman, Lady Grace Mildmay, 1552–1620*, ed. Linda Pollock (London: Collins and Brown, 1993), p. 27. See also Retha M. Warnicke, 'Lady Mildmay's Journal: A Study in Autobiography and Meditation in Reformation England', *The Sixteenth Century Journal: Journal of Early Modern Studies* 1989 Spring 20 (1): 55–68.

2   The composition of the ideal gentlewoman – whose every part connoted the grace of the entire person – was adopted by English sonneteers, and was reflected in the comportment and carriage of the ideal English gentlewoman embodied here by Lady Mildmay. Nancy J. Vickers, in 'Diana Described: Scattered Women and Scattered Rhymes', *Critical Inquiry* 8 (2): 265–79, describes the Petrarchan depiction of women as 'a composite of details' (p. 267) which formed the model for European gentlewomen, as described, for example, by Nicholas Caussin in France: 'A Lady well accomplished is like a starre with fiue rays, which are the fiue virtues, of Deuotion, Modesty, Chastity, Discretion, and Charity. Devotion formeth the interiour; modesty makes it appeare in the exteriour with a requisite comlinesse; Chastity perfecteth both the one, and the other; Discretion applyeth it to the direction of others; and Charity crowneth all her actions'. Nicholas Caussin, extract from 'The holy court, second tome' (1631). Caussin's text, along with many others to be used in this discussion, is quoted from the facsimile collection *Conduct Literature for Women, 1500–1640*, ed. William St Clair and Irmgard Maasen, 6 vols (London: Pickering and Chatto, 2000), vol. 6 (pp. 51–97), p. 79. (Please note: this six-volume text has been reproduced in facsimile. For the sake of a legible script, the Elizabethan '*f*' has been modernized in quotations cited from the facsimiles compiled in these volumes.)

3   Note, for example, Anne Askew's 'Examinations,' edited and 'elucidated' by John Bale: *The Examinations of Anne Askew*, ed. Elaine V. Beilin (New York: Oxford University Press, 1996), and Richard Hyrde's 'Approbation' attached to Elizabeth Jocelin's *The*

Mother's Legacy, *Conduct Literature*, vol. 5, pp. 275–432. See also John Wallington's description of his wife's piety (described later in this chapter).

4   Christina Luckyj explores the relationship between silence and gender in Chapter Two of *A Moving Rhetoricke: Gender and Silence in Early Modern England* (Manchester: Manchester University Press, 2002).

5   In 'Women's Writing and the Self' Elspeth Graham develops an argument that two clusters of ideas can be identified in recent work on the early modern period: one that represents women as negatively defined and lacking positive identity; and the other that focuses on the degree of empowerment permitted to women through relatively fluid gender constructions. If on the one hand women were clearly subordinated as the 'weaker' gender, on the other hand they could manipulate their identities through the fluidity permitted by such a gender distinction. So, for instance, as many accounts of cross-dressing indicate, women – understood to be frailer and more impressionable – could appropriate masculine signs of power, and thus masculine power *itself*, by dressing as men. And this fluidity in turn highlighted the very 'constructedness' of identity: masculine superiority was understood to be imposed rather than intrinsic, a social interpretation rather than a biological necessity. Uncertainty prevailed about the very marks of gender that were relied upon for the functioning of domestic/public duties, and for understandings of propagation and laws of inheritance. 'Women's Writing and the Self', *Women and Literature in Britain, 1500–1700*, ed. Helen Wilcox (Cambridge: Cambridge University Press, 1996), pp. 209–33.

6   This point will be elaborated on later in our argument in considering the feminized union between body and soul that was the contemporary convention for devotional writing, both male and female. For now, it is useful to mention the work of Helen Wilcox, who has written extensively on the kind of female proactivity that might be gleaned from women's devotional writing. Wilcox pays attention, for example, to the effect of inverted syntax, which may highlight a woman's narrative voice although the overt narrative intention is to highlight a scriptural text. As an instance of this kind of female self-assertion, see Wilcox's analysis of the voice of the Quaker missionary Katherine Evans, in 'Selves in Strange Lands: Autobiography and Exile in the Mid-Seventeenth Century', ed. Ronald Bedford, Lloyd Davis and Philippa Kelly, *Early Modern Autobiography: Theories, Genres, Practices* (Ann Arbor: University of Michigan Press, 2006) p. 143.

7   Such analyses at times reveal more about the retrospective analyst than about the event of a particular death itself. Consider, for example, Lucinda Becker's discussion of Ralph Josselin's distaste for a widower's over-hasty wish to remarry. Becker cites Josselin's consecutive diary notes: his counseling of the man to postpone remarriage; the timely death of the woman he wished to remarry; his planting of an apricot tree. Becker's conclusion that the planting of the tree was Josselin's gesture of smug satisfaction that God's will had been done is wildly speculative, given that Josselin, whose diary entries are filled with *non sequiturs*, may have planted an apricot tree for reasons completely unrelated to the matter in hand. (Lucinda M. Becker, *Death and the Early Modern Englishwoman* (London: Ashgate, 2003), pp. 71–2. For a moving discussion of two women's deaths (Katherine Brettargh and Mary Gunter), see Robert Watson, *The Rest is*

Silence: Death as Annihilation in the English Renaissance (Berkeley: University of California Press, 1994), pp. 305–22.

8 For a useful article on the perils of childbirth, see Sharon Howard's discussion of the discourse of martyrdom in Alice Thornton's perilous and painful childbirth: 'Imagining the Pain and Peril of Seventeenth-century Childbirth: Travail and Deliverance in the Making of an Early Modern World', *Social History of Medicine* 16 (3) 2003: 367–82. If figures like Lady Ann Fanshawe indicate something of a norm, the approach of childbirth was a perilous event. Of Fanshawe's 14 pregnancies, only three survived all the way through to maturity. She gave birth to three daughters whom she named Elizabeth, four named Richard, and two named Henry. An interesting light is thrown on the difficulties encountered in pregnancy at the time when we consider that Fanshawe's three children who did survive – Katherine, Margaret and Anne – were all born within the period when she did not have to undergo the exertion of travelling abroad with her husband.

9 For accounts of this, see Christine Peters, *Women in Early Modern Britain, 1450–1640* (Basingstoke: Palgrave, 2003), pp. 45–67; Alison Sim, *The Tudor Housewife* (Montreal and Kingston: McGill-Queen's University Press, 1996), pp. 94–107, and Amy Louise Erickson, *Women and Property in Early Modern England* (London: Routledge, 1993), where she analyzes property law, upbringing and expectations of boys and girls, marriage settlements and inheritance. See also Judith M. Bennett, who takes the involvement of women in brewing as paradigmatic of women's access to, and involvement in, work during the rise of capitalism, and the low social status they were accorded. *Ale, Beer, and Brewsters in England: Women's Work in a Changing World, 1300–1600* (Oxford: Oxford University Press, 1996). One of the most concise and informative accounts of women's employment remains that given by Carol Camden in 1952: *The Elizabethan Woman* (New York and London: Elsevier Press, 1952), pp. 145–8.

10 See Eve Rachele Sanders, *Gender and Literacy in Early Modern England* (Cambridge: Cambridge University Press, 1998), who argues that literacy 'helped to engender new and profoundly different forms of subjectivity' (p. 2). Helen Hackett also offers some useful speculations on women's literacy in *Women and Romance Fiction in the English Renaissance* (Cambridge: Cambridge University Press, 2000). Thomas Salter voices a typical view of women's ideal self-employment when he says, 'how far more conuenient the Distaffe, and Spindle, Nedle and Thimble were for them with a good and honest reputation, then the skill of well ---[word unclear] a penne or wrightyng a loftie vearce with disshame and dishonour, if in the same there be more erudition than vertue…' 'A mirrhor mete for all mothers, matrons, and maidens, intituled the mirrhor of modestie' (1579), *Conduct Literature*, vol. 5, p. 37.

11 For some valuable discussions of these women see the following: on Lady Anne Clifford, see Mary Ellen Lamb, who depicts Clifford as a subject 'split' between her role as an aristocratic heir and a woman who defies contemporary authority in 'The Agency of the Split Subject: Lady Anne Clifford and the Uses of Reading', *English Literary Renaissance* 22 (3): 347–68; Barbara Lewalski, 'Claiming Patrimony and Constructing a Self: Anne Clifford and her *Diary*', in *Writing Women in Jacobean England* (Cambridge, Mass: Harvard University Press, 1993) pp. 125–51, and Lewalski also, 'Re-writing Patriarchy and Patronage: Margaret Clifford, Anne Clifford, and Aemilia

Lanyer', *The Yearbook of English Studies* (21): 87–106. See also Mihoko Suzuki, who argues that Clifford undermined the conventional perception of women as either a passive means of succession (i.e. property) or as unruly obstacles to the steady flow of a male-centred lineage: 'Anne Clifford and the Gendering of History', *CLIO* 30 (2): 195–229. See also Sharon Seelig, *Autobiography and Gender in Early Modern Literature*: *Reading Women's Lives, 1599–1678* (Cambridge: Cambridge University Press, 2006): including Clifford and Hoby in her discussion, Seelig explores the relation between the writers' choices of genre and the stories they chose to tell, tracing a progression in women's writing from simple, factual accounts to more imaginative forms of self-representation. Mildmay and Clifford are also discussed in both Helen Hackett's *Women and Romance Fiction* (reading preferences) and Eve Rachele Sanders's *Gender and Literacy* (the diaries themselves).

12 Lady Margaret married Thomas Posthumous Hoby whose mother had married, on the death of his father, Lord John Russell, uncle to Anne on the maternal side.

13 Bishop Joseph Hall, *The Works of the Right Reverend Joseph Hall*, a new ed. rev. and corr. with some additions, by Philip Wynter. 10 vols (Oxford: Oxford University Press, 1863), p. 644.

14 For a discussion of the expectations of women articulated by conduct publications, see Effie Botonaki, *Seventeenth-Century English Women's Autobiographical Writings: Disclosing Enclosures, Studies in British Literature*, vol. 88 (Lewiston: Edwin Mellon Press, 2004). See Introduction, pp. 1–42.

15 Patrick Hannay, 'A happy husband' (1618), *Conduct Literature,* vol. 4, p. 376.

16 Consider, for example, Thomas Becon, who says, 'An honeste wife ought not behynde her husbandes back to haunt any euell company'. Becon wrote the preface to Miles Coverdale's first English translation of 'The christen state of matrimonye,' by Heinrich Bullinger (1541), which went through eight English translations over the next 35 years. *Conduct Literature*, vol. 2, p. 162. Thomas Salter advises against association with 'kitchine seruauntes' and 'idle housewiues,' who should be "shonned, as infectious diseases" (p. 25). For William Whately, woman's 'impudency and vnwoman-hood, doth track the way to the harlots house'. 'A Bride-Bush: or, A Direction for Married Persons' (1619), *Conduct Literature*, vol. 5, pp. 251–2.

17 The works of Erasmus (1467–1536), *De pueris statim ac liberaliter instituendis declamatio*, trans. Beert C. Verstraete, *Collected Works of Erasmus*, ed. J.K. Sowards, vol. 26 (Toronto: University of Toronto Press, 1985), and Juan Vives (1492–1540), *Vives: On Education, a Translation of the De Tradendis Disciplinis of Juan Luis Vives*, ed. and trans. Foster Watson (Cambridge: Cambridge University Press, 1913), had a great deal of influence on sixteenth- and seventeenth-century pedagogy, and were manifest in such widely consulted works as Sir Thomas Elyot's *The Book Named the Governour* (1531), ed. S.E. Lehmberg (London: Dent, 1970), which dealt with the education of the English governing class. Richard Mulcaster's *Positions Concerning the Training Up of Children* (1581), ed. William Barker (Toronto: Toronto Universty Press, 1994), Thomas Becon's *A New Catechisme* (1564), *Conduct Literature*, vol. 2, pp. 267–328, and Thomas Salter's 'The mirrhor of modestie' (1579), *Conduct Literature*, vol. 5, pp. 1–72 were also influential.

18 *The Autobiography of Thomas Whythorne*, ed. James M. Osborn, modern spelling edition (London: Oxford University Press, 1962) p. 120

19 Sylvia Brown in *Women's Writing in Stuart England* (Phoenix Mill: Sutton Publishing, 1999) has referred to a similar feature in the Mother's Legacy genre. She suggests that the authors of these legacies 'are themselves caught between the contradictory self-assertion which the genre allows, and the self-negation it demands' (p. vii).

20 See Elaine V. Beilin, 'Anne Askew's Dialogue with Authority', *Contending Kingdoms: Historical, Psychological and Feminist Approaches to the Literature of Sixteenth-Century England and France*, ed. Marie-Rose Logan and Peter L. Rudnytsky (Detroit: Wayne State University Press, 1991), pp. 313–22. In another context Helen Wilcox observes of a woman's assumption of the mantle of 'weak' or 'ignorant' subject that she 'is transformed from an obstacle into a source of praise for the God who will deign to use such means for glory'. 'My Soule in Silence', in *Representing Women in Renaissance England*, ed. Claude J. Summers and Ted-Larry Pebworth (Columbia and London: University of Missouri Press, 1997), p. 12.

21 From the papers of Nehemiah Wallington, '"A Faithfull Memoriall of my owne Mother that is deceased", drawn up by her husband, John Wallington'. Printed (with modernized spelling) in *Historical Notices of Events Occurring Chiefly in the Reign of Charles I*, ed. R. Webb from the original MSS, 2 vols (London: Richard Bentley, 1869), vol I, pp. x–xi.

22 Helen Wilcox calls this 'a feminized soul dependent on the power of grace'. 'My Soule in Silence', *Representing Women*, p. 14.

23 Song of Solomon, 1. 13: 'A bundle of myrrh is my wellbeloved unto me; he shall lie all night betwixt my breasts'.

24 Song of Solomon, 1. 2: 'Let him kiss me with the kisses of his mouth: for thy love is better than wine'.

25 In describing God's nurturing love her voice chimes with those of other, later women, often of very different social standings and religious persuasions, for whom God is able to 'annointe' a woman's 'teate', as Elizabeth Grymston puts it. 'For where he purposeth to heale, he spareth not to launce: and if he see thou be fostered by the world thy naturall nurse, he can annoint hir teate with the bitternesse of discontent, to weane thee from hir: for he that bindes the franticke, and awakes the lethargee, is troublesome, but friendly to both.' Elizabeth Grymeston, 'Miscellanea, Meditations, Memoratives' (1604), Brown University Women Writers Project first electronic edition, 2001. Source copy owned by the Bodleian Library, shelfmark: Quarto.E.31.Th.Bs. STC 12407. Later in the century the Quaker Margaret Fell, wife of George Fox, employs God's 'tenderness and the bowels of love' towards women as a powerful argument for female speech and female agency as primary carriers of the Gospel, transforming Mildmay's Tudor conservatism into the radical and revolutionary. Margaret Fell, *Women's Speaking Justified*, 1667. Brown University Women Writers Project first electronic edition, 2002. <http://www.wwp.brown.edu/encoding/research/NASSR/WWP.html>. Source copy owned by Henry E. Huntington Library, shelfmark: 94232, Wing F643. See also Margaret Askew Fell (Fox), 'Women's Speaking Justified: Epistle from the women's yearly meeting at York, 1688' (Los Angeles: Clark Memorial Library, 1979), and Catie Gill, *Women in the Seventeenth-Century Quaker Community* (Aldershot: Ashgate, 2005).

26 See Sylvia Brown, 'General Introduction: The Mother's Legacy', *Women's Writing in Stuart England*, p. vii. C.W. Bynum aptly describes the female model for the religious man: 'The male writer who saw his soul as a bride of God or his religious role as womanly submission and humility was conscious of using an image of reversal. He sought reversal because reversal and renunciation were at the heart of a religion whose dominant symbol is the cross – life achieved through death'. *Fragmentation and Redemption: Essays on Gender and the Human Body in Medieval Religion* (New York: Zone Books, 1991) p. 171.

27 *Female and Male Voices in Early Modern England: An Anthology of Renaissance Writing*, ed. Betty S. Travitsky and Anne Lake Prescott (New York: Columbia University Press, 2000).

28 Richard Rogers, *Two Puritan Diaries, By Richard Rogers and Samuel Ward*, ed. with an introduction by M.M. Knappen (1933) (Gloucester Mass.: P. Smith, 1966), p. 101

29 William Gouge says that a husband's 'superioritie and authoritie hath power to command his wife'. He later stipulates, however, that 'If her husband command her to doe that which God hath expresly forbidden, then ought she by no means to yeeld vnto it: if she doe, it may rather be termed a joint conspiracie of husband and wife together against Gods will'. Gouge,'Of Domesticall Duties', *Conduct Literature*, vol. 5, pp. 171, 173.

30 St Paul in his letter to the Ephesians, 5. 22-4, exhorts: 'Wives, submit yourselves unto your own husbands, as unto the Lord. For the husband is the head of the wife, even as Christ is the head of the church; and he is the saviour of the body. Therefore, as the church is subject unto Christ, so let the wives be to their own husbands in every thing'. Similarly in 1 Corinthians 12.3 he says, ' I would have you know, that the head of every man is Christ; and the head of the woman is the man; and the head of Christ is God'.

31 The reformed theologian Heinrich Bullinger offers the Pauline background for this. He gives a long description of the making of Eve from Adam's flesh, and continues: 'the wyfe is the husbandes flesh and bone ... yet was she not made of the head. For the husband is the head and master of the wyfe' (p. 42). Becon, too, describes Christ who for 'the defence of his church bestowed his bloud and life. And for this cause is man head of the wife, euen as Christ is head of the congregation'. *Conduct Literature*, vol. 2, p. 274. Gouge exhorts wives to practice subjection, meekness and 'mildnesse' of 'countenance, gesture, and ... cariage'. *Conduct Literature*, vol. 5, p. 112.

32 Dorothy Leigh writes to her children of the devil who inhabits the waking world: ' doe not sleepe at night', she says, 'till thou hast humbled they selfe before God on thy knees in prayer; for night is a time when the world leaues a man (as it were) for a while, and when the world leaues him, the diuell hath not so much power ouer him; for the world is a great Instrument for the diuell to worke by. Therefore when the world is asleepe (as it were) the diuells power is weakened, and then bee sure thou prayest to God to deliuer thee from the diuell, and from the world'. 'The Mother's Blessing', in *Women's Writing in Stuart England*, p. 36. Elizabeth Richardson writes of the devil who pervades 'the vaine world', 'my corrupt flesh', and 'sinfull thoughts', tempting her to 'offend with my tongue, or in my actions.' *A Ladies Legacie to Her Daughters* (1645), in *Women's Writing*, pp. 199–200. And Elizabeth Jocelin forewarns her unborn child that the devil is lurking the minute one opens one's eyes: 'At thy first wakinge in the morninge, be carefull of thy selfe that thou harbor in thy brayn no vayn or unprofitable but of all no

ungodly fancy ... but straight frame thy selfe to meditate on the mercies of god ... The devils malice is easily perceived for even now he lyes lurkynge ... The infinit malice of the divell and your own exceedinge weaknes how do you thinke you wear preserved from his snares while you slept or do you thinke he only besets you when you are awake? No be not deceived he is not so fayr an enemy'. *Mother's Legacy*, in *Women's Writing*, p. 112.

33 For more on this, see Christine Peters, *Women in Early Modern Britain*, pp. 132–3, 140.

34 In her famous discourse on the virtues of breastfeeding, for example, the Countess of Lincoln condemns those who rely on wetnurses in order to preserve their own strength and beauty: a woman who refuses to nurse her own children betrays her God-given duty (while also potentially compromising the character of the child, which was believed to be shaped by the milk it suckled – see Christine Peters, *Women in Early Modern Britain*, p. 66). Women, it was insisted, could learn all they needed from their home-coming husbands.

35 While conduct books exhorted women to confine themselves to the home, working guilds were open to young women and to women who continued at least nominally to run them when their husbands deceased. Marriage to a member of a guild conferred rights upon a wife, which she was permitted to retain beyond her husband's death. A few women operated sizeable businesses, although most female shop owners were widows who ran those left to them by their late husbands. Steve Rappaport also makes the point that, given the nature of preindustrial forms of production, 'most women were actively engaged in the production and distribution of goods and services, often working in shops alongside male members of the household', learning economic skills not through apprenticeship but through informal 'on the job' experience. 'Reconsidering Apprenticeship in Sixteenth-Century London', *Renaissance Society and Culture*, ed. John Monfasani and Ronald G. Musto (New York: Italica Press, 1991) p. 240, f. 2. But it is also true that women's work – the major part of which was of low status, like searching the bodies of suspected plague victims, or as an 'unchaste' taverner's servant – 'conferred different degrees of status and economic independence'. Peters, *Women in Early Modern Britain*, p. 65.

36 Sir Thomas Elyot, *The defence of good women, deuised and made by Sir Thomas Elyot knight. Conduct Literature*, vol. 2, pp. 201–66. Elyot's misogynistic character, Caninius, for example, says that 'in woman kinde faithe neuer rested, yet be you still as blinde as your litell god Cupide, for the childish affections which ye beare to your ladies, causeth you to think the thinges which ye se, to be nothing but vanities' (pp. 209–10). Candidus defends the reputation of women against this assault, arguing, 'I haue found women much blamed for their inconstancy: but for mine own knowlage I neuer perceiued any suche lacke to be in them, but rather the contrary' (p. 210).

37 Xantip, the scold, asks what she should do about her stingy, disrespectful husband, who does not allow her to behave well because he 'will not let me haue that which is necessary, but spend that we haue in tipling and swilling, ... and amongst whores and harlots'. This attitude attacks the heart of current opinion about the superior wisdom of husbands, whose wishes should not be contradicted by women's whims. *A Looking-Glasse for Maried Folkes* (1610), *Conduct Literature*, vol. 4, p. 118.

38 See Travitsky and Prescott, *Female and Male Voices*, p. 82.

39 *Jane Anger Her Protection for Women*. PDF document rendering of STC 644 prepared in March 2000 by Wes Folkerth, Dept of English, McGill University. On-line access: <http://www.shakespeare.mcgill.ca/anger.pdf>

40 William Dethick, *The Excellencie of man, his nobilitie, praise, glory, honour and dignitie*, section titled 'Of the Praise and Glorye of Women', Folger Library MS V.b.125, ascribed to Sir William Dethick, c. 1610, pp. 40v–41r.

41 Sir Francis Fane, in Folger MS V.a.180. Commonplace book, compiled c. 1655–6, p. 41.

42 See Carol Thomas Neely, 'Shakespeare's Tragedies and Early Modern Culture', in *Shakespearean Tragedy and Gender*, ed. Shirley Nelson Garner and Madelon Sprengnether (Bloomington: Indiana University Press, 1996), p. 79.

43 See Amy Louise Erickson, *Women and Property*, pp. 53–4. Erickson provides a very good discussion of the range of expectations put upon housewives, as well as the cultivation of housewifery as an art that was not confined to marital situations (pp. 53–5).

44 Joseph Swetnam *The Arraignment of lewde, idle, froward and unconstant women or, the vanity of them, chuse you whether with a commendation of the wise, virtuous, and honest women. Pleasant for married-men, profitable for young-men, and hurtfull to none.* (London: Printed by E.C. for F. Grove, on Snow-Hill, near the Sarazenshead, 1615).

45 Heinrich Bullinger, *The christen state of matrimonye* (1541), *Conduct Literature*, vol. 2, p. 162.

46 Thomas Becon, *Catechisme*, *Conduct Literature*, vol. 2, p. 281.

47 Richard Braithwaite, 'The English Gentlewoman' (1641), *Conduct Literature*, vol. 6, p. 153.

48 John Cotta, quoted by Linda Pollock, *With Faith and Physic*, p. 93.

49 Gervase Markham, *The English Housewife: Containing the inward and Outward virtues which ought to be in a complete woman; as her skill in physic, cookery, banqueting-stuff, distillation, perfumes, wool, hemp, flax, dairies, brewing, baking, and all other things belonging to a household*, ed. Michael Best (Kingston and Montreal: McGill-Queen's University Press, 1986), p. 8.

50 Mary Trye notes how she inherited her medical skills: 'abiding the late great and never-to-be-forgotten pestilential calamity of this city, and undergoing that mortal stroke, in which I lost two of my dearest friends, my father and mother, but surviving them myself, I received a medicinal talent from my father, which by the instruction of so excellent a tutor as he was to me, and my constant preparation and observation of medicines, together with my daily experience by reason of this very great practice; as also being mistress of a reasonable share of that knowledge and discretion other women attain; I made myself capable of disposing such noble and successful medicines, and managing so weighty and great a concern'. 'Medicatrix, OR The woman physician', in *English Women's Voices, 1540–1700*, ed. Charlotte F. Otten (Miami: Florida International University Press, 1992), p. 193.

51 *My ladies looking glasse*, *Conduct Literature*, vol. 4, p. 270.

52 Hoby's first marriage, to Walter Devereux in 1589, ended with his death in 1591 when he accompanied his brother into France and was shot in the cheek and killed. A second marriage was arranged very quickly, in order to avoid the attentions of bounty hunters,

and just two months after becoming a widow, she married Thomas Sidney. He died, however, in 1595, when Margaret was just 25 years of age.

53 Joanna Moody speculates on this in the Introduction to Hoby's published diary, *The Private Life of an Elizabethan Lady: The Diary of Lady Margaret Hoby, 1599–1605*, ed. Joanna Moody (Phoenix Mill: Sutton Publishing, 1998), p. xxix.

54 William, son of Lord and Lady Eure of Malton, called in with some friends on 27 August 1600, presumably in order to rouse anger in Thomas Hoby, who was detested amongst the neighbours for his petty, litigious ways. Custom insisted that the Hobys receive him and his friends, and the young men proceeded to become very drunk, to call Mr Hoby a cuckold, to deprive the Hobys of sleep all night, and to ride off in the morning breaking windows as they went.

55 Elaine McKay, *The Diary Network in Sixteenth and Seventeenth-Century England*, Monash University School of Historical Studies, 2001; on-line access:
    <http://www.arts.monash.edu.au/eras/edition_2/mckay.htm>

56 Given the petty, litigious nature of her third husband, his small stature and raucous ways, it is most unlikely that Lady Margaret – who had been briefly and happily married to the dashing Thomas Sidney – could possibly have fallen in love with Sir Thomas in the eleven months between Sidney's death and her third wedding day. Indeed, she had refused Sir Thomas's hand when he proposed to her in 1591, marrying Thomas Sidney instead. See *Diary*, intro. pp. xiii–xxv.

57 We simply do not know, for example, how prominent her second husband might have remained in her mind. We do know that in the seventeenth century, when people died of natural causes far more frequently than they do today (and many people could not even remember how many children they had conceived) death was more easily accepted. Indeed, the death of Lady Margaret's sister-in-law merits only a brief factual mention in her diary before her discussion of supper and prayers.

58 Dean Ebner, *Autobiography in Seventeenth-Century England* (The Hague: Mouton, 1971), p. 20.

59 See Elaine McKay's astute and concise analysis of these points in *The Diary Network in Sixteenth and Seventeenth-Century England*.

60 This quotation from Clifford is from *The Diaries of Lady Anne Clifford*, ed. David Clifford (Wolfeboro Falls: Alan Sutton, 1991). In his prologue, pp. 1–2, the editor cites this passage from Lady Anne's Great Books. Unless otherwise specified, all other quotations in this essay are from *The Diary of the Lady Anne Clifford*, with an introductory note by V. Sackville-West (London: William Heinemann, 1923).

Chapter 8

Women's Wills

An early modern English life, its possessions and its desired legacy for future generations, could be inscribed in the writing of a will. Because women made approximately 20 per cent of the two million wills that survive from the 1550s–1750s,[1] wills can be regarded as one of the main genres in which women wrote, or dictated, during the period. Wills exemplify less a category of text than a range of factors that encompass stylistic conventions, interpersonal contexts of authorship and response, representing key institutions such as religion, the law, family and gender relations along with practices of textual production, dissemination and reception. A further element underscoring the generic quality of wills is that they must be proven; like all genres and texts, they are subject to interpretation and dispute over meaning and intention. Conceived generically, wills thus mark the interaction of discursive, historical and social factors now regarded as central to notions of textuality and meaning. Thinking about wills in such terms in no way diminishes their importance in legal and social history, nor is it a move aimed simply at substituting one disciplinary approach for another. It does, however, allow wills to be considered as texts that position authors and readers in socially and personally important ways. Wills reveal the workings of powerful institutions and discourses while also contributing to and intervening in them, and they interact with other genres in the period such as plays and advice books.

While the majority of people in the early modern period did not make wills, they were widely known about and their purpose was respected. Wills are a paradoxical kind of text – a part of everyday life and death, they are yet infrequently encountered by the majority of people, and generally in a solemn social context. Wills provide a meeting point between the wishes of those now dead and the wishes of the living: 'An outward and visible sign of wealth and a check upon the "wrongful" disposition of property, [a will] enshrines the wishes of the individual holder as against the demands of the potential heir. It is in effect the written version of the "dying words," the permanent expression of the deathbed wish'.[2] Jack Goody's description captures the life and death drama inherent in making and executing wills as well as the micro and macro effects that they can have, from structuring interpersonal relationships to reproducing the social system.[3] Indeed, as Shakespeare sensed when starting such plays as *Hamlet* and *King Lear* amid crises of family succession and settlement, any system of inheritance – with the laws and codes that implement it – struggles, in J.H. Baker's words, 'to hold a balance between the living, the dead, and the unborn'.[4] Baker's summation of the functions of a will as a legal device mindfully understates what is at stake. Inheritance can perhaps best be theorized as a set of customs produced by different attitudes to death and dying in feudal and early capitalist societies. Since land could only be devised by will after the 1540 Statute of Uses, the genre of the will provides an important illustration of shifting inheritance practices that reflect not only economic and political change but also cultural change in early modern England.

The 'cosmic' significance of wills and succession that drives Shakespeare's great tragedies is also tied to the legal and material aspects of interpersonal, family and gender relations. In this light, wills exemplify the complicated connections among the religious and temporal discourses that pervade everyday life in the period. *The Book of Common Prayer* and tracts such as Thomas Becon's *The Sicke Mans Salve* (1558–59; 28 reprints by 1632), William Perkins's *A Salve for a Sicke Man* (1595), William Perneby's *A Direction to Death* (1599), and Christopher Sutton's *Disce Mori, Learne to Die* (1600) all exhorted readers to die well. An important part of doing so was piously to make a will. Christopher Marsh sums up the tenor of Becon's influential work in this respect as follows: 'it is the Christian's essential duty to settle his estate, on loan from God, in a manner which demonstrates gratitude and faith, and serves to signal – but not cause – his salvation ... The real duty a testator performed in making his will was to dispose of his wealth in a godly fashion'.[5] The godly disposal of wealth implies that religious and moral aspects of will making are fundamentally linked to social and material concerns. The difficult critical-historical task is in part, we suggest, to avoid elevating one set of concerns at the expense of the other and instead to grasp their interdependence. In general it is only when dispute arises over a will that the complex of personal, moral, material and other motives can be revealed and placed under scrutiny. In recounting a court case between family members in Douai in 1434, Martha Howell observes, 'This was ... a suit between intimates, people closely bound to one another by shared experiences, shared property, shared affections'.[6] Her words are an important reminder not only of the cultural conditions in which selves, kinship and property are situated, but also of the experiential and affective facets of people's lives that permeate property relations as much as they are constituted by them.

In the early modern period, the various situations in which married women could make wills are analogous to their many other restricted legal and social rights to hold and exchange property. Sara Mendelson and Patricia Crawford summarize the situation thus:

> unmarried daughters and married women were rare as testators, since each needed male permission – a father or husband, respectively—to dispose of personal property. Married women required a husband's consent to dispose of personal property, apart from bequests of pin money ... A widow's power to bequeath her possessions depended upon how much of the family wealth her husband had left to her.[7]

On this reading, it is impossible not to conceive of married women's wills as framed and ordered by authoritative masculine speech acts of consent, permission and bequest.

Such authority derived from the common law, which restricted married women's rights to hold property and to pursue other modes of social activity. The opening pages of *The Law's Resolutions of Women's Rights* (1632) succinctly sums up the situation for married women: '*baron* and *feme* ... are but one person. And by this a married Woman perhaps may either doubt whether she be either none or no more than half a person'. The author goes on vividly to describe the overarching property rights of the husband:

> the prerogative of the Husband is best discerned in his dominion over all external things, in which the wife by combination divesteth herself of propriety in some sort and casteth it upon her governor ... For thus it is, if before Marriage the Woman were possessed of Horses, Neat, Sheep, Corn, Wool, Money, Plate, and Jewels, all manner of movable substance is presently by conjunction the husband's to sell, keep, or bequeath if he die.[8]

Legal writers also considered situations in which married women were and were not empowered to make wills. Henrie Swinburn suggests that it is just as well that a wife is unable to bequeath real property; if she could, she would more than likely be pressured to 'deuise the same to her husband ... if this gappe were lefte open, fewe children should succeede in the mothers inheritaunce'. Swinburn later observes that a wife can bequeath goods and chattels as long as she has the husband's consent, and that there are some situations in which she can bequeath movables without consent – for example, if a betrothed woman dies before marriage, or if a married woman is an executrix and needs to pay off debts for the deceased.[9] Ultimately, Swinburn compares the position of the *feme covert* with other figures not always able to make testament, including prisoners and 'deafe and dumbe' people. Swinburn does note that single women can make wills involving movables from the age of twelve.[10] Writing later in the seventeenth century, John Godolphin reiterates the general rules and the exceptions: 'That *Women Covert* are Intestable for want of Freedom, is not such a general Rule in Law as to exclude all Exceptions'. The details agree with Swinburn's position that most of the exceptions depend on the husband's consent. Godolphin also points out that 'If a *Feme Sole* make Will, and after take a Husband, the same is Revocation thereof'.[11] Early modern women's wills comprised a highly contingent genre.

But in some respects contingency is a feature of much will making in the period. Though the idea behind a will was generally understood, in legal terms the purposes and consequences of wills were rather uncertain. They had only been recently formally instituted as part of the inheritance system; they had not been allowed under feudal land law, and the legal power to devise land was not introduced until 1540, before which trusts had been used to manipulate this restriction.[12] Theoretically trusts could provide all single and married women with access to separate property, though in practice they applied only to those who belonged to the landed classes. Even this legal strategy did not assure women's positions, however. Any trust might of course be challenged in the Court of Chancery, where the results could not be predicted, and trusts could also be established to benefit males. Susan Staves attributes the employment of trusts to protect a wife's property from the husband less to concerns to secure her position than to satisfy 'the desire of the wife's father to continue to exercise some control over the property he gave the wife to bring into the marriage … to ensure that at least some of it remained for the wife's father's grandchildren'.[13] The gradual development of the succession strategy of strict settlement through the sixteenth and seventeenth centuries (which is discussed in more detail below) is a further sign of the instability of the inheritance system. Existing strategies with conservative patriarchal and dynastic goals were not guaranteed to work, and underwent continuing change and review until a regularly effective device was developed. (Strict settlement continued to be used till the mid-nineteenth century when its effectiveness was curtailed.) Yet despite the potential for financial and familial advantage and sustained moral and religious pressure from the church, it is estimated that less than 20 per cent of the adult population made wills through the period.[14] Though wills had well-known temporal and spiritual benefits, making one was an unusual act, and very unusual for a woman. Men, according to Amy Erickson, were up to six times more likely than women to make wills.[15]

Changing legal and social conditions through the 1500s and 1600s do not diminish the significance of making a will. The fact that relatively few people made wills may increase the value of the ones that were made as documents of attitudes and practices. The total number of wills, with their long-recognized role in interpersonal, familial and social relations, makes them key texts for examining, in Erickson's words, 'the ingenuity of many ordinary women in working within a massively restrictive system' of inheritance and marital property laws.[16] Simultaneously exceptional and unexceptional, private and public, individual and collective, wills exemplify elite and ordinary women's involvement in producing texts, entering discourse, and representing themselves as capable of acting constructively in interpersonal and institutional contexts. Marcia Pointon writes that reconsidering wills made by women during the eighteenth century 'permit[s] a new understanding … of how women felt about the things they owned, and how they employed the fact of their possession in the expectation of exercising influence'.[17] In short, as authors of wills, early modern women of diverse social levels inscribe and exercise agency.

Staging Will-making

A brief account of the role of wills and succession in two popular plays from the early 1600s can demonstrate the struggle over multiple levels of value that were instructively played out on early modern stages. Neither of the comedies, *The Widow's Tears* by George Chapman (c. 1605)[18] and part one of Thomas

Heywood's *The Fair Maid of the West* (c. 1603)[19] ventures into the evocative existential realms of windblown heaths or profound soliloquies. Both plays do, however, stage a range of concerns over the social and personal stakes of inheritance, particularly in relation to women. While at times Chapman's drama resonates somewhat more grandly – near the end a character pronounces, 'in this topsy-turvy world, friendship and bosom-kindness are but made covers for mischief' (V, iv, 33–34) – Heywood's crossdressing adventure enacts a wider range of testatory moves and intrigues. Taken together, the two plays demonstrate many of the prevalent attitudes and practices relating to early modern women's wills and their roles in the inheritance system.

The opening scenes of Chapman's play are dominated by the malcontent Thrasalio, whose scheming echoes that of outsiders like Iago and Edmund. He feels unjustly disadvantaged by the primogeniture system that has privileged his elder brother Lysander: 'you were too forward when you stepped into the world before me, and gulled me of the land that my spirits and parts were indeed born to' (I, i, 45–7). Homosocial conflict, imposed by common law, generates the ensuing sequence of misogynist attitudes and acts by both brothers. First, Thrasalio plots to marry a widow to escape his predicament. His cynicism towards widows, supported by the play's axiomatic title, flows from this family position and legitimates his plan, 'how short-lived widows' tears are … they mourn in their gowns, and laugh in their sleeves' (I, i, 141–4). His second ploy is to undermine Lysander's faith in his wife Cynthia's fidelity. As in *Othello*, the effect is practically immediate and suggests the credit men are prepared to grant male associates over and against the words and actions of women: 'that ill-relished speech … hath taken so deep hold of my thoughts,' Lysander readily admits after hearing Thrasalio's remarks (II, i, 1–3).

This strand of Thrasalio's misogyny again stems from what he perceives as family disenfranchisement. Though he admires Cynthia, he holds that her virtue has so impressed his brother that

> he hath invested her in all his state, the ancient inheritance of our family, and left my nephew and the rest to hang upon her pure devotion, so as he dead, and she matching (as I am resolved she will) with some young prodigal, what must ensue, but her post-issue beggared, and our house, already sinking, buried quick in ruin. (II, iii, 80–85)

By invoking the 'ancient inheritance', Thrasalio couples his own aspirations with the 'dynastic ambition of the house', a motive that largely drove aristocratic succession through strict settlement for over two hundred years.[20] Patently not naming himself, Thrasalio effaces his interest behind that of the family, positioning himself and his nephew, rather than his elder brother, as its authentic heirs. His views about widows, along with the conception of the family that underlies those views, are triply supported through the rest of the action. The widowed countess Eudora initially rejects him for what may sound like overly strong antiromantic reasons: 'am I now so scant of worthy suitors that may advance mine honour, advance my estate, strengthen my alliance (if I list to wed)' (II, iv, 164–6). Yet she soon falls for him after being told of Thrasalio's remarkable potency by the bawd Arsace. Notwithstanding the apparent decline in remarriage rates for widows from the sixteenth to the late seventeenth centuries[21], Eudora's response reinforces the popular misogynist image of the lusty widow, as does Cynthia's desire for a burly soldier soon after briefly grieving for her husband's death. The soldier ends up being Lysander after all, trying to test his wife's chastity. At the last Cynthia manages to turn the tables by claiming she knew who it was all the time (V, v, 84).

The play's sardonic view of husband-wife relationships rests on various assumptions about property, succession and marriage. The primogeniture system leads more or less inevitably to rivalry between males, which is waged in large part through manoeuvring and exploiting women. Thrasalio does not consider working for a living, for he has been imbued with the aristocratic ethos that takes his family's reputation for perpetual realty despite its sinking fortunes.[22] His scheme to wed Eudora (which the Revels editor, writing in the early 1970s, can label 'a good practical purpose'[23]), indicates acceptance that marriage, even if not to a widow, was always the best way for a man 'to improve his financial condition'.[24] More significantly, the justification of antifeminist sentiments about wives and widows through dynastic invocation of house and family suggests the kind of patriarchal class-consciousness that could foster and support the practices of strict settlement. Through avoidance of dower and preference for sons, this mode of succession, so Eileen Spring argues, was primarily responsible for the 'decline of women's rights over land' through the period.[25] Yet notwithstanding its significance, this set of concerns does not tell the whole story of women, wills and property in the period. The antifeminist impacts of strict settlement among the aristocracy and gentry, as Erickson and Cicely Howell note, are often not reproduced in the wills of ordinary people.[26] *The Fair Maid of the West* offers a theatrical version of some of these contrasting attitudes to gender and succession.

As in *The Widow's Tears*, from early on the action in Heywood's play is importantly tied to questions of inheritance and family background. In the opening scenes, Captain Goodlacke admonishes his companion Spencer for being infatuated with the beautiful barmaid, Besse Bridges: 'you forget your selfe, / One of your birth and breeding, thus to dote / Upon a Tanners daughter: why, her father / Sold hydes in Somersetshire, and being trade-falne, / Sent her to service' (I, ii, 15–19). His words assume that personal, moral and material worth can all be equated. Spencer is a gentleman but owns no estate; he is a younger son, like Chapman's Thrasalio, but he has been left financially independent. Forced to flee England, and with no pressing family obligations, Spencer initially leaves all his moveables to beloved Besse: 'Money, apparell, and what else thou findest, / Perhaps worth my bequest and thy receiving, / I make thee mistresse of' (I, iv, 39–41), and then adds a tavern, The Winde-mill, in the Cornish town of Fowey. Besse runs the tavern very profitably – her beauty draws in many customers and she treats her staff well. Her success suggests popular recognition that the *feme sole* or widow faced no legal restraints on trade and could be a thriving entrepreneur.[27]

Meanwhile, overseas a seriously wounded Spencer tells Goodlacke that he has left a will giving Besse £500 per year while she remains chaste (II, ii, 74–5). The terms seem to recall the occasional practice of permitting dower or jointure only while the widow remained unmarried. Besse's continued financial success brings social praise and risks – Goodlacke hopes to lead her into wantonness so he can inherit Spencer's money, and the mayor of Fowey admires and envies her wealth and good name: 'I could wish a match / Betwixt her and mine one and only sonne' (III, iii, 12–13). In particular, Goodlacke's presumption that he might be able to claim the inheritance hints at the vulnerability of heiresses, widows and other female beneficiaries to legal challenge from interested male relatives and parties – a predicament illustrated by the well-known inheritance dispute of Anne Clifford discussed in Chapter 7. Goodlacke perhaps hopes to elevate his own relationship with Spencer to a perfect bond, one that surpasses the love between his friend and Besse. To Spencer's request that he disclose news of the legacy to her, Goodlacke replies, 'I shall performe your trust as carefully, / As to my father, breath'd he' (II, ii, 80–81). He intimates that the ambiguity of masculine friendship and rivalry is akin to the paradox of succession – that in wanting to fulfil the father's will, the son must await his demise.

Desperate at news of Spencer's death (which later proves to be false), Besse resolves to search for her beloved's resting-place. Yet before departing she uses her own will to announce a series of munificent social acts, similar to idealized portrayals of benevolent Elizabethan merchants, such as Simon Eyre in Dekker's *The Shoemaker's Holiday*. Her will is 'committed to the trust of the Mayor and Aldermen of Foy' (IV, ii, 30), and includes bequests 'To set up yong beginners in their trade ... To relieve such as have had losse by Sea ... To every Maid that's married out of Foy, whose name's *Elzabeth* ... [and] To relieve maimed Soldiers' (IV, ii, 32–36), along with legacies to all her servants and to Spencer's own dependants. The terms of Besse's will appear to illustrate recent claims that women tended to bestow charitable legacies more regularly than did men.[28] Like Spencer's initial gift, the will clearly conveys the liberty open to bachelors and single women in making bequests if they had no immediate family responsibilities.[29]

Heywood's *Fair Maid* depicts a number of will- and succession-related situations in which early modern women could find themselves as either beneficiaries or testators. In each case, a degree of vulnerability or exposure to male challenge surfaces. It is the power of Besse Bridges's 'fairness' – her beauty as much as her honesty – that enables her to overcome these threats. Most of her male antagonists end up comparing her to Queen Elizabeth. In this sense, Heywood's play is a useful corollary to Chapman's darker comedy. If the latter shows women largely subject and reactive to men's social and legal manoeuvring, suspect motives and flawed execution, then Heywood's lighter world does allow for female initiative and agency in interpersonal, economic and legal relations. What is perhaps most striking is Besse's ability to act in public. In Chapman's drama Cynthia is constrained by the codes of the 'house' into which she has married. The widowed countess Eudora, though controlling the estate and admitting visitors, remains ensconced in a largely domestic setting and is reliant on her attendants. (In this sense, her position can be compared to that of Olivia in Shakespeare's *Twelfth Night*. Though she is not a widow, with the death of her father and brother Olivia has inherited the estate. Yet apart from enabling her to refuse offers of marriage from Duke Orsino and Aguecheek, Olivia's social power does not seem to extend beyond the household and by the end of the play she is married.) Eudora's submission to Thrasalio takes place within the household and is mysteriously unstaged. The secrecy might suggest the potentially binding force of domesticity and privacy over women's lives. In contrast, Besse almost constantly participates in public activities and discourse. The play opens with her in service, and Spencer's and her own wills dramatically increase her civic role and influence to quasi-queenly status.

Wills, Authorship and Identity

Heywood stages the significant possibility that wills can have striking, determining social outcomes for women. Again, it is partly a generic effect; as noted earlier, wills are at once highly private and public texts – personal sentiments moulded by considerations of family and community expectations, embodied by the presence of witnesses and a notary or scrivener. The content is commonly secret until their announcement, followed by probate in the ecclesiastical courts. Through this process, wills carry their makers, inheritors and the relationships they share from familial and interpersonal to communal and public contexts. The legacies comprise not only real and personal property but also new kinds of identities and roles for the parties involved. In particular, a will characterizes the testator as someone not only with a history of relationships with others but also with social and cultural capital, and, regardless of the amounts, with the power and right to dispense it. People have these attributes before making a will, but doing so places them on the record. A will signifies the past, present and future agency of its author. It exemplifies the remarkable power of texts to mean and do things for oneself and for others, and thereby underscores the capacity for social action that rests with a speaker or author. As authors of wills, even if within a predominantly patriarchal and homosocial system, different kinds of women – single, married and widowed, from disparate class groups and localities with specific customs – were able in varying degrees and ways to act upon their intentions and to participate formally in processes of interpersonal and social exchange. In doing so, they illustrate the role that female authorship, conceived more generally, could play in early modern discourse and institutions.[30]

Wills can be usefully compared to other written genres in the period and the conditions in which they were produced. Some years ago, Margaret Ezell noted that an unwillingness to publish one's writings, and then using the modesty topos when doing so, were not solely traits of female authors.[31] Men too might have reservations about public authorship. Her observations can also be applied to wills.

The reluctance to write one was shared by men and women, and both used formulaic phrases and conventions to convey a final humility. In concert with these customary features, variations in preambles, prefaces and the main parts of wills and other texts mean that a distinct personality can 'break through the set phrases, as when a will transmits what sounds like an authentic voice from the death-bed'.[32] Traces of a particular persona may emerge in conspicuous spiritual formulae being used, though in reality, the person or persons behind these words could be the testator, the scribe or a combination of all those present as the will was made.[33] Personalities also seem to emerge through the care with which certain goods or duties are bequeathed to particular people, while others are named as definitely not to receive bequests. When hearing 'an authentic voice' in such details, it is important for modern scholars to appreciate that the voice and identity do not exist separately from a complicated network of relationships between people, objects and entitlements; wills 'enmesh the personal and individual with the legal and the statutory (of the State) around the crucial issue of accumulated wealth and property'.[34] In this light, women's will-making offers a powerful instance of early modern individuality as social identity in action. The testator's voice seems 'authentic' the more completely it distinguishes, and is mediated by, relationships with others.

The examples of theatrical wills collected by Honigmann and Brock illustrate many of these features. Margaret Spufford has suggested that a key motive in making a will was 'to provide for children who were not yet independent'.[35] This purpose influences the frequent naming of daughters, married or unmarried, as beneficiaries. Margaret Brayne leaves all belongings to her creditor Robert Myles, but charges him to 'keepe, educate & bringe vpp Katherine Brayne my husbandes daughter'.[36] Jane Poley leaves a small annual amount to her eldest son, who may well, like many eldest sons, have received 'preferential treatment by the common law of inheritance'.[37] The large sum of £40 is given to her daughter Frauncis Wibard, 'for the maintenance of her and her poor children and the bringing up of them'. To her apparently childless second daughter, Anne Gibbes, Poley leaves a number of valued personal possessions, including 'a hope ring of gold ... her best petticoat guarded with velvet ... one bolster which belongs to her bed'.[38] Agnes Henslowe, the recent widow of theatre manager Philip, leaves money to a group of 'eighty poor widows and women', with different amounts going to various other people and the 'Rest to only and well beloved daughter Joane Allen'.[39] Elizabeth Condell makes the sharpest discriminations in her will, leaving her 'goodes' to her daughter Elizabeth ffinch and £50 to her granddaughter Elizabeth Cundall. She then declares, 'I doe intend the same as that my said sonne in lawe Mr herbert ffynch shall neuer have possession of the same', and 'I would have no parte of my estate neither prodigally spent, nor lewdly wasted' by her son, William Cundall.[40]

The detail of these bequests is all the more notable because neither the amount of money nor the amount and quality of items is especially huge. The 1686 will of Sarah, Duchess of Somerset, is no less specific in itemizing which female relatives and servants will get what. Yet the mass of goods and clothes that is dispensed seems to cloud the bequest's moral rationale and personal motives.[41] Due to the much smaller quantities of money and property and the specificity with which they are distributed, the wills of ordinary women, Mendelson and Crawford conclude, seem to evince a deep concern for 'both people and things at their deaths'.[42] With limited means, they strive to balance attitudes about each beneficiary's character with the worth and amount of goods and the emotive value they hold for all parties.

In this light, the wills disclose the potential impact of women's moral judgments in the familial and social spheres. They signify the interaction of emotive, ethical and material considerations that guided women's conduct and which, through their texts as much as their behaviour, affected others in and beyond the family network, 'both as permanent legal record and as declaration of sentimental attachment'.[43] Wills are an excellent example of the variable influence that women's texts could have for themselves and for others. In her will, which was written in 1735 and proved in 1742, Dame Rebecca D'Oyly could reassert the power of independent decision-making 'reserved to me in certain articles made on my marriage with the said Sir John D'Oyly'.[44] Dorothy Howard might respect and reward the long years of attention offered by a loyal servant while also conveying a moral message to her relatives:

> as the rest of my estate is very inconsiderable and all my ffriends and near relations greatly provided for and I have a poor servant named Margaret White who in a course of years in sickness and in health has given me undeniable proofs of her honesty uncommon ffidelity and concern for me I am persuaded my friends and relations will not blame me for bestowing upon my said servant all the residue of my estate I do therefore give devise and bequeath unto the said Margaret White all the rest residue and remainder of my goods cloaths moneys or securities.[45]

Howard signed her will in 1748 and it was proved in 1760; through this twelve-year period she combined affection for her kin and friends with an ethical concern that both displayed and modelled a right way to act.

Women's Wills and Advice Books

Mary Prior parallels the increase in the number of women's wills during the seventeenth century with the increase in women's published writings: 'Economic freedom gave to some wives the freedom to make wills, to others the confidence and the cash to write and publish their own work in a way never before possible'.[46] Yet Prior stops short of conceiving writing wills as a mode of female authorship, and so perhaps also occludes the possibility of conceiving of wider material and social effects of women's publishing. She notes, 'No wives who made wills were writers'[47], although one, Dame Mary Compton, was the granddaughter of Elizabeth Jocelin, the author of the 1624 advice book, *The Mothers Legacie*, mentioned in Chapter 7. In revealing this lineage, Prior all but names the final point we wish to raise. As the most consequential form in which women wrote, wills inform many of the issues, relationships and conventions with which female authors were dealing in another notable early modern genre, the mother's advice book or 'legacy' to her children. We suggest that advice books are a kind of discursive adaptation of the will, developing the latter's complex of familial, moral, material concerns and its hybrid private-public address into a personally voiced, socially oriented genre.

It is in fact Jocelin's *Mothers Legacie* which makes the connection between wills and advice books most explicit: 'Our lawes disable those, that are under *Couert-baron*, from dispensing by will and Testament any temporall estate. But no law prohibiteth any possessor of morall and spirituall riches, to impart them vnto others' (sig. A3). A woman who takes up this opportunity becomes a 'truly rich bequeather' (sig. A3v), and the text she produces is a 'will' that is registered 'among the most publique Monuments' (sig. A4v).[48] These lines draw on the material, moral and religious values intrinsic to wills. The ensuing tract is an example and incentive to wives to work around the social-legal restrictions that confront them by using the hybrid legacy genre to enter public discourse. Jocelin goes on to advise her husband and her unborn child on a wide range of social, moral and religious topics. She assumes her mortal justification for authorship: 'I could not chuse but manifest this desire in writing, lest it should please God to depriue me of time to speake … not knowing whether I shall liue to instruct thee when thou art home, let me not be blamed though I write to thee before' (pp. 8–10).

Jocelin's text is analogous to a wife's will that co-opts the husband's consent. In an initial contrast, Dorothy Leigh's *The Mother's Blessing*, first published in 1616, is the work of a widow, intent on continuing her dead husband's paternal nurturing of their sons.[49] Leigh constantly underscores her pious motives as an author, 'to write them the right way that I had truly obserued out of the written Word of God' (sig. A2v). In a prefatory letter to her sons, Leigh stresses how she 'could not chuse but seeke (according as I was by duty bound) to fulfill his will in all things', and the 'care I had to fulfill his will in this' (sig. A5–A5v). She plays on the dual meaning of will as desire and testament to support her assumption of the paternal role. But in fulfilling her husband's will, she gradually asserts a critical perspective on many details of masculine conduct in the world, including hypocrisy, idleness, covetousness and the mistreatment of wives. Finally, her focus turns to the inheritance system itself, and paternal preoccupation with bequeathing estates to sons: 'A thousand waies may separate thy sonnes and their goods farre asunder' (p. 202); 'Seeke ye the heauenly treasure, and a little of this earthly trash will serue the turn' (p. 213). With these words, Leigh attacks the patriarchal values entrenched in early modern society and naturalized by common law. The widow's exclusion from the rules of inheritance affords a critical viewpoint on masculine property and identity, which for all their worldly sway remain subject: for a husband too is 'but a tenant at the will of the Lord' (p. 245).

A later example of the advice book appears less involved in pressuring paternal inheritance than in consolidating succession among women. The title of Elizabeth Richardson's *A Ladies Legacie to Her Daughters* reflects the emphasis on female bequests in the wills of women from all classes.[50] Yet in some significant ways, the text shows that any case of female succession might serve to problematize inheritance norms. Richardson explains the circumstances that led her to publish the book – initially it was conceived as a private work but she was 'over persuaded by some that much desired to have them' (p. 3). The hybrid genre of the legacy is again at issue and grants the author a special licence to write publicly. Richardson positions herself explicitly as a widow, and her text is a counter to those who, since the death of her husband (Sir Thomas Richardson, former Lord Chief Justice to the King's Bench), have worked against her: 'But though I am so unhappy as to be left destitute, not able to raise you portions of wealth, yet shall I joy as much to adde unto the portion of Grace' (p. 4). She hints at a history of legal dispute that has deprived her and her daughters of the estate. Richardson deliberately refrains from addressing her sons, intimating the conflict that could arise between the male heirs and the widow, that so-called 'clog on the estate' in much legal history[51]: 'And howsoever this my endeavour may be contemptible to many, (because a womans) which makes me not to joyne my sons with you; lest being men, they misconstrue my well-meaning; yet I presume that you my daughters will not refuse your Mothers teaching' (p. 6).[52] Like Dorothy Leigh, Richardson shifts the terms of inheritance away from material to spiritual value and in doing so challenges an inheritance system that works against women's right to property. The critique is reinforced within the text in 'A sorrowfull widowes prayer': 'having in thy mercifull goodnesse made me see with comfort all my children, who were left destitute, now by thy provident provision and blessing, well settled for this life ... so may I turne this freedome from the bond of marriage only the more to thy service' (p. 134). Religious, moral, legal and gendered viewpoints come together in subtle but critical response to worldly events.

Freedom from the bonds of marriage and property was perhaps more difficult to achieve through legal and social avenues than through spiritual means. Nonetheless, the way in which such advice book writers as Leigh, Jocelin and Richardson use religious and ethical discourse first to legitimate publishing their texts, then to offer various kinds of critique of patriarchal inheritance and property laws, builds upon the hybrid private-public address of early modern women's wills and the moral authority in interpersonal, familial and social relations signified in the wills' careful bequests. 'I being dead, as if I were alive,' memorably writes Grace Mildmay as she wills her words for the good of her descendants in the document so lengthily discussed in Chapter 7. As a 'testimony' of God's love, her words are designed to 'increase and multiply the gifts of his holy spirit in them, to the perfection of a good life in this world and everlasting blessedness in the kingdom of heaven'.[53] In offering detailed textual evidence of their lives, and carefully thought-out precepts for their children to read, women who wrote advice books pushed beyond the limits of such (usually limited) worldy goods that were in their power to bequeath to descendants. Words of guidance, therefore, served to transgress the financial and material restrictions that might have been imposed on women by virtue of their gender. Advice literature provided a way, not of 'conquering' death but of embracing it as a part of life: of freely entering the eternal realm in the knowledge that one's words of guidance remained in the temporal.

Women's wills are an important example of female social and discursive agency. Through the seventeenth century and beyond, they provide a fundamental context for apprehending ethical and material rights, as well as the capacity to nominate words as actions. As such, wills adumbrated the proliferating genres in which growing numbers of early modern women were starting to write. A woman's will – whether it be in the form of a bestowal of goods or a bestowal of words – enabled her to more effectively participate in a world that was still (by our current standards, at least) highly misogynistic, geared toward women's meek conduct and self-effacement.

Notes

1 Amy Louise Erickson, *Women and Property in Early Modern England* (London: Routledge, 1993), p. 204.

2 Jack Goody,'Inheritance, Property and Women: Some Comparative Considerations', in *Family and Inheritance: Rural Society in Western Europe, 1200–1800*, ed. Jack Goody, Joan Thirsk and E.P. Thompson (Cambridge: Cambridge University Press, 1976), p. 15.

3 Introduction, in Goody, Thirsk and Thompson, p. 1.

4 J.H. Baker, *An Introduction to English Legal History*, 3rd ed. (London: Butterworths, 1990), p. 308.

5 Christopher Marsh, 'In the Name of God? Will-Making in Early Modern England', in *The Records of the Nation: The Public Record Office 1838–1988, The British Record Society 1888–1988*, ed. G.H. Martin and Peter Spufford (London: Boydell, 1990), p. 219.

6 Martha C. Howell, *The Marriage Exchange: Property, Social Place, and Gender in Cities of the Low Countries, 1300–1500* (Chicago: University of Chicago Press, 1998), p. 2.

7 Sara Mendelson and Patricia Crawford, *Women in Early Modern England 1550–1720* (Oxford: Clarendon Press, 1998), p. 197.

8 T. E., *The Law's Resolutions of Women's Rights: Or, the Law's Provision for Women* (1632), in *Sexuality and Gender in the English Renaissance: An Annotated Edition of Contemporary Documents*, ed. Lloyd Davis (New York: Garland, 1998), pp. 373, 388–9.

9 Henrie Swinburn, *A Briefe Treatise of Testaments and Last Willes* (London: 1590) pp. 46, 48–9.

10 Swinburn, pp. 35–6.

11 John Godolphin, *The Orphans Legacy: Or, A Testamentary Abridgment* (1674; London, 1685), pp. 29, 32. Mary Prior notes the case of Margaret Lane, whose will was made 'without the consent of her husband, disposing … freely of money and other goods, and

even of the upbringing of her daughter'. Prior, 'Wives and Wills 1558–1700', in *English Rural Society, 1500–1800: Essays in Honour of Joan Thirsk*, ed. John Chartres and David Hey (Cambridge: Cambridge University Press, 1990), p. 221.

12 Baker, p. 232.

13 Susan Staves, *Married Women's Separate Property in England, 1660–1833* (Cambridge, Mass.: Harvard University Press, 1990), p. 169. On limited class access to trusts, see Baker, p.554; Eileen Spring argues against regarding trusts as unilaterally aiding women: 'Equity protected trusts whatever their purpose, and not all trusts were in favor of women'. *Law, Land, and Family: Aristocratic Inheritance in England, 1300–1800* (Chapel Hill: University of North Carolina Press, 1993), p. 121. A contrasting and positive view of support for women through equity is presented by Maria L. Cioni's *Women and Law in Elizabethan England with Particular Reference to the Court of Chancery* (New York: Garland, 1985).

14 E.A.J. Honigmann and Susan Brock, *Playhouse Wills 1558–1642: An Edition of Wills by Shakespeare and His Contemporaries in the London Theatre* (Manchester: Manchester University Press, 1993), pp. 11–12.

15 Erikson, p. 204.

16 Erikson, p. 20.

17 Marcia Pointon, *Strategies for Showing: Women, Possession, and Representation in English Visual Culture 1665–1800* (Oxford: Oxford University Press, 1997), p. 49.

18 George Chapman, *The Widow's Tears*, ed. Akihiro Yamada, Revels Plays (London: Methuen, 1975).

19 Thomas Heywood, *The Fair Maid of the West, Part 1*, ed. Brownell Salomon (Salzburg: Institut für Englische Sprache und Literatur, 1975).

20 John Habakkuk, *Marriage, Debt, and the Estates System: English Landownership 1650–1950* (Oxford: Clarendon Press, 1994) p. 51.

21 Staves, *Separate Property*, pp. 100–101; Erikson, p. 196.

22 Susan Staves, 'Resentment or Resignation? Dividing the Spoils among Daughters and Younger Sons', in *Early Modern Conceptions of Property*, ed. John Brewer and Susan Staves (London: Routledge, 1995), p. 204.

23 Akihiro Yamada (Revels edn. 1975), p. liv.

24 Erikson, p. 90.

25 Spring, p. 93; cf. Staves, *Separate Property*, p. 69.

26 Erikson; and Cicely Howell, 'Peasant Inheritance Customs in the Midlands, 1280–1700', in Goody, Thirsk and Thompson, pp. 112–55. For example, Cicely Howell observes that provision for the widow was the 'overriding' consideration of husbands in sixteenth- and seventeenth-century Kibworth, in the English Midlands (p. 143); Katharine Warner Swett, in 'Widowhood, Custom and Property in Early Modern Northern Wales', *Welsh History Review* 18 (1996), notes that 'most ordinary north Welshman left their wives with most of their property and their family responsibilities' (p. 199); Amy Erikson concludes that widows were principal beneficiaries in the majority of cases and usually received more than the common law right of dower to one-third of the estate (p. 162).

27 Mary Prior, 'Women and the Urban Economy: Oxford 1500–1800', in *Women in English Society 1500–1800*, ed. Mary Prior (London: Methuen 1985), p. 102.

28 Erikson, pp. 155, 211; Mendelson and Crawford, pp. 173, 198, 221.

29 Howell, 'Peasant Inheritance', p. 141.

30 Cf. Wendy Wall's discussion of the way that various female authors used the 'rhetoric

of will-making' to realize different modes of 'self-authorization' in the period in 'Isabella Whitney and the Female Legacy,' *ELH* 58 (1991): 35–62. See also Jean E. Howard, 'Textualizing an Urban Life: The Case of Isabella Whitney', in *Early Modern Autobiography: Theories, Genres, Practices*, ed. Ronald Bedford, Lloyd Davis and Philippa Kelly (Ann Arbor: University of Michigan Press, 2006).

31 Margaret J.M. Ezell, *The Patriarch's Wife: Literary Evidence and the History of the Family* (Chapel Hill: University of North Carolina Press, 1987), pp. 65, 88.

32 Honigmann and Brock, p. 10.

33 Marsh, p. 247.

34 Pointon, p. 142

35 Margaret Spufford, 'Peasant Inheritance Customs and Land Distribution in Cambridgeshire from the Sixteenth to the Eighteenth Centuries', in Goody, Thirsk and Thompson, p. 171.

36 Honigmann and Brock, p. 61.

37 Erikson, p. 71. Barbara J. Harris likewise suggests that some women 'ignored their eldest sons in their wills or left them only token bequests and used their estates to provide for their other children'. 'Property, Power, and Personal Relations: Elite Mothers and Sons in Yorkist and Early Tudor England', *Signs* 15 (1990): 623.

38 Honigmann and Brock, pp. 65–6.

39 Honigmann and Brock, p. 104.

40 Honigmann and Brock, p. 183.

41 See A. Daly Briscoe, *A Stuart Benefactress: Sarah, Duchess of Somerset* (Lavenham: Terence Dalton, 1973), pp. 213–18.

42 Mendelson and Crawford, p. 198.

43 Pointon, p. 40.

44 Pointon, p. 314.

45 Pointon, pp. 360–61.

46 Prior, 'Wives', p. 223.

47 Prior, 'Wives', p. 223.

48 Elizabeth Jocelin, *The Mothers Legacie, To Her Unborne Childe* (London, 1624).

49 Dorothy Leigh, *The Mother's Blessing: Or, the Godly Counsel of a Gentlewoman, not long since deceased, left behind her for her Children: Contayning many good exhortations, and godly admonitions, profitable for all parents, to leave as a Legacy to their Children*, 4th ed. (London, 1618).

50 Elizabeth Richardson, *A Ladies Legacie to her Daughters* (London, 1645).

51 Staves, *Separate Property*, p. 203.

52 See Harris on the 'delicate' position widows could find themselves in if they disagreed with their eldest sons about the estate, p. 629.

53 *With Faith and Physic: The Life of a Tudor Gentlewoman, Lady Grace Mildmay, 1552–1620*, ed. Linda Pollock (London: Collins and Brown, 1993).

Bibliography

Primary Texts

'A Famous Victory Obtained before the city of Exeter', British Library, Thomason Tracts. E.84 (24)

'The sufferings of Dr John Whynell', Bodleian Library, J. Walker MSS, C.2, ff.252-252v

'True and Joyfull Newes from Exceter', November 1642, British Library, Thomason Tracts. E.128

'Upon the Countesse of Carlisle sitting by a Glasse, and reading in a book'. British Library, Harl 6918 f16

A Pleasant Comedie, called Wily Begvilde (London: Clement Knight, 1606)

Adams, Thomas. *The White Devill: Or, the Hypocrite Uncased* (London, 1613)

An Account of the Death of Walter Devereux, 1st Earl of Essex, in Dublin, Sept. 1576. British Library, Harleian Ms 293, folios 115r–20r

Anger, Jane. *Jane Anger Her Protection for Women*. PDF document rendering of STC 644, prepared in March 2000 by Wes Folkerth, Dept of English, McGill University. On-line access: <http://www.shakespeare.mcgill.ca/anger.pdf>

Ashmole, Elias. Bodleian MS *Ashmole*, 36, printed in *The Diary and Will of Elias Ashmole*, ed. R.T. Gunther (Oxford: Clarendon Press, 1927)

Atkyns, Richard. *The Vindication of Richard Atkyns Esquire* (1669), ed. Peter Young, in *Military Memoirs: The Civil War* (London: Longmans, 1967)

Aubrey, John. *Brief Lives and Other Selected Writings*, ed. Anthony Powell (New York: Charles Scribner's Sons, 1949)

Bacon, Sir Francis. *Bacon's Essays*, fifth edn, ed. Richard Whately (London: John W. Parker, 1860)

———. *Essays or Counsels—Civil and Moral* (1625), Harvard Classics, ed. Charles W. Eliot (New York: Collier, 1969)

Bale, John. *The Examinations of Anne Askew*, ed. Elaine V. Beilin (New York: Oxford University Press, 1996)

Banister, John. *The Historie of Man* (London, 1578)

Barrow, Isaac. *Geometrical Lectures* (London, 1735)

Beard, Thomas. *The Theatre of God's Judgments* (London, 1632)

Becon, Thomas. *A New Catechisme* (London, 1564)

———. *The Sicke Mans Salve* (London, 1558–1559; 28 reprints by 1632)

Birch, Samuel. 'A true and perfect account of the receipts and disbursements of Captaine Samuel Birch in relation to himselfe and company with their charge upon the countrey, marchings, freequarter, etc. since their last raysings', 1648–1650, Historical Manuscripts Commission, Series 29, vol. 3 (London: HMSO, 1891–1931)

Braithwaite, Richard. *The English Gentlewoman* (London, 1641)

Brent, William. *A Discourse upon the Nature of Eternitie* (London, 1655)

Breton, Nicolas. *The Praise of Virtuous Ladies* (London, 1580)

Bridgewater, Elizabeth of. *Diary*, British Library 236 (121r)

Brown, Sylvia (ed.), *Women's Writing in Stuart England: the Mother's Legacies of Dorothy Leigh, Elizabeth Jocelin, and Elizabeth Richardson* (Phoenix Mill: Sutton Publishing, 1999)

Browne, Sir Thomas. *Sir Thomas Browne: The Major Works*, ed. C.A. Patrides (Harmondsworth: Penguin, 1977)

Bruno, Giordano. *Opera latine conscripta* (Florence, 1889)

Bullinger, Heinrich. *A Newe Catechisme* (London, 1541)

Castiglione, Baldassare. *The Book of the Courtier*, trans. Thomas Hoby (Harmondsworth: Penguin, 1967)

Caussin, Nicholas. 'The Holy Court, second tome' (London, 1631)

Cecil, Edward, Viscount Wimbledon. *A Journall, and Relation of the action, which by his Majesties commandement Edward Lord Cecyl, Baron of Putney, and Vicount of Wimbledon, Admirall, and Lieutenant Generall of his Majestys forces, did undertake upon the coast of Spaine, 1625* (London (?): Elliot's Court Press (?), 1626. Facsimile by Da Capo Press, Amsterdam & London: Theatrum Orbis Terrarum Ltd. 1968)

Chapman, George. *The Widow's Tears*, ed. Akihiro Yamada, Revels Plays (London: Methuen, 1975)

Clifford, Lady Anne. *The Diaries of Lady Anne Clifford*, ed. David Clifford (Wolfeboro Falls: Alan Sutton, 1991)

——. *The Diary of the Lady Anne Clifford*, with an introductory note by V. Sackville-West (London: Heinemann, 1923)

Conduct Literature for Women, ed. William St. Clair and Irmgard Maasen, facsimile collection, 6 vols (London: Pickering and Chatto, 2000)

Coryate, Thomas. *Coryate's Crudities*, 2 vols (Glasgow: James MacLehose, 1905)

——. *Greeting from the Court of the Great Mogul* (1616) (Amsterdam and New York: Da Capo, 1968)

Couerte, Robert. *A True and Almost Incredible Report of an Englishman, that ... Trauelled by Land through many unknowne Kingdomes, and Great Cities* (London, 1612)

Cowley, Abraham. *Abraham Cowley, Poetry and Prose*, ed. L.C. Martin (Oxford: Clarendon Press, 1949)

Dallam, Thomas. 'Master Dallam's Mission', ed. J. Theodore Bent, *The Antiquary* 18 (1888)

Darlington Wills and Inventories 1600–1625, ed. J.A. Atkinson et al. (Newcastle-Upon-Tyne: Athenaeum Press, 1993)

Descartes, René. *Meditations and Other Metaphysical Writings*, trans. Desmond M. Clarke (New York: Penguin, 1998)

Dethick, Sir William. *The Excellencie of man, his nobilitie, praise, glory, honour and dignitie*, Folger Library MS V.b.125, ascribed to Dethick, c.1610

Devereux, Robert, second earl of Essex. *Apologie:* preface from Public Record Office, State Papers 12/269/71, fols. 101r–125v. Scribal copy, with marginated heading: 'An apologie of the earle of Essex against those who falsely & maliciously taxe him to be thonely hinderer of the peace & quyet of this kingdome, written to Mr Anthony Bacon' (1598)

Donne, John. *John Donne: Poems* ed. John Carey (Oxford: Clarendon Press, 1990)

Dorney, John. *A Briefe and exact Diurnall, Containing the most materiall and Remarkeable passages that happened in the late well formed Siege laid before the City of Gloucester* (London, 1643)

Dunton, John [Iohn Dvnton]. *A True Journal of the Sally Fleet with the Proceedings of the Voyage* (London, 1637)

Elyot, Sir Thomas. *The Boke of the Governour Devised by Sir Thomas Elyot, Knight* (1531), ed. H. S. Croft, 2 vols (New York: Burt Franklin, 1967)

———. *The Book Named the Governor* (1531), ed. S. E. Lehmberg (London: Dent, 1970)

———. *The defence of good women, devised and made by Sir Thomas Elyot knight* (London, 1545)

Erasmus, Desiderius. *De pueris statim ac liberaliter instituendis declamatio*, trans. Beert C. Verstraete, *Collected Works of Erasmus*, ed. J.K. Sowards, vol. 26 (Toronto: University of Toronto Press, 1985)

Fane, Sir Francis. In Folger MS V.a.180. Commonplace book, compiled c. 1655–1656

Fell, Margaret Askew (Fox). *Women's Speaking Justified* (London, 1667)

Ford, John. *'Tis Pity She's a Whore*, ed. Derek Roper (London: Methuen, 1975)

Fuller, Thomas. *The Worthies of England* (London, 1662); ed. John Freeman (London: George Allen & Unwin, 1952)

Glanville, John. *The Voyage to Cadiz in 1625. Being a Journal Written by John Glanville, Secretary to the Lord Admiral of the Fleet (Sir E. Cecil), Afterwards Sir John Glanville, Speaker of the Parliament, &c., &c.*, ed. Alexander B. Grosart, Camden Society, New Series XXXII, 1883

Godolphin, John. *The Orphans Legacy: Or, A Testamentary Abridgment* (1674) (London, 1685)

Gordon, Patrick. *The Diary of General Patrick Gordon of Auchleuchries in the Years 1635–1699*, 'Russia Through European Eyes' No. 3, gen. ed. A.G. Cross (London: Frank Cass & Co., 1968) (Reprint of Spalding Club edition of 1859.)

Greville, Fulke. *Sonnets from Caelica* (London, 1633)

Grymeston, Elizabeth. *A Sinner's Glasse* (London, 1604)

———. *Miscellanea, Meditations, Memoratives* (London, 1604)

Guylforde, Sir Richard. *The Pylgrymage of Sir Richarde Guylforde Knyght* (London, 1511)

Halkett, Lady Anne. *The Autobiography of Anne Lady Halkett*, ed. John Gough Nichols, Camden Society, 2nd Series 13, 1875

Hall, Joseph. *The Works of the Right Reverend Joseph Hall*, ed. Philip Wynter, 10 vols (Oxford: Oxford University Press, 1863)

Hannay, Patrick. *A Happy Husband* (London, 1618)

Harrison, Thomas. *The Speeches and Prayers of Major General Harrison [et al.]... The Times of their Deaths. Together with Severall occasionall Speeches and Passages in their Imprisonment till they came to the place of Execution* (London, 1660)

Henry, Philip. *Diaries and Letters of Philip Henry, MA, of Broad Oak, Flintshire, A.D. 1631–1696*, ed. Matthew Henry Lee, M.A., Vicar of Hanmer (London: Kegan Paul, Trench and Co., 1882)

Henslow, T. Geoffrey W. *Ye Sundial Booke* (London: W. & G. Foyle, 1935)

Herbert, Edward, Baron of Cherbury. *The Life of Edward, First Lord Herbert of Cherbury, written by himself*, ed. J.M. Shuttleworth (London: Oxford University Press, 1976)

Heywood, Thomas. *Apology for Actors* (1612), in E.K. Chambers, *The Elizabethan Stage*, 4 vols (Oxford: Clarendon Press, 1923), 4

———. *The Dramatic Works of Thomas Heywood*, 6 vols (New York: Russell & Russell, 1964), reprint of 1874 edn

———. *The Fair Maid of the West, Part 1*, ed. Brownell Salomon (Salzburg: Institut für Englische Sprache und Literatur, 1975)

Hoby, Lady Margaret. *The Private Life of an Elizabethan Lady: The Diary of Lady Margaret Hoby, 1599–1605*, ed. Joanna Moody (Phoenix Mill: Sutton Publishing, 1998)

Honigmann, E.A.J. and Susan Brock. *Playhouse Wills 1558–1642: An Edition of Wills by Shakespeare and His Contemporaries in the London Theatre* (Manchester: Manchester University Press, 1993)

Hyde, Edward, 1st earl of Clarendon. *History of the Rebellion and Civil Wars in England*, ed. W.D. Macray (Oxford, 1888)

Hyrde, Richard. Dedicatory letter prefacing *A Devout Treatise Upon the Pater Noster* translated by Margaret Roper from Desiderius Erasmus. 'Richard Hyrde unto the moost studious and virtuous yonge mayde Fraunces. S. sendeth gretynge and well to fare'. Brown University Women Writers Project, first electronic edition, 2001, <http://www.wwp.brown.edu/encoding/research/NASSR/WWP.html>.

Jaggard, William. *A Catalogue of English Books* (London, 1619)

Jocelin, Elizabeth. *The Mothers Legacie, To Her Unborne Childe* (London, 1624)

Jonson, Ben. *Everyman Out of His Humour*, in *The Complete Plays of Ben Jonson*. ed. G.A. Wilkes, vol. I (Oxford: Clarendon Press, 1981)

Josselin, Ralph. *The Diary of Ralph Josselin, 1616–1683*, ed. Alan Macfarlane (London: Oxford University Press, for the British Academy, Records of Social and Economic History, New Series, III, 1976)

———. *The Diary of the Rev. Ralph Josselin, 1616–1683*, ed. E. Hockcliffe, Camden Society, 3rd series, xv, 1908

Lanyer, Aemilia. *Salve Deus Rex Judaeorum*, Brown University Women Writers Project, first electronic edition, 2001

Leigh, Dorothy. *The Mother's Blessing: Or, the Godly Counsel of a Gentlewoman, not long since deceased, left behind her for her Children: Contayning many good exhortations, and godly admonitions, profitable for all parents, to leave as a Legacy to their Children*, 4th edn. (London, 1618)

London, William. *A Catalogue of the most vendible Books in England* (London, 1657–58)

Ludlow, Edmund. *A Voyce from the Watch Tower Part Five: 1660–1662*, ed. A.B. Worden, Camden 4th series, 1978

Madox, Richard. *An Elizabethan in 1582: The Diary of Richard Madox, Fellow of All Souls*, ed. Elizabeth Story Donno (London: Hakluyt Society, 1978)

Markham, Gervase. *The English Housewife: Containing the inward and Outward virtues which ought to be in a complete woman; as her skill in physic, cookery, banqueting-stuff, distillation, perfumes, wool, hemp, flax, dairies, brewing, baking, and all other things belonging to a household*, ed. Michael Best (Kingston and Montreal: McGill-Queen's University Press, 1986)

Marshall, Stephen. *Sermon preach'd November 1640* (London, 1645)

Mildmay, Lady Grace. 'Lady Mildmay's Journal', MS, Northampton Central Library. A modernized and reordered text is printed in Linda Pollock's *With Faith and Physic: The Life of a Tudor Gentlewoman, Lady Grace Mildmay, 1552–1620* (London: Collins and Brown, 1993)

Milton, John. *Milton's Complete Shorter Poems*, ed. John Carey (London: Longman, 1971)

———. *Paradise Lost* (New York: Signet Classics, 1982)

Montaigne, Michel de. *Montaigne's Essayes*, trans. John Florio (1603), 3 vols (London: Dent, 1965)

Moryson, Fynes. *An Itinerary Written by Fynes Moryson, Gent. Containing His Ten Yeers Travell thorow Twelve Dominions* (London, 1617)

Mulcaster, Richard. *Positions Concerning the Training Up of Children* (1581), ed. William Barker (Toronto: Toronto University Press, 1994)

Munda, Constantia. *The Worming of a Mad Dog* (London, 1617)

Norton Anthology of English Literature, ed. M.H.Abrams and Stephen Greenblatt, 2 vols, 7th edn. (New York and London: Norton, 2000)

Norwood, Richard. *The Description of the Sommer Ilands, Once Called the Bermudas*, in *The Journal of Richard Norwood, Surveyor of Bermuda* (New York: Scholars' Facsimiles and Reprints, 1945)

Oglander, Sir John. *A Royalist's Notebook: The Commonplace Book of Sir John Oglander of Nunwell*, ed. Francis Bamford (London: Constable, 1936)

Overbury, Sir Thomas. *Characters, or Wittie descriptions of the properties of sundry Persons*, in *The 'Conceited Newes' of Sir Thomas Overbury and His Friends*, ed. James E. Savage (Gainesville: Scholars' Facsimiles and Reprints, 1968)

Pellham, Edward. *Gods Power and Providence: Shewed, In the Miraculous Preservation and Deliverance of eight Englishmen, left by mischance in Greenland Anno 1630 nine moneths and twelve dayes* (London, 1631)

Perkins, William. 'A Dialogue of the State of a Christian Man', in *The Work of William Perkins*, ed. Ian Breward (Appleford, England: The Courtenay Library of Reformation Classics, 1970)

———. *A Salve for a Sicke Man* (London, 1595)

Perneby, William. *A Direction to Death* (London, 1599)

Peters, Hugh. *A Dying Father's Last Legacy to an Onely Child* (London, 1660)

Pike [Peeke], Richard. *Three to One: Being, An English-Spanish Combat, performed by a* Westerne *Gentleman, of* Tavystoke *in* Devon shire, *with an English Quarter-Staffe, against Three* Spanish *Rapiers and Poniards, at* Sherries *in* Spaine, *The fifteeene day of November, 1625. In the Presence of Dukes, Condes, Marquesses, and other Great Dons of* Spaine, *being the Counsell of Warre. The Author of this Booke, and Actor in this Encounter,* Richard Peeeke (London, 1626)

Prynne, William. *A Divine tragedy lately acted* (London, 1636)

———. *Histriomastix* (London, 1632)

Raleigh, Sir Walter. *The History of the World* (London, 1614)

Reresby, Sir John. *The Memoirs and Travels of Sir John Reresby*, ed. Albert Ivatt, (London: K. Paul, Trench,Trubner, 1904)

Rich, Mary. *Saintly Lives: Mary Rich, Countess of Warwick*, ed. Mary Palgrave, (London: Dent, 1901)

Richardson, Elizabeth. *A Ladies Legacie to her Daughters* (London, 1645)

Rogers, Richard. *Two Elizabethan Puritan Diaries by Richard Rogers and Samuel Ward*, ed. M.M. Knappen (Gloucester, Mass.: Peter Smith, 1966)

Rousseau, Jean-Jacques. *Emile or On Education*, trans. Allan Bloom (New York: Basic, 1979)

Salter, Thomas. *A mirrhor mete for all mothers, matrons and maidens, intituled the mirrhor of modestie* (London, 1579)

Shakespeare, William. *The Norton Shakespeare*, ed. Stephen Greenblatt et al. (New York and London: Norton, 1997)

———. *The Riverside Shakespeare*, gen. ed. G. Blakemore Evans (Boston: Houghton Mifflin, 1974)

Sidney, Sir Philip. *The Defence of Poesy*, ed. Katherine Duncan-Jones (Oxford: Clarendon Press, 1989)

Snawsel, Robert. *A Looking-Glasse for Maried Folks* (London, 1610)

Sowerman, Esther. *Esther Hath Hang'd Haman* (London, 1617)

Speed, John. *A Prospect of the Most Famous Parts of the World* (London, 1631)

Spinoza, Benedict. *Ethics*, trans. W. Hale White, fourth edn (Oxford: Oxford University Press, 1910)

Strange, true, and lamentable Newes from Exceter. And other parts of the Western countreyes (London, 1643)

Sutcliffe, Alice (Woodhouse). *Meditations on Man's Mortality* (London, 1634)

Sutton, Christopher. *Disce Mori, Learne to Die* (London, 1600)

Swetnam, Joseph. *The Arraignment of lewde, idle, froward and unconstant women* (London, 1615)

Swinburn, Henrie. *A Briefe Treatise of Testaments and Last Willes* (London, 1590)

Symonds, Richard. *Diary of the Marches and Moovings of his Majesties Royall Army, Himselfe being personally present*, Add.MSS. British Library, 17062. ed. Charles Edward Long, London: Camden Society, MDCCCLIX

T.E., *The Law's Resolutions of Women's Rights: Or, the Law's Provision for Women* (1632), in *Sexuality and Gender in the English Renaissance: An Annotated Edition of Contemporary Documents*, ed. Lloyd Davis (New York: Garland, 1998)

Taylor, John. *Mad Fashions, Old Fashions, All out of Fashions* (London, 1642)

———. *Mad Verse, Sad Verse, Glad Verse, and Bad Verse* (London, n.d.), British Library, Thomason Tracts, E.46 (i3)

The Anchor Anthology of Sixteenth-Century Verse, ed. Richard S. Sylvester (Garden City: Anchor Press/Doubleday, 1974)

The Sicke Man's Comfort (London, 1590)

The Souldiers Demand (Bristol, 1649) British Library, E.555 (29)

The Woman's Sharp Revenge: Or an answer to Sir Seldome Sober that writ those railing pamphelets called the Juniper and Crabtree Lectures, & c. Being a sound Reply and full confutation of those Bookes: with an Apology in this case for the defence of us women. Performed by Mary Tattle-well, and *Joane Hit-him-home, Spinsters*, 1640, Bodleian Library, STC 23706

Thornton, Alice. 'Autobiography', in *English Women's Voices, 1540–1700*, ed. Charlotte F. Otten (Miami: Florida International University Press, 1992) pp. 232–58

Townshend, Henry. *The Diary of Henry Townshend ... 1640–1663*, ed. J.W. Willis Bund (Worcestershire Historical Society, 1915–20)

Trumbull, Sir William. Public Records Office, State Papers Flanders, SP 77, 18

Vives, Juan. *Vives: On Education, a Translation of the De Tradendis Disciplinis of Juan Luis Vives*, ed. and trans. Foster Watson (Cambridge: Cambridge University Press, 1913)

W.T., *A Discourse of Eternitie* (Oxford, 1633)

Wallington, Nehemiah. *Historical Notices of Events Occurring Chiefly in the Reign of Charles I*, 2 vols, ed. R. Webb (London: Richard Bentley, 1896)

Watson, Thomas. 'Tears of Fancy, or Love Disdained', *Elizabethan Sonnets*, ed. Sidney Lee, vol 1 (London: Archibald Constable and Co., 1904)

Whythorne, Thomas. *Autobiography*, modern spelling and abbreviated edition, ed. James M. Osborn (London: Oxford University Press, 1962)

————. *The Autobiography of Thomas Whythorne*, ed. James M. Osborn (Oxford: Clarendon Press, 1961)

Worthington, John. *The Diary and Correspondence of Dr. John Worthington*, ed. James Crossley (Manchester: Chetham Society, 1847)

Secondary Texts

Atkin, Malcolm and Wayne Laughlin. *Gloucester and the Civil War: A City Under Siege* (Stroud, Glos.: Alan Sutton, 1992)

Baker, J.H. *An Introduction to English Legal History*, 3rd ed. (London: Butterworths, 1990)

Barker, Francis. *The Tremulous Private Body: Essays in Subjection* (London: Methuen, 1984)

Becker, Lucinda. *Death and the Early Modern Englishwoman* (London: Ashgate, 2003)

Bedford, Ronald, Lloyd Davis and Philippa Kelly (eds). *Early Modern Autobiography: Theories, Genres, Practices* (Ann Arbor: University of Michigan Press, 2006)

Beehler, Sharon A. '"Confederate Season": Shakespeare and the Elizabethan Understanding of *Kairos*', in *Shakespeare Matters: History, Teaching, Performance*, ed. Lloyd Davis (Newark: University of Delaware Press, 2003)

Beilin, Elaine V. 'Anne Askew's Dialogue with Authority', in *Contending Kingdoms: Historical, Psychological and Feminist Approaches to the Literature of Sixteenth-Century England and France*, ed. Marie-Rose Logan and Peter L. Rudnytsky (Detroit: Wayne State University Press, 1991)

Bennett, Judith M. *Ale, Beer, and Brewsters in England: Women's Work in a Changing World, 1300–1600* (Oxford: Oxford University Press, 1996)

Benstock, Shari. 'Authorizing the Autobiographical', in *The Private Self: Theory and Practice of Women's Autobiographical Writings*, ed. Shari Benstock. (London: Routledge, 1998)

Birch, Thomas. *The Court and Times of Charles I*, 2 vols (London: Henry Colburn, 1849)

Bloom, Harold. *Shakespeare and the Invention of the Human* (New York: Riverhead Books, 1998)

Botonaki, Effie. *Seventeenth-Century English Women's Autobiographical Writings: Disclosing Enclosures, Studies in British Literature*, vol. 88 (Lewiston: Edwin Mellon Press, 2004)

Bourdieu, Pierre. *Pascalian Meditations*, trans. Richard Nice (Cambridge: Polity Press, 2000)

Briscoe, A. Daly. *A Stuart Benefactress: Sarah, Duchess of Somerset* (Lavenham: Terence Dalton, 1973)

Brissenden, Alan (ed.). *As You Like It*, World's Classics (Oxford: Oxford University Press, 1994)

Brown University Women Writers Project. Available on-line at
<http://www.wwp.brown.edu>

Brown, Sylvia (ed.). *Women's Writing in Stuart England* (Surrey: Sutton Publishing, 1999)

Bruner, Jerome. 'The Autobiographical Process', in *The Culture of Autobiography: Constructions of Self-Representation*, ed. Robert Folkenflik (Stanford: Stanford University Press, 1993)

Burke, Peter. 'Representations of the Self from Petrarch to Descartes', in *Rewriting the Self: Histories from the Renaissance to the Present*, ed. Roy Porter (London: Routledge, 1997)

———. *The Renaissance Sense of the Past* (London: Arnold, 1969)

Burrow, J.A. *The Ages of Man: A Study of Medieval Writing and Thought* (Oxford: Clarendon Press, 1986)

Bynum, C.W. *Fragmentation and Redemption: Essays on Gender and the Human Body in Medieval Religion* (New York: Zone Books, 1991)

Camden, Carol. *The Elizabethan Woman* (New York and London: Elsevier Press, 1952)

Campbell, Lorne. *Renaissance Portraits: European Portrait-Painting in 14th, 15th and 16th Centuries* (New Haven and London: Yale University Press, 1990)

Carlton, Charles. *Going to the Wars: The Experience of the British Civil Wars 1638–1654* (London: Routledge, 1992)

Cioni, Maria L. *Women and Law in Elizabethan England with Particular Reference to the Court of Chancery* (New York: Garland, 1985)

Cipolla, Carlo M. *Clocks and Culture 1300–1700* (New York: Walker & Co., 1967)

———. *Money in Sixteenth-Century Florence* (Berkeley: University of California Press, 1989)

Clark, Arthur Melville. *Thomas Heywood: Playwright and Miscellanist* (Oxford: Basil Blackwell, 1931)

Coleman, Patrick, Jayne Lewis and Jill Kowalik (eds). *Representations of the Self From the Renaissance to Romanticism* (Cambridge: Cambridge University Press, 2000)

Condren, Conal. 'Specifying the Subject in Early Modern Autobiography', in *Early Modern Autobiography: Theories, Genres, Practices*, ed. Ronald Bedford, Lloyd Davis and Philippa Kelly (Ann Arbor: Michigan University Press, 2006)

Dalton, Charles. *The Life and Times of General Sir Edward Cecil, Viscount Wimbledon*, 2 vols (London, 1885)

Davis, Lloyd. 'Cultural Encounters and Self Encounters in Early Modern Travel Autobiographies', *Parergon: Journal of the Australian and New Zealand Association for Medieval and Early Modern Studies*, 2002 (19.2): 151–67.

———. 'Self-Representation and Travel Autobiographies in Early Modern England', in *Mapping the Self: Space, Identity, Discourse in British*

Auto/Biography, ed. Frédéric Regard (Saint-Etienne: Université de Saint-Etienne, 2003)

Delany, Paul. *British Autobiography in the Seventeenth Century* (London: Routledge and Kegan Paul, 1969)

Dictionary of National Biography (Old DNB), ed. Leslie Stephen and Sidney Lee, 22 vols (London: Oxford University Press, 1921–1922)

Dohrn-Van Rossum, Gerhardt. *History of the Hour: Clocks and Modern Temporal Orders*, trans. Thomas Dunlap (Chicago and London: University of Chicago Press, 1996)

Donnelly, Mark P. and Daniel Diehl. *Siege: Castles at War* (Dallas, Tex.: Taylor Pub. Co., 1998)

Dove, Mary. *The Perfect Age of Man's Life* (Cambridge: Cambridge University Press, 1986)

Dragsta, Henk, Sheila Ottway and Helen Wilcox (eds). *Betraying Our Selves: Forms of Self-Representation in Early Modern English Texts* (London: Macmillan, 2000)

Duffy, Christopher. *Siege Warfare: The Fortress in the Early Modern World, 1494–1660* (London: Routledge and Kegan Paul, 1979)

Duncan-Jones, Katherine. *Sir Philip Sidney: Courtier Poet* (New Haven and London: Yale University Press, 1991)

Eakin, Paul John. *Fictions in Autobiography: Studies in the Art of Self Invention* (Princeton: Princeton University Press, 1985)

———. *How Our Lives Become Stories: Making Selves* (Ithaca: Cornell University Press, 1999)

Ebner, Dean. *Autobiography in Seventeenth-Century England: Theology and the Self* (The Hague: Mouton 1971)

Elbaz, Robert. *The Changing Nature of the Self: A Critical Study of the Autobiographical Discourse* (London; Sydney: Croom Helm, 1988)

Elias, Norbert. *Time: An Essay*, trans. Edmund Jephcott (Oxford: Blackwell, 1992)

Erickson, Amy Louise. *Women and Property in Early Modern England* (London: Routledge, 1993)

Ezell, Margaret J.M. *The Patriarch's Wife: Literary Evidence and the History of the Family* (Chapel Hill: University of North Carolina Press, 1987)

Ferry, Anne Davidson. *The 'Inward' Language: Sonnets of Wyatt, Sidney, Shakespeare, Donne* (Chicago: University of Chicago Press, 1983)

Fineman, Joel. *Shakespeare's Perjured Eye: The Invention of Poetic Subjectivity in the Sonnets* (Berkeley: University of California Press, 1986)

Folkenflick, Robert (ed.). *The Culture of Autobiography: Constructions of Self-Representation* (Stanford: Stanford University Press, 1993)

Fosbrooke, T.D. *An Original History of the City of Gloucester* (Gloucester, 1819; reprinted Gloucester, 1986)

Fowler, Alastair. *Spenser and the Numbers of Time* (London: Routledge and Kegan Paul, 1964)

Fox, Alistair. *The English Renaissance: Identity and Representation in Elizabethan England* (Oxford: Blackwell 1997)

Fumerton, Patricia, and Simon Hunt (eds). *Renaissance Culture and the Everyday*, (Philadelphia: Pennsylvania University Press, 1999)

Gagnier, Regenia. *Subjectivities: A History of Self-Representation in Britain, 1832–1920* (New York: Oxford University Press, 1991)

Gill, Catie. *Women in the Seventeenth-Century Quaker Community* (Aldershot: Ashgate, 2005)

Gillies, John. 'Introduction: Elizabethan Drama and Cartographizations of Space', in *Playing the Globe: Genre and Geography in English Renaissance Drama*, ed. John Gillies and Virginia Mason Vaughan (Madison: Fairleigh Dickinson University Press, 1998)

———. *Shakespeare and the Geography of Difference* (Cambridge: Cambridge University Press, 1994)

Goldberg, Jonathan. *Writing Matter: From the Hands of the English Renaissance*, (Stanford: Stanford University Press, 1990)

Goodall, Peter. 'The Author in the Study: Self-Representation as Reader and Writer in the Medieval and Early Modern Period', in *Early Modern Autobiography: Theories, Genres, Practices*, ed. Ronald Bedford, Lloyd Davis and Philippa Kelly (Ann Arbor: Michigan University Press, 2006)

Goody, Jack. 'Inheritance, Property and Women: Some Comparative Considerations', in *Family and Inheritance: Rural Society in Western Europe, 1200–1800*, ed. Jack Goody, Joan Thirsk and E.P. Thompson (Cambridge: Cambridge University Press, 1976)

Grabes, Herbert. *The Mutable Glass: Mirror Imaging in Titles and Texts of the Middle Ages and the English Renaissance* (Cambridge: Cambridge University Press, 1982)

Graham, Elspeth, 'Women's Writing and the Self', in *Women and Literature in Britain, 1500–1700*, ed. Helen Wilcox (Cambridge: Cambridge University Press, 1996)

Graham, Elspeth, et al. (eds). *Her Own Life: Autobiographical Writings by Seventeenth-century Englishwomen* (London: Routledge, 1989)

Greenblatt, Stephen. 'Psychoanalysis and Renaissance Culture', in *Literary Theory/Renaissance Texts*, ed. Patricia Parker and David Quint (Baltimore: Johns Hopkins University Press, 1986)

Greenblatt, Stephen. *Renaissance Self-Fashioning: From More to Shakespeare* (Chicago: University of Chicago Press, 1981)

Gunn, Janet Varner. *Autobiography: Toward a Poetics of Experience* (Philadelphia: University of Pennsylvania Press, 1982)

Gurr, Andrew. *The Shakespearean Stage 1574–1642*, 3rd edn (Cambridge: Cambridge University Press, 1993)

Habakkuk, John. *Marriage, Debt, and the Estates System: English Landownership 1650–1950* (Oxford: Clarendon Press, 1994)

Haber, F.C. 'The Cathedral Clock and the Cosmological Clock Metaphor', *KronoScope: Journal for the Study of Time*, Leyden: Brill, n.d. II.

Hackett, Helen. *Women and Romance Fiction in the English Renaissance* (Cambridge: Cambridge University Press, 2000)

Haley, David. *Shakespeare's Courtly Mirror: Reflexivity and Prudence in 'All's Well That Ends Well'* (Newark: University of Delaware Press, 1993)

Hankins, J.E. *Shakespeare's Derived Imagery* (Lawrence: University of Kansas Press, 1953)

Harris, Barbara J. 'Property, Power, and Personal Relations: Elite Mothers and Sons in Yorkist and Early Tudor England', *Signs* 15 (1990)

Heale, Elizabeth. 'Songs, Sonnets and Autobiography: Self-representation in Sixteenth-century Verse Miscellanies', in *Betraying Our Selves: Forms of Self-Representation in Early Modern English Texts*, ed. Henk Dragstra, Sheila Ottway and Helen Wilcox (London: Macmillan, 2000)

Heale, Elizabeth. *Autobiography and Authorship in Renaissance Verse: Chronicles of the Self* (Basingstoke: Palgrave, 2003)

Hearn, Karen (ed.). *Dynasties: Painting in Tudor and Jacobean England 1530– 1630*, New York: Rizzoli, 1996 (published by order of the Trustees 1995 for the exhibition at the Tate Gallery, 12 Oct 1995 – 7 Jan 1996).

Helgerson, Richard. *Forms of Nationhood: The Elizabethan Writing of England* (Chicago: University of Chicago Press, 1992)

Honigmann, E.A.J. and Susan Brock. *Playhouse Wills 1558–1642: An Edition of Wills by Shakespeare and His Contemporaries in the London Theatre* (Manchester: Manchester University Press, 1993)

Houlbrooke, Ralph. *Death, Religion, and Family in England 1480–1750* (Oxford: Clarendon Press, Oxford Studies in Social History, 1998)

Howard, Sharon. 'Imagining the Pain and Peril of Seventeenth-century Childbirth: Travail and Deliverance in the Making of an Early Modern World' in *Social History of Medicine* 16 (3) (2003): 367–82

Howell, Cicely. 'Peasant Inheritance Customs in the Midlands, 1280–1700', in *Family and Inheritance: Rural Society in Western Europe, 1200–1800*, ed. Jack Goody, Joan Thirsk and E.P. Thompson (Cambridge: Cambridge University Press, 1976)

Howell, Martha C. *The Marriage Exchange: Property, Social Place, and Gender in Cities of the Low Countries, 1300–1500* (Chicago: University of Chicago Press, 1998)

Kelly, Philippa (ed.). *The Touch of the Real: Communing With the Living and the Dead: Essays in Honour of Stephen Greenblatt* (Perth: University of Western Australia Press, 2002)

Knoppers, Laura Lunger. *Historicizing Milton: Spectacle, Power and Poetry in Restoration England* (Athens and London: University of Georgia Press, 1994)

La Belle, Jenijoy. *Herself Beheld: The Literature of the Looking Glass* (Ithaca: Cornell University Press, 1988)

Lacan, Jacques. 'The Mirror Stage as Formative of the Function of the I as Revealed in Psychoanalytic Theory' (1949), in *Ecrits – A Selection* (London, Tavistock Publications, 1977)

Lamb, Mary Ellen. 'The Agency of the Split Subject: Lady Anne Clifford and the Uses of Reading', *English Literary Renaissance* 22 (3) (Autumn 1992): 347–68

Landes, David S. *Revolution in Time: Clocks and the Making of the Modern World* (Cambridge, Mass. & London: The Belknap Press of Harvard University Press, 1983)

Langstone, R. 'Essex and the Art of Dying', *Huntington Library Quarterly* 13 (1950): 109–29

Lejeune, Philippe. *On Autobiography*, trans. Katherine Leary (Minneapolis: University of Minnesota Press, 1989)

Lewalski, Barbara. 'Claiming Patrimony and Constructing a Self: Anne Clifford and her *Diary*', in *Writing Women in Jacobean England* (Cambridge, Mass: Harvard University Press, 1993)

———. 'Re-writing Patriarchy and Patronage: Margaret Clifford, Anne Clifford, and Aemilia Lanyer', *The Yearbook of English Studies* 21 (1991): 87–106

Lockyer, Roger. *Buckingham: The Life and Political Career of George Villiers, First Duke of Buckingham 1592–1628* (London & New York: Longman, 1981)

Luckyj, Christina. *A moving Rhetoricke: Gender and Silence in Early Modern England* (Manchester: Manchester University Press, 2002)

Macfarlane, Alan and Gerry Martin. *Glass, A World History* (Chicago: University of Chicago Press, 2002)

Manning, Brian. 'Military *Coup d'Etat* and Army Mutinies in England, 1648–1649', in *Men, Women and War*, ed. T.G. Fraser and Keith Jeffery (Dublin: The Lilliput Press, 1993)

Marsh, Christopher. 'In the Name of God? Will-Making in Early Modern England', in *The Records of the Nation: The Public Record Office 1838–1988, The British Record Society 1888–1988*, ed. G.H. Martin and Peter Spufford (London: Boydell, 1990)

Martin, Randall (ed.). *Women Writers in Renaissance England* (London: Longman, 1997)

———. 'The Autobiography of Grace, Lady Mildmay', *Renaissance and Reformation* 18 (1994)

Mascuch, Michael. *Origins of the Individualist Self: Autobiography and Self-Identity in England, 1591–1791* (Cambridge: Polity, 1997)

Maurice, Klaus. *Die deutsche Räderuhr. Zur Kunst und Technik des mechanischen Zeitmessers im deutschen Sprachrauum*, 2 vols (Munich, 1976)

Maus, Katherine Eisaman. *Inwardness and Theater in the English Renaissance* (Chicago: University of Chicago Press, 1999)

McKay, Elaine. *The Diary Network in Sixteenth and Seventeenth Century England* (Monash University School of Historical Studies, 2001)

Melchior-Bonnet, Sabine. *The Mirror: A History*, trans. Katharine H. Jewett (New York: Routledge, 2001)

Mendelson, Sara and Patricia Crawford. *Women in Early Modern England 1550–1720* (Oxford: Clarendon Press, 1998)

Miller, Nancy K. *Getting Personal: Feminist Occasions and other Autobiographical Acts* (New York: Routledge, 1991)

Morris, John N. *Versions of the Self* (New York: Basic, 1966)

Mousely, Andrew. 'Renaissance Selves and Life Writing: The *Autobiography* of Thomas Whythorne', *Forum* 26 (1990)

National Portrait Gallery Collection, ed. Susan Foister, Robin Gibson, Malcolm Rogers, and Jacob Simon; introduction by John Hayes (London: NPG Publications, 1988)

Neale, F. and A. Lovell. *Wells Cathedral Clock* (Wells: Wells Cathedral Publications, 1998)

Neely, Carol Thomas. 'Shakespeare's Tragedies and Early Modern Culture', in *Shakespearean Tragedy and Gender,* ed. Shirley Nelson Garner and Madelon Sprengnether (Bloomington: Indiana University Press, 1996)

Newcomb, Lori Humphrey. 'The Triumph of Time: the Fortunate Readers of Robert Greene's *Pandosto*', in *Texts and Cultural Change in Early Modern England*, ed. Cedric C. Brown and Arthur Marotti (Basingstoke: Macmillan, 1997)

Nussbaum, Felicity A. 'Toward Conceptualizing Diary', in *Studies in Autobiography*, ed. James Olney (New York: Oxford University Press, 1988)

———. *The Autobiographical Subject: Gender and Ideology in Eighteenth-Century England* (Baltimore: Johns Hopkins University Press, 1989)

Olney, James (ed.), *Studies in Autobiography* (New York: Oxford University Press, 1988)

———. *Metaphors of Self: The Meaning of Autobiography* (Princeton: Princeton University Press, 1972)

Oppenheim, M. *A History of the Administration of the Royal Navy ... 1509–1660*, introd. K.R. Andrews (Aldershot: Temple Smith, 1988; reprint of London, 1896)

Otten, Charlotte F. (ed.). *English Women's Voices, 1540–1700* (Miami: Florida International University Press, 1992)

Oxford Classical Dictionary, ed. S. Hornblower and A. Spawforth, 3rd edition (Oxford: Oxford University Press, 1996)

Oxford Dictionary of National Biography (New DNB), ed. Brian Harrison and Lawrence Goldman (Oxford: Oxford University Press, 2004)

Oxford English Dictionary (Oxford: Clarendon Press, 1933)

Padgett, Alan G. *God, Eternity and the Nature of Time* (London: Macmillan, 1992)

Pascal, Roy. *Design and Truth in Autobiography* (London: Routledge & Kegan Paul, 1960)

Patrides, C.A. (ed.). *Aspects of Time* (Manchester: Manchester University Press; Toronto: Toronto University Press, 1976)

————. '*The Grand Design of God*': *The Literary Form of the Christian View of History* (London: Routledge and Kegan Paul; Toronto: University of Toronto Press, 1972)

————. *The Phoenix and the Ladder: The Rise and Decline of the Christian View of History* (Berkeley and Los Angeles: University of California Press, 1964)

Pennell, Sara. 'Consumption and Consumerism in Early Modern England', *The Historical Journal* 42 (2) (1999)

Pennington, Donald. 'The War and the People', in *Reactions to the English Civil War, 1642–1649*, ed. John Morrill (London: Macmillan, 1982)

Peters, Christine. *Women in Early Modern Britain, 1450–1640* (Basingstoke: Palgrave, 2003)

Pirnie, Karen Worley. 'Moulsworth, Freud and Lacan', in '*The Birthday of My Self*': *Martha Moulsworth, Renaissance Poet*, ed. Ann Depas-Orange and Robert C. Evans (Princeton: Critical Matrix, 1996)

Pointon, Marcia. *Strategies for Showing: Women, Possession, and Representation in English Visual Culture 1665–1800* (Oxford: Oxford University Press, 1997)

Pollard, Tanya (ed.). *Shakespeare's Theatre: A Sourcebook* (Oxford: Blackwell, 2004)

Popova, S.N. 'Istoria Zerkal' [History of Mirrors], *Voprosy Istorii* [USSR] 1982 (5)

Prior, Mary. 'Wives and Wills 1558–1700', in *English Rural Society, 1500–1800: Essays in Honour of Joan Thirsk*, ed. John Chartres and David Hey (Cambridge: Cambridge University Press, 1990)

————. 'Women and the Urban Economy: Oxford 1500–1800', in *Women in English Society 1500-1800*, ed. Mary Prior (London: Methuen, 1985)

Quinones, Ricardo J. *The Renaissance Discovery of Time* (Cambridge Mass.: Harvard University Press, 1972)

Rappaport, Steve. 'Reconsidering Apprenticeship in Sixteenth-Century London', in *Renaissance Society and Culture*, ed. John Monfasani and Ronald G. Musto (New York: Italica Press, 1991)

Regan, Geoffrey. *Someone Has Blundered: A Historical Survey of Military Incompetence* (London: Batsford, 1987)

Rossi, Mario M. *La Vita, le opere, i tempi di Edoardo Herbert di Chirbury*, 3 vols (Florence, 1947)

Sanders, Eve Rachele. *Gender and Literacy in Early Modern England* (Cambridge: Cambridge University Press, 1998)

Santore, Cathy. 'The Tools of Venus', *Renaissance Studies* (Oxford) 11/3 (1997)

Sawday, Jonathan. '"Mysteriously divided": Civil War, madness and the divided self', in *Literature and the English Civil War*, ed. Thomas Healy and Jonathan Sawday (Cambridge: Cambridge University Press, 1990)

Schneider, Norbert. *The Art of the Portrait: Masterpieces of European Portrait Painting 1420–1670*, trans. Iain Galbraith (Cologne: Benedikt Taschen, 1994)

Scott, George Ryley. *The History of Torture throughout the Ages* (London: T. Werner Laurie, 1940)

Seelig, Sharon. *Autobiography and Gender in Early Modern Literature: Reading Women's Lives, 1599–1678* (Cambridge: Cambridge University Press, 2006)

Shuger, Debora. 'The "I" of the Beholder: Renaissance Mirrors and the Reflexive Mind', in *Renaissance Culture and the Everyday*, ed. Patricia Fumerton and Simon Hunt (Philadelphia: Pennsylvania University Press, 1999)

———. 'Life-writing in Seventeenth-century England', in *Representations of the Self from the Renaissance to Romanticism*, ed. Patrick Coleman, Jayne Lewis and Jill Kowalik (Cambridge: Cambridge University Press, 2000)

Sim, Alison. *The Tudor Housewife* (Montreal and Kingston: McGill-Queen's University Press, 1996)

Smith, C.J. *Historical and Literary Curiosities* (London, 1840)

Smith, Sidonie and Julia Watson (eds). *Getting a Life: Everyday Uses of Autobiography* (Minneapolis: University of Minnesota Press, 1996)

Smith, Sidonie and Julia Watson. *Reading Autobiography: A Guide for Interpreting Life Narratives* (Minneapolis: University of Minnesota Press, 2001)

Spacks, Patricia Ann Meyer. *Imagining a Self: Autobiography and Novel in Eighteenth-century England* (Cambridge, Mass.: Harvard University Press, 1976)

Spengemann, William C. *The Forms of Autobiography: Episodes in the History of a Literary Genre* (New Haven: Yale University Press, 1980)

Spring, Eileen. *Law, Land, and Family: Aristocratic Inheritance in England, 1300–1800* (Chapel Hill: University of North Carolina Press, 1993)

Spufford, Margaret. 'Peasant Inheritance Customs and Land Distribution in Cambridgeshire from the Sixteenth to the Eighteenth Centuries', in *Family and Inheritance: Rural Society in Western Europe, 1200–1800*, ed. Jack Goody, Joan Thirsk and E.P. Thompson (Cambridge: Cambridge University Press, 1976)

Stachniewski, John. *The Persecutory Imagination: English Puritanism and the Literature of Religious Despair* (Oxford: Clarendon Press, 1991)

Stanham, Edward. *The Astronomical Clock in Wimborne Minster Dorset* (Woodmansterne Publications Ltd., 1988)

Staves, Susan. 'Resentment or Resignation? Dividing the Spoils among Daughters and Younger Sons', in *Early Modern Conceptions of Property*, ed. John Brewer and Susan Staves (London: Routledge, 1995)

———. *Married Women's Separate Property in England, 1660–1833* (Cambridge, Mass.: Harvard University Press, 1990)

Stewart, Richard W. 'Arms and Expeditions: the Ordnance Office and the assaults on Cadiz (1625) and the Isle if Rhé (1627)', in *War and Government in Britain, 1598–1650*, ed. Mark Charles Fissel (Manchester: Manchester University Press, 1991)

Stoyle, Mark. *Documentary Evidence for the Civil War Defences of Exeter, 1642–43* (Exeter: Exeter Archaeology, 1992)

————. *The Civil War Defences of Exeter and the Great Parliamentary Siege of 1645–46* (Exeter: Exeter Museums Archaeological Field Unit, 1990)

Strong, Roy. 'Sir Henry Unton and his Portrait: An Elizabethan Memorial Picture and its History', *Archaeologia* XCIX (1965)

————. *Tudor & Jacobean Portraits*, 2 vols (London: Her Majesty's Stationery Office, 1969)

Sturrock, John. *The Language of Autobiography: Studies in the First Person Singular* (Cambridge: Cambridge University Press, 1993)

Suzuki, Mihoko. 'Anne Clifford and the Gendering of History' *CLIO* 30/2 (Winter 2001): 195–229

Swett, Katharine Warner. 'Widowhood, Custom and Property in Early Modern Northern Wales', *Welsh History Review* 18 (1996)

Travitsky, Betty S. and Anne Lake Prescott (eds). *Female and Male Voices in Early Modern England: An Anthology of Renaissance Writing* (New York: Columbia University Press, 2000)

Treadwell, James. *Autobiographical Writing and British Literature, 1783–1834* (Oxford: Oxford University Press, 2005)

Turner, Frederick M. *Shakespeare and the Nature of Time* (Oxford: Oxford University Press, 1971)

Vezzosi, Alessandro. *Leonardo da Vinci: The Mind of the Renaissance* (New York: Discoveries, 1997)

Vickers, Nancy J. 'Diana Described: Scattered Women and Scattered Rhymes', *Critical Inquiry* 8/2 (1981)

Wall, Wendy. 'Isabella Whitney and the Female Legacy', *ELH* 58 (1991)

Waller, G.F. *The Strong Necessity of Time: The Philosophy of Time in Shakespeare and Elizabethan Literature* (The Hague: Mouton, 1976)

Warnicke, Retha M. 'Lady Mildmay's Journal: A Study in Autobiography and Meditation in Reformation England', *The Sixteenth Century Journal: Journal of Early Modern Studies* Spring 20 1 (1989): 55–68

Watson, Robert. *The Rest is Silence: Death as Annihilation in the English Renaissance* (Berkeley: University of California Press, 1994)

Weatherill, Lorna. 'A Possession of One's Own: Women and Consumer Behaviour in England, 1160–1740', *Journal of British Studies* 25/2 (1986)

Whitrow, G.J. 'Time and Measurement', in *Dictionary of the History of Ideas* (Scribner: New York, 1973)

Wilcox, Helen. '"The birth day of my selfe": John Donne, Martha Moulsworth and the emergence of individual identity', in *Sixteenth-Century Identities*, ed. A.J. Piesse (Manchester: Manchester University Press, 2000)

————. 'My Soule in Silence', in *Representing Women in Renaissance England*, ed. Claude J. Summers and Ted-Larry Pebworth (Columbia and London: University of Missouri Press, 1997)

————. 'Selves in Strange Lands: Autobiography and Exile in the Mid-Seventeenth Century', in *Early Modern Autobiography*, ed. Ronald Bedford,

Lloyd Davis and Philippa Kelly (Ann Arbor: University of Michigan Press, 2006)

Woodbridge, Linda. 'Shakespeare and the Carnival of Time', *The Scythe of Saturn: Shakespeare and Magical Thinking* (Urbana and Chicago: University of Illinois Press, 1994)

Young, Peter and Wilfred Emberton. *Sieges of the Great Civil War, 1642–1646* (London: Bell & Hyman, 1978)

Index